JAGUAR
ALL THE CARS

JAGUAR
ALL THE CARS
SECOND EDITION

NIGEL THORLEY

© Nigel Thorley 2003, 2009

Nigel Thorley has asserted his right to be
identified as the author of this work.

First published in September 2003
Reprinted 2005

Second edition published in November 2009

British Library cataloguing-in-publication data:
A catalogue record for this book is
available from the British Library.

Published by Haynes Publishing,
Sparkford, Yeovil, Somerset BA22 7JJ, UK

Tel: 01963 442030 Fax: 01963 440001
Int. tel: +44 1963 442030 Fax: +44 1963 440001

E-mail: sales@haynes.co.uk
Website: www.haynes.co.uk

ISBN 978 1 84425 693 8

Library of Congress catalog card number
2009928026

Haynes North America Inc.
861 Lawrence Drive, Newbury Park,
California 91320, USA

Layout by G&M Designs Limited,
Raunds, Northamptonshire
Printed and bound in Great Britain by
JF Print, Sparkford

Conversion factors

	METRIC	IMPERIAL
Length (distance)		
Inches (in)	x 25.4 = Millimetres (mm)	x 0.0394 = Inches (in)
Feet (ft)	x 0.305 = Metres (m)	x 3.281 = Feet (ft)
Miles	x 1.609 = Kilometres (km)	x 0.621 = Miles
Volume (capacity)		
Cubic inches (cu in; in³)	x 16.387 = Cubic centimetres (cc; cm³)	x 0.061 = Cubic inches (cu in; in³)
Imperial pints (Imp pt)	x 0.568 = Litres (l)	x 1.76 = Imperial pints (Imp pt)
Imperial gallons (Imp gal)	x 4.546 = Litres (l)	x 0.22 = Imperial gallons (Imp gal)
US gallons (US gal)	x 3.785 = Litres (l)	x 0.264 = US gallons (US gal)
Mass (weight)		
Pounds (lb)	x 0.454 = Kilograms (kg)	x 2.205 = Pounds (lb)
Hundredweight (cwt)	x 50.802 = Kilograms (kg)	x 0.020 = Hundredweight (cwt)
Torque		
Pounds-force feet (lbf ft; lb ft)	x 1.356 = Newton metres (Nm)	x 0.738 = Pounds-force feet (lbf ft; lb ft)
Pounds-force feet (lbf ft; lb ft)	x 0.138 = Kilograms-force metres (kgf m; kg m)	x 7.233 = Pounds-force feet (lbf ft; lb ft)
Power		
Horsepower (hp)	x 745.7 = Watts (W)	x 0.0013 = Horsepower (hp)
Speed		
Miles per hour (miles/hr; mph)	x 1.609 = Kilometres per hour (km/hr; kph)	x 0.621 = Miles per hour (miles/hr; mph)
Fuel consumption		
Miles per gallon (mpg)	x 0.354 = Kilometres per litre (km/l)	x 2.825 = Miles per gallon (mpg)

Contents

Introduction

The purpose of this book is to provide a comprehensive, yet concise, guide to all the production cars that have carried the Jaguar name.

Every model is covered, from the first Jaguar (branded SS) to the current models at the time of writing. The reader will find a brief history of each car and its development changes, along with technical specifications, prices when new, years in production, numbers produced, and exterior/interior colour schemes. There is also a visual appraisal in both words and photographs covering key identification points and modifications over the production period, enabling the reader to accurately identify a particular car.

The author has tried to be as precise as possible, but individual owners could, and often did, make specific requests when ordering new cars. Consequently, some vehicles may not conform exactly to the specifications listed in this book.

Over the years Jaguar have produced 18 distinct model ranges spread across the two marques (Jaguar and Daimler), amounting to a total of over 200 models, powered by nine different engine designs, and manufactured in five factories in the UK (some were even assembled abroad at various times). Jaguar's total worldwide sales now exceed two million vehicles.

More books have been written on the Jaguar marque than on any other, and the heritage of the company and its vehicles has remained of paramount importance, both to Jaguar and to the owners of their cars, past and present.

It is hoped that the reader will find much of interest here, not just as an intensive 'read' in its own right but as a handy reference guide to the company's many cars – a tribute to the British motor industry and to the name of Jaguar.

Nigel Thorley
Yorkshire, July 2009

Jaguar heritage

The formative years of Jaguar can be traced back to humble beginnings in Blackpool, under the title of the Swallow Sidecar Company. In 1922 a partnership was formed between one William Lyons and William Walmsley, initially to produce sidecars for the motorcycle trade. Within four years the business had moved to larger premises, also in Blackpool, where stylish bodies were produced for contemporary cars like the Austin Seven. Yet more expansion resulted in the company moving to Coventry – the heart of the British motor industry – in 1928, where it gained access to unlimited supplies of raw materials and skilled labour.

In Coventry (Foleshill at this time) Swallow produced its first complete cars, the SS 1 and SS 2 models of 1931, though these were still very much based on another manufacturer's running gear (that of the Standard Motor Company). In 1934 SS Cars Limited was established as a

Above: *The car that started it all, the Austin Seven with unique Swallow body. Extensive use of curves, two-tone exterior paintwork, and a sporty appearance led to instant success in 1926. A saloon version plus variants on chassis as diverse as Fiat, Wolseley, and Morris followed in the 1930s. So too did a move of production from Blackpool to Coventry.*

Below: *The first car designed and built by Lyons under the SS name, the SS1, here seen in its later 1933 form with swept-back wings but still using Standard running gear.*

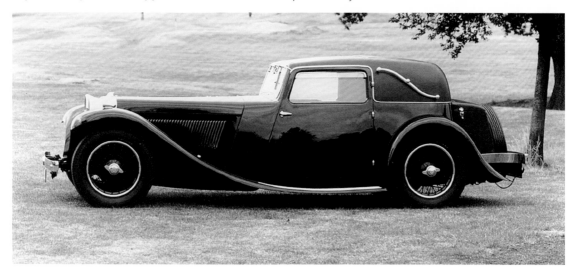

separate company to emphasise the ongoing importance of car production, although sidecars remained a major part of the business up to and including the Second World War.

In 1934 the partnership broke up, William Lyons taking full control of the businesses, and in 1935 the company announced its first car under the 'Jaguar' model name – the SS Jaguar 2½-litre saloon. A unique chassis using an overhead valve version of a Standard six-cylinder engine with a stylish four-door luxury body, this was supplemented by a smaller (four-cylinder) engined model and, later, by a larger 3½-litre car plus two-door drophead coupés and the SS100, a very stylish sports car based on a similar chassis and running gear. Over 20,000 SS Jaguars were produced up to the outbreak of the Second World War.

From 1939 to 1945 production was geared to the war effort, after which the sidecar business was sold off, the 'SS' insignia was dropped, and a new company name appeared – Jaguar Cars Limited. Initially post-war car production revolved around the pre-war models, with some modifications and with the new Jaguar name replacing the 'SS'. The first entirely new model was the Mark V, introduced in 1948. Although using the same pushrod engine, this had an entirely new chassis with independent front suspension and a larger, stylish body, smoothing out the pre-war lines.

In the same year Jaguar introduced the fabulous XK120 Super Sports, utilising the new chassis but with a sophisticated, entirely in-house designed and built twin camshaft six-cylinder engine. This was followed in 1950 by the Mark VII saloon, based on the same running gear. The XK six-cylinder unit would go on to power all subsequent Jaguars up to 1971 and would remain in production until 1992.

A move to a new factory in Allesley was completed by 1952 to expand production. Competition successes in races and rallies in the 1950s led to world recognition and major expansion, with the continued development of new models. In 1955 Jaguar introduced its first car of monocoque (chassis-less) construction, the 2.4-litre saloon, their most successful model up to that time. By 1959 the company was producing three separate model ranges from sports cars through to flagship saloons, and business was booming.

In the swinging sixties Jaguar built some of its most memorable models, like the Mark 2 saloon and E-type sports, both considered icons in the world of motoring even today. Over 90,000 Mark 2s were produced and 72,500 E-types. The company grew into a major group, purchasing other businesses like Daimler, Guy, Henry

The first car to carry the Jaguar name, albeit then as a model rather than the marque – the SS Jaguar 2½-litre saloon. Offering style and 90mph-plus performance at a modest £385, this car remained in production in various forms until 1949, and set the scene for all future saloons carrying the Jaguar name.

Meadows, and Coventry Climax to become one of the most significant parts of the British motor industry, with record exports. Other new models that enhanced the range during the 1960s included the S-type and the 420, while the Daimler name was revitalised with a 2½-litre model and, later, the Sovereign.

In 1968 a merger took place between Jaguar Cars Limited and the British Motor Corporation to form British Motor Holdings, later to become part of the massive British Leyland organisation. During this period Jaguar introduced a one-model policy in the form of the XJ6 saloon, resulting in a total of three series covering six- and twelve-cylinder Jaguar and Daimler saloons and even coupé models – a total of over 400,000 cars produced from 1968 to 1992.

After the E-type the sporting side of the model range continued with the XJ-S grand tourer, in production from 1975 until 1996. Jaguar returned to the competition arena successfully in the 1980s and was highly successful in the European Touring Car Championship and at Le Mans. Finally escaping the grip of British Leyland, the company was privatised in 1984 under the helm of Sir John Egan; the original Jaguar company's founder, Sir William Lyons (knighted in 1956), died in 1985.

In 1986 the XJ40 saloon, the first completely new model since 1975, was introduced and took the company into a new era of success. Alongside the XJ-S, it became the mainstay of production in various forms, and in 1988 Jaguar established a record of building and selling more cars in a single year than ever before, a figure that the company did not better until 1998.

The SS100 was the first true sports car to come from the company. A choice of 2½- or 3½-litre six-cylinder engines meant speeds of up to 100mph, with an incredible 0–50mph acceleration time of 7.5 seconds. Only produced until the outbreak of the Second World War, a mere 308 were made. The SS100 was the first of an esteemed line of Jaguar sports cars, culminating in the E-type, XJ-S, XK8, and new XK.

In 1990 Jaguar became part of the Ford Motor Company, and the first new model derived from Ford's investment was the X-300 saloon car range of 1994, followed by the XK8 (X-100) sports car in 1996. The X-300 saloons were equipped with the multi-valve straight six (AJ16) and V12 power units. With the introduction of the XK8 came a significant new engine, the AJ-V8 power unit, fitted to this and the later (X-308) saloon. These V8 saloons remained in production until 2002, and the XK8 sports cars have since gone through further development and were produced until 2005, in both normally aspirated and supercharged form.

From a relatively simplistic two-model base (XJ saloons and XJS sports) established in the 1970s, Jaguar has expanded their range to the comprehensive four-model line-up available at the time of writing.

Alongside the traditional flagship XJ saloons and performance XK sports cars, the range was supplemented in 1999 by the S-type saloons, the first medium-sized Jaguars since the demise of the Mark 2. Then in 2001 the range was increased again to include the X-type saloons, the first time that Jaguar had ventured into this highly competitive smaller prestige car market.

Jaguar's Mark V saloon was only in production for three years from 1948 to 1951 but was a great success, particularly in overseas markets. It offered updated traditional styling and a new chassis with excellent handling capabilities. It is seen here in rare drophead coupé form.

Since then, entirely new models, offering the very latest technologies, have come on the scene – the new XJ in 2003, and again in 2009, the new XK in 2005 (both with lightweight aluminium bodies), and the XF (replacement for the S-type) in 2008. This decade also saw the introduction and expansion of diesel engine options, a vital move to meet the increasingly stringent demands on manufacturers to offer more fuel-efficient products.

Apart from the X-type, which was produced at Halewood on Merseyside, the production of all other models, at the time of writing, is centralised at Jaguar's Castle Bromwich (Birmingham) factory, although the company still maintains an engine-building facility at the Ford factory in Bridgend, Wales, along with an engineering and development operation at Whitley in Coventry. The head office and main production site at Browns Lane in Coventry was closed in 2005, the buildings being subsequently demolished, and ownership of Jaguar, along with Land Rover, passed from Ford to the Tata Group of India in 2008.

Jaguar has survived the rise and fall of the British motor industry and is still one of the most respected marques in the world.

Chronological order of production (SS and Jaguar models)

The following does not include Swallow sidecars or Swallow-bodied vehicles, nor specialist sports/racing cars and non-production models.

1931–3	SS 1 two light coupé
1931–3	SS 2 two light coupé
1933–6	SS 1 tourer
1933–6	SS 2 tourer
1934–6	SS 1 two light coupé
1934–6	SS 2 four light saloon
1934–6	SS 2 tourer
1934–6	SS 1 airline
1935–6	SS 1 drophead coupé
1935	SS 90 sports
1935–6	SS Jaguar 1½-litre saloon
1935–6	SS Jaguar 2½-litre saloon
1936–40	SS Jaguar 100 2½-litre sports
1937–40	SS Jaguar 100 3½-litre sports
1937–40	SS Jaguar 1.75-litre saloon

1937–40	SS Jaguar 2½-litre ohv saloon
1937–40	SS Jaguar 3½-litre saloon
1937–40	SS Jaguar drophead coupé (1½, 2½, 3½ litres)
1937–40	SS Jaguar 2½-litre tourer
1946–50	Jaguar 1.75-litre saloon
1946–50	Jaguar 2½-litre ohv saloon
1946–50	Jaguar 3½-litre saloon
1947–9	Jaguar drophead coupé (1½, 2½, 3½ litres)
1948–51	Jaguar Mark V saloon (2½, 3½ litre)
1948–51	Jaguar Mark V drophead coupé (2½, 3½ litres)
1948–54	XK120 roadster
1950–8	Mark VII saloon (including Mark VIIM)
1951–4	XK120 fixed-head coupé
1953–4	XK120 drophead coupé
1954–7	XK140 roadster
1954–7	XK140 drophead coupé
1954–7	XK140 fixed-head coupé
1955–9	2.4-litre saloon
1957	XKSS sports
1957–9	3.4-litre saloon
1957–9	Mark VIII saloon
1957–61	XK150 drophead coupé (including S models)
1957–61	XK150 fixed-head coupé (including S models)
1958–61	XK150 roadster (including S models)
1959–61	Mark IX saloon
1959–67	Mark 2 saloon (2.4, 3.4, 3.8 litres)
1960–4	Daimler SP250 sports
1960–7	Daimler DR450/DQ450 Majestic saloons and limousines
1961–4	E-type 3.8-litre sports (roadster/fixed-head coupé)
1961–4	Mark X 3.8-litre saloon
1962–7	Daimler 2.5-litre V8 saloon
1963–8	S-type saloon (3.4/3.8 litres)
1964–6	Mark X 4.2-litre saloon
1964–8	E-type 4.2-litre sports (roadster/fixed-head coupé)
1966–8	E-type 2+2 sports
1966–8	420 Saloon
1966–9	Daimler 420 Sovereign saloon
1967–8	340 saloon
1967–9	240 saloon
1967–9	Daimler V8 250 saloon
1967–70	420G saloon
1968–71	E-type 4.2-litre Series 2 sports (roadster/fixed-head coupé/2+2)
1968–73	XJ6 Series 1 saloons
1968–92	Daimler DS420 limousines
1969–73	Daimler Sovereign Series 1 saloons
1971–4	E-type Series 3 sports (roadster/fixed-head coupé)
1972–3	Jaguar XJ12 Series 1 saloon (including Daimler 66)
1972–3	Daimler Double Six Vanden Plas Series 1 saloon
1974–8	Jaguar XJ6 Series 2 saloons (including Daimlers)
1974–8	Jaguar XJ12 Series 2 saloons (including Daimlers)
1975–7	Jaguar XJ6/12 C coupés (including Daimlers)
1975–90	XJ-S V12 coupé
1978–87	Jaguar XJ6 Series 3 saloons (including Daimlers)
1978–91	Jaguar XJ12 Series 3 saloons
1978–92	Daimler Double Six Series 3 saloon
1983–7	XJ-S 3.6-litre coupé
1983–6	XJ-S 3.6-litre cabriolet
1985–7	XJ-S V12 cabriolet
1986–94	Jaguar/Daimler XJ40 AJ6 saloons
1988–90	XJ-S convertible
1991–6	XJ-S coupé/convertible
1993–4	Jaguar XJ12/Daimler Double Six (XJ40) saloons
1994–7	Jaguar/Daimler X-300 saloons
1996	Daimler Century saloon
1996–2005	XK8 sports
1997–2002	Jaguar XJ8/Daimler saloons
1998–2005	XKR sports
1999–2007	S-type saloons
2001–2009	X-type saloons
2003–2009	XJ6 and XJ8 (X-350) saloons
2003 to date	diesel engine options
2004–2009	X-type estate cars
2006 to date	new XK sports
2007 to date	new XKR sports
2008 to date	XF saloons
2010 to date	new XJ saloons

Jaguar engines

This book is not intended to be a technical publication, but it is worth spending a little time examining the engines designed and built by Jaguar and fitted in its cars. This section provides details of the power units installed in the various Jaguar models and their different applications.

Background

Until the introduction of the SS Jaguar 2½-litre saloon in 1935, the engines fitted to previous SS cars were taken directly from the Standard Motor Company parts bin. With the introduction of the SS Jaguar, however, the engines, although still supplied by Standard, were significantly modified to a superior overhead valve design by renowned engineer Harry Weslake.

These modified engines were subsequently fitted, in various forms, to all SS Jaguar models and post-war Jaguars, up to and including the Mark V saloons until 1951. However, after the Second World War, William Lyons of Jaguar negotiated a deal to purchase all tooling for the six-cylinder engines from Standard, and all later production was done in-house at its Foleshill factory. During the post-war period production of the small 1.75-litre four-cylinder engine also used in the Jaguar saloon was still carried out by Standard, and this unit was subsequently used for other models like the Triumph Roadster and Renown saloon.

During the Second World War, William Lyons and his small team of engineers worked on a design for their first complete in-house engine. This was primarily designed for an entirely new saloon, later to be called the Mark VII. Lyons's specifics for the new engine were that it could comfortably power a large luxury saloon the size of a Jaguar and that it could be sufficiently advanced so as not to require major changes for subsequent models.

Coded X (for experimental), various forms and configurations of engine were tried. The

XK version was the final outcome, since when this designation has remained with the engine to the present day. It was also originally intended that a four-cylinder version of the power unit would be produced, and although some examples were made – one of which, in high compression form, powered the successful 'Goldie' Gardner MG EX135 streamlined record breaker in 1948 at over 175mph – the engine never entered production for a Jaguar motor car.

The XK engine went on to power all Jaguar production models and race cars until 1971, when it was supplemented by a very prestigious V12 power unit. Even then the XK engine remained in production, powering all manner of vehicles from Scorpion tanks to Dennis fire engines and even boats. It continued on until 1992 when the very last car powered by that engine, a Daimler DS420 limousine, left the production line.

With the purchase of the Daimler Motor Company in 1960 Jaguar inherited two of its engines for production cars, a 4.5-litre unit and a 2.5-litre V8. The larger engine remained in production until 1965, during which time it only ever powered the big Majestic Major models; thereafter production ceased with the cars. The little 2.5-litre engine, initially powering just the Daimler SP250 sports, went on to power the first Daimler models designed by Jaguar, the saloons based on the Mark 2 produced from 1962 to 1969.

It wasn't until 1971 that Jaguar introduced another engine, the celebrated V12 power unit, initially introduced in the E-type but intended for the XJ saloons. This engine never replaced the XK six but was retained for use in top-of-the-range models and remained in low volume production until 1997.

In 1983 Jaguar introduced a new six-cylinder power unit, the AJ6. Designed for a new saloon (the XJ40) it was, however, first fitted to the XJ-S sports car from that year. Later increased in capacity to 4.0 litres, it was eventually replaced by a redesigned AJ16 engine which remained in production until 1997.

Jaguar had never made a V8 engine for production until the AJ-V8 design was completed and first launched in 4.0-litre form in the 1996 XK8 sports car. It was then fitted to the equivalent XJ (X-308) saloons along with a 3.2-litre version. Variations on these engines were subsequently fitted to all XJs, XKs, S-types and XF models. They have now been replaced by new Gen III engines of 5.0-litre capacity in both normally aspirated and supercharged forms.

Jaguar introduced a new V6 engine range (AJ-V6) in 1999, initially for the S-type in 3.0-litre form but later expanded to the XJ models and the X-type, in this case in three engine capacities.

In 2003 the first-ever diesel engine was offered in a Jaguar, then of 2.0-litre capacity, for the X-type. Since then the engine range has expanded, initially to a 2.2-litre version, then a much larger 2.7-litre diesel for the S-type and XJ, and then in 2009 with the introduction of the AJ-V6D Generation III 3.0-litre unit.

The XK six-cylinder engine

The XK six-cylinder engine was designed with a conventional iron cylinder block fitted with a massive seven bearing steel crankshaft. An aluminium twin-overhead-camshaft cylinder head was employed with combustion chambers of hemispherical design. A two-stage chain system was used to drive the camshafts employing separate top and bottom chains.

Initially designed as a 3.4-litre capacity engine (3,442cc), the XK was fitted with two 1.75in SU carburettors, had a bore and stroke of 83 x 106mm, and was rated at 160bhp with

195lb ft of torque at 2,500pm. Finally, great emphasis had been put on the look of the engine, with its highly polished alloy cam covers and detail finishing. As many have said in the past and today, it is as good to look at as to drive!

XK engine production car installations

Model	Years	Cubic capacity	Carb/Fuel injection
XK120	1948–54	3,442cc	2 x SU
Mark VII/VIII	1950–8	3,442cc	2 x SU
XK140	1954–7	3,442cc	2 x SU
2.4 (Mark 1)	1955–9	2,483cc	2 x Solex
3.4 (Mark 1)	1957–9	3,442cc	2 x SU
XK150	1957–61	3,442cc	2 x SU
	1958–61	3,442cc	3 x SU
	1959–61	3,781cc	2 x SU
	1959–61	3,781cc	3 x SU
Mark IX	1958–61	3,781cc	2 x SU
2.4 (Mark 2)	1959–67	2,483cc	2 x Solex
3.4 (Mark 2)	1959–67	3,442cc	2 x SU
3.8 (Mark 2)	1959–67	3,781cc	2 x SU
E-type S1	1961–4	3,781cc	3 x SU
Mark X	1961–4	3,781cc	3 x SU
S-type	1963–8	3,442cc	2 x SU
	1963–8	3,781cc	2 x SU
E-type S1	1964–7	4,235cc	3 x SU
Mark X	1964–7	4,235cc	3 x SU
420/Sov	1966–9	4,235cc	2 x SU† partial
340	1967–8	3,442cc	2 x SU†
240	1967–9	2,483cc	2 x SU†
420G	1968–70	4,235cc	3 x SU†
E-type S2	1968–71	4,235cc	3 x SU*†
XJ6 S1	1968–73	2,782cc	2 x SU†
	1968–73	4,235cc	2 x SU†
DS420	1968–92	4,235cc	2 x SU†
XJ6 S2	1974–5	2,782cc	2 x SU†
	1974–8	4,235cc	2 x SU†
	1975–8	3,442cc	2 x SU†
XJ6 S3	1979–87	3,442cc	2 x SU†
	1979–87	4,235cc	Fuel injection†

For certain markets these E-types were instead fitted with Zenith-Stromberg carburettors to reduce emissions.

†*Engines featured ribbed cam covers instead of polished alloy type.*

The original Jaguar six-cylinder XK engine conceived during the Second World War. In various forms, it powered all Jaguars from the XK120 through to the XJ Series 3.

The XK power unit was first fitted to the XK120 Super Sports from 1948, and then to the Mark VII saloon in 1950, at which time production of the old in-line ex-Standard engine was stopped. Very early XK engines fitted to both these models were unique in having their polished camshaft covers secured with chromed studs only at the sides, the front sections covering the timing chains not being secured thus. This led to problems with oil leaks, and from 1951 all engines featured extra studs in these locations, an easy identification feature.

All production applications for the XK power unit from 1948 through to 1978 featured normal carburettor aspiration, either with two or three carburettors. For the majority of engines produced these were of SU manufacture, but Solex and Stromberg were also used in some models. In 1978 electronic fuel injection became available on certain models, initially for the US market only but later for all markets.

Another identification point for an XK engine can be found in the painted area of the cylinder heads where the spark plugs sit. Here the heads were colour coded dependent on engine compression ratio and application, eg gold for E-type and Mark X engines, various shades of blue for twin carburettor engines, etc. Also the polished alloy camshaft covers, a well known feature of the engine's visual appeal, were replaced in 1968 by cast ribbed covers powder coated in black.

XK engines were last fitted to the Daimler DS420 limousine as late as 1992, although mainstream saloon car production ended with the Jaguar XJ6 Series 3 saloon in April 1987.

Daimler 2.5-litre V8 engine

Although not designed or initially built by Jaguar, this engine was inherited when the Daimler Motor Company was taken over in 1960, and was subsequently used in the new Daimler 2.5-litre V8 and V8 250 saloons up to 1969. Designed by Edward Turner, it was an advanced design derived from his motor cycle experience. It was first fitted to a Daimler prototype in 1958 and after going into production was fitted to the SP250 glass fibre sports car introduced at the 1959 British Motor Show.

This engine was well known for its exceptional smoothness and quiet running, and after tests by Jaguar in a Mark 1 saloon following the Daimler take-over it was decided to adapt the engine for installation in the Mark 2 bodyshell, to create a new Daimler.

The V8 engine utilised a cast iron block with light alloy cylinder head and crankcase, the

The Turner-designed Daimler 2.5-litre V8 engine, fitted to the Jaguar-designed 2.5-litre V8 and V8 250 Daimler saloons from 1962 to 1969 – the only non Jaguar-designed engine to be used since the abandonment of the Standard-inspired units of the 1930s and 1940s.

crankshaft being based on five main bearings. Of over-square dimensions (76.2 x 69.85mm), it developed 140bhp at 5,800 rpm. Its compact dimensions made it an ideal installation in the Jaguar Mark 2 bodyshell, where it was fitted with twin SU carburettors.

Daimler 2.5-litre V8 engine production car installations

Model	Years	Cubic capacity	Carb/Fuel injection
2.5-litre V8	1962–7	2,548cc	2 x SU
V8 250	1967–9	2,548cc	2 x SU

V12 engine

The original concept for a V12 Jaguar engine came about with a new sports/racing car, coded XJ13, intended to race at Le Mans in the 1960s. For various reasons the project was never completed, although the only example of the XJ13 to be made still exists today. The engine designed for that car was a four overhead camshaft unit of complex design, far too complex for mass production. Jaguar's engineers therefore set about simplifying the concept.

The reasoning behind such a large engine was to captivate the prized North American market, at the time dominated by home-grown V8s. Jaguar's XK six cylinder engine wasn't as powerful in many cases, and it was thought the prestige of a V12 engine in a Jaguar would open up new markets and set the company apart from both US manufacturers and other competition.

The final outcome was a single overhead camshaft per bank of six cylinders, with a flat cylinder head design of alloy construction, as was the block, this time with an 'open deck' design and an aluminium crankcase. Of 5.3 litres capacity and originally fitted with no less than four Zenith-Stromberg carburettors to keep the engine height low, it also used a new advanced engine ignition system, the Lucas-based OPUS equipment.

This engine, as the XK before it, was first installed in a Jaguar sports car, the E-type. The Series 3 underwent significant redesign in order to accommodate the large V12 engine and first went into production in 1971. The engine was, however, really meant to power Jaguar's XJ saloons, the bodyshells of which were designed to take the V12. The new XJ12 model was announced in 1972, followed by Daimler models under the Double Six name.

From April 1975 the V12 engine became fuel injected by the Lucas-Bosch system, initially just

Jaguar's legendary V12 5.3-litre engine, introduced in 1971 and discontinued in 1997, here seen in original four-carburettor form as fitted to the Series 3 E-type and XJ12 Series 1.

Later 6.0-litre version of the V12 engine, easily identifiable by the ceramic cover over the centre section of the engine, and only fitted to cars from 1993 to 1997.

for the Series 2 XJ coupé models but later for saloons and the XJ-S sports car at its launch. Other modifications to the engine carried on throughout its life, the first being in 1981 when the May 'fireball' cylinder head design was adopted to improve engine efficiency and fuel economy. Later in the 1980s TWR Racing up-rated it to 6.0 litres capacity from 5.3 litres for racing purposes, similar changes later being accommodated into mainstream production for the XJR-S sports cars, then the normal production XJSs and, from 1993, XJ40 saloons.

Low volume production of the V12 engine continued for the last of the XJSs and the X-300 saloons before finally ending in 1997, when it was replaced by the V8s.

Identification points are numerous and complex on this engine. Suffice to say that carburettor and fuel injected versions are easy to identify. The factory produced 6.0-litre V12 engines from 1993 which included many extensive and detail changes; ease of identification issues here are the ceramic ribbed cover over the top of the engine and the significantly smaller air conditioning compressor.

V12 engine production car installations

Model	Years	Cubic capacity	Carb/Fuel injection
E-type S3	1971–4	5,343cc	4 x Stromberg
XJ12/DD6 Series 1	1972–3	5,343cc	4 x Stromberg
XJ12/DD6 Series 2	1973–9 1975	5,343cc	4 x Stromberg Fuel injection
XJ12/DD6 coupé	1975–7 1975	5,343cc	4 x Stromberg Fuel Injection
XJ-S	1975–91	5,343cc	Fuel injection
XJ12 Series 3	1979–91	5,343cc	Fuel injection
DD6 Series 3	1979–92	5,343cc	Fuel injection
XJR-S	1988–9	5,343cc	Fuel injection
XJR-S	1990–3	5,991cc	Fuel injection
XJ-S	1993–5	5,994cc	Fuel injection*
XJ40/DD6	1993–4	5,994cc	Fuel injection*
X-300	1994–7	5,994cc	Fuel injection*

* Ribbed engine cover over the V.

AJ6/16 six-cylinder engines

The XK power unit had been in production for a long time and Jaguar desperately needed a new engine, eventually to replace it. This would be designed specifically with a saloon model – the XJ40 – in mind, but, as with other Jaguar engines, it would first see light of day in a sporting mode, in this case the XJ-S.

Two engines were designed and built under the AJ6 code name, the smaller being a 2.9-litre single camshaft canted six which effectively utilised half the V12 engine with the same bore spacings, valves and camshafts, and high compression combustion chambers. In contrast, the larger 3.6-litre engine used a four-valves-per-cylinder head arrangement, both cylinder heads made from aluminium for lightness. The camshafts were chain driven as on other Jaguar engines, with two chains for the 3.6-litre engine and one for the 2.9. Both engines shared the same basic cylinder block with seven bearing cast iron crank, and both were fuel injected.

With a bore and stroke of 91 x 92mm, the 3.6-litre engine as installed in the XJ-S boasted 221bhp and 248lb ft of torque at 4,000rpm. The 2.9-litre engine was not launched until the introduction of the XJ40 saloon in 1986, at which time, with a bore and stroke of 91 x 74.8mm it supplied 165bhp with 176lb ft of torque at 4,000rpm.

The AJ6 engines were later significantly updated. The 3.6-litre was enlarged to 4.0-litre capacity in 1989, the reasoning behind this being to increase mid-range torque and enhance the feeling of effortless power and refinement. Capacity was increased to 3,980cc by increasing the stroke to 102mm. Peak torque was increased to 250lb ft at 3,750rpm. Revised camshaft profiles were used with a new low-loss air cleaner system, and tappets and valve timing were also improved. The pistons were redesigned too and a forged steel crankshaft replaced the iron one. In addition an entirely new engine management system was adopted with digital control of fuel and ignition.

Next, in 1991, the 2.9-litre AJ6 was discontinued and replaced by a new 3.2-litre engine, derived from the larger twin-cam unit. With a capacity of 3,293cc from a reduced stroke of 83mm, power output was increased to 200bhp thanks to the four-valve head. This 3.2-litre engine was also the first produced by Jaguar to be equipped with a catalytic converter. The major advantages of the 3.2-litre unit were smoothness and increases in performance and fuel economy. Now with 200bhp on tap and torque increased to 220lb ft, this engine was, however, only used in the XJ40 saloons.

In early 1994 came the final development of the AJ6 engine, so modified that it was given a new name (AJ16). Power output was up again, by seven per cent, to 244bhp. A new cylinder head and block were employed with improved

The 2.9-litre AJ6 single cam engine, only fitted to XJ40 saloons from 1986 to 1991.

The 3.6-litre AJ6 engine first fitted in the XJ-S from 1983 and then into XJ40 saloons until 1990, when it was upgraded to 4.0-litre capacity.

porting, cam profiles, higher compression, new pistons, and another new engine management system with sequential fuel injection timing. Perhaps the biggest change was the adoption of individual coils over each cylinder.

The AJ16 engine, although fitted initially to the XJ-S, was really destined for the new X-300 saloons from late 1994. It only remained in production until 1997 when, as with the V12, the V8s replaced it.

As well as being fitted to the X-300 models in normal aspirated form, there was also another variant, a supercharged version of the 4.0-litre engine. An intercooled supercharger boosted inlet manifold pressure by 10.5psi, providing up to 77 extra bhp. The supercharged engines are identified by the plenum arrangement at the side

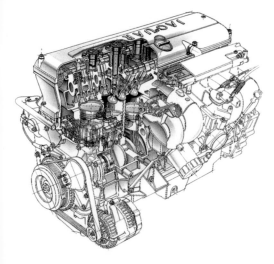

AJ16 4.0-litre engine derived for the X-300 saloon car range, but still based on the earlier AJ6 unit and first fitted to the XJS from 1993.

AJ-V8 engines

The concept of the Jaguar AJ-V8 engine came about in the early 1980s, and after much deliberation it was decided that the 'new' engine to power the next generation of Jaguars must have several attributes. Firstly, it had to achieve outstanding performance with the utmost refinement; secondly, it had to be of sound design and quality to ensure longevity in service; and thirdly, it had to be cost effective both in production terms and in service, including its fuel economy.

Initially coded AJ26 before later becoming the AJ-V8, it was launched in the XK8 in September 1996. It was a 4.0-litre design, with a bore and stroke of 86mm and a twin-camshaft arrangement with four valves per cylinder, the largest valves of any similar-sized engine around. Of alloy design for lightness, weight is also saved in other areas like the inlet manifolding, which is plastic. The very latest electronics technology has been used for engine management and ignition system, with fly-by-wire throttle control and an exceptionally efficient cooling system that permits virtually instant warm-up of the engine. In normal 4.0-litre form it provided 290bhp, with torque of 290lb ft at 4,250rpm and exceptional smoothness, quietness, and excellent fuel economy.

After being fitted in the XK8 sports car, from 1997 it was fitted in the X-308 saloon. The unit's next development came at this time, with a new 3.2-litre version built only for the saloon, as an alternative for the lower priced models. A supercharged version of the 4.0-litre engine was also introduced, this becoming available in the

of the engine finished to the same colour as the cam cover and bearing the words 'XJR6 supercharged' in red.

All the 2.9-litre, 3.2-litre, 3.6-litre, and 4.0-litre AJ6 engines had black powder coated ribbed cam covers. The 2.9-litre had a single cover of the same type as fitted to the V12 engine, the others a double-ribbed single cover incorporating the plug lead orifices. The different twin-cam engines show their litreage in the form of a sticker across the front of the cam cover. In the 1990s these covers were changed to incorporate an integrated oil filler cap.

The AJ16 engine is instantly recognisable by its silver painted, enlarged camshaft cover.

AJ6/16 engine production car installations

Model	Years	Cubic capacity (all fuel injected)
XJ-S	1983–91	3,590cc
XJ40	1986–9	3,590cc
XJ40	1986–91	2,919cc
XJ40	1989–94	3,980cc
XJ40	1991–4	3,239cc
XJ-S	1991–4	3,980cc
XJ-S	1994–6	3,980cc (AJ16)
X-300	1994–7	3,239cc (AJ16)
X-300	1994–7	3,980cc (AJ16)
XJR	1994–7	3,980cc (supercharged AJ16)

The AJ-V8 engine (seen here in its later 4.2-litre supercharged form) was, with the exception of the X-type, fitted to all Jaguar models until 2009 when it was replaced by the 5.0-litre Generation III engine.

XK8 (called the XKR) from May 1998. This supercharged engine developed 370bhp and 387lb ft of torque, ten per cent more than the old V12 and a 27 per cent increase over the standard 4.0-litre V8 engine. A low-maintenance Eaton supercharger is driven by a single belt to increase manifold pressure by up to 12psi. Supercharged engines are identifiable by the silvered plenum chamber on top of the engine, embossed with the words 'V8 supercharged'.

With changes, including the fitment of variable valve timing for the 3.2-litre version, this smaller engine was only fitted to the X-308 saloons until 2002. The 4.0-litre engine remained in use for S-type, XJ, and XK cars until 2002 when it was increased to 4.2-litre capacity, mated to an improved automatic transmission.

For a brief period from 2003 a 3.5-litre version of the AJ-V8 engine was available for the XJ saloons only. The larger 4.2-litre variants ceased production in 2009 to make way for the Generation III 5.0-litre models.

The AJ-V8 Gen III engines of 5.0-litre capacity were introduced in 2009 for the 2010 model year XK and XF models (and later in the entirely new XJ saloons). These engines are built for improved performance and fuel economy, and environmental issues are also addressed since, for the first time, recycled aluminium is used for the heads and high-pressure castings for the blocks.

New technology used in these engines includes a centrally-mounted, multi-hole, spray-guided direct fuel-injection system and a new type of variable camshaft timing system, activated by the positive and negative torques generated by opening and closing the valves, instead of by oil pressure. This allows the engine oil pump to be reduced in size, saving energy and reducing fuel consumption. Another innovation is the 'intelligent' oil pump pressure relief valve, which senses oil pressure deep in the engine's oil galleries to control the oil pump delivery. As a result, oil pump frictional losses are reduced during the warm-up period. There is also an electronic oil level sensor feature, and servicing intervals have been expanded from the traditional 10,000 miles to 15,000 miles.

Changes were also made to the supercharger, providing greater efficiency and lower noise levels.

AJ-V8 engine production car installations

Model	Years	Cubic capacity (all fuel injected)
XK8	1996–2002	3,996cc
X-308	1997–2002	3,248cc
X-308	1997–2002	3,996cc
XJR	1997–2002	3,996cc (supercharged)
XKR	1997–2002	3,996cc (supercharged)
S-type	1999–2002	3,996cc
XK8	2002–9	4,196cc
XKR	2002–9	4.196cc (supercharged)
S-type	2002–8	4,196cc
S-type	2002–8	4,196cc (supercharged)
X-350	2003–5	3,555cc
X-350	2003–9	4,196cc
XJR	2003–9	4,196cc
XF	2008–9	4,196cc
XF	2009 on	5,000cc
XF	2009 on	5,000cc (supercharged)
XK	2009 on	5,000cc
XK	2009 on	5,000cc (supercharged)
XJ	2010 on	5,000cc
XJ	2010 on	5,000cc (supercharged)

The latest petrol engine from Jaguar, the AJ-V8 Gen III 5.0-litre that replaced the 4.2-litre units in 2009.

AJ-V6 engines

After the demise of the AJ16 engine, Jaguar was without a six-cylinder power unit until 1999, when the new medium sized S-type saloon was introduced. Although also equipped with the AJ-V8 4.0-litre engine, this car was always designed to take the smaller V6 engine, called the AJ-V6.

The origins of the AJ-V6 lie in the Ford Duratec engine, but with significant re-engineering by Jaguar's personnel. A lightweight engine of all-aluminium construction, its basic principles follow the V8 power units. Its 2,967cc capacity offers

The first of the AJ-V6 engines of 3.0-litre capacity, as fitted to S-type saloons from 1999 on and now also fitted to X-types and the XJ6.

Diesel Engines

For the very first time in the history of the company, Jaguar introduced its first production diesel engine in 2003, fitted to a new version of the X-type saloon, the 2.0 litre D.

The growth and success of the diesel engine has been unprecedented in recent years and in some particular markets it is vital to have a diesel-engined car in a manufacturer's range. Jaguar, for many years, had been working on the design of such an engine, and at various times the company came close to fitting an oil burning unit to some models. It has taken until 2003 to finally get the right engine for their application.

The origins of the Jaguar 2.0 litre diesel engine (code named X-404) lies in the Ford TDCi unit although, like the V6 petrol engines, it has been significantly enhanced to meet the demands of Jaguar owners and to uphold the characteristics required of a prestige car.

The engine is a four-cylinder unit, has a capacity of 1,998cc and develops peak power of 128bhp at 3,800rpm, and 243lb ft of torque at only 1,800rpm. The engine is made as lightweight as possible, with a stiff cast-iron block with aluminium ladder frame and alloy cylinder head. The fuel system is based on a high-pressure common-rail direct injection system, with a variable-geometry turbocharger.

This very high-tech engine also has a system to detect and reduce combustion noise.

Installation in the X-type is transverse, transmitting power through the standard X-type five-speed manual gearbox to the front wheels

238bhp with excellent torque, and it has variable timing, a sophisticated engine management system, and superb smoothness.

This engine was launched in the S-type conventionally mounted, driving the rear wheels. However, with the launch of the smaller X-type saloon in 2001 a derivative of the engine was introduced, with a capacity of 2.5 litres. Now mounted transversely it was able to provide four-wheel drive in this mode, but only for the X-type. The 3.0-litre V6 is also fitted to the X-type and also offers four-wheel drive. The 2.5-litre engine later became available for the S-type saloon as well, although still with this model's conventional rear wheel drive.

In 2002 another variant of the AJ-V6 engine came on the scene, of 2.0 litres capacity. This was mounted transversely, driving the front wheels only, and was fitted to a lower priced version of the X-type for strategic markets.

The 3.0-litre engine was then fitted to the XJ6 (X-350) saloon from 2003 and to earlier XF models.

AJ-V6 engine production car installations

Model	Years	Cubic capacity (all fuel injected)
S-type	1999–2008	2,967cc
X-type	2001–9	2,967cc
X-type	2001–6	2,495cc
S-type	2002–7	2,495cc
X-type	2002–4	2,099cc
XJ6	2003–9	2,967cc
XF	2008–9	2,967cc

The 2.7 litre V6 diesel engine for the S-type saloon.

19

saloon in 2008, but production of this engine ceased in 2009.

The larger diesel engine was replaced in 2009 by the new AJ-V6D Gen III unit of 3.0-litre capacity, producing 240bhp or, in S form, 275bhp. Performance is therefore boosted over 30 per cent over the 2.7-litre engine, with 12% less emissions and 10 per cent better fuel economy. A key feature of these engines is the parallel sequential turbocharger system, the first of its type to be fitted to a V-engine. A new common-rail direct-injection system is also employed and, by placing the injector crystals deeper into the engine, noise levels are dramatically reduced. Turbo lag is also reduced and service intervals have been extended to 16,000 miles.

Diesel engine production car installations

Model	Years	Cubic capacity (all fuel injected)
X-type	2003–9	1,998cc
XJ6	2004–9	2,720cc
S-type	2004–8	2.720cc
X-type	2005–9	2,198cc
XF	2008–9	2,720cc
XF	2009 on	2,993cc
XJ	2010 on	2,993cc

The 2.0 litre four cylinder diesel engine for the X-type saloon.

only. A significant amount of sound deadening material is fitted, and a full engine cover is fitted to minimise noise.

Jaguar went a stage further with the small diesel engine in providing a 2.2-litre version with the later provision of a six-speed manual transmission for the X-type models.

In 2004 Jaguar introduced a much larger engine, suitable for the S-type and XJ saloons, of 2.7-litre capacity. A joint venture with Ford and Peugeot-Citroën, this was an entirely different unit from the other diesel engines offered and heralded entirely new technology, like the block being made from lightweight compacted graphite iron.

It was a four-camshaft unit with twin turbochargers and 24 valves, providing over 200bhp and with torque exceeding that of the then current 4.2-litre petrol unit. Renowned for quiet running, and over 40 per cent more fuel efficient than the equivalent petrol engine, this unit was carried over to the XF

The latest diesel engine from Jaguar – the 3.0-litre AJ-V6D Gen III that replaced the 2.7-litre unit.

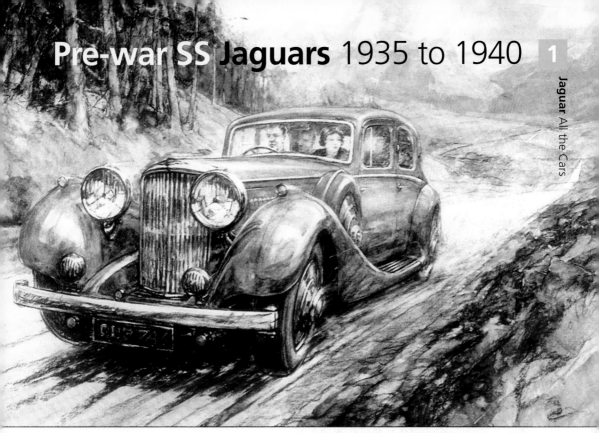

Background

The launch of the Jaguar name came about in September 1935 with the announcement of a new saloon model from SS Cars Limited, the manufacturers of the then current range of cars carrying that insignia, based on Standard Motor Company mechanicals. The new car, although now commonly known as a 'Jaguar', actually used the name purely as a brand model for a new car from SS, and although still based on many components supplied by Standard, the car was a major leap forward for SS and set the scene for all future models they would produce.

The main feature of the new car was an overhead valve version of the Standard six-cylinder engine that the company had already been using in their previous models. The redesign had been carried out by Harry Weslake, a formidable engineer of his day, and the end result was an engine capable of propelling the car to over 90mph. The Standard Motor Company had set up tooling specifically to build the new more powerful engine for SS Cars. The second element was the chassis, which was a revamp of the one supplied by Standard for the SS1 model, although significantly strengthened and with a new braking system incorporated. The third element of the new car was the style of its bodywork. Whilst somewhat similar to the likes of MG, it was nevertheless a major move

forward for SS, and the finished job was immediately well received.

Only two models were launched at the Mayfair Hotel in London prior to the 1935 British Motor Show, the 2½-litre straight six saloon and a 1½-litre four-cylinder version, the smaller-engined car only identifiable externally by the shorter wheelbase and bonnet area.

The only SS1 model to be retained after the introduction of the Jaguar saloons was the tourer, now also carrying the Jaguar name and using the same overhead valve engine but essentially the bodywork of the old SS1. Announced just before the SS Jaguar models was the SS90, a two-seater sports car based on the earlier SS1 model. Only very small numbers were built and it was superseded by the Jaguar SS100 sports car, announced along with the new saloons. The SS100 had the new six-cylinder overhead valve engine in a shortened version of the saloon chassis.

By the start of the Second World War, the range of models had been extended to include an even larger (3½-litre) version of the overhead valve engine in the saloons, and a range of drophead coupés. The SS100 had also gained the larger engine, whilst the tourer had been dropped.

Production of all models stopped with the onset of the war, as SS Cars Limited turned their attention to the war effort.

Model range and development

Models available at launch
SS Jaguar 2½-litre saloon
SS Jaguar 1½-litre saloon
SS Jaguar 2½-litre tourer
SS Jaguar 100 2½-litre sports car

The 'new' SS Jaguar models were very soon upgraded, and by the end of 1936 changes had been made to improve the overall design. By 1937 two extra models had been added to the range – a 1½-litre and 2½-litre drophead coupé. These were extremely attractive, somewhat bespoke built, two-door full hood variants of the saloons. With their introduction, the tourer model was dropped from the range.

All these cars were built around an ash framework in the traditional way, but this was a time-consuming process which proved too slow to meet the heavy sales demand for the cars. Hence, in 1938, production switched to all-steel bodies for the SS Jaguar saloons, which also meant certain changes to the design again. The drophead coupés remained virtually hand-built in the traditional manner.

With the introduction of the steel-bodied cars, SS introduced another new variant to the range, a larger 3½-litre version of the straight-six engine, which boosted performance considerably. A drophead coupé version of the 3½-litre model also became available, and the SS 100 sports car was fitted with the bigger engine. The 1½-litre engine was enlarged to 1.75 litres in late 1937.

Production continued towards the start of the Second World War, with some changes taking effect from late 1939 and early 1940 – the 1.75-litre and the 3½-litre saloons being the last to roll off the production lines (July and December 1940 respectively).

Exterior identification points

General points applicable to pre-war SS Jaguar saloon models
Front view
■ Traditional frontal aspect with separate wings flowing towards the centre and incorporating separately mounted side lights on top. Integrated side light housing incorporated into the wings on 2½-litre models in 1937, standardised with all-steel production on all cars.
■ Bold crested chromed radiator grille with vertical slats incorporating radiator filler cap

A very early example of the SS Jaguar, in this case a 1½-litre model. Note the lack of front door window quarter-lights, the thick waistline trim towards the rear of the car and the door handles situated below the waistline. Being a 1½-litre model, it has a shorter bonnet and the wing-mounted spare wheel protrudes above the bonnet line.

The 1937 SS Jaguar – in this case the longer bonnet 2½-litre version now sporting the front door window quarter-lights and the normal cover for the side-mounted spare wheel.

Frontal view of the 1½-litre saloon with separate chromed horns, smaller headlights and separate side lights on top of the front wings.

and SS Jaguar winged logo on top. 3½-litre models had a wider and deeper radiator grille, and by 1938 the 2½-litre grille was standardised for the 1½-litre models.

- Large Lucas chromed surround, separately mounted headlamps (either side of the radiator grille), later changed to Lucas P100 type on 2½-litre models, but always fitted to 3½-litre cars. In both cases they hinge from the top.
- Twin chrome-plated horns externally mounted above bumper level. From 1940 they were changed in design and hidden out of sight beneath the wing/bumper area.
- Twin fog lamps fitted to all-steel bodied cars, except the 1½-litre models.
- Full-width, single blade, chromed front bumper.
- One-piece flat windscreen with chromed surround and twin wipers.
- Full-depth, two-piece bonnet with piano-hinged centre and chrome finisher. Bonnet lengths vary according to whether 1½ or 2½/3½-litre models.
- Slightly wider track and longer wheelbase for all-steel models.
- All-steel models featured door, bonnet, and bonnet louvre lines all matching the rake of the front screen pillar.

Rear view
- Severe sloping rear bodywork incorporating full-width boot lid, hinged from the bottom.
- Single chromed boot lid T-handle, top centre with lock, replaced in 1940 by a vertically mounted stylised handle and lock.
- Integrated number plate mounting below boot lid with glass cover and flanked each side by single red rear lights.
- Fly-off, chromed petrol filler mounted to the left-hand side of the number plate area below boot lid area.
- Full-width, single blade, chromed rear bumper bar.
- Single exhaust tailpipe emitting from the right-hand side rear.
- Small, two-thirds width rear screen with chromed surround.
- Steel-bodied cars incorporated the spare wheel in a well underneath the boot, accessed by a hinged down panel incorporating the number plate housing. The bumper was hinged to aid removal of the wheel. By 1940 the spare wheel access panel was enlarged to ease the removal of the spare wheel, eliminating the need for the bumper to be hinged.

Side view
- Traditional 1930s style full-length bodywork, incorporating flowing front wing line down to

The slightly later (pre all-steel bodywork) 2½-litre saloon with wider radiator grille, integrated side lights, and the addition of the fog/driving lamps.

The later 3½-litre, displaying yet wider radiator grille with flatter top.

An early example of the SS Jaguar from the rear, showing the simplistic lighting treatment either side of the number plate housing, the sighting for the fuel filler, and the T-handle to open the boot lid. Also note the relationship between the bottom of the boot lid and the rear number plate housing. Finally, the 'J' emblem mounted in the centre of the bumper bar – up to the Second World War some cars carried the 'SS' insignia.

Later rear end design with separate under-panel, accessed via T-keys, housing the spare wheel, and the revised positioning of the fuel filler. Also note the stylised boot lock and handle.

Rear compartment of a pre-war SS Jaguar with the later door trim style (with pockets) and arm-rests above the rear wheel arches.

Early front door trim with Art Deco styling, with wood cappings and window surrounds.

The early 1.5-litre four-cylinder Standard engine fitted to the SS Jaguar saloons.

From 1937, fitted with quarter-lights, this stylish handle wound the draught-excluder open.

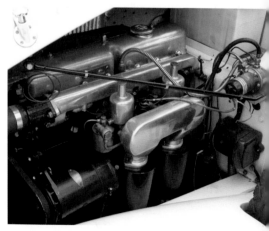

The 2½-litre engine.

running boards and leading to curved rear wings.

- Four-door construction with front doors and rear doors centrally hinged.
- Louvred side panels to bonnet area.
- Waistline chromed trim running from leading edge of bonnet through the doors to spears above the rear wings.
- Door handles mounted below the waistline trim. With all-steel bodies, incorporated within the waistline trim which was of a slightly different style.
- Traffic indicators mounted at the rear edge of front wings.
- Two-light glass arrangement, opening windows to front and rear doors with no quarter-lights. (Quarter-lights fitted to the front doors on post 1937 models.)
- Nearside mounting of spare wheel inset into rear section of front wing with steel cover incorporating chrome finishing, applicable to pre all-steel models only. The 1½-litre cars more recognisable by the spare wheel height proud of the bonnet line.
- Body-coloured wire spoked wheels standard equipment on all models.
- Body length forward of bulkhead differed, 11in longer for 2½/3½-litre models.

SS Jaguar tourer specifics
Front view
- Radiator grille similar but different from earlier SS1 models incorporating a thick centre chromed vane.
- General wing line, and standing of car from the front, much lower than the SS Jaguar saloon equivalent.

Rear view
- Squared-off sloping rear end incorporating the fuel tank and exposed spare wheel.
- Fish-eye rear light unit, reminiscent of earlier SS models above square number plate mounting.

Side view
- Traditional line of earlier SS1 tourer with cut-away single door, hinged at the rear.
- Canvas hood arrangement with hood frame and traditional side-screens.

SS Jaguar 100 specifics
Front view
- Traditional style lower set frontal aspect with separate wings to the saloons.
- Lower set chromed radiator surround incorporating bright mesh insert.
- P100 headlights mounted on chromed 'tripod' bracing, incorporating the '100' insignia in the centre.
- No bumper bar fitted.

An example of the later all-steel bodywork, in this case a 3½-litre saloon. Note the integrated door handles into the waistline trim.

The Lucas P100 headlights, standard equipment on most 2½ and 3½-litre models and an extra cost option on the 1½-litre cars, showing the retaining clips at the bottom, as the surrounds were hinged at the top. Note also the winged badging incorporating the SS Jaguar insignia on the radiator grilles of all these models.

Comparison between the 1½ and 2½-litre models from 1937. Note the height of the spare wheel compared to the bonnet line and the length of the bonnet (the car in the foreground is the 1½-litre model.

Shown for representation only, the SS1 Tourer which was effectively rebadged as an SS Jaguar, most probably to clear body stocks during the early production of the SS Jaguar saloons.

The sculptured seating, unique to the pre-Jaguar SS models, in this Tourer.

The Desmo leaping Jaguar mascot. This was not fitted as standard equipment to the pre-war SS Jaguar models, but was available as an accessory.

The SS Jaguar 100 sports, with a modified body from the early SS90 but fitted to a shortened version of the SS Jaguar saloon chassis and mechanicals.

The dramatic front of the SS100 with pronounced mesh grille and sweeping lines of the wings.

Rear view of an SS100 with the ungainly hood erect. The 'owl eye' rear light unit was also used on earlier SS models like the Tourer.

The drophead coupé version of the SS Jaguar saloons, with only two doors and much wider than the saloons and, in this instance, with the hood in the 'sedanca' position.

A drophead coupé with the hood fully erect. Note the Ace wheel-discs covering the wire wheels, a period option for all models.

Revised rear seating arrangement for drophead coupé models.

Rear view

- Sloping rear end incorporating fuel tank and separately mounted spare wheel.
- Traditional line of earlier SS1 tourer with cut-away single door, hinged at the rear.
- Fold down front screen arrangement.
- Canvas hood arrangement with hood frame and traditional side-screens.
- Fish-eye rear light unit, reminiscent of earlier SS models, above square number plate mounting.
- No bumper bar fitted.

Side view

- Traditional line, similar to earlier SS models with cut-away single door, hinged at the rear.
- Cut-off rear end just aft of the rear wings, emphasising the shortened wheelbase compared to other models.
- Fold-down front screen arrangement with chromed surround.
- Canvas hood arrangement with hood frame and traditional side-screens.

Drophead coupé specifics

Front view

- Lowered roof line, evident above front screen.

Rear view

- Canvas rear hood replacing steel saloon roof.
- Much smaller 'pill-box' style rear screen with chromed surround.

Side view

- Longer, two-door configuration.
- Single door glass area and no rear compartment windows.
- Chromed dummy hood-irons visible at rear side of hood.

Interior identification points

General points applicable to all SS Jaguar saloon models

- Full width wooden dashboard area with centrally mounted instruments, initially the two larger (rev counter and speedometer) flanked by smaller auxiliary gauges. Instruments set into a central black panel with switchgear. From 1937, instruments regrouped with larger rev counter/speedometer on the outside.
- Either side of instrument 'pack' wood finish continued without glove-compartments. Passenger side glove-box fitted from 1937.
- Prominent dashboard top rail in wood, incorporating ashtrays and handle to open the

Rear of the drophead coupé model with the pillar box style rear screen.

The original dashboard layout of the SS Jaguar saloons. The large upper rail mounted handle is to open the windscreen. Note the lack of glove boxes on these early dashboards.

The later dashboard layout with revised instrument positions and addition of glove boxes. Windscreen wipers are now operated by individual controls on the top rail.

windscreen (hinged from the top). Individual wiper controls fitted from 1937.
- Complete dashboard change in 1938 on all-steel cars. Full-width veneered dash with integrated instrumentation in the style that would follow for most other large Jaguar saloons up to the early 1960s. Inset rev counter and speedometer flanked minor gauges in the centre surrounded by switchgear. Glove-boxes (with lids) now featured either side of the dashboard.
- 120mph speedometer fitted to 3½-litre models.
- A heater was added from 1940, mounted in the centre below the dash area which also incorporated venting to the windscreen area.
- Large diameter four-spoke steering wheel incorporating horn push and controls for throttle.
- Soft leather finished door panels with wooden top-rails, chromed handles for door lock and window winder. Front door arm-rests and map pockets incorporated from 1937.
- Bucket-style front pleated leather seating, with better bolster support from 1937, and then also incorporating cut-out areas in the seat back to aid rear compartment legroom.
- From 1940, plain non-pleated leather seating was adopted, incorporating stuffed side-rolls to aid driver/passenger location. Also, from 1940, chromed handles at the front of each seat adjusted the height of that seat.
- From 1940, similar door trim panels fitted.
- Full-width rear bench pleated leather seat, incorporating side armrests over each wheelarch from 1937.
- Rear footwells to allow for passenger feet areas on early cars, eliminated with sloping floor from 1937.
- From 1940, all models featured veneered picnic tables and matching ashtrays incorporated into the front seat backs, and plain leather (instead of pleating) to the seating.
- Boot internal area incorporated plain rubber matting, and from 1940 was supplemented by ribbed rubber guide strips to support luggage.
- The boot lid incorporated a lift-up panel to reveal a fully-equipped tool kit.

SS100 specifics
- Plain (unpleated) bucket seats in the front, no rear seating fitted.
- All metal, painted dashboard in kidney shape with rev counter and speedometer situated in front of the driver along with the oil pressure gauge. Other gauges spread across the passenger side of the dash with switchgear around.

The completely revised dashboard treatment for the late 1930s car, looking somewhat similar to post-war models. It has new style instrumentation, and note the now fitted heater unit beneath the dashboard area.

The integrated tool kit into the boot lid of the SS Jaguar saloons.

Flat, plain, unpleated bucket seating for the SS100 models.

Layout of the SS100 dashboard which was always painted to match body colour.

Technical specifications

	1.5-litre Saloon	1.75-litre Saloon
cc	1,608	1,776
Bore and stroke (mm)	69.5 x 106	73 x 106
Compression ratio	6.1 to 1	7.2 to 1
bhp	52	65
@ rpm	4,300	4,600
Fuelling	Single Solex carb	Single SU carb
Transmission	4-speed (manual)	4-speed (manual)
Wheel size (in)	18, wire	18, wire
Suspension front	Beam axle, half elliptic leaf	Beam axle, half elliptic leaf
Suspension rear	Live axle, half elliptic leaf	Live axle, half elliptic leaf
Brakes	Girling – rod operated	Girling – rod operated
Performance		
0–50mph (sec)	19.6	17
Top speed (mph)	70	72
Average mpg	25	27
Dimensions		
Length (in)	173	173
Width (in)	61.5	65.5
Height (in)	60	60
Wheelbase (in)	108	112.5
Front track (in)	48	52
Rear track (in)	48	55
Weight (cwt)	21	26.5

Optional extras

Ace wheel rimbellishers.
Unique exterior colour schemes.
Lucas chromium-plated fog lamps.
Chromium-plated badge bar.
Radio installation.
Fitted luggage for boot area.
Extra fittings to 1.5-litre models, normally
    standard on other cars.

Technical specifications *cont ...*

	2.5-litre Saloon	3.5-litre Saloon
cc	2,663	3,485
Bore and stroke (mm)	73 x 106	82 x 110
Compression ratio	7.6 to 1	7.2 to 1
bhp	105	125
@ rpm	4,600	4,500
Fuelling	Twin SU carbs	Twin SU carbs
Transmission	4-speed (manual)	4-speed (manual)
Wheel size (in)	18, wire	18, wire
Suspension front	Beam axle, half elliptic leaf	Beam axle, half elliptic leaf
Suspension rear	Beam axle, half elliptic leaf	Live beam, half elliptic leaf
Brakes	Girling – rod operated	Girling – rod operated
Performance		
0–50mph (sec)	10.6	9
Top speed (mph)	87	92
Average mpg	19	18
Dimensions		
Length (in)	186	186
Width (in)	66	66
Height (in)	61	61
Wheelbase (in)	120	120
Front track (in)	54	54
Rear track (in)	56	56
Weight (cwt)	32	32

Colour schemes

Exterior	Details
Olive Green	
Maroon	
Suede Green	
Cream	To 1938
Ivory	From 1938
Dark Blue	
Black	
Lavender Grey	
Mountain Ash Green	From 1938
Birch Grey	From 1938
Battleship Grey	From 1938
Gunmetal	From 1938
Honeysuckle	From 1938

Seat trim colours
Olive Green
Maroon
Red
Suede Green
Dark Blue
Black-Silver Grain
Brown
Pigskin Grain Tan
Beige

Hood colours
French Grey
Black
Dark Sand
Gunmetal Grey

	2.5-litre SS100	3.5-litre SS100
cc	2,663	3,485
Bore and stroke (mm)	73 x 106	82 x 110
Compression ratio	7.6 to 1	7.2 to 1
bhp	102	125
@ rpm	4,600	4,500
Fuelling	Twin SU carbs	Twin SU carbs
Transmission	4-speed (manual)	4-speed (manual)
Wheel size (in)	18, wire	18, wire
Suspension front	Beam axle, half elliptic leaf	Beam axle, half elliptic leaf
Suspension rear	Live axle, half elliptic leaf	Live axle, half elliptic leaf
Brakes	Girling – rod operated	Girling – rod operated
Performance		
0–50mph (sec)	8.8	7.1
Top speed (mph)	94	101
Average mpg	20	21
Dimensions		
Length (in)	153	153
Width (in)	63	63
Height (in)	54	54
Wheelbase (in)	104	104
Front track (in)	54	54
Rear track (in)	54	54
Weight (cwt)	23	23.3

Prices and production volumes

	Price new (£)	1935	1936	1937	1938	1939	1940	Total produced
SS Jag 2.5-litre tourer	375	■	■	■	–	–	–	105
SS Jag 1.5-litre saloon	285	■	■	■	■	–	–	2,250
SS Jag 2.5-litre saloon	395	■	■	■	■	■	■	5,023
SS Jag 2.5-litre dhc	415	–	–	–	■	■	■	279
SS Jag 1.75-litre saloon	298	–	–	–	■	■	■	4,408
SS Jag 1.75-litre dhc	318	–	–	–	■	■	■	677
SS Jag 3.5-litre saloon	445	–	–	–	■	■	■	1,067
SS Jag 3.5-litre dhc	465	–	–	–	■	■	■	241
SS Jaguar 100 2.5-litre	395	–	■	■	■	■	■	191
SS Jaguar 100 3.5-litre	445	–	–	–	■	■	■	118
Total production								**14,359**

Post-war pushrods 1945 to 1951

Background

With the end of the Second World War came the resumption of car production, and the company began getting back to some semblance of normality. But, having had little opportunity during the war to design new models, the pre-war designs had to be resurrected and, like other manufacturers, it was vital for the company to win export sales to secure allocation of essential raw materials. SS Cars Limited had become Jaguar Cars Limited in March 1945, and thereafter the company's cars were Jaguars in their own right rather than SS Jaguars.

A major change affecting the post-war models, and one which secured Jaguar's independence from outside supply, was the acquisition of the tooling to produce the 2.5-litre and 3.5-litre pushrod engines used in the cars – although the production and rights for the smaller four-cylinder unit remained with Standard Motors.

Production started mid-year, and it was limited to the saloons. No decision seems to have been taken at the time, but it soon became apparent that the SS100 (the two-seater sports car built in small numbers before the war) would not reappear. However, the drophead coupé was reintroduced from 1947. All saloons were on offer with all three engine sizes, but drophead coupés were available only with the six-cylinder engines.

Although Jaguar had been working on an entirely new engine, this was not ready for mass production yet, nor was the bodywork for the brand new luxury saloon, to be known as the Mark VII. The latter didn't appear until 1950, whilst the engine was announced to the public at the 1948 British Motor Show, at the time fitted to what was intended to be a low-production

sports car. However, Jaguar desperately needed a new saloon model to maintain their export drive and satisfy the demand at home for new cars. Hence, what would be destined to be called an interim model appeared at the October 1948 motor show – the Mark V saloon.

The designation Mark V came about merely because it was the fifth prototype of the model, and, although it very much looked like the pre-war/post-war design, apart from the carryover of the engine and gearbox everything else about the car was new. A very rigid new chassis (designed for the later all-new saloon in 1950) was used, which incorporated, for the first time on an SS or Jaguar, independent front suspension and, at the rear, more suspension travel with softer springs. A hydraulic braking system was also employed for the first time, but with smaller diameter drums because of the fitment of smaller road wheels.

The Mark V was offered only with the 2.5-litre or 3.5-litre six-cylinder overhead valve engines, with the usual Moss four-speed manual transmission.

Externally the new car was wider, taller, longer, and heavier than the outgoing models, and virtually every internal and external body panel was new, along with much more brightwork. The saloons were again accompanied by two-door drophead coupé models, but these more hand-built cars were produced in very small numbers.

The Mark V proved a very competitive car, both commercially (it represented good value for money) and in motor sport (it did well in major rallies well past the time the model was discontinued from the Jaguar range). The last Mark V left the production lines in 1951 just after the introduction of the new luxury 100mph Mark VII that the chassis had originally been intended for.

Model range and development

Models available at post-war launch
Jaguar 1.75-litre saloon
Jaguar 2.5-litre saloon
Jaguar 3.5-litre saloon

All three Jaguar saloons (and drophead coupés) continued very much as they were before the war. Externally, identification points were thinner waistline chrome trims, new radiator grille badging, and the revised 'Jaguar' insignia (instead of 'SS') on the spinners of the wire wheels. The bonnet was also slightly shorter to make room for a deeper scuttle panel below the windscreen. One of the apparent benefits of this was that it made room to fit modern radio receiver equipment.

Mechanically, all cars now benefited from a new hypoid rear axle and revised gear ratios, and were fitted with a new Girling two-leading-shoe braking system. The Standard four-cylinder engine benefited from a new water-heated inlet manifold.

Internally, the post-war cars saw a return to pleated upholstery, though without the rear seat picnic tables that were fitted to the last of the pre-war models. The heater unit was improved and repositioned, hidden further under the dashboard, with new controls. The steering-wheel-mounted advance and retard controls were no longer fitted to post-war models.

The cars continued virtually unchanged until production finished in 1949, just after the launch of the replacement models – the Mark Vs.

The Mark V represented quite a leap forward for Jaguar. The smoothing out of the body style, while still retaining the previous model's 'look', the extensive use of chrome plating, and the adoption of independent front suspension and hydraulic braking brought the Jaguar range very much up to date. Another change in the running gear was the adoption of a split propeller shaft under the car, thus eliminating the need for a conventional tunnel in the rear compartment, and making for more legroom for rear-seat passengers.

Externally, such features as the sloping bonnet, the faired-in headlights, the massive front bumper, and slimmer 'A' posts to the windscreen made the new car immediately identifiable. From the side the Mark V featured separate chrome on brass window surrounds, and wider doors with substantial push-button handles. Another 'first' was the fitment of full rear wheel spat covers.

At the rear, similar substantial bumper bar treatment was adopted, a much deeper boot lid was fitted (allowing the spare wheel to be

The post-war/pre-war design, now badged on the radiator as a Jaguar and with slimmer waistline trims. This car also carries the Ace rimbellishers and its horns are now completely hidden.

A typical advertisement picture for the post-war Jaguar saloon, in this case a 3.5-litre model. The distance between the rear of the bonnet and the windscreen indicates the slighter deeper scuttle area.

The later post-war dashboard with hidden heater unit and large controls for it on the dashboard.

accommodated behind a hinged panel in the centre of the bumper), and the fuel filler was now concealed under a flush panel built into the nearside rear wing.

Internally, the Mark V was very well equipped and, with yet another change of direction, non-pleated leather seating returned yet again. The whole interior was much larger, and although the dashboard looked somewhat similar to the out-going models it was actually quite different. A new style of four-spoke steering wheel was adopted, a design that would be used on all subsequent Jaguars, in some cases, up to 1961. Some novel features were used that were unique to the Mark V, like the trigger interior door handles.

The drophead coupé models, which were announced at the same time as the saloons, were still to be built with some aspects of traditional coachwork, like ash-framed door panels, for example. Because of the construction method, conventional door handles were also used, and the cars were built for a limited period in very small numbers, and were discontinued well before the demise of the saloons.

Subsequent changes were few on the Mark V as the production run was so small, and all attention was being given to its replacement, the Mark VII – so the Mark V slowly dropped out from the range in late 1950 to early 1951.

Exterior identification points

General points applicable to post-war Jaguar saloon and drophead models
Front view
- P100 headlights with smaller clear centres.
- Headlights now hinged from the bottom instead of the top.
- Revised radiator grille badging, still incorporating the winged logo but now with chromed letters and figures, painted cream for 2.5-litre models, black for 3.5-litre models, and black infilled letters with pale lilac for the 1.5-litre models.

Rear view
- Rear bumper now incorporated the centrally-mounted 'J' emblem, some of which were also fitted to pre-war models.

Side view
- Waistline chromed trim running from leading edge of bonnet through the doors to spears above the rear wings in the same fashion as the pre-war car but of much thinner section.
- Scuttle area between bottom of windscreen and bonnet now wider.

Compare the waistline chrome trims of this post-war car with the earlier, much thicker chrome strips used on the pre-war examples.

Pre-war thicker waistline trims.

Post-war frontal view showing the bottom-hinged headlights and the new 'Jaguar' winged badge on the radiator grille.

- 'SS' insignia wheel spinners replaced with those containing the word 'Jaguar'.

Points only applicable to the Mark V models
Front view
- Lucas 'tripod' headlights faired into the front wings with chrome spears on top.
- Revised radiator grille badging, still retaining the winged emblem with the word 'Jaguar', but now incorporating either 2.5 or 3.5-litre markings.
- Pod-mounted matching chromed fog (driving) lights mounted either side of the radiator grille diagonally below the headlights.
- Traditional Jaguar style chromed radiator grille with vertical chromed slats, and still incorporating the chromed cap screwing directly into the radiator. (Mascots remained an extra cost option with these models.)
- Traditional styled front wings, but now with greater fairing into the main bodywork and still retaining integrated side light units.
- Substantial multi-component chromed bumper bar, forming two separate horizontal bumpers with quarter bumpers and vertical overriders, and number plate mounting, plus body-colour painted closing panels on top to conceal the irons.

Rear view
- Rear styling following the design of the earlier cars, but with deeper boot panel, still hinged at the bottom and incorporating a stylised handle and lock.
- Fuel filler incorporated into the nearside wing under concealed flush body-colour painted panel.
- Substantial bumper bar treatment as at the front, centre section of which folded down to access the spare wheel compartment. Centrally mounted number plate mounting.
- Rear lighting accommodated within the rear quarter bumpers.

Side view
- Although retaining a similar style to the earlier models, body longer and taller.
- Wider doors with separate chrome-plated window surrounds, all doors featuring opening quarter-lights.
- Full length triangular section chromed waistline trims with extended spears over the rear wings, incorporating substantial push-button door handles.
- Rear wheel spats in body colour.
- Steel wheels of smaller (16in) diameter, and chromed hubcaps with centre sections painted to match body colour, and incorporating centre spinner design with 'Jaguar' name.
- Bonnet centre hinged but with separate (detachable) side panels, previously part of the whole bonnet unit.

A much more modernistic approach to the pre-war design in the Mark V saloon. Note the extensive chromework and the smaller 16in wheels (no longer wire wheels) with painted hub-caps to match the exterior bodywork.

Impressive frontal view of the Mark V with faired-in headlights, wing mounted pedestal fog lamps and the substantial bumper bar arrangement incorporating number plate mounting.

Sculptured chromed door handles incorporating push-button operation. Note also the retention of fresh-air ventilation in the scuttle panel.

- Ventilators fitted to the scuttle on either side of the car ahead of the front doors and behind the engine compartment side panels.

Points only applicable to the drophead coupé Mark V models.

- Wider door incorporating conventional pull down door handles.
- Traffic indicators mounted just to the rear of the front doors.

Interior identification points

General points applicable to post-war models

- Return to pleated upholstery in the same style of pre-1940 models.
- Centrally-mounted heater unit, situated further back underneath the dashboard area.
- Heater controls now fitted to the dashboard area.
- Fitment of radio installation could now be carried out in the centre of the dash area.

Points only applicable to Mark V saloon and drophead coupé models

- Plain unpleated leather to all seating.
- Height-adjustable front seats with shaped bolsters to rear squabs.
- Full width bench seating with raised 'wing' areas at sides to meet up with rear doors 'D' posts.
- Flat rear floor area without a transmission tunnel intrusion.
- Plain, padded door panels incorporating trigger-style door handles with turn-buttons to instigate locking mechanism.
- Traditional style to wooden dashboard area but with rearranged switchgear and stylised instrument legends.
- Shallower dashboard top rail without individual wiper controls.
- Radio installation (where fitted) now built into the dashboard lower area, normally occupied by pull-out drawer.
- Under top dash panel 'black violet' reflected lighting for instrumentation.
- Windscreen now fixed.
- Dashboard top rail-mounted rearview mirror.
- 18in Bluemells four-spoke steering wheel with pronounced chrome-edged box incorporating Jaguar head and indicator turn control.
- Conventional front door-mounted swivel draught excluder quarter-lights for most cars, very early examples featured the same type as at the rear.
- Rear door-mounted swivel draught excluder quarter-lights controlled by knurled sliders.

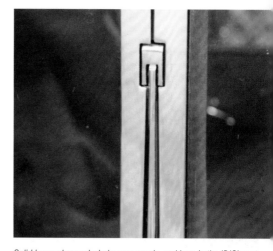

Solid brass chromed window surrounds, and here in the 'B/C' post incorporating the traffic indicator.

Rear of the Mark V with deeper boot lid and substantial bumper arrangement, behind which is a fold-down panel for access to the spare wheel.

The Mark V retained the pre-war style of opening bonnet but now the side panels were separate and detachable.

The Mark V drophead coupé with the hood erect...

... with the hood in the 'sedanca' position.

... with the hood down.

The dashboard layout was similar but with instruments and switches placed differently from the earlier cars. The upper rail hides the black violet lighting. Note the new style steering wheel with prominent centre boss.

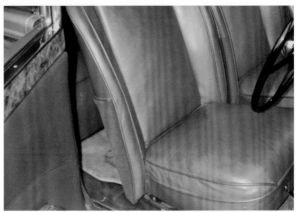

Front seating of the Mark V with stiff bolsters for added support and quite plain door panels.

The rear compartment of the Mark V, again with unpleated upholstery. The inset rear courtesy light (one either side) in the rear quarter of the roof became a regular feature of the big Jaguar saloons into the early 1960s. Also note the quite sophisticated catch to the rear door quarter-lights, new to the Mark V and which became a standard fitment on most subsequent Jaguar saloons well into the 1960s. Also note the trigger door handles with separate locking 'knob'.

Technical specifications

	1.75-litre	2.5-litre
cc	1,776	2,663
Bore and stroke (mm)	73 x 106	73 x 106
Compression ratio	7.6 to 1	7.6 to 1
bhp	65	105
@ rpm	4,600	4,600
Fuelling	Single SU carb	Twin SU carbs
Transmission	4-speed (manual)	4-speed (manual)
Wheel size (in)	18, wire	18, wire
Suspension front	Beam axle, half elliptic leaf	Beam axle, half elliptic leaf
Suspension rear	Live axle, half elliptic leaf	Live axle, half elliptic leaf
Brakes	Girling – rod operated	Girling – rod operated
Performance		
0–50mph (sec)	17	10.6
Top speed (mph)	72	87
Average mpg	27	16
Dimensions		
Length (in)	173	186
Width (in)	65.5	66
Height (in)	60	61
Wheelbase (in)	112.5	120
Front track (in)	52	54
Rear track (in)	55	56
Weight (cwt)	26.5	32

Optional extras

Ace wheel rimbellishers.
Unique exterior colour schemes.
Chromium-plated badge bar.
Radio installation.
Fitted luggage for boot area.
Leaper mascot for radiator grille top.
Chromium-plated wing mirrors.
White-wall tyres.

	3.5-litre
cc	3,485
Bore and stroke (mm)	82 x 110
Compression ratio	7.2 to 1
bhp	125
@ rpm	4,500
Fuelling	Twin SU carbs
Transmission	4-speed (manual)
Wheel size (in)	18, wire
Suspension front	Beam axle, half elliptic leaf
Suspension rear	Live axle, half elliptic leaf
Brakes	Girling – rod operated
Performance	
0–50mph (sec)	9
Top speed (mph)	92
Average mpg	17
Dimensions	
Length (in)	186
Width (in)	66
Height (in)	61
Wheelbase (in)	120
Front track (in)	54
Rear track (in)	56
Weight (cwt)	32.5

Technical specifications *cont ...*

	2.5-litre (Mark V)	3.5-litre (Mark V)
cc	2,663	3,485
Bore and stroke	73 x 106	82 x 110
Compression ratio	7.3 to 1	6.75 to 1
bhp	102	125
@ rpm	4,600	4,250
Fuelling	Twin SU carbs	Twin SU carbs
Transmission	4-speed (manual)	4-speed (manual)
Wheel size (in)	16, wire	16, wire
Suspension front	Independent wishbones, torsion bar, anti-roll bar	Independent wishbones, torsion bar, anti-roll bar
Suspension rear	Live axle, half-elliptic leaf	Live axle, half-elliptic leaf
Brakes	Girling – hydraulic	Girling – hydraulic
Performance		
0–50mph (sec)	10.6	9.9
Top speed (mph)	87	92
Average mpg	16	18
Dimensions		
Length (in)	187	187
Width (in)	69	69
Height (in)	62.5	62.5
Wheelbase (in)	120	120
Front track (in)	56	56
Rear track (in)	56	56
Weight (cwt)	32.5	33

Colour schemes

Exterior	Post-war	Mark V
Olive Green	■	–
Maroon	■	–
Suede Green	■	■
Ivory	■	■
Dark Blue	■	–
Black	■	■
Lavender Grey	■	■
Mountain Ash Green	■	–
Birch Grey	■	■
Battleship Grey	■	■
Gunmetal	■	■
Honeysuckle	■	–
Dove Grey	■	–
Pastel Blue Metallic	■	–
Pastel Green Metallic	■	–

Seat trim	Post War	Mark V
Olive Green	■	–
Maroon	■	–
Red	■	■
Suede Green	■	■
Pale Blue	■	
Dark Blue	–	–
Black	■	–
Silver Black	■	–
Brown	■	–
Pigskin Grain Tan	■	■
Beige	–	–
Biscuit	■	–
Grey	■	–
Hood		
French Grey	■	■
Black	■	■
Dark Sand	■	■
Gunmetal Grey	■	■

Prices and production volumes

	Price new (£)	1945	1946	1947	1948	1949	1950
Jaguar 1.75-litre saloon	684	■	■	■	■	■	–
Jaguar 2.5-litre saloon	889	–	■	■	■	■	–
Jaguar 2.5-litre dhc	1,189	–	–	–	■	–	–
Jaguar 3.5-litre saloon	991	–	■	■	■	■	–
Jaguar 3.5-litre dhc	1,263	–	–	–	■	–	–
Jaguar Mark V 2.5 saloon	1,247	–	–	–	–	■	■
Jaguar Mark V 2.5 dhc	1,247	–	–	–	–	–	■
Jaguar Mark V 3.5 saloon	1,263	–	–	–	■	■	■
Jaguar Mark V 3.5 dhc	1,263	–	–	–	■	■	■

	Price new (£)	1951	Total produced
Jaguar 1.75-litre saloon	684	–	5,761
Jaguar 2.5-litre saloon	889	–	1,749
Jaguar 2.5-litre dhc	1,189	–	101
Jaguar 3.5-litre saloon	991	–	3,860
Jaguar 3.5-litre dhc	1,263	–	498
Jaguar Mark V 2.5 saloon	1,247	■	1,671
Jaguar Mark V 2.5 dhc	1,247	–	29
Jaguar Mark V 3.5 saloon	1,263	■	7,828
Jaguar Mark V 3.5 dhc	1,263	■	971
Total production			**22,468**

3 | The XK sports cars 1948 to 1961

Background

The XK120 was the first entirely new car produced by Jaguar after the Second World War. Announced at the British Motor Show in October 1948, it was only the second sports car ever produced by the company (the first being the SS Jaguar 100 in the 1930s) and was the first car to feature Jaguar's own in-house designed engine, the famous XK straight six power unit.

The XK120 was not so much developed as contrived to bring publicity to Jaguar by showing off its new engine, which was actually intended for a new saloon, eventually to be called the Mark VII. Hasty work in cutting down one of the new saloon chassis and installing the XK power unit, and then hand-crafting an aluminium two-seater roadster body, led to the launch of the car at the motor show before it had ever run.

Initially intended to be sold as a very limited production car with both a 2.0-litre four-cylinder engine and the 3.4-litre six-cylinder engine, no-one – least of all William Lyons – anticipated the public response to the XK120. The quantity of forward orders embarrassed Jaguar, and it soon became clear that they could not meet the demand by producing the car with an alloy body over an ash wooden frame (a typically pre-war method of build). In addition the idea of a four-cylinder version (to be known as XK100) had to be dropped. Few cars (around 200 in total) actually got delivered, while the company worked

towards full-scale production via an all-steel bodyshell, which began in May 1950.

Soon after the supply of XK120s got under way, they were already finding success in competition both on the race track and in road rallies. This eventually led to further development and the XK120 C-type, designed specifically for racing, which further boosted the standing of Jaguar and its XK road-going cars.

Riding on the success of the XK120 two-seater, two further production variants were produced – a fixed-head coupé from 1951, and a drophead coupé from 1953.

Production of the XK120 ceased in 1954 to make way for its replacement, by which time a total of 12,055 of all variants had been produced. That replacement was the XK140, introduced for 1954, which also came in three variants: two-seater, fixed-head, and drophead. Externally the 140s are easily identifiable, although retaining the overall style of the earlier car. Internally the changes were more subtle, except for the moving forward of the engine in the chassis to provide better legroom and, in the fixed-head version, 'occasional' rear seating. Mechanically XK140 models benefited from a more powerful version of the XK engine, improved handling, and the adoption of rack and pinion steering.

The XK140 was superseded in 1957 by the final development of the design, the XK150, a much more radical style although still retaining the styling concept of the original XK120. Externally it was a more slab-sided design with larger glass areas and more interior space. A redesign of the interior meant no veneer, while disc brakes were fitted all round. Initially the XK150 was only available in two body styles, drophead and fixed-head coupés, but in 1958 a two-seater roadster version was added followed by the 'S' high performance versions and larger engined variants.

The XK150 left production in 1961 to make way for the all new E-type. The total production figure for all XKs from 1948 to 1961 amounted to over 30,000.

Model range and development

Only one production model was offered of the XK120 in 1948, although subsequently three variants were produced, all based on the same chassis and basic mechanical configuration.

Models available 1948–54
XK120 open two-seater (roadster)
XK120 fixed-head coupé
XK120 drophead coupé

The principle of the three models stemmed from William Lyons's ability to produce cars catering for different markets, building on the development of an original concept and utilising as many common parts as possible, therefore keeping the cost of production down. This theme continued throughout XK production.

The original two-seater (roadster) was aimed at the true sports car market, offering minimal accommodation and equipment levels with high performance and good handling – typical 'wind in the hair' motoring. In contrast the fixed-head coupé was a true grand tourer in its own right. Still offering the performance and handling capabilities of the two-seater, it provided virtually unheard of benefits to sports car drivers, like an integrated hard top that was part of the overall body design and made the car structurally very robust, lockable doors, wind-up windows, and even a walnut veneered dashboard.

The drophead coupé provided an amalgam of both styles. For those who wanted open air motoring, simply releasing the windscreen catches and folding down the hood provided instant access to the sun; yet the car retained the 'comfort' elements of veneer, wind-up windows, and lockable doors.

The first 200 two-seater models were all of alloy construction, virtually hand-built and therefore very different in detail to later steel-bodied cars. The front wings formed one piece, even including the sidelight housings. Internal

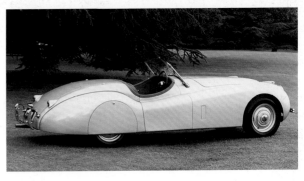

In its original form the XK120 roadster was fitted with steel wheels painted to the body colour with no rimbellishers but with chromed hubcaps. Earlier cars, like this one, featured painted centres to hubcaps to match the exterior paint finish. Also on this early car are the chromed sidelight cowls on the top of the front wings. Full rear spats covered all steel wheel cars when new.

Front view of XK120 clearly showing the slim split-bumper treatment, 'tripod' headlights and, being an early car, chromed sidelight housings. A split-windscreen was common to all XK120 models.

Rear of XK120 model with just over-riders fitted; this was applicable to all models. Slight changes were made to rear lighting and number plate plinths during production – see text.

floors were of plywood construction and wood was also used in the sills. Underneath the alloy structure was an ash wooden frame to support it.

When body construction changed to steel, the bonnet, doors, and boot lid remained in aluminium. Apart from the obvious feel and sound of the metal, the differences in body style between alloy and steel-bodied cars are small. There are slight curvature differences to the front wings, and at the rear the steel wings are slightly less bulbous. The early steel-bodied cars also had chromed sidelight pods on the front wings.

The majority of XK120s were fitted with conventional steel road wheels with fully enclosing rear wheel spats. If wire wheels were specified from new, these spats were not fitted and the rear wings had copper beading fitted as a finisher.

It wasn't until 1951 that the fixed-head coupé was introduced, and SE (Special Equipment) models were offered by the factory the same year. Using an improved power unit with high lift camshafts, lightened flywheel, stiffer rear springs, wire wheels, a dual exhaust system, and benefiting from Jaguar's success in racing, the XK120 SE provided an increase of 20bhp over the 'ordinary' cars.

In 1953, for the last year in production, the XK120 drophead coupé was introduced, offering the enhanced fixed-head interior with the ability to still enjoy open air motoring.

When the XK140 was introduced in 1954 it was significantly modified, although it retained the overall style of the 120. Instantly recognisable from the outside by the fatter bumper bars, heavy cast radiator grille, and larger window areas on the fixed-head coupé, all 140 models utilised the more powerful 180bhp engine and were equipped with rack and pinion steering. In the fixed-head and drophead coupés occasional rear seating was provided. Special Equipment models were also available but now offered a boost in performance to 210bhp. The XK140 was the first Jaguar sports car to become available with the option of automatic transmission.

Models available 1954–7
XK140 two-seater (roadster)
XK140 fixed-head coupé
XK140 drophead coupé

The XK140 only stayed in production for three years, being replaced by the XK150 in 1957. Although following the basic styling features of both the earlier models the XK150 had a wider bonnet, another new grille, a flattened out wing line, and a curved one-piece windscreen for the first time on an XK. Mechanically disc brakes were the major technological advance. Interior trim was also modified again.

Interior of XK120 roadster showing four-spoke steering wheel with prominent centre horn push and fabric-covered dashboard only applicable to roadster models. Note the cut-away doors, also found only on roadster models.

Later XK120 roadster showing the painted sidelight housings and the hood erect. Perspex side-screens were used on all XK120 roadster models. Inset is a rear view of the hood and rear screen design.

XK120 fixed-head coupé.

Models available at launch 1957
XK150 3.4-litre fixed-head coupé
XK150 3.4-litre drophead coupé

Initially there was not a two-seater (roadster) version of the XK150, this coming on line late in 1958 with a much more accentuated rear deck area compared to earlier two-seater XKs. This was also accompanied by an 'S' model with triple carburettors and a straight port cylinder head boasting an output of 250bhp. By 1959 'S' models were also available in the other two body styles. Then Jaguar introduced an extra, larger engine for the XK, of 3.8 litres capacity, either with conventional twin carburettors or with triples, the latter boosting performance again to 265bhp.

All this amounted to no less than 12 models, plus SE types; and this is where the XK150 model list becomes confusing. Early literature states that 'standard' models of the XK150 were available, supposedly with drum brakes and steel wheels (with full rear body spats) and lacking the front valance mounted fog lamps.

XK150s were available with a choice of manual, manual with overdrive, or automatic transmission. Production of all models finally ceased in 1961.

Exterior identification points

General points applicable to all XK120s
Front view
- Twin slim-line bumper bars, between which were situated the chromed oval radiator grille containing vertical slats.
- Steel number plate mounting below the radiator on UK cars, but on the side under or over-bumper for other markets.
- Tripod headlights.
- Growler badge to forward centre of bonnet top in bronze against a cream background, with the words 'Jaguar Cars Ltd Coventry'.
- Split windscreen with chromed surround.
- In September 1952 the front wing sidelight pods changed from chrome to body colour.

Rear view
- Twin vertical over-riders to outside areas of body.
- Twin single red rear light lenses mounted in chrome plinths.
- Full depth boot lid with operating handle to extreme base, with separate number plate surround above which incorporated a chromed reversing light/number plate illumination panel.
- Single tail pipe exhaust systems were fitted to 'standard' cars, a twin pipe arrangement to SE models.

Different interior design for fixed-head and drophead coupé XK120 models, with wood-veneered dashboard and enhanced door trim panels.

Drophead coupé XK120 model. Note revised door and hood treatment compared to that of the roadster models.

XK140 styling differed at the front from that of the 120 (behind it) by having a more prominent cast radiator grille, revised 'J' lighting, and a substantial ribbed bumper bar. Fog lights were an extra cost fitment to these cars.

Side view
- Cars with steel wheels had chromed hub caps with centre sections painted to body colour, with wheels to match.
- Where fitted, wire wheels were of the 54-spoke type, painted either to body colour or silver and held in place by chromed eared hub spinners depicting the Jaguar name.
- Full body spats were fitted over the rear disc wheels (no covers on wire wheel equipped cars).
- From February 1951 front wing ventilators were added to aid intake of cool air to the cockpit.

XK120 model specifics
XK120 two-seater (alloy cars)
- Rear number plate plinth mounted onto the boot lid from the exterior.
- Wheel-arches had wired edges to add strength to the aluminium.
- Fuel filler cover lock fitted to rear bodywork.

XK120 two-seater (steel cars)
- Rear number plate plinth bolted to the boot lid from the inside with no visible fixings on the outside; this was hereafter true of all 120s, regardless of body style.
- Fuel filler cover lock fitted to the cover itself.
- From 1951 the hood extended further back, permitting the rear window to be unzipped.

XK120 fixed-head coupé
- Revised doors accommodating exterior chromed handles, locking on the driver's side, and with chromed on brass fixed window frames with quarter-lights.
- Additional quarter-lights behind the doors.

XK120 drophead coupé
- Unlike the two-seater, the front split windscreen was held within steel surrounds with a header panel, part of the main body structure, and was painted to match.
- Fuel filler moved rearwards on the body to allow room for hood retraction.
- External door handles were smaller and more rounded than fixed-head coupé models, and the window glass, frames, and quarter-lights were of a different style.
- The hood was of a different style, incorporating a larger rear window that unzipped to fold down.

General points applicable to all XK140s
Front view
- As XK120 except for chromed cast oval radiator grille with only seven vertical slats.
- Red circular enamel badge carrying the words 'Jaguar Cars Ltd' above a growler head, and the word 'Coventry' under it.

The fixed-head coupé XK140 was easily identifiable from the XK120 by its pronounced bumper bar treatment, heavy chromed centre boot trim, and enlarged window areas with wider doors.

XK140 roadster with hood erect.

Above left: Interior of XK140 roadster, very similar but subtly different to the earlier XK120 model (see the picture on page 44).

Above right: Interior design for fixed- and drophead coupé XK140 models. Note the flat horn boss to the steering wheel, an easy identification point, as are the interior door handle slides.

- Deep single chromed ribbed front bumper bar with prominent chromed over-riders either side of a black-painted metal number plate plinth.
- Bumper to front body distance was covered with a steel valance painted to body colour, which accommodated twin Lucas fog lamps where fitted.
- Revised headlights (not tripods) with 'J' insignia in centre.
- Separate circular indicator lenses with chromed surrounds to the lower section of the front wings.
- Chromed centre bonnet strip.

Rear view
- Deep split rear chrome bumpers with over-riders with centre section to provide metal number plate plinth and access to spare wheel.
- Number plate illumination/reversing light attached to lowermost area of boot lid (now shorter than the XK120 style).
- Vertically mounted chromed boot handle with chrome finisher running centrally up the boot lid.
- Unique chromed badge in red with silver lettering depicting the Jaguar badge, winged badge, and the 1951 win at Le Mans.
- Rear light lenses fitted in extended chromed plinths.

Side view
- Where disc wheels were fitted, hub caps were all chromed.
- As later XK120s except for specifics noted below.

XK140 model specifics
XK140 two-seater
- As XK120 equivalent, but look for wrap-around effect of front and rear bumpers.
- Where steel wheels were fitted, hub caps were entirely chrome.
- At the rear the central chrome strip up the boot continues over rear deck area.

XK140 fixed-head coupé
- Raised roof line (1½in) and elongated passenger area (6½in) shows in larger window areas all round compared to XK120.
- 4in shorter in front wings and bonnet area as engine was moved forward in the chassis compared to XK120 fhc.
- Lengthened doors with new style larger door handles mounted lower in the door.
- Steel wheel hub caps were chromed, not painted.

XK140 drophead coupé
- Longer hood and door window area because of occasional rear seating.

XK140 drophead coupé. Note that all XK120 and XK140 dropheads feature glass side windows.

Rear view of XK140 showing the bumper bar treatment and unique badging to the boot panel, indicating appropriate Le Mans victories. Twin exhausts only applied to high-performance models.

XK150 fixed-head coupé, of a completely different styling approach to earlier models and easily identifiable by its very large side window areas and slab-sided body look.

As with other 140 models look for wrap-around effect of front and rear bumper bar arrangement.

General points applicable to all XK150s

Front view

- Revised wider oval radiator grille with 16 slats incorporating a new red plastic badge depicting the growler head and the words 'Jaguar' and 'XK150' in silver.
- Similar style bumper bar to XK140 but dished in the centre to accommodate the new radiator grille.
- Wider bonnet with raised centre section with full length chrome finisher.
- Metal valance behind bumper bars now formed two separate panels.
- One-piece curved windscreen with slimmer surrounds.

Rear view

- Single wrap-around rear bumper bar with twin over-riders.
- New boot lid mounted number plate surround, with chromed illumination/reversing light also mounted on the boot lid. Post-1959 models with revised rake.
- Revised position of boot handle with shorter centre chromed trim and new style badging depicting Jaguar's subsequent wins at Le Mans during the lifespan of the car (initially four wins, on later cars five).
- Rear lights initially mounted on elongated chromed plinths, later changed to significantly larger plinths and lens units incorporating separate indicator and reflector lenses.
- Rear bumper now one-piece with matching over-riders. Positions of latter altered with revised lighting.

Side view

- Front wing, door, and rear wing line raised and flattened.
- On 'S' specification models, a chromed 'S' badge appeared on the doors.
- Door handles repositioned on fhc and dhc models.
- Larger window areas all round.

XK150 model specifics

XK150 two-seater

- Windscreen moved 4in rearward.
- Bonnet longer, extending rearwards towards new bulkhead and screen.
- The first XK Roadster to feature glass wind-up windows.
- Curved top to door window glass structure with chrome finisher. No quarter-lights.
- Exterior door handles, a first for an XK Roadster, in this case matching the style used on the XK140 fhc.
- Hood slimmer in style, with enlarged rear window and single chromed trim above.

XK150s were the only XKs to feature a one-piece wrap-around windscreen. The bumper bar treatment was similar to the XK140, but with a wider grille.

Rear view of the XK150 with one-piece bumper bar and an integrated reversing light plinth/number plate surround within the boot lid. This is a later model with larger rear light units featuring separate indicator lenses (the colour varied according to market). Earlier XK150s featured the same lighting treatment as the XK140 (see the picture on page 47).

Revised boot badge for XK150 models with updated list of Le Mans victories.

XK150 fixed-head coupé
- Larger glass in new chromed brass window frames.
- Revised shape to front and rear quarter-lights.
- Larger rear window.

XK150 drophead coupé
- Neater hood style with chromed rain gutters and enlarged rear window (still unzippable).
- Folded hood rests higher up on rear deck area.

Interior identification points

XK120 two-seater (all models)
- Split-bench style leather seats with ten pleats, with matching leather centre section over transmission tunnel.
- Door trim panels included a covered pocket and pull strap for door opening (early alloy cars had a knob towards the front of the trim panel).
- Leather-covered dashboard to match trim colour. Passenger side grab handle fitted to steel-bodied cars only.
- A Bluemel 18in cast black (or white in some export cars) steering wheel was fitted with four spokes that would become a standard feature on all Jaguars for many years. In the case of all XK120s this featured a protruding black horn push containing a side view of a jaguar face with chromed surround.

XK120 fixed-head coupé
- Door trims had no pockets and incorporated chromed window winding and door handles plus walnut-veneered cappings to the top section.
- Wooden cappings continued to the door frame surround securing a woollen head lining.
- Wooden cappings continued to the front screen surround and to the dashboard which was of a totally different design to the two-seater's. Walnut veneered with lockable glove-box, pull-out drawer (also used to accommodate a radio), flip-up ashtray, and trimmed upper section incorporating demisting vents. Switchgear and some instruments changed in 1952, most noticeable from the knurled lighting switch in the centre of the dash. Switches and warning lights changed again in 1954, along with a movement of the instrument positions.
- Behind the seats a storage locker with lid was provided, trimmed to match the interior.
- Two tinted Perspex sun visors were fitted just to this model.

XK120 drophead coupé
- As fixed-head coupé but full-width map pockets to both front door trims along with hand-pulls within the wooden cappings.

This side view of a drophead coupé XK150 clearly shows the slab sided look of the body.

When XK150s were ordered new, wire wheels were still an extra cost option. Full rear wheel spats applied, but are rarely seen these days if the car is fitted with steel wheels.

The roadster XK150 had a pronounced 'rear deck' as it was strictly a two-seater. The boot luggage rack was a period extra.

- No sun visors fitted.
- The hood mechanism was completely different to the two-seater, enabling it to be folded down quickly and easily to rest on the rear storage locker.

XK140 (all models)
- More interior accommodation due to the engine being moved forward in the chassis.
- The smaller 17in steering wheel now used a flat horn push depicting gold growler image.

XK140 two-seater
- Interior styling remained mostly as XK120 two-seater. Dashboard now moved closer to the occupants. Direction indicator stalk moved from steering wheel boss to outboard of the column.

XK140 fixed-head coupé
- Occasional rear seating in the form of two individual cushions and backrests replaced XK120's locker.
- Behind the seats a panel could fold down, giving access to the boot area for storage of larger items.
- After 1955 centre upholstered section between the front seats featured full depth pleating.
- Revised door trims incorporating a chromed slider instead of conventional door handle.
- Slimmer seat back rests to provide more space in the rear compartment.
- Veneered dashboard now incorporated two ashtrays and chromed direction indicator switch to top centre below rear-view mirror.

XK140 drophead coupé
- As fixed-head coupé but with a fully lined hood. The shaping of this (although longer overall) was same as on the XK120.
- Larger rear window, but screen, side windows, and quarter-lights remained as on the XK120.

XK150 (all models)
- Wider, more airy interior without any veneered woodwork on any models.
- Similar seating arrangement to XK140s, and all three variants of the 150 carried the same style of trim.
- Door trim panels of different style to earlier cars, with chromed horizontal finishers and arm-rests and, until 1958, a trimmed pull-open ashtray to each door, changed later to a single chromed ashtray on the transmission tunnel.
- Entirely new dashboard design incorporating soft padded trim. Some instruments and switchgear also new, all in a revised layout. The passenger side glove-box had a lid, but on the driver's side it was open.

XK150 two-seater (roadster)
- Wind-down windows incorporated fixed chrome surrounds.
- A fixed tonneau cover could be pulled over the hood when down (previously a separate item on other XKs).

XK150 fixed-head coupé
- Larger window areas to previous fhc models.

See accompanying photographs for more detail.

XK150 dashboard layouts were the same regardless of model. Now without wood, they had a padded covering.

Comparison of frontal aspects: XK150 (left), XK140 (centre), and XK120 (right).

Rear comparison views of roadster models: XK120 (right), XK140 (centre), and XK150 (left).

Technical specifications

	XK120	XK140
cc	3,442	3,442
Bore and stroke (mm)	83 x 106	83 x 106
Compression ratio	8:1 (7:1/9:1 optional)	8:1 (7:1/9:1 optional)
bhp	160 (180 SE)	190 (210 SE)
@ rpm	5,000 (5,300 SE)	5,500 (5,750 SE)
Torque (lb ft)	195 (203 SE)	210 (213 SE)
@ rpm	2,500 (4,000 SE)	2,500 (4,000 SE)
Fuelling	2 x SU carbs	2 x SU carbs
Transmission	4-speed (3 synchro)	4-speed (3 synchro)
Wheel size (in)	16, steel or wire	16, steel or wire
Suspension front	Ind wishbone, torsion bar	Ind wishbone, torsion bar
Suspension rear	Live axle, leaf springs	Live axle, leaf springs
Brakes	4 wheel drum	4 wheel drum
Performance		
0–60mph (sec)	10	8.4
Top speed (mph)	124.6 ots (120.5 fhc; 119.5 dhc)	121.1
Average mpg	19.8 (17.2 fhc, 14.5 dhc)	16–18
Dimensions		
Length (in)	174	176
Width (in)	61.5	64.5
Height (in)	52.5 (53.5 fhc)	52.5 (55 fhc)
Wheelbase (in)	102	102
Front track (in)	51	51.5
Rear track (in)	50	51.375
Weight (cwt)	26 (27 fhc, 27.5 dhc)	28 (29 dhc)

Optional extras

XK120

Lucas fog lamps.
Fitted luggage (two suitcases to match trim).
Boot lid chromed luggage rack.
Choice of seven Radiomobile radios with fitting kits.
Auxiliary (larger) fuel tank.
Aero screens to replace full-length split screen.
Underbody steel shield for adverse road conditions.
Bucket front seats.
Dunlop Racing tyres.

External (boot) spare wheel mounting.
Heater unit (only until 1952, then standard equipment).
High lift camshafts.
C-type cylinder head.
2in H8 SU carburettors.
Close ratio gearbox.
Wire wheels.
Dual exhaust system.
Chrome wheel rimbellishers for steel wheels.
White-finished Bluemel steering wheel.
Racing clutch.

Technical specifications *cont ...*

	XK150 3.4	XK150 3.8
cc	3,442	3,781
Bore and stroke (mm)	83 x 106	87 x 106
Compression ratio	8:1 (7:1/9:1 optional), 9:1 'S'	8:1 (7:1/9:1 optional), 9:1 'S'
bhp	210 (250 'S')	220 (265 'S')
@ rpm	5,500	5,500
Torque (lb ft)	216 (240 'S')	240 (260 'S')
@ rpm	3,000 (4,500 'S')	3,000 (4,000 'S')
Fuelling	2 x SU carbs (3 'S' models)	2 x SU carbs (3 'S' models)
Transmission	4-speed (3 synchro)	4-speed (3 synchro)
Wheel size (in)	16, steel or wire	16, steel or wire
Suspension front	Ind wishbone, torsion bar.	Ind wishbone, torsion bar.
Suspension rear	Live axle, leaf springs	Live axle, leaf springs
Brakes	4 wheel disc	4 wheel disc
Performance		
0–60mph (sec)	8.5 (7.8 'S')	7.6 ('S')
Top speed (mph)	123.7 (132 'S')	125 (136.3 'S')
Average mpg	20.5 (18.6 'S')	13–19
Dimensions		
Length (in)	177	177
Width (in)	64.5	64.5
Height (in)	55.5 fhc (54 two-seater)	55.5 fhc (54 two-seater)
Wheelbase (in)	102	102
Front track (in)	51.25	51.25
Rear track (in)	51.25	51.25
Weight (cwt)	28.5	29

Optional extras *cont ...*

XK140

Windscreen washers (later standard equipment).
Lucas fog lamps.
Fitted luggage (two suitcases to match trim).
Boot lid chromed luggage rack.
Choice of Radiomobile radios with fitting kits.
Aero screens to replace full-length split screen.
Underbody steel shield for adverse road
    conditions.
Bucket front seats.
Dunlop racing tyres.
Dunlop Road Speed whitewall tyres.
High lift camshafts.
C-type cylinder head.
2in H8 SU carburettors.
Close ratio gearbox.
Wire wheels.
Dual exhaust system.
Chrome wheel rimbellishers for steel wheels.
White-finished Bluemel steering wheel.
Cut-away rear spats for wire-wheeled cars.

XK150

Lucas fog lamps.
Fitted luggage (two suitcases to match trim).
Boot lid chromed luggage rack.
Choice of Radiomobile radios with fitting kits.
Underbody steel shield for adverse road
    conditions.
Bucket front seats.
Dunlop Racing tyres.
Dunlop Road Speed whitewall tyres.
Sundym tinted windscreen.
Close ratio gearbox.
Dual exhaust system.
Chrome wheel rimbellishers for steel wheels.
White-finished Bluemel steering wheel.
Jaguar leaping mascot for bonnet.
Thornton Powr-Lok differential.
Chromed badge bar.
Bluemel wood rim steering wheel.
Weathershields sunroof (fixed head coupé only).
Full-length tonneau cover for drophead coupé
    model.
Radiator blind.

Colour schemes

Exterior colour	Years	Interior Two-seater	Interior Soft top	Interior Fhc	Interior Dhc	Interior Soft top
Bronze	To 1952	Black/Tan	Fawn	Tan		
Birch Grey		Biscuit/Red	French Grey	Red	Red	
Birch Grey	1952–6	Red (140 only)	Black	Dark Blue	Dark Blue	French Grey
				Light Blue	Light Blue	Black
				Grey (140)		
Suede Green		Suede Green	French Grey	Suede Green	Suede Green	Black
			Black			
Black	To 1952	Biscuit/Pigskin	Black			
			Sand			
Black		Biscuit/Red	Black	Red		
			Sand			
Black	1952–6	Tan	Black	Tan	Tan	
Black	From 1956	Tan		Red	Red	Sand
		Red		Tan	Tan	Black
		Grey		Grey	Grey	
				Biscuit	Biscuit	
Red		Biscuit/Red	Fawn	Red	Red	Black
			Black			Fawn (140)
Red	From 1952	Red	Black	Red	Red	Black
			Fawn			Fawn
Silver	To 1952	Red	Fawn	Red		
			Black			
Silver	To 1952	Light/Dark Blue	Fawn	Light Blue		
			Black			
Pastel Blue Metallic	To 1952	Light/Dark Blue	Fawn	Light Blue		
			Black			
Pastel Green Metallic	To 1952	Suede Green	Fawn	Suede Green		
Cream	To 1952	Biscuit/Red	Fawn	Red		
Cream	To 1952	Biscuit/Pigskin	Fawn			
Pastel Blue	1952–6	Light/Dark Blue	French Grey	Light Blue	Pale Blue (140)	French Grey
			Black	Dark Blue (140)	Dark Blue (140)	Black
			Dark Blue			Blue (140)
Pastel Green	1952–6	Suede Green	Fawn	Suede Green	Suede Green	Fawn
			Black		Grey	Black
Old English White	1952–6	Biscuit/Red	Fawn	Red	Red	Fawn
	From 1952	Red	Black		Pale Blue	Black
			Blue		Dark Blue	Blue
British Racing Green	From 1952	Tan	Gunmetal	Tan	Tan	Gunmetal
		Suede Green	Black	Suede Green	Suede Green	Black
Battleship Grey	1952–6	Biscuit/Red	Gunmetal	Red	Red	Gunmetal
		Red (140 only)	Black	Grey	Grey	Black
					Biscuit	

Colour schemes *cont* ...

Exterior colour	Years	Interior Two-seater	Interior Soft top	Interior Fhc	Interior Dhc	Interior Soft top
Lavender Grey	1952–6	Red	Fawn	Red	Red	Fawn
		Suede Green	Black	Suede Green	Suede Green	Black
		Pale Blue		Pale Blue (140)	Pale Blue	
		Black Blue (140)		Dark Blue (140)	Dark Blue (140)	
Dove Grey	1952–6	Tan	Fawn	Tan	Tan	Fawn
		Biscuit	Sand	Biscuit	Biscuit	Sand
		Black		Black		
Pacific Blue	1952–6	Blue	Blue	Blue	Blue	Blue
		Grey	Black	Grey	Grey	Black
		Dark Blue (140)		Dark Blue (140)	Dark Blue (140)	
		Light Blue (140)		Light Blue (140)	Light Blue (140)	
Pearl Grey	From 1952	Red	Blue	Red	Red	Blue
		Blue	Black	Blue	Blue	Black
		Grey	French Grey	Grey	Grey	French Grey
		Light Blue		Light Blue	Light Blue	
		Dark Blue		Dark Blue	Dark Blue	
Mediterranean Blue	1952–6	Blue		Blue	Blue	
		Grey		Grey	Grey	
Maroon	1952–6	Red (140 only)	Black	Red (140 only)	Red (140 only)	Black
		Biscuit (140)	Sand	Biscuit (140)	Biscuit (140)	Sand
Arbor Green	1952–6	Suede Green		Suede Green	Suede Green	
Carmine Red	1952–6	Red		Red	Red	
Indigo Blue	From 1956	Light Blue	Blue	Light Blue	Light Blue	Blue
		Dark Blue	Black	Dark Blue	Dark Blue	Black
		Grey		Grey	Grey	
Claret (maroon)	From 1956	Red	Black	Red	Red	Black
		Maroon	Sand	Maroon	Maroon	Sand
Cotswold Blue	From 1956	Dark Blue	Blue	Dark Blue	Dark Blue	Blue
		Grey	Black	Grey	Grey	Black
Mist Grey	From 1956	Red	French Grey	Red	Red	French Grey
		Light Blue	Black	Light Blue	Light Blue	Black
		Dark Blue		Dark Blue	Dark Blue	
		Grey		Grey	Grey	
Sherwood Green	From 1956	Tan	French Grey	Tan	Tan	French Grey
		Suede Green	Black	Suede Green	Suede Green	Black
Carmen Red	From 1956	Red	Black	Red	Red	Black
Cornish Grey	From 1956	Red	French Grey	Red	Red	French Grey
		Light Blue	Black	Light Blue	Light Blue	Black
		Dark Blue		Dark Blue	Dark Blue	
		Grey		Grey	Grey	
Imperial Maroon	From 1956	Red	Sand	Red	Red	Sand
		Maroon	Black	Maroon	Maroon	Black

Prices and production volumes

	Price new (£)	1948	1949	1950	1951	1952	1953
XK120 two-seater (alloy)	1,263	■	■	■	–	–	–
XK120 two-seater (steel)	–	–	–	–	■	■	■	■
XK120 fixed-head coupé	1,694	–	–	–	■	■	■
XK120 drophead coupé	1,616	–	–	–	–	–	■
XK140 two-seater	1,598	–	–	–	–	–	–
XK140 fixed-head coupé	1,616	–	–	–	–	–	–
XK140 drophead coupé	1,644	–	–	–	–	–	–
XK150 two-seater	1,666	–	–	–	–	–	–
XK150 fixed-head coupé	1,763	–	–	–	–	–	–
XK150 drophead coupé	1,793	–	–	–	–	–	–

	Price new (£)	1954	1955	1956	1957	1958	1959
XK120 two-seater (alloy)	1,263	–	–	–	–	–	–
XK120 two-seater (steel)	–	■	–	–	–	–	–
XK120 fixed-head coupé	1,694	■	–	–	–	–	–
XK120 drophead coupé	1,616	■	–	–	–	–	–
XK140 two-seater	1,598	■	■	■	–	–	–
XK140 fixed-head coupé	1,616	■	■	■	–	–	–
XK140 drophead coupé	1,644	■	■	■	–	–	–
XK150 two-seater	1,666	–	–	–	■	■	■
XK150 fixed-head coupé	1,763	–	–	–	■	■	■
XK150 drophead coupé	1,793	–	–	–	■	■	■

	Price new (£)	1960	1961	Total produced
XK120 two-seater (alloy)	1,263	–	–	240
XK120 two-seater (steel)	–	–	–	7,374
XK120 fixed-head coupé	1,694	–	–	2,680
XK120 drophead coupé	1,616	–	–	1,767
XK140 two-seater	1,598	–	–	3,347
XK140 fixed-head coupé	1,616	–	–	2,798
XK140 drophead coupé	1,644	–	–	2,790
XK150 two-seater	1,666	■	–	2,264
XK150 fixed-head coupé	1,763	■	–	4,448
XK150 drophead coupé	1,793	■	–	2,673
Total production				**30,381**

3

Production changes

1948
XK120 two-seater launched.

1950
XK120 all-steel bodies introduced.
Curved wiper arms fitted.
Starting handle operation deleted.
Shorter dashpots fitted to SU carburettors.

1951
XK120 fixed-head coupé announced.
XK120 SE models available.
Heater became standard fitment.
Front wing ventilators added.
Chrome to body front sidelight housings.
Hood frame changed from chrome to grey paint finish.
Zipped fasteners to hood rear window added.

1952
Window-winders and door interior handles changed.
Additional studs fitted to camshaft covers at the front.
Revised instrument panel fitted.
Hood style extended further back.
Windscreen washers introduced.
Hardura boot mat fitted instead of carpet.

1953
XK120 drophead coupé announced.
(Late) Doors on dhc changed from alloy to steel.
Rear wing piping changed to body colour.

1954
XK120 dashboard style changed.
Rear reflectors added to XK120 cars for UK market.
XK140 models introduced.
(Late) Overdrive option on manual transmissions available for 140.
(Late) 140 boot lid handle changed.

1956
Auto transmission available on fhc and dhc.
Steel door skins replace alloy on fhc and dhc.
Fly-off handbrake changed to normal push-button release type.

1957
XK150 fhc and dhc models announced.

1958
XK150 two-seater announced.
XK150 two-seater 'S' introduced.
Improved heating system introduced.
Fuel filler lid opening changed to rearward.
Indicator operating stalk fitted to steering column.
Larger rear light units fitted.
Over-riders on rear bumper moved inwards.
Boot badge altered to show 1957 Le Mans win.
Pull armrests added to internal door trims.

1959
XK150 fhc and dhc 'S' introduced.
XK150 3.8-litre engines introduced.

1961
End of XK150 sales.

Chassis numbers

Model	Right/Left Drive	Chassis/Vin Nos Commencing
XK120 OTS	RHD	660001
	LHD	670001
XK120 FHC	RHD	669001
	LHD	679001
XK120 DHC	RHD	667001
	LHD	677001
XK140 OTS	RHD	800001
	LHD	810001
XK140 FHC	RHD	804001
	LHD	814001
XK140 DHC	RHD	807001
	LHD	817001
XK150 OTS	RHD	820001
	LHD	830001
XK150 FHC	RHD	824001
	LHD	834001
XK150 DHC	RHD	827001
	LHD	837001

Background

This was the first entirely new style saloon car produced by the company after the Second World War, and the first saloon to use the still relatively new XK power unit.

After the War a change of company name to Jaguar Cars Limited (from SS) meant the re-emergence of what were basically pre-war designs for the saloons, though now bearing the Jaguar name. It wasn't until 1948 that a new model – known as the Mark V – appeared, which only lasted until 1951. Although using a new chassis and suspension layout, the Mark V still utilised the straight six push-rod engine derived from Standard designs, while its bodyshell still resembled the pre-war style.

The Mark V's release was a deliberate ploy by Jaguar to retain an important area of the luxury saloon market until the appearance of the 'all new' Mark VII in 1950 – the car that the XK power unit was originally designed for, with a new chassis design (temporarily used in the Mark V), independent front suspension, and an all-enveloping steel body not that far removed from the gorgeous XK120 sports car style launched in 1948.

Jaguar's Mark VII offered a new standard of luxury, refinement, style, performance, and handling to anything else on the market at the time, and at a very competitive price. Introduced at the British Motor Show in 1950, there was only one model, and at under £1,000 before purchase tax it was an instant success. It would prove to be the most prolific model produced by the company up to the introduction of a smaller saloon in 1956.

Despite its size and weight the Mark VII was very successful in competition, in circuit racing, and in rallying, and in 1956 actually won the Monte Carlo Rally. It was particularly well-liked in the United States, where one journalist called it 'The Prima Ballerina'. Jaguar later offered automatic transmission, and in 1954 the car was upgraded to the Mark VIIM with many significant improvements. In 1957 further development resulted in it being supplemented and renamed the Mark VIII, and then in 1958 it became the Mark IX when the engine was enlarged and it was equipped with power-assisted steering and all-round disc brakes to keep the car abreast of newer competition.

The Mark IX remained in production until 1961, when it was eventually superseded by another all-new design, the Mark X. The Mark VII to IX models were the flagships of the Jaguar range for more than a decade and justly deserved the company's slogan of the period: 'Grace, Space and Pace'. In total over 46,000 of these cars were sold.

Model range and development

The first truly new saloon to carry the Jaguar name, the Mark VII was always designed to take the XK six-cylinder power unit, the earlier XK120 merely being intended as a low production car to publicise the engine. When announced at the British Motor Show in 1950 the Mark VII was available as a simple, single model. Of 3.4 litres engine capacity, it was only available with a four-speed manual gearbox, in one trim form, and with hardly any variation to suit different markets around the world, although it was clear, from the outset, that the car was designed to 'hit' the American market.

It was certainly the most luxurious model Jaguar had produced up to that time, and there is also no doubt that it was designed to captivate a wider market, offering a higher standard of trim, performance, and value for money than any of the home-grown competition, from Lagonda to Armstrong Siddeley and even Rolls-Royce.

The underpinning of the car was a new low-slung chassis with independent front suspension, clad with a very stylish all-steel body emphasising a design style that every model from the XK120 through to the XK150 and Mark 2 would follow into the 1960s. Performance of up to 100mph was guaranteed from the 160bhp straight six engine, with sufficient room to carry five people in the utmost comfort of leather and walnut veneer plus the largest boot space of any contemporary car.

Despite the gargantuan size of the Mark VII, over 16ft in length, chrome adornment had been kept to a minimum. To provide more internal accommodation the engine was moved 5in further forward than in the previous model, and for better safety the brakes (although still drums) were servo assisted.

An instant success in America, sales boomed, and in 1952 the paint finish changed from cellulose to synthetic enamel. Jaguar had been experiencing problems in supply of the Moss four-speed gearbox and this tied in with the Americans' need for an automatic transmission version of the car. As such a Borg Warner automatic transmission became available as an option, with the quadrant and control lever fitted rather clumsily above the steering column set into the dashboard. This took effect from 1953 and where fitted a bench-type front seat could also be specified.

Numerous minor changes took place to engine and suspension and then in January of 1954 a Laycock de Normanville overdrive unit was made available at extra cost for the manual transmission. Operating on top gear only it brought the

The Mark VII in its original 1950–4 form. Note the double ribbing to the bumper bars and the painted hubcap centres. All Mark VIIs are identified by their split windscreen and full spats covering the rear wheels. In the background is the last variant of the style, the Mark IX, dating from 1961.

Lighting treatment changes in the Mark VII design. The central picture shows an earlier car with flush-mounted fog lamps; above is the later Mark VIIM model, with separate Lucas fog lights, chromed grilles for the horns, and separate indicator lenses (orange for some markets or white, as here, for certain overseas markets).

ratio down to 3.54:1, allowing effortless low speed cruising.

Later in 1954 (September) a revised version of the Mark VII came onto the market, called the Mark VIIM, although never badged as that. This model was externally recognisable by the wider profile ribbed bumper bars (very similar to the XK140 sports car), 'J' headlights, and separate fog lamps and indicators. More prominent rear lights were also fitted, along with a wrap-around rear bumper style.

Internally, improved seating and a new steering wheel centre boss (like the XK) were other visual changes, but the most important enhancement came in the mechanics: a close ratio gearbox, high lift camshafts, and standardised 8:1 compression ratio boosting bhp to 190 from 160. Stiff torsion bars also helped the handling. This was a much improved car to the original Mark VII.

October 1956 saw the introduction of another new model, the Mark VIII. Visually this was easily identifiable from the earlier models by its prominent radiator grille, leaping Jaguar mascot on the bonnet, single piece windscreen, and chrome side trims allowing the car to be finished in a choice of two-tone paint schemes.

Internally the Mark VIII was improved with sculptured rear seating with thicker seats all round, fitted veneered picnic tables in the rear of the front seats, and even a magazine rack where a bench-seat was specified. Many other smaller trim changes were carried out and the more luxurious approach to the whole interior of the Mark VIII was epitomised by the fitting of no less than three cigar lighters. Mechanically the Mark VIII was fitted with Jaguar's B-type cylinder head, which gave a good increase in top speed and a general performance improvement which was helped by the fitting of a dual exhaust system.

Surprisingly the Mark VIII never carried a model identification badge on the boot lid. The Mark VIIM remained in production alongside it until July 1957.

During 1956 all automatic transmission models were fitted with a new Jaguar innovation, the Intermediate Speed Hold switch which allowed the intermediate gear to be held indefinitely by a switch mounted on the dashboard in front of the driver.

The Mark VIII was the rarest of these cars, and despite being in production until December 1959 another new model, the Mark IX, was introduced alongside it at the October 1958 British Motor Show. Externally the Mark IX looked exactly like the Mark VIII except for a discreet 'Mark IX' badge on the boot lid . Internally the differences were also very subtle. Mechanically, however, the Mark IX offered a new standard, adopting power-assisted steering as standard equipment

Mark VII and VIIM models did not feature a chromed bonnet mascot but instead had this cast head, wings, and Jaguar emblem.

Rear view of Mark VII model with double-ribbed bumper bar. Very early cars did not feature a 'Jaguar' scripted badge on the rear and early lighting was basic (it was later revised to the Mark VIIM design – see Mark VIII lights). A single exhaust pipe also featured on Mark VII models.

Originally Mark VII models had trafficators instead of lights. Later versions with conventional indicators used a chrome finisher (see inset) until the arrival of the Mark VIIM, which was fitted with a new steel panel without finisher.

and also becoming the first Jaguar saloon to be provided with all-round disc brakes as standard. Further performance was enhanced by the fitting of a new 3.8-litre configuration (3,781cc) of the XK power unit with a new block design incorporating liners but using the existing B-type cylinder head. This boosted horse power to 220bhp with an increase in torque of over 11 per cent. Other changes included a larger heating and ventilation system, necessitating the fitment of two six volt batteries under the bonnet instead of one 12 volt.

Over the years a few chassis-only vehicles were supplied to outside coachbuilders, and at least one Mark IX was built into a hearse. Jaguar themselves produced a half-way house model based on the Mark VIII with some Mark IX modifications, called the Mark VIIIB. Intended for specialist work with the army and other services, including ministerial and ambassadorial work, the model looked like any conventional Mark VIII/IX but normally featured a low compression version of the 3.4-litre engine and a revised interior with bench front seat and glass division for the rear compartment.

The well-known coachbuilding firm of Harold Radford also offered an enhanced version of the Mark VIII and IX models called the Countryman, with a centre division, seats that could be folded down to form a bed, and picnic hamper and tables, etc, in the boot. It is not known how many were actually produced.

Over 46,000 Mark VII to IX models were produced from 1950 through to 1961. These were the only Jaguar saloons offered between 1950 and 1956.

Exterior identification points

General points applicable to all models
Front view
- Full-width chromed bumper bar with twin vertical over-riders mounted towards the centre of the body, with the number plate mounting between, fitted on the bumper.
- Vertical chromed radiator grille with vertical slats flanked by single headlights with chromed surrounds.
- Below the headlights flush mounted fog/spot lights, or on later cars chromed horn grilles.
- Sidelight units moulded into the top of each front wing, painted in body colour.
- Chrome trim running full length of the bonnet centre.

Rear view
- Shallow rounded rear window with chromed surround.

Internal rear view of Mark VII (and VIIM) with bench-seating, plain rear coverings to the front seats, and built-in ashtrays in the door woodwork.

Front interior view of Mark VII. Note the pronounced horn push boss in the steering wheel and the equally pronounced area of the centre dashboard top rail.

Mark VII dashboard instrument layout remained the same throughout production of the later models, although the top rail altered in shape and style, as did the warning lights and the rear-view mirror.

- Severe sloping one-piece boot lid and rear wings, the former hinged at its rear.
- Lighting units mounted at the base of each rear wing.
- Fuel fillers (one per side) mounted at top of rear wings with lockable covers painted in body colour.
- Boot-mounted rear number plate with chrome illumination/reversing light plinth. To each side were chromed, vertically mounted lockable boot handles.
- Full-width ribbed rear bumper bar with twin vertical over-riders.

Side view
- Body curvature and swage line follow XK style, sweeping down from front wing through door lines to lift again over rear wings.
- Chrome on brass window frame surrounds with quarter-lights front and rear.
- Heavy chromed horizontal trim running along entire length of bonnet sides, over bulkhead, across doors, between chromed handles, to 'spear' on rear wing.
- Rear wheel spats fitted to all models.

Specifics
Mark VII
- Tripod headlights.
- Flush-mounted fog lamps under headlamps.
- Triple-ribbed front and rear bumper bars.
- Radiator grille with narrow surround. At the top a winged badge with Jaguar head at centre of bonnet.
- Chromed strip running full length of bonnet centre.
- Split front windscreen with chromed surround.
- Painted B/C post with trafficators.
- Hubcaps chromed with body-coloured centre sections.
- Fully enclosed rear wheel spats.
- Single exhaust pipe system.
- Single circular rear light units, from 1953 fitted with additional circular reflectors above.
- Jaguar scripted badge to boot lid on all but very earliest cars.
- Earlier cars featured front wing ventilators to bring air into the footwells, later deleted.

Mark VIIM
- As above except thicker double-ribbed front and rear bumper bars (wrap-around at rear) with differing over-riders.
- 'J' headlights.
- Separate Lucas fog lamps mounted on valance.
- Circular indicator lights to base of front wings.
- Vertical slatted horn grilles below headlights replaced the Mark VII's flush fog lamps.
- Apart from earliest Mark VIIMs, hubcaps were entirely in chrome.

Mark VIIM interior, in this case fitted with automatic transmission with control quadrant above the steering wheel. Only when equipped with auto transmission was an umbrella-style handbrake fitted (below the dash, far right). Normally a pull-on handbrake was sited between the front seats. Note also map pockets in the front door trims.

The later Mark VIIM design is identified externally by its double-ribbed bumper bars and revised lighting/horn grilles.

Mark VIII models utilised the same rear styling as the Mark VIIM (double-ribbed wrap-around bumper bar). Mark VIIMs and Mark VIIIs also featured 'Jaguar' script to the boot lid. Swage line chromed trims enabled the use of two-tone paintwork, and Mark VIIIs (and IXs) now featured cut-away rear wheel spats.

- Larger rear light lenses on chromed plinths.
- 'Automatic' scripted badge (where automatic transmission was fitted) below the 'Jaguar' name on boot lid.
- Trafficators eliminated from the B/C post.

Mark VIII

- More prominent chromed surround to radiator grille, incorporating winged badge and Jaguar name at top leading to chrome leaping mascot at tip of bonnet and revised centre strip running the entire length of the bonnet centre.
- Single-piece windscreen with revised wiper parking.
- Side swage line chrome trims running the entire length of the body, curving down and across rear wheel spats.
- Rear spats now cut-away at base to reveal hubcaps.
- Dual pipe exhaust system with chromed tailpipes.
- Mark VIIIs did not feature any special badging at the rear. Other aspects of rear view as Mark VIIM.

Mark IX

- Exactly as Mark VIII above except for discrete 'Mk IX' badging to bottom right-hand side of boot lid.
- Later Mark IX's featured enlarged rear light units, similar to XK150 models though with larger chrome plinths, with individual lenses for reflectors and indicators.

Interior identification points

Mark VII

- Leather trimmed front bucket seats with vertical pleating and chromed height adjustment handle.
- Rear bench similarly upholstered with centre fold-down armrest.
- Walnut-veneered dashboard with twin-lidded glove-boxes, that on the passenger side lockable.
- 17in Blumels black cast steering wheel, with pronounced centre boss containing Jaguar head and circular surround (as XK120).
- Handbrake situated between front seats.
- Trimmed door panels with wooden cappings and armrests to all doors, with hidden trigger release door handles/pulls. Tool kits incorporated into both front door trims at lower level.
- Centrally mounted front ashtray to dashboard top rail also incorporating rear view mirror.
- Rear door trim wooden cappings incorporating ash trays.

Both Mark VIII and IX models were exactly the same externally except for a unique 'Mk IX' boot badge on the latter. Frontal treatment was revised from the Mark VIIM, with prominent radiator grille surround, Jaguar leaping mascot on the bonnet, and the single-piece windscreen.

Rear view of the Mark IX saloon. This was exactly the same as the Mark VIII except for the 'Mk IX' badge on the boot lid and, where fitted, the 'automatic' script. All Mark VIIIs and IXs featured a twin exhaust pipe system. This is a late Mark IX model, with larger rear lighting units with separate indicator lenses, never fitted to Mark VIIIs and only fitted to Mark IXs from late 1959.

Bench-seating was standard on Mark VIII/IX automatic transmission models with fold-down picnic tables and magazine rack in the rear compartment. Early Mark VIIIs featured 'open' rack. Rear seating took the form of a split back arrangement, and ashtrays were moved to the door panel trim area.

Mark VIIM

■ As Mark VII except deeper Dunlopillo filled seating all round.

■ Bench front seat available for automatic transmission models with plain veneer cappings.

■ Revised steering wheel with flat boss incorporating gold growler head and circular surround (as XK140).

■ Map pockets incorporated into front door trims.

Mark VIII

■ Revised wooden dashboard and layout with less prominent top rail and new rear view mirror.

■ Chromed grab handle to dashboard top rail on passenger side and map holder below glovebox area, on passenger side.

■ Removal of dashboard mounted ashtray.

■ Two ashtrays, one in each front door trim.

■ Deeper Dunlopillo filled seating all round with revised shaped front individual seating and/or bench arrangement.

■ Revised rear door wooden cappings without ashtrays, also removed to positions within door trims.

■ Rear of front seats carried veneered picture tables (two) plus, on bench-seat, a magazine rack in the centre with square-faced clock.

■ Rear seat redesigned to simulate individual seats with revised shape to squab and centre armrest.

■ Provision of nylon over-rug to rear compartment, trimmed to match interior colour.

■ Boot fully Hardura covered, including spare wheel and with trimmed interior to boot lid.

Mark IX

■ As Mark VIII except for removal of handbrake from between front seats, replaced by umbrella type to extreme driver's side under dash area.

■ Removal of indicator switch from steering wheel to stalk on steering column.

■ Slightly revised instrumentation and warning lighting.

Mark VIIIB

■ As Mark VIII except bench front seat arrangement with centre cut-away to accommodate manual gearbox lever.

■ Umbrella style handbrake as Mark IX.

■ Centre division to bench-seat with sliding glass panels at top, magazine rack, and picnic tables to rear.

■ Revised rear bench-seating with longer centre armrest.

Manual transmission models with individual bucket front seats were available on the Mark VIII and IX, as shown here. A lambswool over-carpet was fitted to all these cars.

This is a rare Mark VIIIB model, built during the time of the Mark VIII/IX models, specifically for use as a limousine. As such a front bench-seat was fitted, but with a cut-away section for the gear lever. Layout of the dashboard follows normal Mark VIII/IX practice, with less pronounced top rail and removal of the indicator switch from the steering wheel to a stalk on the column.

Rear compartment of the Mark VIIIB limousine, with centre division and longer centre armrest.

Technical specifications

	Mark VII	Mark VIIM
cc	3,442	3,442
Bore and stroke (mm)	83 x 106	83 x 106
Compression ratio	8:1 (7:1 optional)	8:1 (7:1/9:1 optional)
bhp	160	190
@ rpm	5,200	5,500
Torque (lb ft)	195	203
@ rpm	2,500	3,000
Fuelling	2 x SU carbs	2 x SU carbs
Transmission	4-speed (3 synchro)	4-speed (3 synchro)
		BW 3-speed auto
Wheel size (in)	16, steel	16, steel
Suspension front	Ind wishbone, torsion bar	Ind wishbone, torsion bar
Suspension rear	Live axle, leaf springs	Live axle, leaf springs
Brakes	4 wheel drum	4 wheel drum
Performance		
0–60mph (sec)	13.7	13.6
Top speed (mph)	101	102
Average mpg	17.6	17–24
Dimensions		
Length (in)	196.5	196.5
Width (in)	73	73
Height (in)	63	63
Wheelbase (in)	120	120
Front track (in)	56	56.5
Rear track (in)	57.5	58
Weight (cwt)	34.5	34.75

Optional extras

Mark VII/VIIM
Fitted luggage (available from several sources).
Choice of Radiomobile radios with fitting kits.
Underbody steel shield for adverse road
    conditions.
Dunlop Racing tyres.
High lift camshafts.
C-type cylinder head.
2in H8 SU carburettors.
Close ratio gearbox.
Chrome wheel rimbellishers for wheels.
Dunlop Road Speed whitewall tyres.

Sundym tinted windscreen.
Thornton Powr-Lok differential.
Chromed badge bar.
Radiator blind.
Oil bath air cleaner system.
Straight through exhaust system.
High ratio steering box.
Wing mirrors.
Witter tow bar.
Cut-away rear spats to aid brake cooling.
Ace Turbo wheel trims.

	Mark VIII	Mark IX
cc	3,442	3,781
Bore and stroke (mm)	83 x 106	87 x 106
Compression ratio	8:1 (7:1 optional)	8:1 (7:1/9:1 optional), 9:1 'S'
bhp	210	220
@ rpm	5,500	5,500
Torque (lb ft)	216	240
@ rpm	3,000	3,000
Fuelling	2 x SU carbs	2 x SU carbs
Transmission	4-speed (3 synchro) BW 3-speed auto	4-speed (3 synchro) BW 3-speed auto
Wheel size (in)	16, steel	16, steel
Suspension front	Ind wishbone, torsion bar	Ind wishbone, torsion bar.
Suspension rear	Live axle, leaf springs	Live axle, leaf springs
Brakes	4 wheel drum	4 wheel disc
Performance		
0–60mph (sec)	11.6	11.3
Top speed (mph)	106.5	114.3
Average mpg	17–22	13.5
Dimensions		
Length (in)	196.5	196.5
Width (in)	73	73
Height (in)	63	63
Wheelbase (in)	120	120
Front track (in)	56.5	56.5
Rear track (in)	58	58
Weight (cwt)	36	35.5

Mark VIII/IX

Fitted luggage (available from several sources).
Choice of Radiomobile radios with fitting kits.
Underbody steel shield for adverse road conditions.
Dunlop Racing tyres.
High lift camshafts.
C-type cylinder head.
2in H8 SU carburettors.
Close ratio gearbox.

Chrome wheel rimbellishers for wheels.
Dunlop Road Speed whitewall tyres.
Sundym tinted windscreen.
Thornton Powr-Lok differential.
Chromed badge bar.
Radiator blind.
High ratio steering box.
Wing mirrors.
Witter tow bar.
Ace Turbo wheel trims.

Colour schemes

Exterior colour Single	Duotone	Details	Interior trim
Suede Green			Suede Green
Ivory		To 1952	Red
			Pale Blue
Birch Grey		To 1956	Red
			Grey
			Pale Blue
Battleship Grey		To 1956	Red
			Grey
			Biscuit
Lavender Grey		To 1956	Red
			Suede Green
			Pale Blue
Gunmetal Grey		To 1952	Red
			Grey
			Pale Blue
Black			Red
			Tan
			Grey
			Biscuit
Pastel Green		To 1952	Suede Green
			Grey
Pastel Blue		To 1956	Pale Blue
Dove Grey		To 1956	Tan
			Biscuit
Twilight Blue Met		To 1952	Blue
Cream		1952–3	Red
			Red
			Biscuit
Mediterranean Blue		1953/4 only	Blue
			Grey
British Racing Green		From 1952	Tan
			Suede Green
Pacific Blue		From 1952	Light Blue
			Dark Blue
Old English White		From 1953	Red
			Pale Blue
Indigo Blue		From 1954	Light Blue
			Dark Blue
			Grey
Maroon (Imperial)		From 1956	Red
			Maroon

Exterior colour Single	Duotone	Details	Interior trim
Cornish Grey		From 1956	Red
			Light Blue
			Dark Blue
			Grey
Sherwood Green		From 1956	Tan
			Suede Green
Mist Grey		From 1956	Red
			Light Blue
			Dark Blue
			Grey
Claret		From 1956	Red
			Maroon
Cotswold Blue		From 1956	Dark Blue
			Grey
Pearl Grey		From 1956	Red
			Light Blue
			Dark Blue
			Grey
Claret	Imperial Maroon	From 1956	Red
			Maroon
Indigo Blue	Cotswold Blue	From 1956	Dark Blue
			Light Blue
			Grey
Cornish Grey	Mist Grey	From 1956	Red
			Light Blue
			Dark Blue
			Grey
British Racing Green	Forest Green	1956–8	Suede Green
			Tan
Black	Claret	From 1956	Red
			Maroon
			Grey
Black	Forest Green	1956–8	Suede Green
			Red
Carmen Red		From 1959	Red
Cotswold Blue	Mist Grey	From 1959	Red
			Light Blue
			Dark Blue
			Grey
British Racing Green	Suede Green	From 1959	Suede Green
			Tan

Prices and production volumes

	Price new (£)	1950	1951	1952	1953	1954	1955
Mark VII saloon	1,276	■	■	■	■	■	–
Mark VIIM saloon	1,680	–	–	–	–	■	■
Mark VIII saloon	1,997	–	–	–	–	–	–
Mark IX saloon	1,994	–	–	–	–	–	–

	1956	1957	1958	1959	1960	1961	Total produced
Mark VII saloon	–	–	–	–	–	–	20,937
Mark VIIM saloon	■	■	–	–	–	–	10,060
Mark VIII saloon	■	■	■	■	–	–	6,247
Mark IX saloon	–	–	■	■	■	■	10,002
Total production							**47,246**

Production changes

1950
Mark VII launched.

1952
Extra studs fitted to front of cam covers.
Two-speed wipers fitted.
5.5in steel wheels replace 5in.
Moulded rubber wiper blades fitted.

1953
Automatic transmission became available.
Telescopic rear shock absorbers fitted.
Different locks fitted to boot/glove-box and to
    ignition.
Larger eight-bladed cooling fan fitted to engine.
New horns fitted to radiator area instead of
    valances.

1954
Overdrive available on manual models.
Mark VIIM announced.
Trafficators eliminated from all markets.
Orange lenses fitted to all indicator lights at front.

1955
Front wing ventilators eliminated.

1956
Mark VIII introduced.
Intermediate Speed Hold added to automatic cars.

1957
(July) Mark VIIM finally discontinued.
Die-cast radiator shells replaced brass.

1958
Reutter reclining front seats available.
Power-assisted steering option for US market.
(October) Mark IX introduced.

1959
Mark VIII finally discontinued.

1960
Brake warning light added to dashboard.

1961
Mark IX production discontinued.

Chassis numbers

Model	Right/ Left Drive	Chassis/ Vin Nos Commencing
Mark VII	RHD	710001
	LHD	750001
Mark VIIM	RHD	722755
	LHD	738184
Mark VIII	RHD	760001
	RHD	780001
Mark IX	RHD	770001
		790001

Background

Since the introduction of Jaguar's first 'in-house' engine, the XK, in 1948 – launched in the XK120 sports car – the company had grown significantly, both in size and stature, with increased sales and competition successes. From 1950 however, all saloon car sales (the backbone of the business) had concentrated on one prestigious large model: the Mark VII. If Jaguar were to make greater inroads into the car market they needed a smaller, cheaper, and higher volume saloon. Welcome the 2.4-litre.

William Lyons at Jaguar worked on the same principle he did back in the 1930s, to capitalise on as many mechanical parts as possible from existing models in order to keep costs down and enhance profits. Hence the starting point for the new model was the XK power unit, mated to the existing Moss manual gearbox and developments of existing suspension, steering, and trim layouts. Despite this the new small Jaguar would encompass new ideas and technology far in advance of what Jaguar had used before.

It would be built around monocoque (chassisless) construction, with the body itself providing the necessary rigidity and supporting the mechanics. A separate front subframe was designed to carry the suspension, steering, and the weight of the engine. This allowed for a much lighter structure and enabled significant strength to be built into the whole body, which

was very carefully designed yet still looked like a Jaguar. Styling cues were taken from the existing XK140 sports car frontal aspect and scaled down curves from the Mark VII saloon.

Of much smaller dimensions – only 15ft in length and just over 5ft in width – the new Jaguar saloon was still a luxurious five-seater, trimmed to the usual Jaguar standard. But it was powered by a new configuration of the XK power unit, of only 2.4 litres capacity, producing 112bhp and a top speed of just over 100mph, sufficient for a car of this size and better than the competition. This was Jaguar's particular advantage: except for a rather traditional Daimler Conquest, the avant-garde Armstrong Siddeley 234/236, and an assortment of lesser machines such as the Ford Zodiac, Vauxhall Cresta, and Humber Super Snipe, there was little competition in this area of the market.

An incredible success when launched for the 1956 model year, the Jaguar saloon was followed in 1957 by a larger 3.4-litre engined version offering up to 120mph performance, also becoming available with all-round disc brakes. The 2.4- and 3.4-litre saloons remained in production until 1959, by which time over 35,000 had been produced, more than any other model in such a short period of time.

In 1959 the model range was significantly enhanced by the introduction of three totally revised cars, now called Mark 2s, of 2.4-litre, 3.4-litre and 3.8-litre engine capacities. These put right complaints about the earlier models, which were well known for their skittish handling resulting from a narrow rear track. More power, better handling, improved vision, and enhanced trim made the Mark 2s even more popular than their predecessors.

The top of the range 3.8-litre model was, at the time, the fastest production saloon car in the world, offering 125mph performance with acceleration to match. Available in manual, manual with overdrive, or automatic transmission form, along with the other two models this wide choice and good design meant that sales would exceed anything Jaguar had experienced before, with nearly 90,000 being produced up to 1967.

The Mark 2 was also to generate another new model in 1962, the Daimler 2.5-litre V8. With Jaguar's purchase of the Daimler Motor Company in 1960, this marque was in desperate need of a new model, and the cunning mating of Daimler's superb little V8 engine to the Jaguar Mark 2 bodyshell produced a car with an entirely different character. This was to find its own successful market throughout the 1960s, ending up as the most successful model produced by Daimler up to that time.

In the mid-1960s Jaguar was up against stiffer competition from other marques and was hard at work developing a new saloon car for later in the decade (the XJ6). During this same period the need to revitalise models to improve flagging sales resulted in changes being made to the entire range, not least the Mark 2s. In 1967 the range was reduced, equipment levels changed, and prices reduced to hold their market. Out went the 3.8-litre Mark 2, and the other two cars were re-badged as the 240 and 340, both having changes in trim to keep costs down. Engines were improved with straight port cylinder heads to enhance performance. Similar trim changes were made to the Daimler model. However, sales never recuperated, each model being slowly dropped from the range, the 340 first in 1968, the 240 next in 1969, and finally, later that year, the Daimler V8.

The compact Jaguar saloons of the 1950s and 1960s were the company's most successful cars up to that time, having identified an important new market for car producers which other manufacturers were eager to cater for and would eventually dominate. It would take Jaguar until 1999 to re-invent the compact luxury saloon car with the S-type.

Model range and development

First announced at the UK's 1955 Motor Show, just two models were introduced for the 1956 model year.

Frontal view of early 2.4-litre saloon. The cast radiator grille was only used on this model until 1958. For certain overseas markets the chromed leaping mascot did not feature on the bonnet.

2.4-litre saloon as supplied new, with steel wheels, chromed hubcaps with no rimbellishers, and full spats over the rear wheels. This is a later model with the wider radiator grille standardised with the 3.4-litre model to aid cooling and rationalise the parts bin.

Rear view of the 2.4-litre saloon, showing the small rear light units, wrap-around bumper bar, and 'Jaguar' script on the boot lid. The cut-away spats over the rear wheels were standardised on 3.4-litre models and on 2.4s towards the end of production. This picture clearly shows the reduced width track of the rear wheels.

Models available at launch
2.4-litre standard saloon
2.4-litre saloon

Although Jaguar initially promoted the car as a two model line-up, there was really only one. The so-called 'standard' model never went into serious production, but was offered – as the XK100 sports car had been in 1948 – as a more economical alternative. Mechanically the same as the higher priced model, it lacked some of the refinements expected of a Jaguar, such as a well-equipped dashboard, or even windscreen washers. The production 2.4, however, offered the usual Jaguar 'package' of leather and walnut interiors, with the XK engine mated to the usual Moss manual gearbox. At launch this model was offered with or without overdrive.

With excellent worldwide response, Jaguar soon developed the new car and in February 1957 announced the addition of a second model to the range, this time utilising the 3.4-litre XK engine taken from the XK140 sports car with the B-type cylinder head. Offering 210bhp this provided much more punch and subsequently made the model exceptionally popular on both the race circuits and rally routes of Europe.

Correspondingly in 1957 Jaguar also offered all-round disc brakes on the smaller Jaguars and most 3.4-litre cars were so equipped. The 3.4s were also identified by a wider radiator grille – to aid cooling to the larger engine – and cut-away spats over the rear wheels, also to aid cooling, this time to the brakes. Both these features were later adopted by the 2.4-litre models as well. Both models also became available with automatic transmission. They remained in production until 1959, by which time over 37,000 had been sold.

At the 1959 Motor Show Jaguar announced three new models to replace the 2.4 and 3.4-litre cars, called Mark 2s. This subsequently led to the earlier models becoming known as Mark 1s, although this title was never officially recognised by the factory, nor does it show on any badges or in any literature relating to these cars.

Using the existing 2.4-litre, 3.4-litre, and the fairly new 3.8-litre versions of the XK six-cylinder engine, the Mark 2s were a significant improvement over the earlier cars, although retaining their overall style. Widening the rear track improved handling and the inclusion of the larger engine turned the 3.8-litre Mark 2 into the fastest production saloon car in the world at that time.

Externally the Mark 2s were easily identifiable by their much larger window areas, chromed side window frames, and that wider rear wheel track. Internally they were virtually all new, with revised seats (with picnic tables in the rear), new trim, and an entirely new dashboard layout, with the

Dashboard layout of the 2.4- and 3.4-litre (Mark 1s) followed later XK practice, but with wood surrounds. When automatic transmission was fitted the control quadrant was attached to the lower dash area, made of Bakelite, as seen here.

Above left: Front interior trim of the 2.4- and 3.4-litre models with bucket seating and four-spoke steering wheel.

Above right: A choice of split-bench or bucket seats was available on Mark 1 models from 1957, when automatic transmission became available. Rear seating followed normal bench practice.

Frontal styling differences between the Mark 1 (2.4- and 3.4-litre models) and the Mark 2 design from 1959 to 1967. On the left, the Mark 2 shows revised lighting treatment with flush-mounted fog lights, separate indicator lenses (different colours dependent on market), and pronounced vertical centre rib to the grille.

speedometer and rev counter directly in front of the driver and all switches and ancillary gauges grouped in the centre – a theme that would be adopted on all future Jaguar models from there on in until the 1970s.

The Jaguar Mark 2s proved an even bigger success than the 1950's 2.4 and 3.4 and, apart from minor changes, remained in production until 1967, during which time a further model was introduced in 1962. This was the Daimler 2.4-litre V8, which, as already mentioned, married Daimler's own 2.5-litre V8 engine to a Mark 2 bodyshell, initially mated to a Borg Warner Model 35 automatic transmission (later a standard manual box alternative became available). This model offered a greater degree of refinement, with performance just slightly better than the 2.4-litre Jaguar version.

Externally the Daimler benefited from a fluted radiator grille and rear boot plinth plus new badging, while internally it used a better quality of walnut veneer and split-bench type seating (without the Mark 2's picnic tables), along with other slight changes to the trim. Aimed at the more professional market place, such as solicitors, consultants, and the gentry, it never infringed on the market for the more sporty Jaguar Mark 2s.

Sales for the smaller Jaguars had proved excellent in the early 1960s and development continued throughout their years in production. All-synchromesh gearboxes were available from later in 1964, and by 1966 trim had changed in an effort to bring prices down when sales eventually started to decline. The Mark 2 spawned other medium-sized Jaguar models like the S-type and 420 which must have had some effect on sales, as did more modern machinery coming from its competitors by this time.

Because of declining sales and the need to continue the existing range until an all new saloon could become available in 1968, Jaguar redesigned the Mark 2s in 1967, at the same time reducing the number of models on sale. First to be discontinued was the 3.8-litre, its sales already overtaken by the 420, while the two smaller-engined Mark 2s (the 2.4 and 3.4) were re-badged as the 240 and 340 and offered at reduced prices.

The 240 and 340 models now used a straight port cylinder head and the 2.4-litre model got SU carburettors instead of Solex, which improved performance somewhat, although the trim was reduced to keep prices down. Out went leather upholstery (and picnic tables) as standard, to be replaced by Ambla material (with leather as an extra cost option). Externally the broad ribbed bumpers, so characteristic of Jaguars from the Mark VII on, were replaced by a slimline type reminiscent of the Mark X and S-type models of the period. Even items like fog lamps became an

Side view comparison between the Mark 2 (right) and the earlier Mark 1. Note the instantly identifiable larger window areas with chromed surrounds of the later car.

Rear view changes between the Mark 1 and Mark 2 models. The later car (in the foreground) shows the larger rear light units with separate indicator lenses and revised badging. Note also the larger rear window of the later car.

This picture shows the pronounced difference in window areas between the two cars and the revised door trim treatment.

extra cost option. The Daimler received similar treatment, being renamed the V8 250, although to keep the 'quality edge' of the Daimler marque fog lamps and leather trim remained standard features.

Although sales were boosted slightly the 'new' compact model range had a limited lifespan, the 340 being the first to meet its demise in 1968, followed in 1969, after the introduction of the XJ6, by the 240. Because there was initially no other Daimler available, the V8 250 stayed in production longer.

Apart from the standard production cars the Jaguar dealers Coombs in Surrey produced their own limited number of competition modified cars, mainly Mark 2s with enhanced performance and handling characteristics. Jaguar also at one time commissioned a special estate car version called the County, which was used extensively by the factory in the 1960s and later sold off, but the model never went into production.

Near the end of production a few examples of the 340 model were produced to special order with a 3.8-litre engine with the straight port cylinder head.

Exterior identification points

General points applicable to all pre-Mark 2 models

Front view

- Ribbed bumper and over-rider treatment similar to XK150, with dish in centre section to accommodate radiator grille base. Steel number plate mounting in centre mounted on bumper.
- Oval chromed radiator grille, with prominent surround and vertical slats and incorporating Jaguar growler badge with the word 'Jaguar' and the appropriate litreage of the engine.
- Oval, vertical mounted sidelight housings at the base of each front wing (also incorporating indicator bulbs).
- Two chromed, flush mounted horn grilles with vertical slats below headlights.
- Separate Lucas fog/spot lights mounted on lip of front wings between bumper bar and wings.
- Leaping Jaguar chromed mascot atop the leading edge of the bonnet, with full length chrome trim in the centre. (The mascot was eliminated for certain overseas markets.)

Rear view

- Severe sloping bodywork reminiscent of Mark VII to IX models.
- Shallow curved rear screen with chromed surround.

Radiator grille badging showed the size of the engine fitted to the car and was colour coded – a black background for the 2.4, red for the 3.4, and maroon for the 3.8. On the boot lid of Mark 2 models litre identification appeared, but not for the 2.4-litre model.

Close-up of Mark 2 frontal view with revised lighting and grille treatment.

Rear view of the Mark 2 shows wider track to the rear wheels, revised lighting, the use of a 'Mk 2' badge on the boot lid, and a 'disc brake' badge in the centre of the rear bumper bar.

- One-piece boot lid hinged at the rear, with centrally mounted number plate with chrome surround and chromed illumination/reversing light plinth.
- Integrated rear light units to base of each rear wing with chromed plinth surround.
- Chromed boot lid button and escutcheon in the centre above bumper bar, below boot lid.
- Scripted 'Jaguar' name to centre of boot lid.
- Ribbed rear bumper to match front, wrapping around the curved sides of the wings and incorporating vertically mounted over-riders.
- Single exhaust pipe (not chromed).

Side view

- Slab-sided but taking styling cues from both the Mark VII and XK140. Did not feature pronounced swage line as on other models.
- Chrome waist-line trim ran entire length of the car, from bonnet sides, along the doors (between chromed door handles), and sweeping down the rear wings to meet the bumper bar.
- Solid window frame surrounds as part of doors without normal chrome on brass frames. Chrome edging to window frames. Quarter-lights front and rear.
- Spats covering rear wheels.
- Pronounced narrower track of rear wheels to front.
- Fuel filler mounted on left-hand side within rear wing (when looking from the rear), with cover painted to body colour.
- Wheels finished to body colour with chromed hubcaps.

Mark 1 specifics

2.4-litre (Mark 1)

- Heavy cast oval chromed radiator grille with just eight slats, incorporating plastic circular badge in black with Jaguar growler logo and words 'Jaguar 2.4 litre' surrounding it. From 1958 the grille changed to 3.4-litre style (see below and photographs).
- Rear wheel spats completely enclosed wheels. Later changed to 3.4-litre style (see below and photographs).

3.4-litre (Mark 1)

- As above but with a wider, thinner (16) slatted radiator grille (also fitted to the 2.4-litre model from 1958), with revised red badge bearing the words 'Jaguar 3.4 litre'.
- From the side all 3.4-litre models were fitted with cut-away rear wheel spats, later adopted for 2.4-litre cars as well.
- At the rear 3.4-litre models carried '3.4' badging below the Jaguar script on the boot lid.
- Twin exhaust pipe system emerging from the left-hand side of the car.

Frontal treatment of the Mark 2 interior, with pronounced centre console arrangement, flatter seats, and completely revised dashboard with main instruments in front of the driver and ancillaries in the centre against a matt black painted panel up to 1960 (black fabric covered for later models). The steering wheel design shows that this is a pre 1964 model. See the later photograph of a Daimler interior on page 76 for the style of steering wheel used after 1964.

Above left: Rear seating arrangement for Mark 2 models, with revised flatter front seats with fold-down picnic tables.

Above right: From 1962 a Daimler model became available, identified by its pronounced fluted radiator grille and Daimler badging, with similar treatment at the rear.

Mark 2s were always available with either steel wheels or wire wheels, both chromed or painted.

General points applicable to Mark 2s, Daimlers, and subsequent models

Front view
▦ Bumper bar treatment very similar to Mark 1 models.
▦ Enlarged oval chromed radiator grille with prominent thick centre vertical vane now incorporating the growler badge at the top.
▦ Flush-mounted Lucas fog lamps below headlights.

Rear view
▦ Enlarged rear window with chromed surround.
▦ Enlarged rear light units with chromed plinths, incorporating separate reflectors and indicator lenses.
▦ 'Disc Brake' badge to centre of rear bumper bar.
▦ Litreage badge (except 2.4) featured on boot lid.
▦ 'Jaguar' letters badge on boot lid, not scripted.

Side view
▦ Enlarged window areas with chrome on brass surrounds, quarter-lights front and rear.
▦ Chromed rain gutters along roof area.
▦ Sculptured door handles.
▦ All Mark 2s featured cut-away rear wheel spats.
▦ Wider rear wheel track.

Mark 2 and allied models specifics

2.4-litre Mark 2
▦ This model featured the black background badge to the radiator grille bearing the words 'Jaguar 2.4 litre'.
▦ At the rear there was *no* 2.4-litre badge on the boot lid.
▦ A single exhaust pipe system exited from the left-hand side of the car.

3.4-litre Mark 2
▦ Red radiator grille badge bearing the words 'Jaguar 3.4 litre'.
▦ At the rear a '3.4' chromed badge appeared below the Jaguar emblem in the centre of the boot lid.
▦ Dual exhaust system.

3.8-litre Mark 2
▦ Maroon radiator grille badge bearing the words 'Jaguar 3.8 litre'.
▦ At the rear a '3.8' chromed badge appeared below the Jaguar emblem in the centre of the boot lid.
▦ Exhaust system as 3.4-litre Mark 2.

Daimler 2.5-litre V8
▦ As Mark 2 except, from the front, a closer knit (20-slat) radiator grille incorporating a fluted surround with no badging.

From 1967 the Mark 2 models were re-badged '240' and '340', with revised slimmer bumper bars, new style hubcaps to the steel wheels, and the replacement of the fog lamps with horn grilles (unless the former were fitted).

Rear view of the 240/340 model with revised badging and slimmer bumper bar, necessitating a deeper rear valance.

Later Daimler model, now known as the V8 250. Chromed rimbellishers with new-style hubcaps and the Daimler emblem were standard on this model, which was otherwise unidentifiable from 240/340 models from the side.

- Atop the leading edge of the bonnet a swept 'D' emblem leading to a full-width centre bonnet chrome strip of triangular section.
- From the side the only difference to Jaguar models was the use of scripted 'D' emblems on the centres of the hubcaps and the fitting of chrome rimbellishers as standard equipment to the steel wheels.
- From the rear a fluted chromed rear number plate/reversing light plinth.
- Scripted 'Daimler' badge in the centre of the boot lid.
- A chromed 'V' incorporating an '8' also on the boot lid.
- A twin exhaust system, one pipe from each side of the car at the rear with chromed tailpipes.

Daimler V8 250

- As 2.5 except at the front the adoption of the slimline bumper bars fitted to Jaguar 240/340 models.
- New style hubcaps to steel wheels, still incorporating the 'D' emblem.
- At the rear a slimline bumper and revised 'V8 250' badging to bottom right-hand side of the boot lid.

Jaguar 240

- As Mark 2 except, at the front, replacement of fog lamps for flush-fitting dished chromed grilles.
- Slimline bumper bar front and rear with revised over-riders.
- From the side a revised style of chromed hubcap with pronounced centre section incorporating growler badge on black background.
- At the rear revised badging in most cases eliminating the word 'Jaguar' and with the figure '240' sited on the right-hand side bottom area of the boot lid.
- Twin exhaust pipes as earlier 3.4- and 3.8-litre models.

Jaguar 340

- As 240 except '340' badging to boot lid.

Interior identification points

2.4/3.4-litre

- Walnut-veneered dashboard with central layout of instruments. Passenger side lockable glove-box, driver's side open cubby.
- Bluemel black-enamelled four-spoke steering wheel with flat horn push incorporating growler badge (as per XK140).
- Separate bucket type front seats trimmed in leather (split-bench type arrangement for cars

Daimler frontal treatment for the post-1967 model. The fitment of fog lights was standard on Daimler models at all times.

Different style of badging used on Daimler models, and the fluted plinth for reversing light/number plate illumination. Daimler models with the V8 engine featured a twin exhaust pipe system emitting from either side at the rear.

Above left: Unique to Daimler models was this scripted 'D' emblem on the bonnet.

Above right: Daimler V8 250 interior showing the later style of steering wheel, also fitted to Jaguar Mark 2 models. Flatter front seats of the split-bench variety applied to Daimler, which also lacked a centre console arrangement.

equipped with automatic transmission) with rear seat bench.
- ▨ Wood surrounds to all door windows, with vinyl upholstered door trims and armrests to match interior trim colour.
- ▨ Handbrake between driver's seat and front door mounted on floor.
- ▨ Automatic transmission models with centrally mounted 'quadrant' under dashboard.

Mark 2

- ▨ Walnut-veneered dashboard with centre layout of auxiliary gauges and rocker switch gear. Speedometer and rev counter positioned in front of driver. Centre console arrangement leading down from dashboard incorporating radio speaker, radio and heater controls along with covered ashtray, console continuing rearward between the front individual seats to extractor vent for rear compartment. Lockable glove-box to passenger side of dashboard.
- ▨ Two-spoke black-coated steering wheel incorporating chromed half horn ring and centre badging depicting growler. (Design changed to Mark X style from 1964.)
- ▨ Front seats still individual but with flatter cushions (no split-bench option). Fold-down picnic tables in rear of front seats.
- ▨ Rear bench-seat similar but different stitching to earlier cars.
- ▨ Door trims incorporating armrests and elasticated map pockets to the front, open pockets at the rear. Wooden cappings to all door trim tops.
- ▨ Swivel action rear quarter-light catches.

Daimler 2.5 V8

- ▨ As Mark 2s except for split-bench front seating (regardless of transmission) and replacement of centre console by revised ashtray, radio mounting in wood veneer set below centre section of dashboard incorporating heater controls.
- ▨ Scripted 'D' to centre steering wheel boss.
- ▨ No picnic tables in rear of front seats.

Daimler V8 250

- ▨ As 2.5 except for black vinyl-covered dashboard top rail.
- ▨ Vinyl trim door panel tops with simple stained wood topping.
- ▨ Aerated leather upholstery.

240/340

- ▨ As Mark 2 except majority of cars featured non-leather Ambla upholstery throughout.
- ▨ Some very late cars featured V8 style padded front dashboard top rail and simplified wooden fillets to door trim panels.

The dash layout of Daimler models followed Mark 2 practice except for the removal of the centre console in favour of this separate unit for the radio, speakers, and heater controls. This very late model shows padded dash top rail.

Rear seating on Daimler models also followed Mark 2 practice, although no picnic tables were fitted and door trims were different.

Above left: Late 240 Jaguar model. All 240/340 models normally featured Ambla upholstery instead of leather, with no picnic tables in the rear of the front seats à la Daimler.

Above right: The dash area to the side of the main instruments was used for auxiliary controls on Mark 2 and Daimler models. A brake warning light always featured, as did the slider control for the manual choke arrangement that applied to 2.4 and Daimler models. The rear window heater and switch was an extra cost option.

Technical specifications

	2.4-litre	3.4-litre
cc	2,483	3,442
Bore and stroke (mm)	83 x 76.5	83 x 106
Compression ratio	8:1 (7:1 optional)	8:1 (7:1/9:1 optional)
bhp	112	210
@ rpm	5,750	5,500
Torque (lb ft)	140	216
@ rpm	2,000	3,000
Fuelling	2 x Solex carbs	2 x SU carbs
Transmission	4-speed (3 synchro) Later BW 3-speed auto	4-speed (3 synchro) BW 3-speed auto
Wheel size (in)	15, steel, wires optional	15, steel, wires optional
Suspension front	Ind semi trailing wishbone, coil springs, anti-roll bar	Ind semi trailing wishbone, coil springs, anti-roll bar
Suspension rear	Live axle, Panhard rod, leaf springs	Live axle, Panhard rod, leaf springs
Brakes	4 wheel drum, later 4 wheel disc	4 wheel drum, later 4 wheel disc
Performance		
0–60mph (sec)	14.4	9.1
Top speed (mph)	101.5	120
Average mpg	18.3	15–22
Dimensions		
Length (in)	180.75	180.75
Width (in)	66.75	66.75
Height (in)	57.5	57.5
Wheelbase (in)	107.375	107.375
Front track (in)	54.6	54.6
Rear track (in)	50.25	50.25
Weight (cwt)	27	28.5

	2.4-litre Mark 2	3.4-litre Mark 2
cc	2,483	3,442
Bore and stroke (mm)	83 x 76.5	83 x 106
Compression ratio	8:1 (7:1 optional)	8:1 (7:1/9:1 optional)
bhp	120	210
@ rpm	5,750	5,500
Torque (lb ft)	144	216
@ rpm	2,000	3,000
Fuelling	2 x Solex carbs	2 x SU carbs
Transmission	4-speed (3 synchro) Later all synchro BW 3-speed auto	4-speed (3 synchro) Later all synchro BW 3-speed auto
Wheel size (in)	15, steel, wires optional	15, steel, wires optional
Suspension front	Ind semi trailing wishbone, coil springs, anti-roll bar	Ind semi trailing wishbone, coil springs, anti-roll bar
Suspension rear	Live axle, Panhard rod, leaf springs	Live axle, Panhard rod, leaf springs
Brakes	4 wheel disc	4 wheel disc
Performance		
0–60mph (sec)	17.3	11.9
Top speed (mph)	96.3	120
Average mpg	18	16
Dimensions		
Length (in)	180.75	180.75
Width (in)	66.75	66.75
Height (in)	57.75	57.75
Wheelbase (in)	107.375	107.375
Front track (in)	55	55
Rear track (in)	53.375	53.375
Weight (cwt)	28.5	29.5

Technical specifications *cont …*

	3.8-litre Mark 2	240
cc	3,781	2,483
Bore and stroke (mm)	87 x 106	83 x 76.5
Compression ratio	8:1 (7:1/9:1 optional)	8:1 (7:1 optional)
bhp	220	133
@ rpm	5,500	5,500
Torque (lb ft)	240	146
@ rpm	3,000	3,700
Fuelling	2 x SU carbs	2 x SU carbs
Transmission	4-speed (3 synchro)	4-speed (3 synchro)
	Later all synchro	Later all synchro
	BW 3-speed auto	BW 3-speed auto
Wheel size (in)	15, steel, wires optional	15, steel, wires optional
Suspension front	IInd semi trailing wishbone,	Ind semi trailing wishbone,
	coil springs, anti-roll bar	coil springs, anti-roll bar
Suspension rear	Live axle, Panhard rod,	Live axle, Panhard rod,
	leaf springs	leaf springs
Brakes	4 wheel disc	4 wheel disc
Performance		
0–60mph (sec)	8.5	12.5
Top speed (mph)	120.4	106
Average mpg	15.7	18.4
Dimensions		
Length (in)	180.75	180.75
Width (in)	66.75	66.75
Height (in)	57.75	57.75
Wheelbase (in)	107.375	107.375
Front track (in)	55	55
Rear track (in)	53.375	53.375
Weight (cwt)	30	28.5

	340	V8
cc	3,442	2,548
Bore and stroke (mm)	83 x 106	76.2 x 69.85
Compression ratio	8:1 (7:1 optional)	8.2:1
bhp	210	140
@ rpm	5,500	5,800
Torque (lb ft)	216	155
@ rpm	3,000	3,600
Fuelling	2 x SU carbs	2 x SU carbs
Transmission	4-speed (3 synchro) Later all synchro BW 3-speed auto	4-speed (3 synchro) Later all synchro BW 3-speed auto
Wheel size (in)	15, steel, wires optional	15, steel, wires optional
Suspension front	Ind semi trailing wishbone, coil springs, anti-roll bar	Ind semi trailing wishbone, coil springs, anti-roll bar
Suspension rear	Live axle, Panhard rod, leaf springs	Live axle, Panhard rod, leaf springs
Brakes	4 wheel disc	4 wheel disc
Performance		
0–60mph (sec)	8.8	13.5
Top speed (mph)	124	110
Average mpg	17–22	17
Dimensions		
Length (in)	180.75	180.75
Width (in)	66.75	66.75
Height (in)	57.75	57.75
Wheelbase (in)	107.375	107.375
Front track (in)	55	55
Rear track (in)	53.375	53.375
Weight (cwt)	30	29

Optional extras

2.4-litre saloon

Choice of three radio installations with or
without rear parcel shelf mounted speaker.
Laminated windscreen.
Chromium plated wheel rimbellishers for steel
wheels.
Ace Turbo wheel trims for steel wheels.
Witter tow bar.
Le Mans 40/45-watt headlight bulbs.
Locking petrol filler cap.
Front seat belts.
Driver's seat bracket to raise seat height.
Split-style front seat arrangement (manual
transmission cars).
Radiator blind.
Choice of radial, town and country, or whitewall
tyres.
Borg Warner automatic transmission.
Overdrive (for non overdrive equipped manual
transmission cars).
Cut-away rear wheel spats for earlier cars not so
fitted.
Wire wheels with conversion kit for hubs, etc.
Conversion kit to change drum braked cars to
disc braked.
Conversion kit to change earlier disc braked cars
to later 'quick change' type.
High ratio steering box.
Lightened flywheel.
Competition clutch.
Fire extinguisher.
Chromed grab handle to passenger side of
dashboard.
Powr-Lok differential.
Rear window demister.
White-finished steering wheel (export).
Gear lever extension piece.
Rheostat for dashboard lighting.
Vanity mirror for passenger sun visor.
Stiffened shock absorbers.
Heavy duty anti-roll bar.
Twin windtone horns.
Close ratio gearbox.
Twin pipe exhaust system (for 2.4-litre only).
Stage 1 tuning kit, increasing bhp to 119.
Stage 2 tuning kit, increasing bhp to 131.
Stage 3 tuning kit, increasing bhp to 150.
High lift camshafts.
Sundym tinted windscreen.
Wing mirrors.

3.4-litre saloon

Choice of three radio installations with or
without rear parcel shelf mounted speaker.
Laminated windscreen.
Chromium plated wheel rimbellishers for steel
wheels.
Ace Turbo wheel trims for steel wheels.
Witter tow bar.
Le Mans 40/45-watt headlight bulbs.
Locking petrol filler cap.
Front seat belts.
Split-style front seat arrangement (manual
transmission cars).
Radiator blind.
Choice of radial, town and country, or whitewall
tyres.
Borg Warner automatic transmission.
Overdrive (for non overdrive equipped manual
transmission cars).
Wire wheels with conversion kit for hubs, etc.
Conversion kit to change drum braked cars to
disc braked.
Conversion kit to change earlier disc braked cars
to later 'quick change' type.
High ratio steering box.
Lightened flywheel.
Competition clutch.
C-type cylinder head.
Fire extinguisher.
Chromed grab handle to passenger side of
dashboard.
Powr-Lok differential.
Rear window demister.
White-finished steering wheel (export)
Rheostat for dashboard lighting.
Vanity mirror for passenger sun visor.
Stiffened shock absorbers.
Heavy duty anti-roll bar.
Twin windtone horns.
Close ratio gearbox.
High lift camshafts.
Sundym tinted windscreen.
Wing mirrors.

Mark 2 (all models)

Choice of five radio installations with or without rear parcel shelf mounted speaker.
Laminated windscreen.
Chromium plated wheel rimbellishers for steel wheels.
Ace Turbo wheel trims for steel wheels.
Witter tow bar.
Locking petrol filler cap.
Front seat belts.
Choice of radial, town and country, or whitewall tyres.
Borg Warner automatic transmission.
Overdrive (for non overdrive equipped manual transmission cars).
Wire wheels with conversion kit for hubs, etc.
High ratio steering box.
Lightened flywheel.
Competition clutch.
C-type cylinder head.
Fire extinguisher.
Powr-Lok differential.
Rear window demister.
Heavy duty anti-roll bar.
Close ratio gearbox.
High lift camshafts.
Sundym tinted windscreen and side windows.
Wing mirrors.
Childproof locks to rear doors.
Integrated ignition/starter switch to steering column.
Reclining front seats.
Steel sunroof (only offered from new from factory with differing bodyshell).
Power-assisted steering.

Daimler V8 models

Choice of five radio installations with or without rear parcel shelf mounted speaker.
Laminated windscreen.
Ace Turbo wheel trims for steel wheels.
Witter tow bar.
Locking petrol filler cap.
Front seat belts.
Choice of radial, town and country, or whitewall tyres.
All synchromesh manual gearbox for later cars.
Overdrive (for non overdrive equipped manual transmission cars).
Wire wheels with conversion kit for hubs, etc.
Fire extinguisher.
Sundym tinted windscreen and side windows.
Wing mirrors.
Childproof locks to rear doors.
Integrated ignition/starter switch to steering column.
Reclining front seats.
Power-assisted steering.

240/340 models

Choice of five radio installations with or without rear parcel shelf mounted speaker.
Laminated windscreen.
Chromium plated wheel rimbellishers for steel wheels.
Ace Turbo wheel trims for steel wheels.
Witter tow bar.
Locking petrol filler cap.
Front seat belts.
Leather upholstery.
Choice of radial, town and country, or whitewall tyres.
Borg Warner automatic transmission.
Overdrive (for non overdrive equipped manual transmission cars).
Wire wheels with conversion kit for hubs, etc.
High ratio steering box.
Fire extinguisher.
Powr-Lok differential.
Rear window demister.
Close-ratio gearbox.
Sundym tinted windscreen and side windows.
Wing mirrors.
Childproof locks to rear doors.
Integrated ignition/starter switch to steering column.
Reclining front seats.
Power-assisted steering.

Colour schemes

Exterior colour	Details	Interior trim
2.4- and 3.4-litre saloons		
Suede Green		Suede Green
Birch Grey	To 1957	Red
		Grey
		Pale Blue
Battleship Grey	To 1957	Red
		Grey
Lavender Grey	To 1957	Red
		Suede Green
		Pale Blue
Black		Red
		Tan
		Grey
		Biscuit
Pastel Green	To 1957	Suede Green
		Grey
Pastel Blue	To 1957	Pale Blue
		Grey
Dove Grey	To 1957	Tan
		Biscuit
British Racing Green		Tan
		Suede Green
Old English White		Red
		Pale Blue
Dark Blue	From 1958	Light Blue
		Dark Blue
		Grey
Maroon (Imperial)		Red
		Maroon
		Biscuit
Cornish Grey	From 1957	Red
		Light Blue
		Dark Blue
		Grey
Sherwood Green	From 1958	Suede Green
		Tan
Mist Grey		Red
		Light Blue
		Dark Blue
		Grey
Claret	From 1958	Red
		Maroon

Exterior colour	Details	Interior trim
Cotswold Blue	From 1958	Blue
		Grey
Pearl Grey		Red
		Light Blue
		Dark Blue
		Grey
Forest Green	1958 only	Suede Green
Carmine Red		Red
Mark 2 and Daimler 2.5 V8		
Pearl Grey	To 1966	Red
		Light Blue
		Dark Blue
		Grey
Warwick Grey	From 1964	Red
		Tan
Dove Grey	To 1966	Red
		Tan
		Grey
Mist Grey	To 1962	Red
		Grey
Carmen Red	To 1966	Red
		Black
Imperial Maroon		Red
Old English White		Red
		Tan
Primrose Yellow	From 1964	Red
		Tan
		Black
Honey Beige	From 1966	Red
		Tan
British Racing Green		Suede Green
		Tan
		Champagne
Sherwood Green	To 1966	Suede Green
		Tan
Willow Green	From 1966	Suede Green
		Black
		Champagne
Cotswold Blue	To 1965	Dark Blue
		Grey

Exterior colour	Details	Interior trim
Indigo Blue	From 1964	Light Blue
		Dark Blue
		Grey
Black		Red
		Tan
Opalescent Dark Green	From 1961	Suede Green
		Tan
		Champagne
Opalescent Blue	From 1961	Dark Blue
		Light Blue
		Grey
		Red
Opalescent Gunmetal	From 1961	Red
		Tan
Opalescent Silver Grey	From 1961	Red
		Tan
		Grey
Opalescent Silver Blue	From 1961	Dark Blue
		Light Blue
		Grey
		Red
Opalescent Bronze	From 1961	Red
		Tan
Opalescent Golden Sand	From 1966	Red
		Tan
Opalescent Maroon	From 1966	Red
		Champagne
		Tan

Exterior colour	Details	Interior trim
240, 340 and V8 250		
Willow Green		Suede Green
		Black
British Racing Green		Suede Green
		Black
		Beige
Signal Red		Black
		Red
		Beige
Regency Maroon		Red
		Beige
Old English White	Replaced by 'White' in 1968	Black
		Red
Warwick Grey		Black
		Red
		Dark Blue
Ascot Fawn		Black
		Red
Sable Brown		Beige
		Red
		Black
Indigo Blue		Black
		Red
		Dark Blue
Pale Blue		Dark Blue
		Red
		Black
Primrose Yellow		Black
Black		Red
		Dark Blue
		Beige

Prices and production volumes

	Price new (£)	1955	1956	1957	1958	1959	1960
2.4-litre saloon	1,344	■	■	■	■	■	–
3.4-litre saloon	1,672	–	–	■	■	■	–
2.4-litre Mark 2	1,534	–	–	–	–	■	■
3.4-litre Mark 2	1,669	–	–	–	–	■	■
3.8-litre Mark 2	1,779	–	–	–	–	■	■
Daimler 2.5-litre V8	1,568	–	–	–	–	–	–
240 saloon	1,365	–	–	–	–	–	–
340 saloon	1,442	–	–	–	–	–	–
Daimler V8 250	1,850	–	–	–	–	–	–
Total production							

Production changes

1955
2.4-litre introduced.

1956
Rear axle ratio changed to 4.27 on non-overdrive cars.
Shroud fitted to scuttle vent to prevent ingress of dirt.
Pressed steel sump fitted instead of alloy.

1957
3.4-litre introduced.
New radiator fitted with revised filling neck.
(September) Wider grille fitted including revised front wings.
Automatic transmission became available.
(September) Rear-view mirror moved to roof on 3.4s.
Disc brakes introduced and later standardised.

1958
Metal toggle overdrive switch replaced plastic.
60 watt brighter headlight bulbs introduced.
Cut-away rear spats fitted to 2.4s.

1959
Revised 'quick change' bridge brake calipers fitted.
72-spoke wire wheels replaced 60-spoke.
Vacuum reservoir tank fitted to front wing area.
(October) Mark 2s introduced.

1960
60lb oil pressure gauge replaced 100lb.
Position of steering column stalks changed over.
Oil bath air cleaners replaced by paper on 3.4/3.8.
Black-painted centre dash area replaced with Rexine.
Wider steel wheels fitted.
Organ type accelerator replaced by pendant.
Soft sun visors replaced hard type.
Strengthening added to chromed window frames.

1962
Front seat-belt anchorages fitted.
Sealed beam headlight fitted.
Waso steering ignition/lock available.

1963
(Late) Mark X style revised steering wheel fitted.
Extra cut-away area in rear of front seats to increase legroom.

1964
One-piece front carpets fitted.
PVC heel pads fitted to carpets.
'Automatic' emblem on boot lid eliminated on all models.
Larger radiator fitted.
4.27 rear axle ratio fitted to V8 models instead of 4.55.
D1 and D2 positions on auto box for V8 models.

1961	1962	1963	1964	1965	1966	1967	1968	1969	Total produced
–	–	–	–	–	–	–	–	–	19,705
–	–	–	–	–	–	–	–	–	17,280
■	■	■	■	■	■	■	–	–	26,322
■	■	■	■	■	■	■	–	–	29,531
■	■	■	■	■	■	■	–	–	27,848
–	■	■	■	■	■	–	–	–	13,018
–	–	–	–	–	–	■	■	■	4,430
–	–	–	–	–	–	■	■	–	2,804
–	–	–	–	–	–	■	■	■	4,897
									145,835

1965
Hazard light system for export models.
All-synchromesh manual gearbox fitted.
Revised clutch to fit above gearbox.
Limited slip differential now extra cost on
    Daimlers.

1966
240/340/250 introduced.
Ambla upholstery standardised on Jaguars.
Rear of front seat picnic tables deleted.
S-type style heading and visors fitted.
Fog lamps deleted as standard equipment on
    Jaguars.
3.8-litre Mark 2 discontinued.

1967
(February) Manual transmission available on V8
    models.
(June) 2.5-litre V8 discontinued.
Reclining front seats standardised on Daimler
    models.
Power-steering standard on V8s.

1968
Non-earred spinners fitted to wire wheel cars (all
    markets).
Revised water temperature gauge fitted with
    coloured segments.
(September) 340 model discontinued.

1969
(April) 240 model discontinued.
(July) V8 250 model discontinued.

Chassis numbers

Model	Right/ Left Drive	Chassis/ Vin Nos Commencing
2.4 (Mk.1)	RHD	900001
	LHD	940001
3.4 (Mk.1)	RHD	970001
	LHD	985001
2.4 (Mk.2)	RHD	100001
	LHD	125001
3.4 (Mk.2)	RHD	150001
	LHD	175001
3.8 (Mk.2)	RHD	200001
	LHD	210001
240	RHD	1J 1001
	LHD	1J 30001
340	RHD	1J 50001
	LHD	1J 80001
Daimler 2.5 V8	RHD	1A 1001
	LHD	1A 20001
Daimler V8 250	RHD	1K 1001
	LHD	1K 30001

E-type Series 1, 2 and 3 sports cars
1961 to 1974

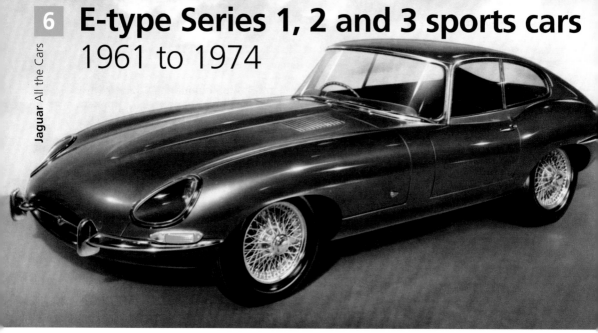

Background

Jaguar had developed a well established sports car market since 1948 with its XK range of cars, culminating in the XK150 produced from 1957 until 1961. Although offering good performance, the styling of these was still heavily based on the original XK120 of 1948 and designs were moving ahead elsewhere in the market place.

This changed with Jaguar's successes at Le Mans, won in 1955 and 1957 by its aerodynamically styled D-types. It was these cars which were to help Jaguar and its aerodynamicist Malcolm Sayer to cultivate the design that we now know as the E-type.

Launched in March 1961 at the Geneva Motor Show, the 'new' sports car, now officially known as the E-type, met the motoring world head-on and became the most talked-about car of the decade. Though offering the good old XK six-cylinder engine in XK150 3.8-litre S triple carburettor form, mated to the same old Moss gearbox, the car did herald in an entirely new independent rear suspension system that would adorn all future Jaguar models until the late 1980s. The aerodynamic body-style was new but had its gestation in the D-type sports/racing car, and introduced monocoque (chassisless) construction to Jaguar road-going sports cars for the first time. A new interior with dash layout based on the Mark 2 was also adopted and the car was available in two body styles, open and closed.

Needless to say, demand exceeded supply for some considerable time and it wasn't until 1964 that any major changes were made to the overall

design. Stylistically the car stayed the same but with better seating and, mechanically, gaining a few litres in engine capacity and a better braking system and gearbox.

In 1966 came a new addition to the range, offering an extra two occasional rear seats on a longer wheelbase bodyshell and, for the first time in the E-type, an automatic transmission, just for that model. The E-type survived substantial upgrades to meet ever more stringent safety and environmental regulations from the US, most of which appeared on the car with little ceremony. Then in 1968 came a 'new' E-type, known as the Series 2, with revised external and internal styling and many mechanical modifications. The three models, roadster, coupé, and 2+2, continued in production until 1971.

In 1971 a third generation of E-type appeared, the Series 3, for the first time showing off Jaguar's new 12-cylinder engine in a wider bodyshell specially adapted to accept the new power unit, which also meant upgraded brakes, steering, and styling features. However, the Series 3 only remained in production until 1974, by which time the whole car was a little long in the tooth, particularly for the American market, where inevitably there was a demand for more refinement and safety.

The final E-type left the production lines in 1974 after a total production run of 72,500 vehicles over 13 years. Since that time the E-type has remained the epitome of the finest in Jaguar sports car design, a design that even current sports car producers refer back to – an icon of the 'sixties and of Jaguar sports car design for ever.

Model range and development

When it was launched the E-type was only available in one engine size with manual transmission and a choice of two body styles.

Models available at launch
E-type 3.8-litre roadster
E-type 3.8-litre fixed-head coupé

The E-type was a direct replacement for the XK150 and it was considered that just two models catered for all needs. The 3.8-litre triple carb engine pushed the performance level beyond that of the competition as, under the right conditions, the E-type genuinely could achieve 150mph, with acceleration to match.

The roadster model was a mere two-seater with a quick fold-down hood mechanism and a cover to hide the hood when down. With wind-up glass windows it offered all the accommodation found in the previous XK150 roadster. The boot space was minimal, but fitted suitcases or a chromed luggage rack were available for touring purposes.

The fixed-head coupé model was of an entirely new design, being one of the first production cars to offer a third wide opening rear door (akin to today's hatchbacks), providing a relatively flat loading area for an extensive amount of luggage. Interior accommodation was similar to the roadster, both being cars fitted out to a high specification. The fastback styling of the fixed-head coupé was particularly handsome and emphasised the styling features of the design, more so than the roadster; it was Sir William Lyons's favourite model.

Following the theme of the XK150, the E-type displayed no woodwork inside the car at all, instead relying on soft trim, and black and figured aluminium for centre areas of the dashboard and console. There were tightly gripping bucket seats, and an entirely new style of steering wheel (a drilled three-spoke design with a wood rim) that became a highly recognisable feature of the E-type over many years.

The E-type instantly became a success on the race tracks too, in the hands of well-known exponents like Graham Hill and Roy Salvadori, and demand continued to exceed supply for some time.

The only major changes in the first couple of years of production were to alter the design of the floorpan to allow for better legroom and to fit internal locking mechanisms to the bonnet, other changes being mainly cosmetic until 1964. That year saw significant improvements in the

Very early E-type Series 1 roadster showing the external bonnet lock escutcheon, soon replaced by internal chromed locks. The chrome finisher to the upper section of the door was only fitted to roadster models.

Fixed-head coupé model. All cars were fitted as standard with wire wheels, either chromed, body colour, or silver-painted. White wall tyres were an extra, as was the Webasto sun-roof seen on this example.

Series 1 E-type frontal aspect with covered headlights, chromed centre bar to the radiator intake with growler badge, and bonnet-mounted stick-on number plate. Some US cars featured a sprung number plate mounting at low level.

design with less stylish but more comfortable seating and a move away from brash alloy finish of the interior to matt black. Mechanically the 3.8-litre engine was enlarged to 4.2 litres capacity, providing better mid-range torque, and with a new all-synchromesh gearbox and better brakes the E-type was an infinitely better drive overall, although some mourned the passing of the free revving 3.8-litre engine.

The next major change came in 1966 when Jaguar added a third model to the range, this time catering for a different market by attempting to hold on to sports car drivers longer, after they had got married and had kids. The 2+2, as it became known, was a lengthened and raised version of the E-type designed to accommodate the addition of a pair of occasional seats in the rear compartment. With the lengthening of the body by 9in it was also possible to fit a Borg Warner automatic transmission so this became available at the same time, a godsend to the valuable US market.

Due to changes in US regulations the E-type needed to adapt, so during 1967 and early 1968 a special Federal model became available, features of which ended up on European cars as well. This model, now (and still unofficially) known as the Series 1½, was identifiable by the exposed headlamp treatment and, mechanically, by an adapted version of the XK engine with Zenith-Stromberg emissions carburettors instead of the British SU type, as well as by the recycling of gases across the manifold and back into the engine. It suffered somewhat in performance and to many was never as aesthetically pleasing as the earlier cars.

This model later developed into the Series 2 E-type from 1968, again to meet changes in legislation but also to bring it up to date. This was externally identifiable by its exposed headlights (different to the Series 1½ type), larger front and rear lighting units, and significantly enlarged air intake to improve cooling. Internally there was a new layout, with rocker switches, a degree of crash padding, and revised door trims. Mechanically the car was more practical, particularly so in hot climates, and with improved brakes and the availability of air conditioning and emissions controls it proved another highly successful version of the E-type, which was still available in all three body styles.

In 1971 Jaguar announced the final phase of the E-type, the Series 3, which was originally intended to have been made available with both the existing six-cylinder XK engine and the brand new V12 unit. Designed primarily for a new upmarket saloon, the V12 engine was, as with the first XK engine, mated to a sports car initially, in this case the E-type, which had to be significantly modified to take it. The XK-engined

Rear view of Series 1 roadster. The '4.2' badging on the boot only applied to post-1964 models with the larger engine. The 3.8-litre models had no such badging.

Rear view of the 4.2-litre Series 1 fixed-head coupé, showing the tailgate area.

Jaguar produced a glass fibre hard-top for the Series 1, 2 and 3 roadster models which could be painted either black or body colour dependent on year of production. Series 3 hard-tops are longer with an air extractor vent.

version of the Series 3, although listed, never actually went into production.

The Series 3 was available in just two body styles, roadster and fixed-head coupé. Both were built on the long wheelbase 2+2 floorpan, though only the fhc offered the occasional rear seating. Widened to take enlarged wheels and tyres and with another enlarged 'mouth' on the bonnet, the Series 3 was instantly recognisable from other E-types, particularly as the bonnet 'mouth' carried a chromed radiator grille as well.

Another interior redesign, now replacing the quite large wood rim steering wheel with a smaller all-leather version, the Series 3 E-type was a much more refined car all round and moved the model somewhat away from its true sports car up-bringing. Quieter, softer sprung, and with power-steering, it was quicker than the Series 2 but not quite so fast as the original Series 1 models.

The fixed-head coupé design only lasted until mid-1973, when it was discontinued, followed by the roadster in 1974 when sales floundered, leaving Jaguar with no model to replace it until late in 1975, when the XJ-S appeared.

Despite the varied fortunes of the E-type, caused more than anything else by legislation, over 72,500 cars were sold, making this Jaguar sports car significantly more successful than the old XK.

In addition Jaguar hand-built 12 3.8-litre E-types for competition purposes. Now known as lightweights, these had aluminium panels and enhanced performance. The Italian coachbuilder Frua also produced a modified version of the E-type which didn't enter production; nor did a more radical design by Bertone for the *Telegraph* newspaper.

Exterior identification points

General points applicable to E-type Series 1s

Front view

■ Aerodynamically shaped curved long bonnet sloping down at front to nose section with elongated air intake mouth, the latter with chromed splitter bar incorporating red circular growler badge.

■ Twin headlight units with glass covers styled into body shape.

■ Integral sidelights and indicator lenses set below headlights, above the bumper bars.

■ Chromed quarter bumpers wrap-around to side of bonnet to meet wheel-arches, with small vertical over-riders close to bonnet mouth at front.

■ Pronounced bulge to bonnet, forward hinged and incorporating louvred panels either side of

Interior layout of the 3.8-litre Series 1 E-type with figured alloy brightwork on the central console and instrument panel. The traditional three-spoke wood-rim steering wheel applied to all E-types up to Series 3.

4.2-litre Series 1 interior showing revised seating and the replacement of figured alloy by black fabric.

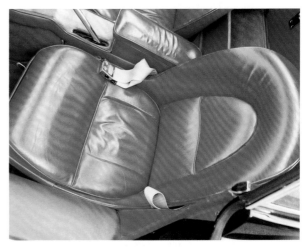

Bucket seats in the 3.8-litre models were replaced by a flatter design in 4.2-litre cars.

the bulge to aid cooling of the engine compartment.
- Majority of E-types featured 'stick-on' number plates to the leading edge of the bonnet above the mouth. Some cars, particularly in the US, were fitted with metal support plates to one side that hinged as the bonnet was raised.
- One-piece curved windscreen with chromed surround and three wiper blades.

Rear view
- Curved and tapered body areas, with indented area in the centre for number plate and illumination. Reversing light set centrally beneath. Severe curvature of under-bonnet allowed view of rear suspension and exhaust system.
- One-piece rear-hinged boot lid or side-opening door with rear screen on fixed-head coupé model.
- Fuel filler to one rear wing with cover painted to body colour.
- Twin exhaust pipes emit from centre of car under number plate area.
- Chromed quarter bumper bars to match front with over-riders, wrapping around to meet rear wheel-arches.
- Integral chromed horizontal light units set above bumpers on rear wings.

Side view
- Very early 3.8-litre cars featured chromed escutcheon external bonnet locks, one per side to lower edges of rear of bonnet.
- Aerodynamic style followed through from bonnet area to rear of car with pronounced haunch over rear wing.
- Stylised chromed door handles apply to all models.
- 72-spoke wire wheels fitted to all cars, either body colour, silver enamel, or chromed, all with chromed eared hubcaps depicting 'Jaguar' name.
- Later non 'flat floor' models identifiable by view of lowered floorpan area beneath sill area of car.

E-type Series 1 specifics
E-type 3.8/4.2-litre roadster
- Door frames incorporate chromed horizontal finisher at waist height.
- Door windows of curved glass with no support framework except at front.
- Fabric hood clipped to windscreen top rail and affixed to rear deck of bodywork.
- Perspex rear screen to hood with chromed finisher above.
- One-piece rear-hinged door lid with no external lock mechanism.
- Chromed 'Jaguar' badge to centre of boot lid.

Coupé boot with fold-down frontal area.

1967 mid-term model, now known as the Series 1½, with exposed headlights.

Series 2 E-types are identifiable from the front by the enlarged air intake area, raised bumper bar level, larger side/indicator lights, and exposed headlights with different surrounds to the Series 1½.

■ Chromed '4.2' badge below 'Jaguar' on boot lid. No badging on 3.8-litre models.

E-type Series 1 fixed-head coupé
■ As above but doors do not have chromed waist trim.
■ Chrome on brass window surround to glass accompanied by matching rear opening quarter-lights and chromed rain gutters to steel roof.
■ Extended steel roof slopes back (fastback) to form a large side-opening door with glass rear screen with chromed surround. No external locks or hinges.
■ Badging as roadster model.

E-type Series 1 2+2
■ As fixed-head coupé but with a steeper rake and greater curvature to the windscreen.
■ 3in increase in roof height.
■ 9in extra length to the wheelbase, all taken up in lengthened doors and chromed window frames.
■ Chromed waistline trim to doors with matching finisher on rear wing area in stepped style.

E-type Series 1½ specifics
■ Front open headlights (without glass covers), necessitating a redesign of chrome trim on the bonnet side tops and around the headlamp units themselves.
■ Most wire wheel equipped cars by this time fitted with 'easy-clean' flat centre hubs.

General points applicable to E-type Series 2s
Front view
■ Redesigned nose section of bonnet with 70 per cent larger mouth.
■ Front bumper bar continued across centre of air intake, incorporating splitter bar with new oval badge depicting growler.
■ Open headlights similar to Series 1½ cars but with revised chrome trim surrounds, much deeper on top.
■ Sidelight/indicator units enlarged and moved to new position beneath bumper area.

Rear view
■ Full-width bumper now running across the top of the rear bodywork above number plate area.
■ Enlarged rear lighting units placed beneath the bumper level along with a new stainless finishing panel incorporating the reversing lights (two) and square number plate above the exhaust tailpipes.

Side view
■ All Series 2 cars equipped with wire wheels

From late in 1967 the curved centre hubs of wire wheels above were changed to the 'easi-clean' style shown at the top.

Rear of Series 2 model, with full-width bumper bar treatment, alloy background panel incorporating larger lights, spread tail-pipes and, usually, square number plates.

used the 'easy-clean' type of flat hub accompanied by non-eared hub spinners. Some cars fitted with conventional steel road wheels, either silver or chromed, with conventional Jaguar hubcaps depicting centrally mounted growler badge.
▓ Series 2s easily identifiable by open headlights and under bumper.

E-type Series 2 specifics
E-type Series 2 2+2
▓ As other Series 2 models except windscreen enlarged and moved further forward, virtually eliminating a scuttle area between screen and bonnet.

General points applicable to E-type Series 3s
Front view
▓ Enlarged bonnet air intake mouth area now incorporating slatted grille with gold growler badge in the centre and a chromed trim scoop area below mouth. Rubber-faced over-riders (or Nordel impact absorbing units on US cars).
▓ Wider aspect to bonnet area with pronounced flares to bonnet sides in wheel-arch areas.
▓ Lighting as Series 2 models.
▓ One-piece curved windscreen with chromed surround and two windscreen wipers.

Rear view
▓ Series 2 style but revised siting of reversing lights and reversal to rectangular number plates (in most markets).
▓ New four exhaust tailpipes in fishtail style, later replaced by twin pipe system.
▓ Badging on rear depicting 'Jaguar' and 'E-type' emblems with enlarged 'V' incorporating figure '12' in chrome.

Side view
▓ Only built on the long wheelbase 2+2 floorpan so recognisable by the extra length to both roadster and coupé models, particularly in the door areas.
▓ Flared wheel-arches front and rear.
▓ Chrome door finisher on both models, similar to 2+2 style but not the same.

E-type Series 3 specifics
Fixed-head coupé 2+2
▓ Rear tailgate incorporates chromed air extractor grille above badging.

Interior identification points
E-type Series 1 3.8-litre (all models)
▓ Dashboard in black finish with speedometer and rev counter directly in front of driver, with ancillary gauges and toggle switches on centre panel finished in figured alloy.
▓ Open glove-box to passenger side of dashboard.

2+2 model, in this case a Series 2 car with US-style repeater indicator lights on the side of the bonnet. 2+2s are instantly identifiable by the longer bodyshell, with wider doors and chromed finisher across the top of them.

Revised interior for Series 2 models, with rocker switches on the centre panel, and revised door trims and handles.

Series 3 roadster based on the longer wheelbase (2+2) floorpan. It can be identified from the side by the wider wheel-arches and chromed trim along the top of the doors (which are also wider).

- Figured alloy centre console extending down, incorporating chromed ashtray, radio, gear lever, and handbrake (fly off).
- Sculptured bucket seating with wide pleating.
- Wood-rim three-spoke drilled steering wheel incorporating horn push centre boss with gold, white, and black chequered flag, laurels, and 'E-type' script.
- Upholstered door panels and sill areas with horizontal chrome trims and handles to each door.

E-type Series 1 3.8-litre roadster
- Centre chromed vertical stay rod to screen area to accommodate the sliding rear view mirror fitted to roadster models.
- Mohair hood with beige interior lining affixed to screen via three toggle clamps.
- No sun visors fitted.
- Boot lid opened from behind driver's seat, with hardura covering and wooden floor removable to gain access to tools and spare wheel.

E-type Series 1 3.8-litre fixed-head coupé
- Conventional roof-mounted rear view mirror.
- Trimmed rear deck area with rails for luggage, with removable panel to access spare wheel and tools.
- Fold-down forward section to provide extra load area, chrome trimmed.
- Upholstered rear side-opening door with lock access from behind driver's seat and stay bar. Covered door hinges on later models.

E-type Series 1 4.2-litre (all models)
- Flatter front seat arrangement to 3.8-litre models with closer horizontal and vertical pleating.
- Replacement of alloy dash and console panels with black figured Rexine on centre dash panel and leather to match interior trim on centre console.
- Console now incorporated a leather clad armrest and lidded glove-box area between seats.
- Door trims now incorporated armrest and pulls with chrome trim.

E-type Series 1 4.2-litre roadster
- Boot locking handle behind driver's seat now incorporated a locking mechanism.
- Better quality trim to rear compartment.

E-type Series 1 4.2-litre fixed-head coupé
- Extensive use of Rexine and Moquette to rear compartment.
- Extended trim coverings to protect luggage from catches, etc, in the rear compartment.

E-type Series 1 4.2-litre 2+2 coupé
- As fixed-head coupé but at the front parcel

All Series 3 E-types were fitted with the V12 engine necessitating a larger air intake, now with a chromed grille. Larger under-bumper lighting and wider wheel-arches also differentiate this model.

Styling cues at the rear of the Series 3 are taken from the Series 2 six-cylinder models. Prominent V12 badging on the tailgate and ventilation grille was also used on the fixed-head coupé model. The chromed steel wheels with hubcaps and black centres were used on Series 2 and 3 models except where wire wheels were specified.

Different tail-pipe arrangements on the E-type Series 3. A four pipe system was initially fitted (inset), later changed to twin pipes as seen in the main picture.

shelves were fitted below dashboard area for storage.

■ Slightly revised centre console to accommodate rear seating arrangement.

■ Rear seating in leather with matching pleats, trimmed side panels below rear quarter-lights, and a fold-down top section of the seat for extra luggage accommodation.

E-type Series 1½ (all models)

■ Front seats provided with adjustable squabs and positive locking arrangement.

■ Burst-proof door locks with recessed door handles and chromed window winders incorporating black plastic knobs.

■ Wider seats necessitating slightly recessed centre console sides.

■ Plastic surround to rear view mirror.

■ During production of this model the centre dash layout changed to incorporate new style rocker switches in place of toggle type.

E-type Series 2 (all models)

■ Changes as the later Series 1½ models including rocker switches on dashboard, revised door trims, rear view mirror, etc.

■ Reclining front seats with fitting to accept headrests.

■ Aerated perforated leather trim to seats.

■ Simplified moulded centre console for radio now incorporated cigarette lighter.

■ Re-siting and redesign of ashtray to centre console in front of armrest.

■ Horn now operated from steering column mounted stalk and not steering wheel boss.

E-type Series 3 (all models)

■ Smaller diameter leather covered three-spoke steering wheel fitted with black growler centre boss motif.

■ Revised seating from Series 2 models but still with aerated leather seat centres.

■ Vacuum-formed black centre console.

■ Speaker grilles in rear compartment panelling.

■ Revised door interior trims with square recessed areas for handles and squared off armrests/pulls.

E-type Series 3 roadster

■ Deeper tonneau cover fitted when hood down, extending forward to rear of front seats.

■ Trimmed box area behind front seats for luggage, with hinged lid.

E-type Series 3 fixed-head coupé

■ Only available as a 2+2 seating arrangement.

■ Extended front seat adjustment levers to enable rear seat passengers to move the seat backs.

Interior revision of Series 3 models incorporated a small, leather-rimmed steering wheel.

Air conditioning became available on later E-types, usually for the US market, and was fitted as shown here.

2+2 seating arrangement.

Technical specifications

	3.8-litre	4.2-litre Series 1
cc	3,781	4,235
Bore and stroke (mm)	87 x 106	92.07 x 106
Compression ratio	9:1 (8:1 optional)	9:1 (8:1 optional)
bhp	265	265
@ rpm	5,500	5,400
Torque (lb ft)	260	283
@ rpm	4,000	4,000
Fuelling	3 x SU carbs	3 x SU carbs
Transmission	4-speed (3 synchro)	4-speed all synchro 2+2 BW 3-speed auto
Wheel size (in)	15, wire	15, wire
Suspension front	Ind wishbone, torsion bar	Ind wishbone, torsion bar
Suspension rear	Ind lower wishbone, upper driveshaft link, radius arms, coil springs	Ind lower wishbone, upper driveshaft link, radius arms, coil springs
Brakes	4 wheel disc, rear inboard	4 wheel disc, rear inboard
Performance		
0–60mph (sec)	7.1	7.0 (8.9 2+2)
Top speed (mph)	149.1	150 (136.2 2+2)
Average mpg	19.7	18.5 (18.3 2+2)
Dimensions		
Length (in)	175.5	175.5 (184.5 2+2)
Width (in)	64.25	66.75
Height (in)	47 (48 fhc)	50.5 2+2
Wheelbase (in)	96	96 (105 2+2)
Front track (in)	50	50
Rear track (in)	50	50
Weight (cwt)	24	25.1 (27.7 2+2)

Optional extras

E-type Series 1 3.8 litre models
Choice of three radio installations with fitting kits.
Two choices of bonnet-mounted wing mirrors.
Locking petrol filler cap.
Front seat safety belts.
Clear glass rear door (fhc).
Sundym tinted glass.
Detachable glass fibre hardtop for roadster model.
Alternative choices of tyres.
Chromium plated wire wheels.
Competition wire wheels.

E-type Series 1 and 1½ 4.2-litre models
Choice of three radio installations with fitting kits.
Two choices of bonnet-mounted wing mirrors.
Locking petrol filler cap.
Front seat safety belts.
Rear seat safety belts for 2+2 model.
Clear glass rear door (fhc).
Electrically heated rear screen for 2+2 model.
Sundym tinted glass.
Detachable glass fibre hardtop for roadster model.
Alternative choices of tyres.
Chromium-plated wire wheels.
Competition wire wheels.
Steering column lock and ignition switch.

Technical specifications *cont ...*

	4.2-litre Series 2	**Series 3**
cc	4,235	5,343
Bore and stroke (mm)	92.07 x 106	90 x 70
Compression ratio	9:1 (8:1 optional)	9:1
bhp	265	272
@ rpm	5,400	5,850
Torque (lb ft)	283	304
@ rpm	4,000	5,600
Fuelling	3 x SU carbs, 3 x Stromberg (US)	4 x Stromberg carbs
Transmission	4-speed all synchro	4-speed all synchro
	2+2 B/W 3-speed auto	B/W 3-speed auto
Wheel size (in)	15, wire/steel option	15, wire/steel option
Suspension front	Ind wishbone, torsion bar	Ind wishbone, torsion bar
Suspension rear	Ind lower wishbone, upper driveshaft link, radius arms, coil springs	Ind lower wishbone, upper driveshaft link, radius arms, coil springs
Brakes	4 wheel disc, rear inboard	4 wheel disc, rear inboard
Performance		
0–60mph (sec)		6.4 (6.8 2+2)
Top speed (mph)		146 (142 2+2)
Average mpg		14.5
Dimensions		
Length (in)		184
Width (in)		
Height (in)		
Wheelbase (in)		105
Front track (in)		54.5
Rear track (in)		53
Weight (cwt)		28.8 (29.5 2+2)

Optional extras *cont ...*

E-type Series 2 models

Choice of three radio installations with fitting kits.
Two choices of bonnet-mounted wing mirrors.
Locking petrol filler cap.
Front seat safety belts.
Rear seat safety belts for 2+2 model.
Front seat headrests.
Electrically heated rear screen.
Sundym tinted glass.
Alternative choices of tyres.
Chromium-plated wire wheels.
Competition wire wheels.
Chromium-plated steel wheels.
Air conditioning.

E-type Series 3 models

Choice of three radio installations with fitting kits.
Electric radio aerial.
Three choices of bonnet- or door-mounted mirrors.
Locking petrol filter cap.
Front seat safety belts.
Rear seat safety belts for 2+2 model.
Front seat headrests.
Electrically heated rear screen.
Sundym tinted glass.
Alternative choices of tyres.
Wire wheels.
Chromium-plated wire wheels.
Chromium-plated steel wheels.
Detachable hardtop for roadster model.
Air conditioning.

Colour schemes

Exterior colour Single	Details	Interior trim	Details
E-type 3.8-litre models			
Pearl Grey		Red	
		Dark Blue	
Mist Grey		Red	
Carmen Red		Red	
		Biscuit	
Imperial Maroon	1961–2 only	Tan	
Claret	1961–2 only	Beige	
Old English White		Red	
		Black	
		Cream	
Primrose Yellow	From 1963	Black	
		Beige	
British Racing Green		Suede Green	
		Tan	
		Beige	
		Light Tan	
Sherwood Green		Suede Green	
		Light Tan	
		Tan	
Cotswold Blue		Dark Blue	
Indigo Blue	1963/4 only	Light Blue	
		Red	
Black		Red	
		Grey	
		Light Tan	
		Tan	
Opalescent Dark Green		Suede Green	
		Tan	
		Beige	
		Light Tan	
Opalescent Blue		Dark Blue	
		Red	
Opalescent Gunmetal		Red	
		Light Blue	
		Dark Blue	
		Beige	
Opalescent Silver Grey		Red	
		Light Blue	
		Grey	
		Dark Blue	
Opalescent Silver Blue		Dark Blue	
		Grey	

Colour schemes *cont* …

Exterior colour Single	Details	Interior trim	Details
Opalescent Bronze		Red	
		Beige	
		Tan	
Opalescent Golden Sand	From 1963	Black	
		Beige	
Opalescent Maroon	From 1963	Maroon	
		Beige	
E-type Series 1 4.2 and 1½ models			
Carmen Red		Red	To 1965
		Black	
		Biscuit	To 1965
Old English White		Red	
		Black	
		Cream	To 1965
Primrose Yellow		Black	
		Beige	
Sherwood Green		Suede Green	
		Light Tan	
		Tan	
Dark Blue		Light Blue	
		Grey	
		Red	
Black		Red	
		Grey	
		Light Tan	
		Tan	
Opalescent Dark Green		Suede Green	
		Tan	
		Beige	
		Light Tan	
Opalescent Blue		Dark Blue	
		Red	
Opalescent Gunmetal		Red	
		Light Blue	
		Dark Blue	
		Beige	
Opalescent Silver Grey		Red	
		Light Blue	
		Grey	
		Dark Blue	
Opalescent Silver Blue		Dark Blue	
		Grey	

Exterior colour Single	Details	Interior trim	Details
Opalescent Golden Sand		Black	To 1965
		Beige	To 1965
		Red	From 1965
		Light Tan	From 1965
Opalescent Maroon		Maroon	
		Beige	
Warwick Grey		Red	
		Light Tan	
		Dark Blue	
Willow Green	From 1967	Grey	
		Suede Green	
		Light Tan	
		Beige	
Beige	From 1967	Red	
		Suede Green	
		Tan	
		Light Tan	
British Racing Green	From 1967	Suede Green	
		Beige	
		Light Tan	
		Dark Tan	
E-Type Series 2 models			
Old English White		Red	To 1969
		Black	
Primrose Yellow		Black	
		Beige	
Dark Blue		Light Blue	
		Grey	
		Red	
Black		Red	
		Grey	
		Cinnamon	
Warwick Grey		Red	
		Cinnamon	
		Dark Blue	
Willow Green		Grey	
		Suede Green	
		Cinnamon	
		Beige	
British Racing Green		Suede Green	
		Beige	
		Cinnamon	

Colour schemes *cont* ...

Exterior colour Single	Details	Interior trim	Details
Ascot Fawn		Red	
		Beige	
		Cinnamon	
Sable Brown		Beige	
		Grey	
		Cinnamon	
Light Blue		Dark Blue	
		Light Blue	
		Grey	
Regency Red		Beige	
		Grey	
Signal Red	To 1970	Black	
		Red	
		Beige	
E-Type Series 3 models			
Old English White		Red	
		Dark Blue	
		Light Blue	
		Black	
Primrose Yellow		Black	
		Beige	To 1972
		Biscuit	From 1972
		Red	From 1972
Dark Blue		Light Blue	To 1972
		French Blue	From 1972
		Russet Red	From 1972
		Grey	To 1972
		Red	
Black	Special order from 1972	Red	
		Grey	
		Cinnamon	
Warwick Grey	To 1972	Red	
		Cinnamon	
		Dark Blue	
Willow Green	To 1972	Grey	
		Suede Green	
		Cinnamon	
		Beige	
British Racing Green		Suede Green	To 1972
		Beige	To 1972
		Biscuit	From 1972
		Moss Green	From 1972
		Cinnamon	

Exterior colour Single	Details	Interior trim	Details
Ascot Fawn	To 1972	Red	
		Beige	
		Cinnamon	
Sable Brown	To 1972	Beige	
		Grey	
		Cinnamon	
Light Blue	To 1972	Dark Blue	
		Light Blue	
		Grey	
Regency Red		Beige	To 1972
		Grey	To 1972
		Biscuit	From 1972
		Cinnamon	From 1972
		Russet Red	From 1972
Signal Red		Black	
		Red	To 1972
		Beige	To 1972
		Biscuit	From 1972
		Dark Blue	From 1972
Fern Grey	From 1972	Moss Green	
		Olive	
		Tan	
Turquoise	From 1972	Tan	
		Terracotta	
		Cinnamon	
Green Sand	From 1972	Tan	
		Olive	
		Cinnamon	
Heather	From 1972	Maroon	
		Antelope	
		Cerise	
Lavender Blue	From 1972	French Blue	
		Biscuit	
		Dark Blue	
Azure Blue	From 1972	Dark Blue	
		Biscuit	
		Cinnamon	
Silver Metallic	Special order from 1972	Black	
		Red	
		Biscuit	

Prices and production volumes

	Price new (£)	1961	1962	1963	1964	1965	1966
3.8-litre roadster	2,098	■	■	■	■	–	–
3.8-litre fixed-head coupé	2,197	■	■	■	■	–	–
4.2-litre roadster	1,896	–	–	–	■	■	■
4.2-litre fixed-head coupé	1,992	–	–	–	■	■	■
4.2-litre Series 1 2+2	2,385	–	–	–	–	–	■
Series 2 roadster	2,163	–	–	–	–	–	–
Series 2 fixed-head coupé	2,273	–	–	–	–	–	–
Series 2 2+2	2,512	–	–	–	–	–	–
Series 3 roadster	3,139	–	–	–	–	–	–
Series 3 2+2	3,383	–	–	–	–	–	–
Total production							

Production changes

1961
E-type 3.8-litre models introduced.
(October) Automatic handbrake pad adjustment.
Exterior bonnet fastening deleted.

1962
Revised bonnet hinges.
Steering lock/ignition switch available.
Heated rear screen available on fhc models.
(June) Heel wells fitted to floorpans.
(June) Chrome finisher added to roadster window
      front surround.
(November) Alloy dash finisher pattern altered.

1963
Centre armrest fitted.
One-piece luggage floor matt for fhc.
(November) Longer blades fitted to wipers.

1964
Sealed beam headlamps fitted for most countries.
E-type Series 1 4.2-litre models introduced.
Plastic screen wash reservoir fitted.

1966
Vanity mirror fitted to passenger sun visor.
2+2 model introduced.
Green indicator dash backlight replaced blue.

1967
Switch and warning light adopted for heated rear
      screen.
Series 1½ models phased in.
Ribbed cam covers phased in.

1968
Easi-clean wire wheel hubs adopted.
Series 2 models introduced.

1967	1968	1969	1970	1971	1972	1973	1974	Total produced
–	–	–	–	–	–	–	–	7,818
–	–	–	–	–	–	–	–	7,663
■	■	–	–	–	–	–	–	9,551
■	■	–	–	–	–	–	–	7,771
■	■	–	–	–	–	–	–	5,586
–	■	■	■	–	–	–	–	8,641
–	■	■	■	–	–	–	–	4,878
–	■	■	■	–	–	–	–	5,329
–	–	–	–	■	■	■	■	7,982
–	–	–	–	■	■	■	–	7,310
								72,529

1971
Series 3 models introduced.

1972
Revised heater controls.
Remote control door mirror now available.
Waso steering lock adopted.

1973
Modified Borg Warner Model 12 auto
    transmission fitted.
Twin exhaust pipe outlets replaced four branch.
Fixed-head coupé model discontinued.

1974
Last 50 commemorative models produced.

Chassis numbers

Model	Right/Left Drive	Chassis/Vin Nos Commencing
E-type 3.8	RHD	850001
OTS	LHD	875001
E-type 3.8	RHD	860001
FHC	LHD	885001
E-type 4.2 S1	RHD	1E 1001
OTS	LHD	1E 10001
E-type 4.2 S1	RHD	1E 2001
FHC	LHD	1E 30001
E-type 4.2 S1	RHD	1E 50001
2 + 2	LHD	1E 75001
E-type S2	RHD	1R 1001
OTS	LHD	1R 7001
E-type S2	RHD	1R 20001
FHC	LHD	1R 25001
E-type S2	RHD	1R 35001
2 + 2	LHD	1R 4000
E-type S3	RHD	1S 1001
OTS	LHD	1S 20001
E-type S3	RHD	1S 50001
2 + 2	LHD	1S 70001

The Mark X/420G saloons
1961 to 1970

Background

Although Jaguar had expanded its saloon car range in the 1950s with the introduction of the compact models, updated to the Mark 2 from 1959, the large flagship saloon design based on the Mark VII had reigned supreme since 1950, and a replacement was badly needed. Development work on the E-type enabled Jaguar to take advantage of some of the new sports car's technology, and within a few months of the E-type's launch in March 1961 a brand new luxury saloon was announced at the British Motor Show in October.

The Mark VII having grown into the Mark VIII and then the Mark IX, and it was logical that the next new model would take the name Mark X, even though it owed nothing to the earlier cars except for the by then legendary XK six-cylinder twin camshaft engine. Those who used to think the Mark VII was large were to be somewhat surprised when the Mark X was announced as an even longer and wider car – the widest production car ever produced in the UK until the introduction of Jaguar's own XJ220 supercar in the 1990s. The Mark X was a big car in every way except for its height, which emphasised the length even more, and the whole styling concept was obviously designed with the valued North American market in mind.

William Lyons had attempted to retain much of Jaguar's traditional touches but within an all-new style, although this was to have limited success. The 'old' engine and gearbox were mated to the new E-type independent rear suspension to enhance handling and ride. The extra body length and width made for interior dimensions of gargantuan size and the Mark X was never lacking in equipment levels. The bodywork was of monocoque construction, allowing the car to sit much lower and reducing its overall height, and it was a tribute to Jaguar's engineers that it was even more structurally rigid than the outgoing Mark IX.

The styling, however, was not to meet with universal acclaim. Though aimed at the highly profitable US market, American buyers considered the Mark X to be too much like their own cars, lacking the traditional style and stature of a luxury European car. British buyers did not respond well to the new car either, because it was just too large and bulbous. Even in the early 1960s few home garages were long enough or wide enough to accommodate a vehicle of this size, and it was difficult to park and to handle in confined country lanes, leading to a substantial number of cars suffering from scratched and dented sides.

Even though the Mark X 3.8-litre model didn't sell as well as the early Mark VIIs did in the 1950s, it was updated alongside the E-type in 1964 with 4.2-litre engine and other changes, although sales continued to decline. With Jaguar's policy of revamping its whole range in 1966 the Mark X also received some minor modifications, amongst which was a change of name to 420G. Sales marginally improved, helped by the fact that the car's replacement, the XJ6, wasn't announced until September 1968 and, even then, stocks remained in short supply well into 1969, allowing production and sales of the 420G to continue into 1970.

Never considered to be one of Jaguar's better designs, the Mark X did carry its style and proportions well and was an immensely strong car overall. Many would say it was the last of the traditional Jaguars, with chrome on brass window frames and some of the traditional touches characteristic of previous models.

In total only just over 25,000 Mark X/420G models were produced from 1961 to 1970, pro rata the lowest production figure per year of any Jaguar saloon style ever.

Model range and development

When introduced at the British Motor Show in 1961 there was only one model of the Mark X, with manual four-speed transmission (with or without overdrive) or Borg Warner three-speed automatic gearbox.

Model Available at Launch
3.8-litre Mark X saloon

The Mark X Jaguar offered a high standard of specification, incorporating the E-type's 3.8-litre XK power unit, complete with triple SU carburettors developing 265bhp, an 11 per cent increase over the outgoing Mark IX model. Although both gearboxes were essentially the same as the Mark IX, the new independent rear suspension and the lower centre of gravity improved the handling and, to a degree, the ride.

Externally the Mark X still dripped in chrome, with the usual Jaguar leaping mascot atop the bonnet (although of smaller dimensions). Even the traditional grille was retained, cleverly adapted to fit a much lower body line by leaning it forward from the vertical position. All-new lighting adopted the latest idea of four headlamps (only really seen in the US in the previous couple of years), and due to its overall size the Mark X had a magnificent boot capable to swallowing virtually anything.

Internally the accepted Jaguar touches of veneer and leather were retained, though the dashboard took on the overall style of the Mark 2 and E-type but in a much lighter hue of walnut than before. Enormous seating in the front formed a split-bench arrangement with reclining mechanisms, and Jaguar retained the occasional picnic tables in the rear as a mark of respect to the earlier cars. However, although aimed at the executive and even chauffeur-driven markets, to enable the car to sit a lot lower the floorpan fell below the sill level, which necessitated occupants having to step over enormous sills to get in and out.

Hardly anything changed during the life of the 3.8-litre Mark X except for the adoption of an improved heating system late on. Then in 1964,

after a mere 12,500 had been produced, the Mark X received the same revision treatment that the E-type got. In came the 4.2-litre version of the XK engine to improve torque, along with much improved power assistance to the brake system and a new Varamatic power-steering system to provide greater 'feel'. The by this time archaic manual gearbox was improved with all-synchromesh, and even the automatic transmission was changed for the smoother Model 8 unit. The resulting 4.2-litre Mark X was virtually identical in looks to the old model except for the 4.2-litre badging on the boot lid.

At the same time Jaguar announced a new addition to the Mark X range, the limousine model. Exactly the same mechanically and dimensionally as the standard saloon, this model did offer a centre division arrangement ideally suited to a chauffeur-driven car. A brief black and white brochure was produced on this model, which was only produced to special order. In fact only 18 were made.

The next move came in October 1966 when Jaguar announced a rationalisation of its saloon models, the simplification of trim, and re-badging. The Mark X became the 420G and was only changed externally by the addition of a prominent centre vertical rib to the radiator grille, the fitting of front wing side indicator repeater lights, revised badging at the rear, and new style hubcaps. Two-tone colour schemes also became available, accompanied by a swage coachline separating the colours. When cars were painted in a single colour chromed swage line trims were fitted. Internally 420G models were identified by the black Ambla covered dashboard top rail incorporating a rectangular clock, a pull-out wooden tray under the centre dash panel, and aerated centre leather panels to the seats. Jaguar continued to offer a limousine model alongside the saloon but only 24 were produced, including the example used by Sir William Lyons himself as a company vehicle.

The 420G soldiered on into 1970 and a few cars were still unsold in 1971, resulting in a grand total of only 25,212 being produced since its conception back in 1961.

Exterior identification points

General points applicable to all Mark X/420G models
Front view
- Low set frontal aspect with twin headlight arrangement (inner ones smaller than outer).
- Circular sidelights and elongated oval wrap-around indicator units inset into corners of front wings.
- Chromed horn grilles (similar to those fitted to Mark VIII/IX models) below the centre pair of headlights.

- Traditional but shallow version of Jaguar chromed radiator grille sloping forward from the top with vertical slats and carrying Jaguar winged badge.
- Slimline chromed bumper with matching over-riders sloping forwards, with number plate centrally mounted.
- One-piece forward-hinged bonnet incorporating grille, inner headlights, and horn grilles.
- Reduced size Jaguar leaping mascot atop the bonnet with full-length centrally mounted chrome trim.
- One-piece wrap-around windscreen incorporating chromed surround and two wiper blades.

Rear view

- Rear wrap-around screen with chrome surround.
- Twin fuel tanks with lockable covers, one per side atop rear boot surround panel.
- One-piece boot lid incorporating chromed number plate/reversing light plinth and chromed number plate surround.
- 'Jaguar' script and, where applicable, 'automatic' script centrally mounted.
- Integrated rear light units with chrome surround and reflectors.
- Slimline bumper wrapping around rear wings fitted with over-riders to match front.
- Twin exhaust pipes emerging separately in centre of car below bumper and rear valance level.

Side view

- Elongated style very low with bulged sides incorporating swage indentation at mid-level.
- Sculptured door handles fitted sloping upwards from top of doors.
- Chrome on brass window frames with quarter-lights front and rear.
- Chromed rain gutters and horizontal thin trims at window level above door handles.
- Unique 14in steel wheels painted to body colour with chromed rimbellishers and hubcaps similar to other early 1960s models in the Jaguar range, incorporating pronounced centre section with Jaguar badge.

Mark X/420G specifics

Mark X 4.2-litre model

- Exactly as 3.8-litre except for '4.2' chrome script below Jaguar in centre of boot lid. No '3.8' litre badging featured on previous model.

420G model

- Pronounced chromed centre rib to radiator grille.
- Revised hubcaps similar to those used on the 240/340 models, incorporating more

In 3.8-litre and 4.2-litre form the Mark X was identical externally except for a '4.2' badge on the boot lid of the latter. This body style was only used for these and the later 420G models and is instantly recognisable from any other Jaguar saloon. Pre-420G models featured the usual chromed Jaguar hubcaps containing a 'Jaguar' emblem, and chromed rimbellishers were a standard fitment.

The Mark X radiator grille featured vertical slats of equal size. For certain overseas markets the Jaguar leaper on the bonnet (of a smaller size to that used previously on other cars) was not fitted.

Up to 1964 the interior design of the Mark X was unchanged, as seen here with Mark 2/E-type layout, except for wood-veneered centre section and pull-out occasional tray below with chromed handle. The three black push-buttons on the centre console controlled the vacuum air flow/heating system.

pronounced centre section and growler image on black badge.
- Indicator repeater lenses to forward edge of front wings.
- Painted coachline to swage area for cars in two-tone exterior paint finishes.
- Chromed trims along the entire side length of the body from front wing (behind indicator repeater) to rear wing. This trim used on single colour models.
- Revised '420G' badging on boot lid.

NB: There were no exterior differences at all between production saloons and special order limousines.

Interior identification points

Mark X/420G (all models)
- Dashboard layout similar to Mark 2 and E-type models with speedometer and rev counter directly in front of driver and ancillary gauges and switchgear on centre panel slightly recessed, in the case of the Mark X models finished in matching veneer to the rest of the dashboard.
- Wrap-around veneered top rail and lower panels of dashboard, meeting doors at extreme ends with chrome finishers.
- Passenger side lockable glove-box with chromed handle.
- Under dashboard full-length oddments shelf.
- Further shelves on front sides of the car below dashboard.
- Steering column mounted indicator stalk and, where fitted, automatic transmission quadrant (or overdrive switch).
- One-piece black plastic-coated steering wheel with two-spoke centre boss incorporating gold growler badge and surround, and half horn ring (with centre boss also operational for horn use).
- Substantial trimmed central console incorporating two chrome surround radio speakers to the side, vacuum heater control buttons, veneered ashtray and audio area and gear lever (manual models), console extending rearward between front bench-style seats to rear compartment heater extractor vents with on/of switch.
- Umbrella-style handbrake sited next to centre console speaker trim on driver's side.
- Padded door trims to match interior finish with veneered cappings and chromed door and window winder handles plus shaped armrests.
- Front seats sculptured to bench style with individual centre armrests that folded away, vertical pleating, and reclining adjustment for seat backs.

From 1964 the last of the 3.8-litre Mark Xs and all 4.2-litre Mark Xs were fitted with a revised heating system with enhanced controls as seen here.

Above left: *The rear compartment of Mark X/420G models did not change except for the use of aerated leather upholstery centre panels on the 420G models from 1967.*

Above right: *When equipped with electrically operated windows, a centre veneered panel was fitted to the console in the front of the car with separate chromed buttons in the rear doors.*

With the introduction of the revised model from 1967, re-badged 420G, a prominent centre vane was added to the radiator grille, and side indicator repeater lights were incorporated into the front wings. Where single colour exterior paint schemes were applied, a chromed swage line trim ran the entire length of the body.

- Rear compartment trimmed to match, with bench-seat arrangement with central armrest.
- Rears of front seats incorporate veneered picnic tables and matching ashtrays.
- Carpeted throughout with vinyl trimmed sill areas.
- Boot entirely Hardura covered including spare wheel with full tool box affixed to offside of boot between spare wheel and trim.

NB: Where cars were specified with electric windows the rear doors incorporated chrome window switches. The centre console incorporated a veneered switch panel with four chromed switches to operate any of the four windows electrically.

Mark X 3.8-litre
- Very late 3.8-litre models featured revised heater controls (see 4.2-litre below).

Mark X 4.2-litre models
- As 3.8 except for revised heater controls with four control levers in a veneered surround at the top of the centre console, above the ashtray and below the oddments shelf. These controlled air flow to each side of the car.

Mark X 4.2-litre limousine models
- As other Mark Xs except for central glass sliding division above front seats.
- Front seats have a solid bench back rest.
- Rear of back rest is fitted out with same picnic tables as saloons, and ashtrays, but with enhanced veneering along the full width.
- In the centre of the back of the front seat a solid wood (veneered) magazine rack incorporating two cigarette lighters (removed from the B/C post areas on saloons) and an auxiliary rectangular clock.
- At least one car was fitted with a cocktail cabinet arrangement instead of the above.

420G models
- Restyled dashboard top rail incorporating centrally mounted rectangular clock flanked by padded black Ambla trim on either side offering a degree of crash padding.
- Padding to top full-width oddments tray now always finished in black instead of trim colour.
- Automatic transmission quadrant control lever on steering column (where fitted) extended and with round black ball tip.
- Aerated leather centre trims to front and rear seats.
- Sill coverings now carpet instead of Ambla.

420G limousine models
- As Mark X limousines except for other 420G changes, listed previously, and revised rear magazine rack design.

Above left: With the introduction of the 420G, coinciding with other model changes within Jaguar, this new style of hubcap was fitted, now depicting a growler head emblem instead of the word 'Jaguar'.

Above right: 420G rear compartment with aerated leather panels. All Mark Xs and the 420G featured the lighter hue to woodwork.

The 420G was also available with two-tone exterior paint finishes, when a simple coachline was added to separate the two colours instead of the chromed trim.

A very small number of Mark X 4.2 and 420G limousines were produced. These had a centre division and a magazine rack or radio compartment fitted.

Technical specifications

	3.8-litre	4.2-litre
cc	3,781	4,235
Bore and stroke (mm)	87 x 106	92.07 x 106
Compression ratio	8:1 (7:1/9:1 optional)	8:1 (7:1/9:1 optional)
bhp	265	265
@ rpm	5,500	5,400
Torque (lb ft)	260	283
@ rpm	4,000	4,000
Fuelling	3 x SU carbs	3 x SU carbs
Transmission	4-speed (3 synchro) BW 3-speed auto	4-speed (all synchro) BW 3-speed auto
Wheel size (in)	14, steel	14, steel
Suspension front	Ind semi trailing wishbones, coil springs, anti-roll bar	Ind semi trailing wishbones, coil springs, anti-roll bar
Suspension rear	Ind lower wishbone/upper driveshaft link, radius arms, coil springs	Ind lower wishbone/upper driveshaft link, radius arms, coil springs
Brakes	4 wheel disc, rear inboard	4 wheel disc, rear inboard
Performance		
0–60mph (sec)	9.1	9.9
Top speed (mph)	119.5	121.5
Average mpg	14.1	14.5
Dimensions		
Length (in)	202	202
Width (in)	76	76
Height (in)	54.75	54.75
Wheelbase (in)	120	120
Front track (in)	58	58
Rear track (in)	58	58
Weight (cwt)	37	37

Optional extras

Choice of three radio installations with or without rear parcel shelf mounted speaker.
Electric radio aerial.
Wind-up radio aerial.
Electrically operated windows (front and rear).
Laminated windscreen.
Witter tow bar.
Heated rear screen (earlier cars).
Front seat belts.
Choice of radial, town and country, or whitewall tyres.

Borg Warner automatic transmission.
Overdrive (for non overdrive equipped manual transmission cars).
Fire extinguisher.
Sundym tinted windscreen and side windows.
Wing mirrors.
Integrated ignition/starter switch to steering column.
Limousine appointments (only available on ordering a new car).

Colour schemes

Exterior colour Single	Details	Interior trim	Details
Mark X 3.8-litre models			
Pearl Grey		Red	
		Grey	To 1964
		Light Blue	To 1964
		Dark Blue	
Mist Grey		Red	
		Light Blue	To 1964
		Dark Blue	To 1964
		Grey	To 1964
Old English White		Red	To 1964
		Black	
		Light Blue	To 1964
		Dark Blue	To 1964
Carmen Red		Red	
		Beige	To 1964
		Black	1964
Sherwood Green		Suede Green	
		Light Tan	
		Tan	To 1964
		Cinnamon	1964
Cotswold Blue	To 1964	Dark Blue	
		Light Blue	
		Grey	
Black		Red	
		Grey	
		Light Tan	
		Tan	To 1964
		Cinnamon	1964
Opalescent Dark Green		Suede Green	
		Tan	
		Beige	
		Light Tan	To 1964
		Cinnamon	1964
Opalescent Blue		Dark Blue	
		Light Blue	To 1964
		Grey	To 1964
		Red	
Opalescent Gunmetal		Red	
		Light Blue	To 1964
		Dark Blue	
		Grey	To 1964
		Beige	

Exterior colour Single	Details	Interior trim	Details
Opalescent Silver Grey		Red	
		Light Blue	To 1964
		Grey	
		Dark Blue	
Opalescent Silver Blue		Dark Blue	
		Grey	
Opalescent Bronze	From late 1962	Red	
		Beige	
		Tan	
Opalescent Golden Sand	From 1963	Black	
		Beige	
Opalescent Maroon	From 1963	Maroon	
		Beige	
British Racing Green	1964	Suede Green	
		Beige	
		Light Tan	
		Cinnamon	
Mark X 4.2-litre models			
Carmen Red		Black	
Old English White		Black	
		Maroon	
Primrose Yellow		Black	
		Beige	
Sherwood Green		Suede Green	
		Light Tan	
		Cinnamon	
Dark Blue		Red	
		Grey	
Black		Red	
		Grey	
		Light Tan	
		Cinnamon	
Opalescent Dark Green		Suede Green	
		Cinnamon	
		Beige	
		Light Tan	
Opalescent Silver Grey		Red	
		Dark Blue	
		Grey	
Opalescent Silver Blue		Dark Blue	
		Grey	
Opalescent Golden Sand		Red	
		Light Tan	

Colour schemes *cont …*

Exterior colour Single	Details	Interior trim	Details
Opalescent Maroon		Maroon	
		Beige	
Warwick Grey		Red	
		Light Tan	
		Dark Blue	
420G models			
Old English White		Red	
		Light Blue	
		Dark Blue	
Dark Blue		Light Blue	
		Grey	
		Red	
Black		Red	
		Grey	
		Light Tan	To 1968
		Cinnamon	
Warwick Grey		Red	
		Cinnamon	
		Dark Blue	
Willow Green		Beige	
		Suede Green	
		Cinnamon	
		Grey	
British Racing Green		Suede Green	
		Beige	
		Cinnamon	
Beige	To 1968	Red	
		Light Tan	
		Cinnamon	
Sable Brown	From 1968	Beige	
		Grey	
		Cinnamon	
Light Blue	From 1968	Dark Blue	
		Light Blue	
		Grey	
Regency Red	From 1968	Beige	
		Grey	
Opalescent Golden Sand	To 1968	Red	
		Light Tan	
Opalescent Silver Blue	To 1968	Dark Blue	
		Grey	

Exterior colour Single	Details	Interior trim	Details
Opalescent Silver Grey	To 1968	Red	
		Light Blue	
		Dark Blue	
		Grey	
Opalescent Maroon	To 1968	Maroon	
		Beige	
Ascot Fawn	From 1968	Red	
		Beige	
		Cinnamon	

Duotones Exterior top	Exterior bottom	Details	Interior
Black	Silver Grey	To 1968	Red
			Grey
			Light Tan
			Cinnamon
Black	Golden Sand	To 1968	Red
			Grey
			Light Tan
			Cinnamon
British Racing Green	Willow Green		Suede Green
			Beige
			Light Tan
			Cinnamon
Dark Blue	Silver Blue		Red
			Light Blue
			Grey
Black	Ascot Fawn	From 1968	Red
			Grey
			Cinnamon
Black	Warwick Grey	From 1968	Red
			Grey
			Cinnamon

Prices and production volumes

	Price new (£)	1961	1962	1963	1964	1965	1966
Mark X 3.8-litre	2,392	▪	▪	▪	▪	–	–
Mark X 4.2-litre	2,156	–	–	–	▪	▪	▪
420G	2,237	–	–	–	–	–	▪

	Price new (£)	1967	1968	1969	1970	Total produced
Mark X 3.8-litre	2,392	–	–	–	–	12,961
Mark X 4.2-litre	2,156	–	–	–	–	5,672
420G	2,237	▪	▪	▪	▪	5,542
Total production						**24,175**

Production changes

1961
Mark X 3.8-litre introduced.

1962
Oval ashtray on centre console replaced by
   rectangular style.
Heated rear screen fitted.

1963
Larger brake pedal fitted to automatic
   transmission cars.
'Live' centre boss horn button fitted to steering
   wheel.

1964
Separate radiator header tank fitted.
Revised heating system fitted.
4.2-litre Mark X introduced.

1966
Separate on/off switch added for heated rear
   screen.
Air conditioning system now available.
420G model introduced.
(December) 4.2-litre Mark X discontinued.

1969
XJ6 type brake servos fitted.
Electric dash clock replaced battery driven type.

1970
(June) 420G discontinued.

Chassis numbers

Model	Right/ Left Drive	Chassis/ Vin Nos Commencing
Mark X 3.8	RHD	300001
	LHD	350001
Mark X 4.2	RHD	1D 50001
	LHD	1D 75001
420G	RHD	GID 53720
	LHD	GID 76961

The S-type and 420 saloons
1963 to 1969

Background

Jaguar had undergone terrific expansion in the 1960s, beginning with the successful launch of the Mark 2 saloons late in 1959, then with the E-type sports car and Mark X models in 1961, plus a rebirth of the Daimler marque in the form of the 2.5-litre V8 saloon based on the Mark 2.

For 1963 William Lyons introduced another new model, this time as a 'filler' to bridge the gap between the very sporty Mark 2 saloon and the flagship Mark X, utilising as many mechanical parts as possible in order to keep the cost of production down and be able to market the new model at a reasonable price. The result – the S-type saloon.

The marketing strategy proved a good idea, for although total production numbers were far from those of the Mark 2, the S-type provided an opportunity for those who wanted something more sophisticated and upmarket, and perhaps less sporty, to stay with the Jaguar marque and avoid the big Mark X, a car not to everyone's liking, particularly if you didn't need one that size. Announced in September 1963 and only in production until 1968, 25,000 S-types were produced, effectively 25,000 more sales than Jaguar might have achieved without this model.

Though based heavily on the larger-engined Mark 2 saloons, slightly improved interiors, a better equipment level, and a bigger boot, plus the sophisticated independent rear suspension of the E-type and Mark X, allowed Jaguar to sell the S-type at a premium price.

With the reasonable success of the S-type, Jaguar looked to another interim model to boost sales further and to cater for yet another wider sector of the luxury market. Enter the 420. Substantially based on the S-type, the 420 arrived in October 1966 with the bigger 4.2-litre XK engine, further enhancements to the interior trim, and a completely revised front end treatment more in keeping with the Mark X. Costing more than the S-type, the 420 created a 'notch up' for the Jaguar driver who wanted to enhance his or her image without, again, entering the big Mark X market.

Another significant move with the 420 was the availability of a Daimler model. Like the Daimler version of the Mark 2, the Sovereign (as the 420 car was called) featured external details emulating the Daimler marque. However, for the first time this car was to be very much a badge-engineered Jaguar, and was the first Daimler to be fitted with the Jaguar XK power unit.

By this time (1966) the Jaguar saloon car range had expanded to no less than nine models, offering a wide choice to the luxury car buying public. But in line with Jaguar's later policy of model reduction, and leading up to the introduction of the XJ6, in mid 1968 the 3.8-litre S-type was dropped, and in August, just one month before the announcement of the XJ6, the 3.4-litre car was also discontinued. By September the Jaguar 420 had also disappeared from the listings, although the Daimler Sovereign version remained available well into 1969 – that is, until a Daimler XJ6 was available.

The S-type and 420 models are often overlooked by enthusiasts these days as they are not as sporty and sought-after as the Mark 2s. Nevertheless, they made an important addition to the Jaguar range in the 1960s and were actually very good cars in their own right. Over 40,000 examples were produced, which in total accounts for a significant number of saloon car sales in the 1960s.

Model range and development

When the S-type was announced in September 1963 it was based on just two versions with manual/manual with overdrive or automatic transmissions.

Models available at launch
S-type 3.4-litre saloon
S-type 3.8-litre saloon

Aimed, as it was, at another sector of the market to the Mark 2, it was only ever offered with either the 3.4-litre or 3.8-litre versions of the XK engine, in performance terms exactly the same as the Mark 2 equivalent. These were mated to the same transmissions and front suspension but with the sophisticated independent rear subframe assembly taken from the Mark X saloon. Twin fuel tanks were fitted at the rear, one in each wing instead of the single boot-mounted type in the Mark 2. The steering lock to lock was also slightly improved.

Externally the design was true to Jaguar, with an amalgamation of ideas from the Mark 2 and Mark X. The latter donated the style of the rear end – and thus an enlarged boot area to the Mark 2 – while the centre section was taken virtually exactly from the Mark 2, although with a slightly longer and flatter roof line, and at the front a smoothing out and to some little extent modernising of the Mark 2 'look' with peaked headlights, wrap-around indicators, slimline bumper treatment, and more pronounced radiator grille.

Internally the dash layout took its style from the Mark X, with the centre section in wood veneer with a similar split-bench seat arrangement yet without rear picnic tables. A prominent centre console arrangement also echoed the Mark X, with trim detail taken from that and the Mark 2. Never intended as a real sporting model, the S-type was available with wire wheels but, unlike the Mark 2, it never entered competition during its production life.

Manufacture of the S-type slowed down in 1968, resulting in the demise of the larger-engined model in June that year and the 3.4-litre model two months later. During the time of its production very little changed on the model, although later on fog lamps were replaced by

The 1960s S-type is identifiable from the Mark 2 – from which it was derived – and the later 420 by the frontal treatment seen here: slightly cowled headlights with inset fog lamps without heavy surrounds of the Mark 2 style, wrap-around indicator lights with inset sidelights, and slim-line bumper bar treatment, similar to later 240/340 models. The radiator grille also has a more prominent surround.

From the side, the S-type is instantly identifiable by its elongated rear wings and larger boot area, and the absence of spats over the rear wheels. Wire wheels were an extra cost option when new.

grilles, and Ambla upholstery became the norm instead of leather just as the Mark 2s changed over to the 240/340.

The 420 arrived mid-stream during S-type production, in October 1966, as a further enhancement to the Jaguar saloon car range. Essentially from the windscreen back the car was pure S-type externally, and even internally only benefited from minor styling changes. At the front, however, the 420 took on the styling of the Mark X, being more angular with four headlamp treatment and a traditional grille leaning forward.

Under the skin the 420 was only available with the 4.2-litre, twin carburettor XK power unit, mated to either a manual (all-synchromesh) gearbox, with or without overdrive or automatic transmission. An improved cooling system was also adopted and the power-assisted steering (still an extra cost option) was of the Marles Varamatic type seen on the later Mark Xs. As the basic 420 cost about £200 more than the 3.8-litre S-type, it provided another move up the ladder for Jaguar drivers aspiring to a better car.

The 420 was also the first Jaguar to get effectively badge-engineered into a Daimler model, called the Sovereign. With no mechanical changes at all, the Sovereign merely took on traditional Daimler features like the fluted grille, badging, etc, but again sold at a slightly higher price, allowing it to appeal to another market just as the V8 had done earlier in the decade. A Daimler Sovereign with automatic transmission cost £2,198, very close to the price of the larger 420G.

No significant changes took place in 420 design during its relatively short lifespan, and with Jaguar's change in marketing strategy in the late 1960s it was dropped from the range in September 1968, although the Daimler Sovereign continued on into 1969. Over 15,000 420s and Sovereigns were produced in this short period, which equated to roughly the same annual sales as the S-type, both models serving to expand Jaguar's customer base using mostly the same mechanical parts.

Exterior identification points

General points applicable to all S-types
Front view
- Similar frontal aspect to Mark 2 except for removal of sidelights to lower section of wings with accompanying wrap-around indicator lenses.
- Inset fog lamps below headlights which feature 'eyebrows'.
- Radiator grille has a more prominent chrome surround than Mark 2 with the appropriate 'litre' badge centre top.
- Slimline bumper treatment as 240/340.

From the rear the S-type shows its larger boot area, similarly designed to the Mark X/420G. It also used the Mark X style of rear lights and number plate surround. Twin tailpipes emitted from underneath in the centre, as with the Mark X, rather than at the sides like the Mark 2.

Above left: Front interior layout of the S-type differed from the Mark 2, with flatter semi-split bench seating, revised plusher door trims, and enhanced centre console area. There was also now an under-dash parcel shelf, not seen on Mark 2s but found on Mark Xs.

Above right: The S-type dashboard layout followed normal 1960s Jaguar practice, in this case with wood-veneered centre panel and oddments tray à la Mark X.

Rear compartment of the S-type, similar to but subtly different from the Mark 2, with different seat patterning, revised door trims, and no occasional fold-down tables.

Rear view
- At the rear it was a smaller version of the Mark X/420G model design, with the same exhaust and trim treatment.
- Cars carried the usual 'Jaguar' script on the boot lid plus litreage, 'S-type', and 'automatic' badging as applicable.
- Enlarged rear window area with chromed surround.

Side view
- Quickly identifiable by the wrap-around front indicator lenses and extended rear wings.
- Elongated rear wings showing most of the rear wheels (no spats fitted).
- Each rear wing featured a lift-up panel for access to fuel filler caps.
- A flatter roof section, but otherwise all other aspects as the Mark 2.

General points applicable to all 420s
Front view
- Similar frontal aspect to the Mark X although on a smaller scale. Four headlight treatment (no fog lamps).
- Same sidelights and indicator units as Mark X/S-type.
- Squared-off forward-leaning chrome radiator grille with vertical slats.
- Rectangular horn grilles fitted below each inner headlight.
- Slimline bumper bar with matching forward-leaning over-riders but without curved centre section of the S-type. Centrally mounted number plate plinth.
- Revised front wings to accommodate outer headlights with more pronounced shaping.
- New bonnet pressing, flatter in appearance and terminating back from the grille.

Rear view
- As S-type except for the badging never showing litreage.

Side view
- As S-type except for pronounced squaring-off of front wings.
- All 420s were fitted with the later chromed hubcaps used on the 420G/240, 340, etc.

420 saloon specifics
Jaguar 420
- Mark X style radiator grille with pronounced top section incorporating winged badge.
- Small (Mark X sized) leaper mascot mounted on in-fill panel between radiator grille and bonnet.
- '420' badging on centre of boot lid accompanying 'Jaguar' and, where applicable, 'automatic'.

The 420 model took styling features from the Mark X, adding them to the existing S-type style. It was identifiable from the S-type by its four headlight treatment and wider rectangular forward-leaning radiator grille, and from the Mark X by its smaller dimensions and rectangular horn grilles.

The second Jaguar design to be engineered into a Daimler, the 420 Sovereign utilised a traditional fluted radiator grille.

The rear of the 420 is visually the same as the S-type except for badging, this example being a Daimler Sovereign. This was the first Daimler model not to feature a rear number plate plinth in fluted form.

Daimler Sovereign

- Fluted radiator grille with pronounced centre chrome strip terminating at the edge of the bonnet.
- Daimler scripted 'D' in chrome featured at edge of bonnet, continuing back in the form of a centre chrome strip the full length of the bonnet.
- Scripted 'D' insignia on hubcap centres.
- At the rear a number plate light/reversing light plinth features the Daimler name.
- 'Daimler' and 'Sovereign' badging on boot lid, plus 'automatic' where applicable.

Interior identification points

S-type (all models)

- Centre dashboard section in wood veneer with pull-out veneered tray beneath legend.
- Steering wheel of the later Mark X style with active centre horn push and half horn ring.
- Full-width parcel shelf beneath dashboard with chromed heater controls in centre section.
- Mark X style centre console with side-mounted speaker grilles, veneered ashtray and audio position, plus push-button ventilation controls (as Mark X).
- Flatter section split-bench style front seating with vertical pleats (aerated on later models). Reclining and fore and aft movement provided some degree of height adjustment.
- Front door trims incorporated elasticated map pockets.
- Rear compartment with more sculptured bench-seat arrangement to Mark 2, with fold-down centre armrest.
- Rear of front seats plain (without pull-down picnic tables).
- Rear door trims with built in armrests and wider pockets than Mark 2.
- Interior door locks activated by chromed 'knobs' as used on Mark VII to IX models.

420 (all models)

- As S-type except centre veneered dash panel sits flush with left- and right-hand panels.
- Dashboard woodwork surrounded by black vinyl crash padding, at the top centre a rectangular clock fitted as 420G model.
- Seats of slightly different proportions to S-type although looking very similar.
- Door trim panels feature only top cappings in wood with similar treatment at the rear.

Daimler Sovereign

- As 420 except for scripted 'D' in centre horn push boss on steering wheel.

Rear three-quarter view of the 420, demonstrating the same profile as on the S-type except for the shape at the leading edge of the front wings.

Comparison of S-type and 420 front views.

Above left: 420 and Sovereign models featured subtle changes to the interior trim, with slimmer wood cappings to the door panels and a soft padded dashboard top rail, continued around the edges of the dashboard to form a degree of crash padding. As well as other minor control changes the clock was relocated to the top centre of the dashboard.

Above right: Seat design of S-type and 420 models.

Technical specifications

	3.4-litre S-type	3.8-litre S-type
cc	3,442	3,781
Bore and stroke (mm)	83 x 106	87 x 106
Compression ratio	8:1 (7:1/9:1 optional)	8:1 (7:1/9:1 optional)
bhp	210	220
@ rpm	5,500	5,500
Torque (lb ft)	216	240
@ rpm	3,000	3,000
Fuelling	2 x SU carbs	2 x SU carbs
Transmission	4-speed (3 synchro), later all synchro BW 3-speed auto	4-speed (3 synchro), later all synchro BW 3-speed auto
Wheel size (in)	15, steel, wires optional	15, steel, wires optional
Suspension front	Ind semi trailing wishbones, coil springs, anti-roll bar	Ind semi trailing wishbones, coil springs, anti-roll bar
Suspension rear	Ind lower wishbones/upper driveshaft link, radius arms, coil springs	Ind lower wishbones/upper driveshaft link, radius arms, coil springs
Brakes	4 wheel disc, rear inboard	4 wheel disc, rear inboard
Performance		
0–60mph (sec)	13.9	10.2
Top speed (mph)	119	121
Average mpg	14–17	15.4
Dimensions		
Length (in)	187	187
Width (in)	66.25	66.25
Height (in)	55.75	55.75
Wheelbase (in)	107.5	107.5
Front track (in)	55.25	55.25
Rear track	54.25	54.25
Weight (cwt)	32	33

Optional extras

Choice of three radio installations with or without rear parcel shelf mounted speaker.
Laminated windscreen.
Witter tow bar.
Front seat belts.

Choice of radial, town and country, or whitewall tyres.
Borg Warner automatic transmission.
Overdrive (for non overdrive equipped manual transmission cars).

	420/Sovereign
cc	4,235
Bore and stroke (mm)	92.07 x 106
Compression ratio	8:1 (7:1/9:1 optional)
bhp	245
@ rpm	5,500
Torque (lb ft)	283
@ rpm	3,750
Fuelling	2 x SU carbs
Transmission	4-speed (3 synchro), later all synchro BW 3-speed auto
Wheel size (in)	15, steel, wires optional
Suspension front	Ind semi trailing wishbones, coil springs, anti-roll bar
Suspension rear	Ind lower wishbones/upper driveshaft link, radius arms, coil springs
Brakes	4 wheel disc, rear inboard
Performance	
0–60mph (sec)	9.9
Top speed (mph)	123
Average mpg	15.7
Dimensions	
Length (in)	187.5
Width (in)	67
Height (in)	56.25
Wheelbase (in)	107.75
Front track (in)	55.25
Rear track	54.5
Weight (cwt)	33

Wire wheels with conversion kit for hubs, etc.
Fire extinguisher.
Sundym tinted windscreen and side windows.
Wing mirrors.

Integrated ignition/starter switch to steering column.
Power-assisted steering.

Colour schemes

Exterior colour	Details	Interior trim
Pearl Grey	To 1966	Red
		Light Blue
		Dark Blue
		Grey
Warwick Grey	From 1966	Red
		Tan
Dove Grey	To 1966	Red
		Tan
		Grey
Carmen Red	To 1966	Red
		Black
Imperial Maroon	To 1966	Red
Old English White		Red
		Tan
Primrose Yellow	From 1964	Red
		Tan
		Black
Honey Beige	From 1966	Red
		Tan
British Racing Green		Suede Green
		Tan
		Champagne
Sherwood Green	To 1966	Suede Green
		Tan
Willow Green	From 1966	Suede Green
		Black
		Champagne
Indigo Blue		Light Blue
		Dark Blue
		Grey
Black		Red
		Tan
Opalescent Dark Green	To 1966	Suede Green
		Tan
		Champagne

Exterior colour	Details	Interior trim
Opalescent Blue	To 1966	Dark Blue
		Light Blue
		Grey
		Red
Opalescent Gunmetal		Red
		Tan
Opalescent Silver Grey		Red
		Tan
		Grey
Opalescent Silver Blue	To 1966	Dark Blue
		Light Blue
		Grey
		Red
Opalescent Golden Sand	1966 only	Red
		Tan
Opalescent Maroon	From 1966	Red
		Champagne
		Tan
Signal Red	From 1966	Black
		Red
		Beige
Regency Maroon	From 1966	Red
		Beige
Old English White	Replaced by 'White' in 1968	Black
		Red
Ascot Fawn	From 1966	Black
		Red
Sable Brown	From 1966	Beige
		Red
		Black
Pale Blue	From 1966	Dark Blue
		Red
		Black

Prices and production volumes

	Price new (£)	1963	1964	1965	1966	1967	1968
3.4-litre S-type	1,669	■	■	■	■	■	■
3.8-litre S-type	1,758	■	■	■	■	■	■
420 saloon	1,930	–	–	–	■	■	■
Daimler Sovereign	2,121	–	–	–	■	■	■

	Price new (£)	1969	Total produced
3.4-litre S-type	1,669	–	9,928
3.8-litre S-type	1,758	–	15,065
420 saloon	1,930	–	10,236
Daimler Sovereign	2,121	■	5,824
Total production			**16,060**

Production changes

1963
S-type 3.4- and 3.8-litre saloons introduced.

1964
One-piece front carpets fitted.
PVC heel pads fitted to carpets.

1965
Hazard light system for export models.
All-synchromesh manual gearbox fitted.
Revised clutch to fit above gearbox.

1966
240/340/250 introduced.
420 models introduced.
Ambla upholstery fitted to S-types.
Fog lamps deleted on S-type models.

1967
Power-assisted steering standardised on Daimler
Sovereign.

1968
Non-earred spinners fitted to wire wheel cars (all
markets).
Revised water temperature gauge fitted with
coloured segments.
S-types and 420 discontinued.

1969
Damiler Sovereign discontinued.

Chassis numbers

Model	Right/ Left Drive	Chassis/ Vin Nos Commencing
S-type 3.4	RHD	1B 1001
	LHD	1B 25001
S-type 3.8	RHD	1B 50001
	LHD	1B 75001
420	RHD	1F 1001
	LHD	1F 25001
Daimler Sov 420	RHD	1A 30001
	LHD	1A 70001

Background

Launched in 1968, the XJ6 was arguably the most important model ever produced by Jaguar up to that time – a car that set new standards of refinement and a car by which others would be judged for many years to come. It also brought to fruition a one-model policy, effectively replacing all other saloons produced by Jaguar at that time, namely the 240/340/V8 250, the 420/Sovereign, and the 420G. This policy could have been devastating for the company, yet proved to be an incredible success.

Surprisingly there was nothing really new about the XJ6. It still used the XK six-cylinder engine (in 420 form), linked to the same gearboxes and independent rear suspension. There was a second version with a new (2.8-litre) configuration of the XK power unit, intended to help sales in tax/engine size conscious countries. At the front the XJ did feature a new suspension with anti-dive characteristics, and with new technology Jaguar was able to isolate the body from road noise significantly better than anyone else at the time. Dunlop designed new tyres for the car which also helped.

Stylistically it was still a Jaguar, with the typical four headlight treatment but, for the first time since the Mark VII, without a prominent, typically Jaguar radiator grille – instead a rather egg-crate design was decided upon. The car also displayed a new 'hump' in the rear quarters and a more angular rear end style. Internally it was all new except for the layout of the dashboard, although even here new technology had been used and there was more concern for safety and crash padding.

At only £1,897 for the 2.8-litre model Jaguar had done it again, offering the ultimate in

refinement and handling at a bargain basement price. Compared to the competition of the day – even the Rolls Royce Silver Shadow – the XJ6 was quieter, faster, even more refined, and handled significantly better.

The marketing ploy of effectively offering just two cars, both virtually identical except for the engine size, paid off handsomely for Jaguar. Few people at the time missed the smaller saloons, as the XJ6 was so far ahead in driveability. It was initially envisaged that there would also be a base 'standard' model, offered without many of the by then common extras, but very few were actually made and it was never available as a production model. Even the 2.8-litre model didn't sell as well as expected, and in service problems were experienced with the engine anyway.

It wasn't until 1969 that a Daimler derivative was offered, taking the Sovereign name from the old 420. From here the range of models expanded dramatically when Jaguar announced in 1972 that there was to be a V12 engined version, the same engine seen a year earlier in the E-type sports car. Then, with XJ6 and XJ12 models in both Jaguar and Daimler guise, there were even two sizes of wheelbase available, and a top of the range Vanden Plas saloon for the ultimate in luxury and equipment. V12 Series 1 XJs were only ever available with automatic transmission.

Over 98,000 of the Series 1 XJs were produced up to 1973 when, mainly due to the ongoing demands of safety and environmental issues abroad, the car developed into the Series 2. All the models followed suit from the Series 1 cars except for the 2.8-litre engine, which was dropped in favour of another new configuration (3.4 litres). On top of this Jaguar announced another new body style, the coupé, based on the shorter wheelbase floorpan and built with only two doors, with pillarless window surrounds and a vinyl roof. Difficulties in production resulted in the coupé models appearing on the market late, and they were discontinued early on for the same reason and because of the need to expand production of the four-door models, which by this time were selling better than ever.

For the first time in their history Jaguar chose to ask an outside coachbuilder to redesign the XJ saloon to bring it more up to date, and Pininfarina did a fine job in revitalising the style to become the Series 3 from 1978. Although looking very similar to the old Series 2 design it was significantly improved, with more window space, a higher roof line, flush-mounted door handles, new trim, and a better interior. Once again it was made available in all four-door forms, from base 3.4-litre Jaguar to Daimler Vanden Plas, in both six- and 12-cylinder variants.

Jaguar experienced many problems of poor build quality and lack of mechanical reliabilty in the 1970s, an image that stuck throughout the company's British Leyland period. It wasn't until Jaguar was privatised in the 1980s that matters started to improve, helped by its then new boss John Egan. The Series 3 XJs saw the company through this period and not only into profit but, with an incredibly improved product and reputation, from success to success.

The models were continually updated. The Jaguar name was taking prominence over Daimler by this time, and Jaguar lost the right to use the Vanden Plas name in the UK, although retaining it in the US. The Series 3 remained in production until 1987 for the six-cylinder models, 1991 for the V12 Jaguars, and 1992 for the V12 Daimlers – long after the appearance of a completely new replacement model (the XJ40) in 1986.

The XJ Series Jaguars must be considered a tribute not only to Sir William Lyons, who saw the car through to production in 1968, but also to the revival of the Jaguar marque in the 1980s. Even today the XJ is still considered to be one of the company's classic designs. With over 400,000 produced from 1968 to 1992, it has left a legacy that even today Jaguar refer back to.

Model range and development

All models were initially available with manual, manual with overdrive, or automatic transmission.

Models available at launch
Jaguar XJ6 2.8-litre standard saloon
Jaguar XJ6 2.8-litre saloon
Jaguar XJ6 4.2-litre saloon

The Series 1 XJ models were available in both short and long wheelbase models, the latter being identifiable by its wider rear doors, as here. This model is the Daimler Vanden Plas version, identified by its vinyl roof covering (always black) and chromed swage line trim.

The Series 1 XJ6 is identified from the front by the 'egg-crate' style of radiator grille with gold growler badge. The Daimler versions featured a more pronounced fluted radiator grille with vertical slats and a chrome centre line running the entire length of the bonnet.

XJ12 Series 1 models are identified from the front by the vertical slatted grille with 'V' emblem.

Although originally listed, the 'standard' model never went into serious production and it is generally considered that only prototypes were actually made.

Perhaps not surprisingly only about a third of the Series 1 cars sold had the 2.8-litre engine, and after some time on the road they acquired a bad reputation for 'holing' a piston. This ultimately also affected resale values. In contrast the 4.2-litre model was building on previous success and offered better performance, smoother running, and improved handling than the 420G that it replaced.

Overall the Series 1 XJ6 was very well accepted, which is reflected in its sales, and apart from minor manufacturing changes little was altered during the first year of full production. In 1969 the company introduced a wider range of models, capitalising on the Daimler name at the same time by replacing the 420 Sovereign. The choice of engine size now covered both marques and production was made much easier by the effective badge-engineering of the two brands from what was ultimately the same car.

The XJ6 bodyshell had always been designed with the V12 engine in mind but, in keeping with Jaguar policy, the new engine was 'trial launched' in a lower volume sports car first – in this case the E-type. The V12 XJ, known as the XJ12, didn't therefore appear until July 1972. It offered buyers a slightly higher specification of equipment (air conditioning as standard, etc), all-round improved mechanics to cope with the power, and a much more attractive vertical slatted radiator grille.

Along with the XJ12 came the natural progression to Daimler, and in September 1972 the first of the long wheelbase bodyshells appeared with another new model, the Daimler Double Six Vanden Plas, resurrecting Daimler's old Double Six model name from the 1920s. This was effectively a hand finished car by the VDP coachworks in London, with enhanced interior and exterior trim. The long wheelbase shell provided substantially more legroom in the rear compartment for passengers, something the shorter wheelbase model lacked compared to the old Mark X/420G design. The release of the Double Six was followed a month later by the introduction of long wheelbase bodyshells for the other models, resulting in quite an extensive range of cars, but all still based on the one base design.

Just a year later the whole XJ range was substantially altered to become the Series 2, with an improved bodyshell with side impact bars, a virtually sealed off front bulkhead from the passenger compartment, and new technology like fibre optic lighting and multi-pin plug connections. Externally the car benefited from a make-over, more because of changing

Rear view of the Series 1 XJ model. Apart from badging the same view applied to all Jaguar models, although this is a post-1969 model with different reflector lighting and curved tail-pipes. The inset picture shows one of the earliest cars, with reflectors set into the reversing light units. Early cars also had straight pipe exhausts.

Daimler Series 1 models differed at the rear in their badging and the fluted plinth surmounting the boot lock.

Steel wheels were the norm on Series 1 XJs of all models. Basic 2.8-litre cars did not feature chromed rimbellishers, although other models did.

regulations over safety, bumper height, etc, in the United States than for aesthetic reasons. The Series 2 models are easily identifiable by their shallower radiator grille and raised bumper level at the front. The internal layout was revised and redesigned and a proper air conditioning system was introduced for the first time.

The range announced at launch was extensive, although some of the cars didn't actually appear until much later. Short and long wheelbase versions were offered throughout, as were 4.2 and 5.3 (V12) engines. Although originally listed the 2.8-litre wasn't made in any great numbers and was totally replaced by a new 3.4-litre engined model in April 1975. Aimed at a possible fleet market, the specification and trim level were down and the car was only available in short wheelbase form, other short wheelbase models dropping from the range by the end of 1974.

An entirely new concept for the Series 2 was a short wheelbase two-door coupé model, also offered in both Jaguar and Daimler forms and with 4.2- or 5.3-litre engines. Although originally announced back in September 1973, it took until 1975 to get the car into viable production, which must have affected its popularity to some extent as few were actually made compared to four-door saloons. Constant problems over supply and build quality resulted in the early demise of the coupé versions in late 1977, although demand for conventional saloons held up remarkably well, even given changing circumstances at Jaguar under British Leyland ownership.

Jaguar announced the next generation of XJ saloons, known as the Series 3, at the end of 1978, although the Series 2 models were still produced until February 1979. As mentioned above, the new models were significant make-overs stylistically, with the help of Pininfarina in Italy. Only a single (long) wheelbase shell was available initially, in all three engine sizes and both Jaguar and Daimler guizes, plus the Vanden Plas (now expanded to include both six- and 12-cylinder models).

Series 3 models are easily recognisable by the raised roofline and larger window areas plus the flush-mounted door handles and rubber-faced bumper bars. The essence of the design was a lighter passenger compartment, slightly more angular approach to external styling, and general updating.

While Jaguar remained in British Leyland ownership there were problems over build quality with the Series 3, and in particular with its exterior paint finishes. With new man John Egan at the helm, however, things started to improve. The first major change came in 1981, when the V12 models were made more economical by the fitment of the May-designed cylinder head, subsequent models being called 'HE' denoting high efficiency.

Above left: *For the Series 1 XJ12 and Daimler Double Six models these ventilated wheels became available, to the same specification as were fitted to E-type Series 2 and 3 models.*

Above right: *Chromed ventilated wheels were also available at extra cost. Both types of ventilated wheels also became the standard fitment on Series 2 XJs.*

Above left: *Front compartment of the Series 1 XJ6, a later model with black instrument surrounds. Daimler and XJ12 models did not feature the bright alloy finishes to the centre console, which were replaced by black fabric. A manual choke also applied to V12 models, along with different door panel trims.*

Above right: *Earlier Series 1 XJ6s featured chromed surrounds to the instruments as shown here.*

Above left: *The specially fitted rear compartment of the Daimler Double Six Vanden Plas included individualised seating, lambswool over-rugs, boxwood inlays to woodwork, and enhanced door trims.*

Above right: *Daimler Vanden Plas, showing revised front seating and trim.*

A new five-speed manual gearbox was briefly available on the Series 3 six-cylinder cars but was never as popular as the automatic transmission variants, and was dropped later in production.

At the end of 1982 Jaguar lost its right to use the Vanden Plas name in the UK, and with the demise of the VDP Coachworks in London anyway production of these upmarket versions of the Series 3 XJ had been done on the normal assembly lines in Coventry. A move away from the Daimler marque was envisaged too, so the range of cars was reduced and the 'Sovereign' name was moved over to a new up-market Jaguar model from 1984. This was fitted with a host of extras as standard equipment, including cruise control, on-board computer, and a new style 'pepperpot' alloy wheel.

In 1985 the 3.4-litre was revamped with tweed instead of leather upholstery, straight grain wood veneer, and other alterations to keep the price down. Six- and 12-cylinder models continued selling better than ever, allowing the company more time to develop their ultimate replacement saloon, the XJ40. This new car would finally arrive in late 1986, although initially production of the Series 3 saloons continued. It wasn't until April 1987 that the last XJ6 Series 3 left the line, while V12 models soldiered on considerably longer because the XJ40 was never intended to take this engine. The Series 3 twelves therefore complimented the X40 range for some time, the very last Jaguar XJ12 leaving the line at the end of 1991 and the Daimler Double Six continuing in production until the end of 1992.

Over 400,000 Series XJs were produced from 1968 to 1992, a phenomenal number, making them the most successful models produced by the company up to this time. More of this basic body design have been made than any subsequent saloon at the time of writing, and it is a tribute to the Series that current models continue to reflect some of the design features from those days.

Exterior identification points

General points applicable to all Series 1 models
Front view
- Overall frontal style taken from Mark X/420G/420 models with twin headlight arrangement.
- Uniquely styled radiator grille without prominent chromed surround.
- Rectangular horn grilles below inner headlights.
- Combined rectangular wrap-around indicator/sidelight units below outer headlights.

Unique to V12-engined Series 1 models was this gold-plated emblem on the centre console.

The Series 2 XJs are identified from the front by the shallower radiator grille with enhanced surround, higher bumper bar level, and revised lighting and valance treatment. For the US market a 'federal' rubber-faced bumper bar was fitted.

Daimler models of the Series 2 design were differentiated as usual by a fluted radiator grille. The fog lamps were a period extra cost option. Daimler models, as Series 1 variants, also featured a centre line chromed bonnet trim.

- Slimline bumper bar with forward-leaning over-riders continuing usual Jaguar design from late 1960s, with centrally mounted number plate.
- Under bumper valance contained chromed air intake grille beneath number plate plinth and between over-riders.
- One-piece forward-hinged bonnet incorporating grille and inner headlight units. Pronounced hump in centre of bonnet, no chromed adornment or leaping mascot fitted.
- One-piece curved windscreen with chromed surround and twin wipers.

Rear view
- Angular rear-end styling with tapering of rear wings.
- Combined light clusters for indicators, rear and brake lights vertically mounted in rear wings.
- Separate horizontal light clusters on boot lid for reversing lights/reflectors (reflectors later moved to other light clusters in rear wings).
- Slimline bumper treatment as front with number plate illumination panel within bumper bar.
- Twin exhaust pipes with chromed surrounds (initially straight pipes, later changed to curved), emerging through the rear under valance below bumper level.
- Chromed winged escutcheon to circular boot lock in centre of boot lid above number plate.
- One-piece boot lid with vertical section forming rear of car containing number plate, chromed surround, and badging.
- Badging initially just litreage in chrome. Later 'Jaguar' added, and other changes according to model.
- Twin fuel tanks, mounted one in each rear wing, accessed by wing top mounted lockable chrome filler caps.
- One-piece curved rear screen with chromed surround.

Side view
- Emphasised the swage line on body with haunch over rear wing. More angular aspect of styling with higher roof line to previous (420G) model.
- Chromed window surrounds with quarter-lights at the front. Rear quarter-lights incorporated into rear doors.
- The first Jaguar to depict a leaper badge at the base of the front wings.
- Hubcaps and chrome rimbellishers followed normal Jaguar practice at the time.

Series 1 specifics
XJ6 Series 1 2.8-litre models
- Chromed radiator grille with both vertical and horizontal slats, incorporating at centre top a circular plastic growler badge in gold.

Front interior compartment of a Series 2 saloon. Note the different dashboard layout, now with all the instruments in front of the driver, and the revised steering wheel, centre console surround, and door trims.

Rear view of the Series 2 model, in this case a Daimler Vanden Plas with fluted plinth.

Above left: Jaguar models featured this style of boot plinth.

Above right: In certain markets the XJ6 Series 2 was known as the 'Executive', with appropriate badging on the radiator grille and boot lid.

■ '2.8' litre badging on boot lid.
■ Standard models (few actually made) did not feature chromed rimbellishers to the steel wheels.

XJ6 Series 1 4.2-litre models
■ Radiator grille as 2.8-litre model above.
■ '4.2' litre badging to boot lid.

Daimler Sovereign Series 1 models
■ All models as XJ6 except for the more prominent chromed surround and fluted radiator grille incorporating vertical slats only, with wider centre slat. Scripted 'D' badge in centre of grille top.
■ Chromed central trim running the entire length of the bonnet.
■ 'D' emblem in centre of hubcaps.
■ At the rear prominent fluted chromed plinth on boot lid above number plate area, incorporating lock mechanism.
■ 'Daimler' and 'Sovereign' badges to boot lid.

Series 1 long wheelbase models
■ As normal bodyshell except for longer rear doors compared to front doors.
■ On Jaguar models an 'L' chromed insignia appeared on the boot lid next to the litre size.

XJ12 Series 1 models
■ Revised radiator grille with only vertical slats and prominent wider centre slat containing 'V12' emblem.
■ From the side a slightly lower look to the car, due to wider profile wheels and tyres.
■ At the rear 'XJ12' badging on the boot lid.

Daimler Double Six Series 1 models
■ As normal Daimler Sovereign except for 'Double Six' badging to boot lid.
■ 'V12' emblem to the top of radiator grille replacing scripted 'D'.
■ Wider profile wheels and tyres gave a slightly lower look to the car.

Daimler Double Six Vanden Plas Series 1 models
■ As Sovereign except for bespoke range of exterior colour schemes.
■ Integrated fog/spot lights instead of horn grilles at front (also an extra on other models).
■ Chromed swage line trims along entire length of body sides.
■ Fitment of driver's door mirror as standard.
■ Black vinyl-covered roof with chromed finisher on D post at rear.
■ Ventilated steel wheels incorporating chrome rimbellishers and conventional Daimler hubcaps.
■ At the rear as Sovereign except for 'Vanden Plas' badging.

Detail of the entirely new dashboard layout and design for the Series 2 XJ models.

Rear seating of Series 2 saloons, very similar to earlier cars except for the colour schemes.

The Series 2 coupé model is easily identified by its two-door configuration, with wider doors and a black vinyl roof. At various stages all the Daimlers and most of the Jaguar V12s featured the chromed swage line trim. Chromed wheels were an extra cost item.

General points applicable to all Series 2 XJs

Front view

- Overall style of cars remained very close to Series 1 models with twin headlight units, but with new-style slimline front bumper arrangement and under-riders with rubber inserts fitted.
- Bumper height raised to just below headlights, necessitating under bumper fitment of integrated wrap-around indicator/side light units.
- Enlarged under-valance chrome air intake panel.
- Reduced depth radiator grille, still with vertical and horizontal slats but with prominent chromed surround.

Rear view

- Revised rear end treatment with chromed number plate illumination plinth also incorporating boot lock, eliminating the need for separate illumination within bumper bar.

Side view

- Although utilising, for example, different front wings, the body line followed Series 1 styling almost exactly. Series 2 quickly identifiable by raised level of front wrap-around bumper bar.
- Ventilated steel wheels now fitted, silver in colour.

XJ Series 2 specifics

XJ Series 2 six-cylinder models

- Growler badge fitted to centre top of radiator grille.
- Rear boot number plate plinth smooth finished.
- Appropriate litreage badging according to model on boot lid.

Daimler Sovereign Series 2 models

- As XJ6 except for fluted treatment to more prominent surround to reduced depth of radiator grille, featuring only vertical slats with wider centre slat. 'D' script on top centre.
- Centre bonnet chrome strip as Series 1 Sovereigns.
- 'D' emblem to hubcaps.
- Boot lid has fluted chromed plinth incorporating boot lock.
- Daimler associated badging to boot lid.

Series 2 Long Wheelbase models

- Majority of Series 2 models made on long wheelbase bodyshell, identified by wider rear doors.

XJ12 Series 2 models

- As XJ6 models except for 'V' emblem to centre of radiator grille centre vane.

Above left: These Kent alloy wheels became available on later Series 2 cars, usually Vanden Plas and V12-engined models.

Above right: Initially all Series 2 models were equipped with these stainless steel wheel covers as standard, although the style and colour changed according to model, eg V12-engined cars had a black centre.

Series 3 XJs are identified from the side by their raised roof level, enlarged glass area, and flush-mounted door handles.

Comparison between the Series 2 front on the left and the Series 3 on the right. The latter had rubber-faced energy absorbing bumper bars, revised radiator grilles with vertical slats only, and a new-style under-valance with improved 'mouth'. Note also the deeper windscreen.

- Similar rear badge treatment to identify as XJ12 models.

Daimler Double Six and VDP Series models
- As other Daimler Series 2 models except for 'V' emblem on radiator grille badge.
- Appropriate badging on boot lid.
- Exterior trim of VDP models (also now available with 4.2-litre engine) as Series 1 VDP model.

XJ and Daimler coupé models
- All models based on the short wheelbase Series 1 bodyshell identifiable from the side by the lack of chromed window surrounds, allowing all windows to be wound down to reveal an open side view.
- Significantly wider front doors (no rear doors). Doors incorporate no quarter-lights or window frame surrounds.
- Vinyl roof with chromed rain gutters fitted to all production coupé models.
- No coupé badging on boot lid.
- Daimler and Jaguar trim followed saloon practice.

NB: Kent five-section alloy wheels with black centres appeared during this period and were available as an extra cost option on all models. Chromed swage line trim was at various times fitted as standard equipment to some V12 models including coupés and Vanden Plas cars. Vinyl roofs were also at one time provided as standard equipment on some V12 Jaguar models.

General points applicable to Series 3 XJs
Front view
- Retention of overall design features of previous Series 2 models except for revised bumper bar treatment with black rubber surround incorporating indicator lenses and centrally mounted number plate with full width chrome finisher blade to the top.
- Under-valance incorporated an enlarged air intake section.
- New vertical slated chrome radiator grille with prominent surround and growler badge on top within a black background. Grille more angular and pronounced than Series 2 style.
- Twin headlight arrangement which now incorporated sidelights in outer units.
- Taller windscreen with chromed surround and twin wiper arms.

Rear view
- The same rubber bumper features as front, incorporating twin red hazard warning lights.
- New style rear light units incorporating reversing lights and reflectors with chrome surrounds.

Rear view of the Series 3 model, with rubber-faced bumper bar, built-in hazard warning lights, flatter boot lid plinth, revised badging, and sharper edged rear lighting.

This comparison between V12-engined XJ saloons, Series 3 on the left and Series 1 on the right, clearly shows the differences.

Daimler treatment of the Series 3s involved the usual fluted plinths and grilles and always retained scripted badging.

This early Series 3 interior shows better quality seating than in Series 2 models and a slightly modified dash layout, with new-style centre console and steering wheel.

- Revised flatter chrome boot plinth with hidden boot lock beneath.
- Heavy chrome/plastic script badging to boot lid according to model.
- Enlarged wrap-around rear screen with chrome surround.

Side view
- Series 3 models instantly identifiable from previous Series XJs by higher roof line, larger window areas, and wrap-around rubber-faced bumper bars.
- Side indicator repeater lenses to front corner of wings.
- Enlarged (taller) glass areas with raised and flatter roof.
- Inset flush-mounted chromed 'pull' door handles within black surrounds.
- Steel wheels completely enclosed within stainless steel ventilated trims held in position by wheel nuts. Centre of trims colour keyed according to engine size.

XJ Series 3 specifics
Jaguar XJ Series 3 six-cylinder models
- Revised boot lid badging according to litreage. Later many changes in script style according to model (see photographs).

Daimler Sovereign Series 3 models
- As Jaguar except for revised Daimler and Sovereign badging.
- New radiator grille incorporating usual fluted surround and chrome bonnet trim. Eliminated on later cars.

XJ12 Series 3 models
- As XJ6 and Daimler models except for revised badging only on boot lid.

Daimler Vanden Plas Series 3 models
- By this time produced in-house at Jaguar. Externally they were only identifiable from standard Daimler models by the swage line chrome trims running the entire length of the body sides.
- Kent alloy wheels fitted, although alternative trims could be specified.
- 'Vanden Plas' badging on the boot lid.

Later Series 3 identifiable changes
Daimler Series 3 models (post-1992)
- With the discontinuing of the VDP models the Daimler range was restricted but took on revised exterior features. Chrome swage line trims previously fitted only to VDP and some other V12 models now fitted.
- New style stainless steel wheel trims incorporating conventional hubcaps and 'D' script in centre.
- Chrome bonnet strip discontinued.

Detail of the pre-1983 centre console area in a Series 3 saloon. Daimler models again benefited from a black-finished radio/heater control panel.

From 1984 Jaguar models took over the Sovereign name for up-market versions like this one. Otherwise very similar externally to the Daimler Sovereign, the badging changed, as did the wheel treatment.

The new pepperpot alloy wheels were designed for the Jaguar Sovereign model but could also be specified for Daimler cars.

Jaguar XJ Series 3 Sovereign models

■ From 1984 up-market Jaguar model identified by silver 'pepperpot' perforated alloy wheels.

■ 'Sovereign' badging on boot lid, style along with 'Jaguar' badge changed later (see photograph).

NB: Wheels for the various models changed throughout production and were also available as extra cost options (see photographs). Rear badging also changed (see photographs).

Interior identification points

XJ6 Series 1 (all models)

■ Standard dash layout with main instruments in front of driver but now within curved veneered surrounds with padding (similar to 420 saloons), with major instruments flanking central warning light unit.

■ Central auxiliary gauges mounted on ribbed black plinth with rocker type switches as Series 2/3 E-type.

■ Through flow black circular air vents to either end of fascia.

■ Black vinyl surround to dash area with top-mounted central radio speaker grille and two directional air vents to screen.

■ Lockable glove-box on passenger side.

■ Two-spoke black plastic-covered steering wheel with half horn ring and oval central growler badge on black background.

■ Column/dash mounted combined ignition starter switch.

■ Centre console incorporating oddments shelf above, below heating/ventilation controls, radio and, if fitted, radio speaker balance control.

■ Gear lever (incorporating overdrive switch on top) or automatic transmission quadrant with black surround, flanked by twin chromed flip-open ashtrays either side and cigarette lighter behind.

■ Where fitted independent electric window controls mounted on console where it rises to form centre armrest and rear-hinged glove-box.

■ Under dashboard parcel shelves either side.

■ Umbrella-style handbrake close to centre console as Mark X/420G.

■ Door trims incorporate only thin wooden cappings on top, soft trimmed vinyl side trims with flush-mounted chromed door handles, chromed window winders, and chrome/black knurled knob to open front quarter-lights.

■ Integrated armrests and door pockets, alternative design according to model.

Daimler models continued in luxury class only, normally with Kent alloy wheels though a revised stainless steel trim, incorporating a conventional hubcap, could also be specified. Chromed swage line trims appeared on all Daimler models to the end of production.

Above left: From 1986 rear badging was revised to this embossed style except for Daimler models.

Above right: Later style interior for Series 3 models incorporated a totally revised centre console with further wood veneer. Earlier Daimler-style door trim panels were also adopted for all models.

Above left: Daimler models continued to feature alternative seating long after the Vanden Plas name had disappeared.

Above right: Bench-style seating could be specified by special order for Daimler Series 3 models.

- Individual front seating with vertical pleats and aerated upholstery centre sections. Provision for headrests from later models. Seats with adjustable recline mechanism.
- Rear compartment bench style seating to match front style with folding centre armrest.
- Rear through flow ventilation outlet in centre of console with on-off controls and flip-top chromed ashtray.
- Rear door trims match front.
- Where fitted electric window lift controls in chrome set into door armrests.
- Rear parcel shelf incorporated centre raised section on all but the very early cars to aid through flow of air from cabin extracted via boot surround.

Later style seating for Jaguar saloons, here seen in a Sovereign model with enhanced woodwork.

Daimler Sovereign Series 1 models
- Wider pleating to seating without aerated sections.
- Longer diagonally mounted door pulls/armrests to front doors with separate black trimmed top section to door trim.
- Scripted 'D' badge to steering wheel centre boss.

Daimler Double Six Vanden Plas Series 1 models
- High quality burr walnut veneer to all woodwork with boxwood inlay around edges of dashboard.
- More substantial veneered woodwork to door trims also incorporating boxwood inlays, the wood implanted in black vinyl surround.
- Centre console as Sovereign except for inclusion of gold plated 'V12' badge to centre below gear lever quadrant. Black figured vinyl covering to console instead of alloy.
- More substantial seating with deeper backs and bolsters. Wide vertical pleating with no aeration. Fitted headrests to front seats also in better quality leather, rear of front seats incorporating elasticated leather pockets.
- Rear of centre console revised to include cigarette lighter.
- Better quality Wilton carpeting all round.
- Rear door trims also of amended type, both front and rear incorporating separate armrests and pockets plus built-in speaker grilles for enhanced audio equipment.
- Rear seats similar in design to front, with the appearance of being individual with pronounced centre armrest and centre in-fill.

XJ12 Series 1 models
- Revised door trims to XJ6 models, similar to but not the same as Daimlers, trimmed completely in one colour.
- Replacement of alloy centre console covering with black figured vinyl, with gold-plated 'V12' badge as Double Six.

New-style cloth upholstery could also be specified.

- Heater and allied controls have matt black surrounds instead of chrome.

XJ6 & XJ12 Series 2 (all models)
- Entirely different dashboard layout to Series 1 models, with smaller speedometer and rev counter and, although still mounted in front of the driver, now flanked either side by auxiliary gauges.
- Rectangular through flow air vents, one to each extreme end of dashboard.
- Ignition/starter moved to opposite side of steering column flanked by combined lighting control on other side.
- New style (flatter) steering column stalks controlling wipers, washers, main beam etc.
- Centre of dash now occupied by large rectangular heater/air conditioning vents in three sections, either end adjustable.
- Passenger side lockable glove-box.
- Centre console incorporated more prominent oddments tray, below which new rectangular push button switches operated auxiliary controls like hazard lights, fuel change over etc. In the centre was a rectangular clock within satin surround to match instruments.
- Radio and heating/air conditioning controls similar to Series 1 models, as were gear lever surrounds and ashtrays, although electric window lift switches now larger and black plastic instead of chrome finished.

- Two-spoke steering wheel with enlarged padded black centre section incorporating oval growler image.
- Umbrella handbrake as before.
- Front and rear seating similar to Series 1 models (dependent on model).
- Door trims revised with more complex heat pressing design and with no wood veneer at the top at all.

Daimler Sovereign and Vanden Plas Series 2 models

- Apart from changes identified above for Jaguars, VDP followed same style as Series 1 and Sovereign cars. Still featured unique style door trims, etc.

Coupé models

- As conventional Jaguar or Daimler models except for wider door trims incorporating elongated armrest-pulls.
- Electrically operated window lifts.
- Front seats incorporated black and chrome mechanisms to release the seat back, moving it forward to gain access to the rear compartment.
- Rear seating narrower than saloons with revised side trims with armrests, pockets, and black pull out ashtrays each side.

NB: Specifications for interior trim changed over the production life of the Series 2. Nylon trim offered as standard on cars like the 3.4-litre base model was also available for other models. Similarly head restraints to the front seats were available as standard and/or extra cost items, dependent on model and year produced. See accompanying photographs for more detail.

XJ6/12 Series 3 (all models)

- Although retaining the overall style of Series 2 models, Series 3 interiors looked better quality and were. The same dash layout continued but with a different lighting switch (more pronounced black surround), uniform graphics, and with the warning lights incorporated into the major instruments.
- A new twin-spoke black steering wheel of smaller circumference with thicker rim and rectangular style soft-padded centre section incorporating the growler image.
- Steering column stalks changed over with indicators now on the left (right on all previous models).
- Although bright alloy was chosen for the centre console vertical section incorporating heater/air conditioning controls and radio, the lower horizontal section used black figured vinyl.
- More supportive and substantial seating both front and rear without aerated panels but with

wider pleating and fitted headrests at the front as well as the provision of lumber support adjustment.
- Simplified door trims similar to those featured on Series 2 models but with no heat pressing design.
- New one-piece glass fibre backed head lining and, for the first time on an XJ, recessed sun visors.
- Better quality carpeting and hidden inertia reel seat belts fitted on all front seats.

Daimler Sovereign Series 3 models

- As Jaguar except for top section above chrome strip of door trims, still finished in black instead of trim colour.
- Black surround to radio console area instead of alloy.
- 'D' badging to steering wheel centre boss.

Daimler Vanden Plas models

- As Sovereign except for flatter type seating as previous VDP models, wider pleating, and individual rear seating as before.
- VDP style door trims as before with wood veneer.
- No boxwood inlay to dashboard veneer.
- The last VDP Series 3 model was registered in 1983. Thereafter the same model became known simply as a Double Six, but interior spec remained the same as for the VDP.

Jaguar XJ6/12 Series 3 Sovereign models

- Only introduced in 1984, taking the Sovereign name from Daimler. As other XJs except interior better equipped as standard. Wood veneer with boxwood inlay to door trims, now taking design of trim from the VDP and later models.
- Standard equipment included on–board computer, rectangular unit crackle finished in centre of console with digital readout (see note below regarding centre console layout).

Jaguar XJ6 (post-1984) Series 3 3.4-litre models

- The intended fleet model supplied as standard, with the same style seating to XJ6 models but with Rachelle cloth covering instead of leather.
- Straight grain woodwork instead of figured walnut veneer.

NB: Style of centre console area on all Series 3 models changed from 1983 to incorporate a flat vacuum-formed oddments tray above, with revised veneered onto metal panelling below incorporating new controls and clock position, to accommodate the on-board computer panel where fitted. Wood veneer panelling also affixed to horizontal section of centre console.

Technical specifications

	2.8-litre Series 1	4.2-litre Series 1
cc	2,792	4,235
Bore and stroke (mm)	83 x 86	92.7 x 106
Compression ratio	9:1 (7:1/8:1 optional)	9:1 (7:1/8:1 optional)
bhp	180	245
@ rpm	6,000	5,500
Torque (lb ft)	182	283
@ rpm	3,750	3,750
Fuelling	2 x SU carbs	2 x SU carbs
Transmission	4-speed all synchro, BW 3-speed auto	4-speed all synchro BW 3-speed auto
Wheel size (in)	15, steel	15, steel
Suspension front	Ind semi trailing wishbones, coil springs, anti-roll bar	Ind semi trailing wishbones, coil springs, anti-roll bar
Suspension rear	Ind lower wishbones/upper driveshaft link, radius arms, coil springs	Ind lower wishbones/upper driveshaft link, radius arms, coil springs
Brakes	4 wheel disc Rear inboard	4 wheel disc Rear inboard
Performance		
0–60mph (sec)	11	8.8
Top speed (mph)	117	124
Average mpg	16–20	15.3
Dimensions		
Length (in)	189.5	189.5 (194.75 long wheelbase)
Width (in)	69.25	69.25
Height (in)	54	54
Wheelbase (in)	108.75	108.75 (112.75 long wheelbase)
Front track (in)	58	58
Rear track (in)	58.5	58.5
Weight (cwt)	32	33 (34 long wheelbase)

Technical specifications *cont ...*

	5.3-litre Series 1	3.4-litre Series 2
cc	5,343	3,442
Bore and stroke (mm)	90 x 70	83 x 106
Compression ratio	9:1	8.8:1
bhp	253	161
@ rpm	6,000	5,000
Torque (lb ft)	302	189
@ rpm	3,500	3,500
Fuelling	4 x Stromberg carbs	2 x SU carbs
Transmission	BW 3-speed auto	4-speed all synchro
		BW 3-speed auto
Wheel size (in)	15, steel/chrome	15, steel/chrome
	Alloys optional	Alloys optional
Suspension front	Ind semi trailing wishbones, coil springs, anti-roll bar	Ind semi trailing wishbones, coil springs, anti-roll bar
Suspension rear	Ind lower wishbones/upper driveshaft link, radius arms, coil springs	Ind lower wishbones/upper driveshaft link, radius arms, coil springs
Brakes	4 wheel disc	4 wheel disc
	Rear inboard	Rear inboard
Performance		
0–60mph (sec)	7.4	10.9
Top speed (mph)	145	117
Average mpg	15.7	16.7
Dimensions		
Length (in)	189.5 (194.75 long wheelbase)	189.5 (194.75 long wheelbase)
Width (in)	69.25	69.25
Height (in)	54	54
Wheelbase (in)	108.75 (112.75 long wheelbase)	108.75 (112.75 long wheelbase)
Front track (in)	58	58
Rear track (in)	58.5	58.5
Weight (cwt)	35 (36 long wheelbase)	32

	4.2-litre Series 2	5.3-litre Series 2
cc	4,235	5,343
Bore and stroke (mm)	92.7 x 106	90 x 70
Compression ratio	8:1 (7:1/9:1 optional)	9:1
bhp	170	285
@ rpm	4,500	5,750
Torque (lb ft)	231	294
@ rpm	3,500	3,500
Fuelling	2 x SU Cabs	4 x Stromberg carbs
Transmission	4-speed all synchro BW 3-speed auto	BW 3-speed auto Later GM 3-speed auto
Wheel size (in)	15, steel/chrome Alloys optional	15, steel/chrome Alloys optional
Suspension front	Ind semi trailing wishbones, coil springs, anti-roll bar	Ind semi trailing wishbones, coil springs, anti-roll bar
Suspension rear	Ind lower wishbones/upper driveshaft link, radius arms, coil springs	Ind lower wishbones/upper driveshaft link, radius arms, coil springs
Brakes	4 wheel disc Rear inboard	4 wheel disc Rear inboard
Performance		
0–60mph (sec)	8.9	7.8
Top speed (mph)	125	147
Average mpg	15	13.2
Dimensions		
Length (in)	189.5 (194.75 long wheelbase)	189.5 (194.75 long wheelbase)
Width (in)	69.25	69.25
Height (in)	54	54
Wheelbase (in)	108.75 (112.75 long wheelbase)	108.75 (112.75 long wheelbase)
Front track (in)	58	58
Rear track (in)	58.5	58.5
Weight (cwt)	33 (34 long wheelbase)	35 (36 long wheelbase)

Technical specifications *cont ...*

	5.3-litre Series 2	3.4-litre Series 3
cc	5,343	3,442
Bore and stroke (mm)	90 x 70	83 x 106
Compression ratio	9:1	8.8:1
bhp	285	161
@ rpm	5,750	5,000
Torque (lb ft)	294	189
@ rpm	3,500	3,500
Fuelling	4 x Stromberg carbs Later Fuel Injection	2 x SU carbs Later Fuel Injection
Transmission	BW 3-speed auto	5-speed all synchro
Wheel size (in)	15, steel/chrome Alloys optional	15, steel Later alloys
Suspension front	Ind semi trailing wishbones, coil springs, anti-roll bar	Ind semi trailing wishbones, coil springs, anti-roll bar
Suspension rear	Ind lower wishbones/upper driveshaft link, radius arms, coil springs	Ind lower wishbones/upper driveshaft link, radius arms, coil springs
Brakes	4 wheel disc Rear inboard	4 wheel disc Rear inboard
Performance		
0–60mph (sec)	7.8	10.9
Top speed (mph)	147	117
Average mpg	13.2	16.7
Dimensions		
Length (in)	189.5 (194.75 long wheelbase)	194.75
Width (in)	69.25	69.25
Height (in)	54	54
Wheelbase (in)	108.75 (112.75 long wheelbase)	112.75
Front track (in)	58	58
Rear track (in)	58.5	58.5
Weight (cwt)	35 (36 long wheelbase)	34

	4.2-litre Series 3	5.3-litre Series 3
cc	4,235	5,343
Bore and stroke (mm)	97.07 x 106	90 x 70
Compression ratio	8:1	9:1
bhp	200	285
@ rpm	5,000	5,750
Torque (lb ft)	236	294
@ rpm	2,750	3,500
Fuelling	Fuel Injection	Fuel Injection
Transmission	5-speed all synchro BW 3-speed auto	GM 3-speed auto BW 3-speed auto
Wheel size (in)	15, steel Later alloys	15, steel or alloys
Suspension front	Ind semi trailing wishbones, coil springs, anti-roll bar	Ind semi trailing wishbones, coil springs, anti-roll bar
Suspension rear	Ind lower wishbones/upper driveshaft link, radius arms, coil springs	Ind lower wishbones/upper driveshaft link, radius arms, coil springs
Brakes	4 wheel disc Rear inboard	4 wheel disc Rear inboard
Performance		
0–60mph (sec)	10.5	7.8
Top speed (mph)	128	147
Average mpg	15.7	13.2
Dimensions		
Length (in)	194.75	194.75
Width (in)	69.25	69.25
Height (in)	54	54
Wheelbase (in)	112.75	112.75
Front track (in)	58	58
Rear track (in)	58.5	58.5
Weight (cwt)	35.4	36

9 # Optional extras

Series 1 saloons

2.8-litre standard saloons

Heated rear screen.
Overdrive for manual gearbox.
Automatic transmission.
Power-assisted steering.
Electrically operated windows.
Flush-fitting fog/spot lights.
Front seat belts, or front and rear.
Laminated windscreen.
Sundym tinted glass.
Two choices of radio equipment.
Chrome wheel rimbellishers.
Wing mirrors.
Front seat headrests (from 1969).
Witter tow bar.

2.8-litre de luxe saloons

Heated rear screen.
Overdrive for manual gearbox.
Automatic transmission.
Electrically operated windows.
Flush-fitting fog/spot lights.
Front seat belts, front and/or rear.
Laminated windscreen.
Sundym tinted glass.
Two choices of radio equipment.
Chrome wheel rimbellishers.
Wing mirrors.
Front seat headrests (from 1969).
Mud flaps.
Witter tow bar.

4.2-litre saloons

Heated rear screen (standard from 1972).
Overdrive for manual gearbox.
Automatic transmission.
Electrically operated windows.
Flush-fitting fog/spot lights.
Air conditioning.
Front seat belts, front and/or rear.
Laminated windscreen.
Sundym tinted glass.
Two choices of radio equipment or radio/cassette or cartridge unit.
Philips radio/cassette and recorder with microphone.
Electrically operated radio aerial.
Wing mirrors.
Front seat headrests (from 1969).
Mud flaps.
Witter tow bar.

V12 saloons

Flush-fitting fog/spot lights (standard on Vanden Plas).
Air conditioning (standard on Vanden Plas).
Front seat belts (standard on Vanden Plas) and/or rear.
Laminated windscreen (standard on Vanden Plas).
Sundym tinted glass (standard on Vanden Plas).
Two choices of radio equipment or radio/cassette or cartridge unit (last standard on Vanden Plas)
Philips radio/cassette and recorder with microphone.
Electrically operated radio aerial.
Chrome-plated ventilated steel wheels.
Wing mirrors (not Vanden Plas).
Passenger side remote door mirror (Vanden Plas only).
Front seat headrests (standard on Vanden Plas).
Mud flaps.
Witter tow bar.

Series 2 saloons

3.4-litre saloons

Heated rear screen.
Overdrive for manual gearbox.
Automatic transmission.
Electrically operated windows.
Under bumper fog/spot lights.
Halogen headlights.
Air conditioning.
Rear seat belts.
Laminated windscreen.
Sundym tinted glass.
Radio and/or radio/cassette system with electric aerial.
Wing mirrors.
Driver's door mirror.
Front seat headrests.
Mud flaps.
Leather upholstery.
Witter tow bar.

4.2-litre saloons

Overdrive for manual gearbox.
Automatic transmission.
Under bumper fog/spot lights (standard on Vanden Plas).
Halogen headlights.
Air conditioning (standard on Vanden Plas).
Rear seat belts (standard on Vanden Plas from 1975).
Sundym tinted glass (standard on Vanden Plas and all models from 1978).
Radio and/or radio/cassette system with electric aerial (standard on Vanden Plas).
Kent alloy wheels.
Whitewall tyres.
Driver's door mirror (standard on Vanden Plas).
Rear seat headrests (only on Vanden Plas).
Mud flaps.
Limited slip differential.
Cloth upholstery.
Witter tow bar.

V12 saloons

Under bumper fog/spot lights (standard on Vanden Plas).
Halogen headlights.

Air conditioning (standard on Vanden Plas and on other Daimler V12s from 1975).
Rear seat belts (standard on Vanden Plas from 1975).
Sundym tinted glass (standard on Vanden Plas and all V12s from 1976).
Choice of two radio and radio/cassette systems with electric aerial (standard on Vanden Plas and from 1976 on DD6 coupé).
Kent alloy wheels.
Whitewall tyres.
Driver's door mirror (standard on Vanden Plas).
Rear seat headrests (only on Vanden Plas).
Mud flaps.
Limited slip differential.
Cloth upholstery.
Witter tow bar.

Series 3 saloons

3.4-litre saloons
Heated rear screen (standard from 1982).
Automatic transmission (standard from 1981).
Electrically operated windows.
Under bumper fog/spot lights.
Halogen headlights.
Air conditioning.
Rear seat belts (standard from 1985).
Sundym tinted glass.
Premier stereo radio/cassette system.
Kent alloy wheels.
Pepperpot alloy wheels.
Electrically operated door mirrors.
Rear seat headrests (from 1983).
Mud flaps.
Cruise control (late production).
Electric front seat height adjustment.
Electric steel sunroof.
Roof rack with or without specialist fittings (from 1985).
Electric headlight wash/wipe system.
On-board computer.
Leather upholstery.
Tailored over-mats.
Witter tow bar.

4.2-litre saloons
Automatic transmission (standard from 1981).
Under bumper fog/spot lights (standard on Daimlers from 1983).
Halogen headlights (standard from 1979).
Air conditioning (standard on Vanden Plas and on all Daimlers from 1983 plus Jaguar Sovereigns).
Rear seat belts (standard on Daimlers and on Jaguars from 1984).
Premier stereo radio/cassette system (standard on Vanden Plas, lesser powered standard on Sovereign models from 1984).
Kent alloy wheels.
Pepperpot alloy wheels (standard on Sovereign models).
Stainless steel rimbellishers with stainless steel hubcaps (standard on some Daimlers).

Whitewall tyres.
Electrically operated door mirrors (standard on all Daimlers and Sovereigns from 1984).
Rear seat headrests (standard on Jaguar Sovereign, Vanden Plas, and later Daimlers).
Mud flaps.
Cruise control (standard on Daimlers).
Electric front seat height adjustment (standard on Daimlers and Jaguar Sovereign from 1983).
Electric steel sunroof.
Roof rack with or without specialist fittings (from 1985).
Electric headlight wash/wipe system (standard on Vanden Plas from 1979 and all Daimlers from 1985).
On-board computer (standard on Jaguar Sovereign and Daimlers from 1983).
Cloth upholstery.
Tailored over-mats.
Witter tow bar.

V12 saloons
Under bumper fog/spot lights (standard on Daimlers from 1983).
Halogen headlights (standard from 1979).
Air conditioning (standard on Vanden Plas and on all Daimlers from 1983 plus Jaguar Sovereigns).
Rear seat belts (standard on Daimlers and on Jaguars from 1984).
Premier stereo radio/cassette system (standard on Vanden Plas, lesser powered standard on Sovereign models from 1984).
Integrated hi-fi radio/cassette and CD player system (from 1991).
Kent alloy wheels (standard on Daimlers from 1984).
Pepperpot alloy wheels (standard on Sovereign models).
Stainless steel rimbellishers with stainless steel hubcaps (standard on some Daimlers).
Whitewall tyres.
Electrically operated door mirrors (standard on all Daimlers and Sovereigns from 1984).
Rear seat headrests (standard on Jaguar Sovereign Vanden Plas and later DD6).
Mud flaps.
Cruise control (standard on Daimlers and Jaguar Sovereign).
Electric front seat height adjustment (standard on Daimlers and Jaguar Sovereign from 1983).
Electric steel sunroof (standard on Daimlers from 1986).
Roof rack with or without specialist fittings (from 1985).
Electric headlight wash/wipe system (standard on Vanden Plas from 1979, Jaguar Sovereign from 1983, and all Daimlers from 1985).
Cloth upholstery.
Tailored over-mats.
Witter tow bar.
Mobile phone installation (from 1988).

Colour schemes

Exterior colour	Details	Interior trim
XJ6 Series 1 2.8-litre		**Ambla**
Special order leather as 4.2-litre models below		
Old English White		Red
		Dark Blue
		Black
Warwick Grey	To 1992	Red
		Dark Blue
		Beige
Ascot Fawn	To 1992	Red
		Beige
Willow Green	To 1992	Beige
Dark Blue		Red
		Dark Blue
		Beige
Sable Brown		Beige
Light Blue	To 1992	Dark Blue
		Black
British Racing Green		Beige
Regency Red		Beige
		Red
Black		Red
		Beige
Signal Red*		Black
		Beige
		Red
Pale Primrose*		Red
		Beige
		Black
Azure Blue*		Dark Blue
		Beige
Light Silver*		Red
		Beige
		Dark Blue
Fern Grey	From 1972	Green
		Olive
		Beige
Turquoise	From 1972	Tan
		Beige
Greensand	From 1972	Tan
		Olive
		Beige

Exterior colour	Details	Interior trim
Heather Pink	From 1972	Maroon
		Antelope
		Cerise
Lavender	From 1972	Tan
		Dark Blue
XJ Series 1 4.2/5.3-litre		**Leather**
Old English White		Red
		Dark Blue
		Light Blue
Warwick Grey	To 1992	Red
		Dark Blue
		Cinnamon
Ascot Fawn	To 1992	Red
		Cinnamon
		Beige
Willow Green	To 1992	Beige
		Suede Green
		Grey
		Cinnamon
Dark Blue		Red
		Light Blue
		Grey
Sable Brown		Beige
		Grey
		Cinnamon
Light Blue	To 1992	Dark Blue
		Light Blue
		Grey
British Racing Green		Beige
		Suede Green
		Cinnamon
Regency Red		Beige
		Grey
Black	To 1992	Red
		Grey
		Cinnamon
Signal Red*		Red
		Beige
Pale Primrose*		Red
		Beige
		Black

Exterior colour	Details	Interior trim
Azure Blue*		Dark Blue
		Cinnamon
		Beige
Light Silver*		Red
		Beige
		Dark Blue
		Black
Fern Grey	From 1972	Moss Green
		Olive
		Tan
Turquoise	From 1972	Tan
		Cinnamon
Greensand	From 1972	Tan
		Olive
		Cinnamon
Heather Pink	From 1972	Maroon
		Antelope
		Cerise
Lavender	From 1972	Biscuit
		Dark Blue
		French Blue

Exterior colour	Details	Interior trim
Vanden Plas (Series 1 and 2)		Leather
Silver Sand		Chamois
		Tuscan
		Deep Olive
Caramel		Chamois
		Tuscan
		Deep Olive
Coral		Chamois
		Tuscan
		Deep Olive
Aegean Blue		Chamois
		Tuscan
		Deep Olive
Sage Green		Chamois
		Tuscan
		Deep Olive
Morello Cherry		Chamois
		Tuscan
		Deep Olive
Aubergine		Chamois
		Tuscan
		Deep Olive

Exterior colour	Details	Interior trim	Details	Interior trim	Details
XJ Series 2 models		Leather		Cloth	
Old English White		Red	To 1974	Garnet	
		Russet	From 1974	Sand	
		Dark Blue	To 1975	Ebony*	
		French Blue	To 1974		
		Cinnamon	From 1974		
Dark Blue		Red	To 1974	Garnet	
		Russet	From 1974	Sand	
		Dark Blue	1974–5	Ebony*	
		French Blue	To 1974		
		Biscuit			
Sable Brown	To 1975	Biscuit			
		Moss Green			
		Cinnamon			
British Racing Green		Biscuit		Sand	
		Moss Green	To 1975	Ebony*	
		Cinnamon			

Colour schemes *cont …*

Exterior colour	Details	Interior trim	Details	Interior trim	Details
Regency Red	To 1987	Biscuit		Sand	
		Cinnamon		Ebony*	
		Red	To 1974		
		Russet	1974–5		
Black*		Red		Ebony*	
		Russet	To 1974		
		Grey	1974–5		
		Cinnamon			
Signal Red*		Red	To 1974	Ebony*	
		Russet	1974–5		
		Beige			
Pale Primrose*		Red		Ebony*	
		Beige			
		Black			
Azure Blue*	To 1975	Dark Blue		Ebony*	
		Cinnamon			
		Beige			
Light Silver*		Red	To 1974	Ebony*	
		Russet	1974–5		
		Beige			
		Dark Blue			
		Black			
Fern Grey	To 1975	Moss Green			
		Olive			
		Cinnamon	1974–5		
		Tan	To 1974		
Turquoise	To 1975	Tan			
		Cinnamon			
		Terracotta			
Greensand	To 1975	Tan	To 1974		
		Cinnamon			
		Olive			
Heather Pink	To 1975	Maroon			
		Antelope			
		Cerise			
Lavender	To 1975	Biscuit			
		Dark Blue			
		French Blue	To 1974		
		Cinnamon	1974–5		
Juniper Green	From 1975	Biscuit		Sand	
		Cinnamon			
Carriage Brown	From 1975	Biscuit		Sand	
		Cinnamon			

Exterior colour	Details	Interior trim	Details	Interior trim	Details
Moroccan Bronze	From 1975	Biscuit		Sand	
		Cinnamon			
Squadron Blue	From 1975	Dark Blue		Sand	
		Biscuit		Navy	
XJ Series 3 models		**Leather**		**Cloth**	
Tudor White	To 1986	Russet		Garnet	To 1985
		Biscuit		Sand	
Cotswold Yellow	To 1980	Cinnamon		Sand	
		Dark Blue		Navy	
Damson Red	To 1980	Russet		Garnet	
		Cinnamon		Sand	
Racing Green Metallic	To 1985	Biscuit		Sand	
Racing Green	1986–8	Cinnamon			
Silver Frost	To 1980	Russet		Garnet	
	and 1989 on	Dark Blue		Sand	
		Doeskin	From 1989		
Cobalt Blue	To 1986	Cinnamon		Sand	
		Dark Blue		Navy	
Quartz Blue	To 1980	Biscuit		Sand	
		Dark Blue		Navy	
Chestnut Brown	To 1983	Cinnamon		Sand	
		Biscuit			
Sebring Red*	To 1986	Biscuit		Sand	
Standard from 1981		Dark Blue		Navy	
Black*		Biscuit	To 1987	Garnet	
Standard from 1981		Russet	To 1981	Sand	
		Barley	From 1988		
Indigo Blue	1981–3	Biscuit†	From 1981	Beige†	From 1981
Grosvenor Brown	1984–5	County Tan†	1981 to 1983	Amber†	1981–3
Portland Beige	1981–3	Isis Blue†		Fleet Blue†	From 1981
Rhodium Silver	1981–6	Black†	1981 to 1986	Graphite†	From 1981
Sapphire Blue (light)	1981–5	Doeskin†	1981 on	Parchment†	1985 only
Coronet Gold	1981–5	Burnt Umber†	1981 to 1983		
Sable Brown	1981–3	Buckskin†	1984 on	**Wool Tweed**	From 1986
Claret	1981–6	Mulberry†	1984 on	Cheviot†	From 1986
Silversand	1981–6	Savile Grey†	1984 on	Chiltern†	From 1986
Clarendon Blue	1984–5	Barley†	1986 on	Cotswold†	From 1986
Cirrus Grey	1984–6	Magnolia†	1986 on	Pennine†	From 1986
Cranberry	1984–6	Charcoal†	1987 on		
Antelope	1984–6				
Sage Green	1984–6				
Regent Grey	1984–6				
Windsor Blue	1986				

Colour schemes *cont …*

Exterior colour	Details	Interior trim	Details	Interior trim	Details
Steel Blue	1986				
Curlew Brown	1986				
Nimbus White	1987				
Grenadier Red	1988	Buckskin	From 1988		
Alpine Green	1987				
Arctic Blue	From 1987	Magnolia	From 1988		
Bordeaux	From 1987	Savile Grey	1988		
		Mulberry	From 1989		
Crimson	1987				
Dorchester Grey	1987–9				
Moorland Green	1987–9				
Satin Beige	1987–9	Parchment	From 1988		
Silver Birch	1987–9				
Solent Blue	From 1987	Magnolia	From 1988		
Sovereign Gold	1987				
Talisman Silver	1987–9	Doeskin	From 1988		
Tungsten Grey	From 1987	Doeskin	From 1988		
Jaguar Racing Green	From 1987	Charcoal	From 1988		
Glacier White	From 1988	Biscuit	1988		
		Charcoal	From 1989		
Westminster Blue	From 1987	Doeskin			
Savoy Grey	From 1988	Isis Blue			
Jade Green	From 1988	Savile Grey	1988		
		Parchment	From 1989		
Gunmetal	From 1988	Savile Grey	1988		
		Parchment	From 1989		
Regency Red	From 1988	Savile Grey			
Brooklands Green	From 1989	Doeskin			
Diamond Blue	From 1988	Magnolia			
Oyster	From 1989	Magnolia			
Tuscany Bronze	From 1989	Savile Grey			
			Contrast Piping		
			(available from 1988)		
			Isis Blue		
			Mulberry		
			Sage Green		
			Mid Grey		
			Buckskin		
			Barley		

† = open choice

* = special order only

Exterior colour	Details	Interior trim	Details	Interior trim	Details
Vanden Plas Series 3		**Leather**		**Cloth**	
Silversand		Chamois			
		Tan			
		Olive			
Caramel		Chamois			
		Tan			
		Olive			
Coral		Chamois			
		Tan			
		Olive			
Biascan Blue		Chamois			
		Tan			
		Olive			
Mistletoe		Chamois			
		Tan			
		Olive			
Mink		Chamois			
		Tan			
		Olive			
Amethyst		Chamois			
		Tan			
		Olive			

Prices and production volumes

Series 1

	Price new (£)	1968	1969	1970	1971	1972	1973
Jaguar XJ6 2.8-litre standard	1,797	■	–	–	–	–	–
Jaguar XJ6 2.8-litre de luxe	1,897	■	■	■	■	■	■
Daimler Sovereign 2.8	2,336	■	■	■	■	■	■
Jaguar XJ6 4.2-litre	2,254	■	■	■	■	■	■
Jaguar XJ6 4.2 L	3,464	–	–	–	–	■	■
Daimler Sovereign 4.2	2,713	■	■	■	■	■	■
Daimler Sovereign 4.2 L	3,954	–	–	–	–	■	■
Jaguar XJ12	3,725	–	–	–	–	■	■
Jaguar XJ12L	4,052	–	–	–	–	■	■
Daimler Double Six	4,398	–	–	–	–	■	–
Daimler DD6 Vanden Plas	5,363	–	–	–	–	■	■
Total Series 1 production							

Series 2

	Price new (£)	1968	1969	1970	1971	1972	1973
Jaguar XJ6 2.8-litre	–	–	–	–	–	–	■
Jaguar XJ6 4.2-litre	3,674	–	–	–	–	–	■
Daimler Sovereign 4.2-litre	–	–	–	–	–	–	■
Daimler Sovereign 4.2 L	4,766	–	–	–	–	–	■
Jaguar XJ6 4.2 L	4,124	–	–	–	–	–	■
Jaguar XJ12 L	4,702	–	–	–	–	–	■
Daimler Double Six L	5,612	–	–	–	–	–	■
Jaguar XJ6 coupé	4,260	–	–	–	–	–	–
Daimler Sovereign 4.2 coupé	4,898	–	–	–	–	–	–
Jaguar XJ12 coupé	5,181	–	–	–	–	–	–
Daimler Double Six coupé	6,131	–	–	–	–	–	–
Daimler DD6 Vanden Plas	7,333	–	–	–	–	–	■
Daimler Sovereign 4.2 Vanden Plas	–	–	–	–	–	–	–
Jaguar XJ6 3.4-litre	4,795	–	–	–	–	–	–
Daimler Sovereign 3.4-litre	–	–	–	–	–	–	–
Total Series 2 production							

1974	1975	1976	1977	1978	1979	Total produced
–	–	–	–	–	–	Not known
–	–	–	–	–	–	19,322
–	–	–	–	–	–	3,233
–	–	–	–	–	–	59,077
–	–	–	–	–	–	874
–	–	–	–	–	–	11,522
–	–	–	–	–	–	386
–	–	–	–	–	–	2,474
–	–	–	–	–	–	754
–	–	–	–	–	–	534
–	–	–	–	–	–	351
						98,527

1974	1975	1976	1977	1978	1979	Total produced
–	–	–	–	–	–	170
■	–	–	–	–	–	12,147
■	–	–	–	–	–	2,435
■	■	■	■	■	■	14,531
■	■	■	■	■	■	57,804
■	■	■	■	■	■	16,010
■	■	■	■	■	■	2,608
■	■	■	■	–	–	6,487
■	■	■	■	–	–	1,677
■	■	■	■	–	–	1,855
■	■	■	■	–	–	407
■	■	■	■	■	■	1,726
–	■	■	■	■	■	883
–	■	■	■	■	■	6,880
–	■	■	■	■	■	2,341
						127,961

Prices and production volumes *cont ...*

	Price new (£)	1979	1980	1981	1982	1983	1984
Series 3							
Jaguar XJ6 3.4-litre	11,189	▪	▪	▪	▪	▪	▪
Jaguar XJ6 4.2-litre	12,326	▪	▪	▪	▪	▪	▪
Jaguar XJ12	15,014	▪	▪	▪	▪	▪	–
Daimler Sovereign 4.2-litre	12,983	▪	▪	▪	▪	▪	–
Daimler Double Six	15,689	▪	▪	▪	▪	▪	▪
Daimler 4.2 Vanden Plas	17,208	▪	▪	▪	▪	–	–
Daimler DD6 Vanden Plas	20,277	▪	▪	▪	▪	–	–
Jaguar 4.2 Sovereign	18,500	–	–	–	–	▪	▪
Jaguar V12 Sovereign	21,000	–	–	–	–	▪	▪
Total Series 3 production							
Total production all series							

Production changes

1968
XJ6 2.8- and 4.2-litre models introduced.

1969
Daimler Sovereign models introduced.
Curved tail pipes introduced to exhaust system.
Front seat headrest fitments made available.
Borg Warner Model 12 auto transmission fitted
    to 4.0-litre models.

1970
Air intake grilles incorporated into front outer
    headlight surrounds.
Satin-finished scuttle ventilator replaced chrome
    type.
Boot spare wheel/fuel pump covers changed
    (tools now inside boot).
'Jaguar' treadplates fitted to sills.

1971
Rear one-piece bumper changed to three-piece.
Radio aerials no longer possible to fit on front
    wings.

1972
XJ12 and DD6 models introduced.
Vanden Plas Double Six introduced.
Long wheelbase bodyshell available on most
    models.

1973
(September) Production of short wheelbase
    bodyshells ceased.

1974
Series 2 models introduced.
Last 2.8-litre engines produced.
XJ coupé models announced but not available.

1975
Coupé models became available at end of 1974.
3.4-litre XJ6 introduced.
Daimler Vanden Plas 4.2-litre model introduced.
Kent alloy wheels introduced.
Fuel injection for V12 engines introduced.
Vinyl roofs fitted to all V12 saloons.
Chrome side strips offered as option on V12 models.

1977
General Motors GM400 auto transmission fitted
    to V12s.
(November) Last coupés built.

1978
Fuel injection introduced on 4.2-litre models.
Sidelights moved to outer headlights/new
    indicator lenses below bumper.

1979
'XJ6' badging replaced for most markets by 'XJ
    4.2' etc.
(March) Series 3 models introduced.
Five-speed manual box became available on six-
    cylinder cars.
Flat-faced headlamps fitted for cars with
    wash/wipe system.
Pirelli tyres offered as an alternative to Dunlop.

1985	1986	1987	1988	1989	1990	1991	1992	Total produced
■	■	■	–	–	–	–	–	5,799
■	■	–	–	–	–	–	–	97,349
–	–	–	–	–	–	–	–	5,408
–	–	–	–	–	–	–	–	11,516
■	■	■	■	■	■	■	■	41,497
–	–	–	–	–	–	–	–	1,953
–	–	–	–	–	–	–	–	402
■	■	■	–	–	–	–	–	16,346
■	■	■	■	■	■	■	–	7,235
								177,244
								403,732

1980
Dunlop Supersport D7 tyres fitted to V12s.
Merlin flush-fitting rear wing radio aerials fitted.

1981
HE engines fitted to V12 models.
Cigar lighter fitted to rear compartment in
  Daimler models.
Door puddle lights fitted to all models.
Rear compartment reading lights fitted to all
  Daimler models.
Black vinyl covering to centre console horizontal
  areas.
Chrome side strips fitted to all Daimlers, optional
  on Jaguar V12s.
Battery cooling fan deleted from six-cylinder models.

1982
Childproof locks fitted to rear doors.
Borg Warner Model 66 auto transmission fitted
  to six-cylinder cars.
Minor instruments supplier changed to Veglia.
Pepperpot alloy wheels introduced.
Individual rear seating standardised on Daimler
  models.
Daimler marque dropped from European markets.

1983
Rachelle cloth seats introduced.
Jaguar Sovereign models introduced.
Linestone headlining standardised for all cars.
Revised style of centre console with veneer on
  metal, new switches, etc.

On-board computer became available.
Revised radiator grille (no bonnet trim), new wheel
  trims, and hubcaps fitted to Daimler models.
New style front wing leaper badge fitted.

1984
Acrylic paint system adopted.

1985
Herringbone tweed upholstery standard on 3.4,
  optional on other models.
Veneered door fillets provided on 3.4-litre models.
Straight grain woodwork fitted to 3.4s.
Stainless steel treadplates fitted to all models.
'HE' script dropped from badges on V12s, and all
  badges now rectangular 'solid' on boot lid.
Mark III air conditioning system fitted.

1987
Last XJ6 left factory.

1989
V12s engined from factory converted to lead-free
  fuel.

1990
ABS brakes introduced.

1991
Last Jaguar V12 produced.

1992
Last Daimler Double Six produced.

Chassis numbers

Model	Right/Left Drive	Chassis/Vin Nos Commencing	Model	Right/Left Drive	Chassis/Vin Nos Commencing
XJ6 S1 2.8	RHD	1G 1001	XJ12 S2 (lwb)	RHD	2R 1001
	LHD	1G 50001		LHD	2R 50001
Daimler Sov S1 2.8	RHD	1T 1001	Daimler Sov S2 DD6	RHD	2K 1001
	LHD	1T 50001	(lwb)	LHD	2K 50001
XJ6 S1 4.2 (swb)	RHD	1L 1001	Daimler S2 VDP DD6	RHD	2P 1001
	LHD	1L 50001		LHD	2P 50001
XJ6 S1 4.2 (lwb)	RHD	2E 1001	XJ6 Coupé	RHD	2J 1001
	LHD	2E 50001		LHD	2J 50001
Daimler Sov S1 4.2 (lwb)	RHD	2D 1001	XJ12 Coupé	RHD	2G 1001
	LHD	2D 50001		LHD	2G 50001
Daimler S1 VDP	RHD	2B 1001	Daimler Coupé 4.2	RHD	2H 1001
	LHD	2B 50001		LHD	2H 50001
XJ12 S1 (swb)	RHD	1P 1001	Daimler Coupé DD6	RHD	2F 1001
	LHD	1P 50001		LHD	2F 50001
XJ12 S1 (lwb)	RHD	2C 1001	XJ6 S3 3.4	RHD	Vin No. (see table 1*)
	LHD	2C 50001		LHD	Vin No. (see table 1*)
Daimler DD6 S1 (swb)	RHD	2A 1001	Daimler S3 3.4	RHD	Vin No. (see table 1*)
	LHD	2A 5000		LHD	Vin No. (see table 1*)
XJ6 S2 3.4	RHD	3A 1001	XJ6 S3 4.2	RHD	Vin No. (see table 1*)
	LHD	3A 50001		LHD	Vin No. (see table 1*)
Daimler Sov S2 3.4	RHD	3B 1001	Daimler Sov S3 4.2	RHD	Vin No. (see table 1*)
	LHD	3B 50001		LHD	Vin No. (see table 1*)
XJ6 S2 4.2 (swb)	RHD	2N 1001	Daimler S3 VDP 4.2	RHD	Vin No. (see table 1*)
	LHD	2N 50001		LHD	Vin No. (see table 1*)
Daimler Sov S2 4.2 (swb)	RHD	2M 1001	Daimler S3 VDP DD6	RHD	Vin No. (see table 1*)
	LHD	2M 50001		LHD	Vin No. (see table 1*)
Daimler Sov S2 4.2 (lwb)	RHD	2S 1001	Daimler S3 DD6	RHD	Vin No. (see table 1*)
	LHD	2S 50001		LHD	Vin No. (see table 1*)
Daimler S2 VDP -4.2	RHD	3C 1001	XJ12 S3	RHD	Vin No. (see table 1*)
	LHD	3C 50001		LHD	Vin No. (see table 1*)
XJ6 S2 4.2 (lwb)	RHD	2T 1001			
	LHD	2T 50001			

*Table 1 appears on page 316.

Background

In 1960 Jaguar purchased the Daimler company and its existing model range, namely the SP250 sports car and the Majestic Major saloon, continued in low volume production until the mid-1960s under Jaguar control. Jaguar's first improvements to the range came with the introduction of a longer wheelbase 'limousine' model based on the Majestic Major. Coded the DR450, this also remained in production until the mid-1960s, but saw a total of only 865 cars produced. None of these models fall within the bounds of this publication.

However, with the merger of Jaguar Cars and the British Motor Corporation to form British Motor Holdings, the need was identified for a new 'carriage trade' limousine to replace both the Daimler Majestic and the ageing Austin Princess (later the Vanden Plas Princess). Apart from independently produced 'stretched' models of existing saloons, the only true limousine available 'off the shelf' by that time was the Rolls Royce Phantom, which was too expensive for many private companies, embassies, or the trade to buy.

As Jaguar owned the Daimler name and already manufactured a vast floorpan for the Mark X/420G, and the British Motor Corporation owned the Vanden Plas Coachworks in London, it was a natural progression for the company to produce a new vehicle based heavily on Jaguar parts but utilising the prestigious Daimler name and the specialist coachbuilding abilities of VDP. The resultant DS420 limousine, as it became known, came out in 1968, virtually coinciding with the amalgamation of the British motor industry into British Leyland. The Jaguar 420 engine (with twin carburettors) had been mated to other

Jaguar mechanical aspects from the Mark X and the XJ6. Other Jaguar input included the 420G floorpan and many inner panels, along with much of the trim from the same model, down to instruments, brightwork, and so on.

The body, designed by Vanden Plas, was reminiscent of the halcyon days of Hooper-bodied Daimlers, and there is no doubt that the overall styling met with the approval of everyone. At 18ft 10in long and weighing in at around 42cwt it was no lightweight, but interior accommodation was what a limousine was all about and the DS420 fitted the bill remarkably well, particularly at £4,425.

The DS420 was offered as either a limousine model or a chassis only, allowing individuals to have their own bodywork hand-crafted. A hearse equivalent became available which proved very popular with the carriage trade. Just a couple of chassis-only vehicles were supplied for very special bodies, which were adapted to landaulette style. A saloon model was also considered, but it was felt that there would be little demand for such a traditionally styled car in the late 1960s.

The cars were initially built at the Vanden Plas Coachworks in London and were sold through normal Daimler channels, but with the closure of VDP in 1981 production moved to a special limousine shop facility at the Jaguar Browns Lane Plant in Coventry.

The DS420 was regularly updated to meet the demands of the market and to coincide with changes to other Jaguar and Daimler models, specifically in order to keep down the cost of production, which was very high, the car still being essentially hand-built.

The limousine's peak year was 1970, when 489 were sold. Production finally ceased at the end of 1992 when it became impractical to continue making such a car, both financially and because of changing regulations. A total of 5,043 cars were produced, a not insignificant figure compared to previous Daimler limousines, or indeed Rolls Royce sales, The DS420 remains very popular in the 'trade' and retains a prestige that is sadly lacking in the current crop of 'stretched' saloons.

Model range and development

The DS420 was announced in April 1968 and was available initially in just two forms. On its announcement at the British Motor Show that year it received a Silver Medal for coachwork design.

Models available at launch
Daimler DS420 limousine (standard equipment)
Daimler DS420 chassis (for private coachbuilders)

There is no definitive DS420 model. The 'standard' limousine offered in 1968 amounted to a long wheelbase bodyshell with a fixed front and rear bench-seat arrangement, occasional pull-up rear seating for additional passengers, and automatic transmission. At the price you didn't get such features as air conditioning, electrically-operated windows, or even full leather upholstery.

Right from the start chassis were supplied to various outside organisations, mostly for conversion to hearses, the height of the front screen and long wheelbase being ideally suited to this form of vehicle.

Due to a drop in demand, poorer quality control, and the final demise of the separate Vanden Plas coachbuilding facility, production moved to Jaguar's factory in 1981, when various changes took place in trim construction to cater for quicker and easier production methods. At this time the gearbox was changed to the modern and more refined General Motors unit, and the general equipment levels were improved with air conditioning as standard.

The basic essence of the DS420 remained unchanged throughout production, although specification and equipment levels were constantly improved and updated to meet the demands of the market, individual tastes and, of course, the Jaguar parts bin. No other models were ever produced and the last car (a chassis to be built as a hearse) left the Browns Lane works in November 1992. The next to last car went to the Jaguar Daimler Heritage Trust, where it remains to this day.

The Daimler DS420 limousine filled a gap in the market for a highly specialised vehicle which some would say still exists to this day.

Styled by Vanden Plas, built around Jaguar parts, the DS420 takes cues from the Mark X/420G models. Differences from the front amount to the enlarged radiator grille surround with Daimler flutes and the scripted 'D' emblem on the bonnet.

Side view reveals the sheer size of the DS420, which is instantly identifiable from any other Jaguar/Daimler model.

The rear of the DS420 is unique but again takes styling cues from the Mark X/420G, using the same lighting and bumper bar. However, the over-riders changed throughout production. The boot-mounted number plate plinth/illumination panel initially used the Mark X plinth with Daimler badge, which was changed in the 1970s to this unique Daimler plinth.

Exterior identification points

General points applicable to early DS420s
Front view
■ Frontal aspect similar to Mark X/420G with twin headlight treatment. Wrap-around indicator lenses, horn grilles, and slimline bumper bar with over-riders and centrally mounted number plate plinth.
■ Prominent rectangular radiator grille with vertical chrome slats and typical Daimler flutes to the upper section.
■ Alligator style opening bonnet with prominent swept 'D' mascot and full-length centrally located chrome strip along bonnet.
■ Steeply raked one-piece windscreen with chromed surround and two windscreen wipers.

Rear view
■ One-piece rear screen with chromed surround.
■ Severe sloping rear wings and rear-hinged one-piece boot lid.
■ Adapted light clusters from Mark X/420G.
■ Daimler 420 Sovereign style rear number plate/reversing light plinth mounted centrally on boot lid.
■ Slimline rear bumper as Mark X/420G.
■ No badging apart from scripted 'Daimler' on boot lid.
■ Twin exhaust pipes emerged underneath bumper bar and rear valance as Mark X/420G.

Side view
■ Softened razor edged styling, long wheelbase, with severe slope to rear wings and boot area.
■ Significant use of chrome including waistline trim running the entire length of the body from the front wing, across the doors between the handles, and sloping down following the wing line to the rear.
■ Traditional chrome on brass window surrounds with enlarged rear side windows with quarter-lights.
■ Steel wheels painted either to body colour or silver with standard equipment chrome rimbellishers and conventional chromed hubcaps following later Daimler design.

General changes to DS420 during production
Front view
■ Horn grilles changed initially to a horizontally slatted simpler circular design. Later changed again to rectangular style.
■ Sidelight/indicator units changed to a rectangular style, affixed in the same position.

Changes to the bumper bar, over-riders, and other exterior trim occurred throughout the life of the DS420. The car on the left is to the original design with Mark X bumper/over-riders and 240/340 horn grilles. The car on the right is a post-1970 model with rubber-faced over-riders and plainer horizontal slatted horn grilles.

Another later version of the external trim, with rubber-faced energy absorbing bumper bars, adapted from the Series 3 XJ design from the mid-1980s, which necessitated revised rectangular sidelight units and XJ Series 1 horn grilles.

Above left: Initially, up until the end of the 1980s, DS420s came as standard with steel painted wheels with conventional Jaguar hubcaps. Nearing the end of production Kent alloy wheels were used, these being adapted to take hubcaps.

Above right: Interior layout and fitments were always down to personal order requirements. A 'conventional' model would include a rear bench trimmed in either leather, cloth, or other material, with extra occasional seating as seen here. Wind-up windows were the norm, electrics, including division etc, being down to special order. In this very late model Series 3 adapted trim was used for the door panels.

- Over-riders changed to smaller chromed style with rubber buffers.
- Later model bumper bar changed to adapted style from Series 3 XJ, of rubber-fronted style with chrome top finisher blade, and indicator lenses mounted within the rubber.

Rear view

- Later cars fitted with bespoke extended chrome fluted number plate/reversing light plinth.
- Mid-term bumper bar featured smaller over-riders with rubber buffers. Later models featured Series 3 rubber-faced bumper bar incorporating rear fog lamps and with chrome finisher blades.

Side view

- Significant use of chrome including waistline trim running the entire length of body from the front wing, across the doors between the handles, and sloping down following the wing line to the rear. Simplified on later models.
- Steel wheel design changed at various stages, sometimes without chromed rimbellishers. Later cars equipped with adapted Kent alloy wheels but still with chromed hubcaps.

Interior identification points

DS420 (early models)

- Mark X/420G style dashboard layout with or without black padded top dashboard roll.
- Steering wheel and column as Mark 420G, including automatic transmission quadrant and indicator stalk.
- Door and other soft trimming adapted from Mark X/420G style.
- Initially a bench-type front seat arrangement trimmed to match Mark X style.
- Rear compartment on standard limousine has bench-seat arrangement with vertical pleating and fold-away centre armrest.
- Door and other soft trimming adapted from Mark X model with wood cappings to upper sections and rear window surrounds.
- Occasional fold-away seating to centre section of the rear compartment trimmed to match.
- Conventional manual sliding glass partition between front and rear compartment trimmed in vinyl and wood.

Identifiable changes during production

- Design, layout, and type of instrumentation changed throughout production, moving away from pure 420G original.
- Very late cars featured manually-operated choke control on dashboard.
- Later steering wheels and columns adapted from Series 3 Daimler model.

- Door and other soft trimming simplified to a style unique to DS420.
- Mid-term split-bench front seat arrangement, later changed to individual front seats with full adjustment.
- Automatic transmission quadrant re-positioned to floor, centrally mounted within black fibre console.
- Centrally situated E-type Series 3 chromed handbrake replaced umbrella style.
- Door and other soft trimming in rear compartment simplified to match front.

NB: Most DS420 models were made to special order so interior trim will vary dramatically from car to car, including the use of non-leather upholstery, electric divisions, side curtains, etc. See accompanying photographs and other details within the production changes listing for some of these features.

More elaborate interiors were fitted like this 'mobile office' … or a veneered and fully fitted cocktail cabinet.

Above left: *Most of the trim for the driving compartment came directly from the Mark X/420G, with adaptations which included a centre console to accept the later style of automatic transmission control. Earlier cars used a steering column mounted control as found on Mark Xs.*

Above right: *Front compartment seating varied from a simple vinyl-covered bench through to fully adjustable separate leather seats on the later models, and, again, similarities can be seen with other Jaguar/Daimler models, like the 420 and Mark X.*

Technical specification

	DS420
cc	4,235
Bore and stroke (mm)	92.07 x 106
Compression ratio	7:1 (8:1 optional
bhp	245
@ rpm	5,000
Torque (lb ft)	283
@ rpm	3,500
Fuelling	2 x SU carbs
Transmission	BW 3-speed auto
Wheel size (in)	15, steel, later alloy
Suspension front	Ind semi trailing wishbones, coil springs, anti-roll bar
Suspension rear	Ind lower wishbones/upper driveshaft link, radius arms, coil springs
Brakes	4 wheel disc, rear inboard
Performance	
0–60mph (sec)	13.4
Top speed (mph)	109
Average mpg	14.8
Dimensions	
Length (in)	226
Width (in)	77.5
Height (in)	63.5
Wheelbase (in)	141
Front track (in)	58
Rear track	58
Weight (cwt)	42

Optional extras

Choice of two types of radio installations for front and rear compartment.
Electric radio aerial.
Electrically operated front and rear windows.
Electrically operated rear quarter windows.
Electrically operated centre division.
Chromium-plated flag mast for bonnet.
Adjustable reading lamps in the rear compartment.
Nylon over-rugs for the rear compartment.
Rubber fitted matting for the front compartment.
Laminated windscreen.
Heated rear screen.
Front seat belts.
Rear seat belts.
Fire extinguisher.
Sundym tinted windscreen and side windows.
Wing mirrors.
Integrated ignition/starter switch to steering column (earlier cars).
Fog/spot lamps.

Electrically heated rear screen.
Rear compartment footrests.
Chromium-plated badge bar.
Sony colour TV in veneered cabinet.
Single or dual tone colour finishes and interior trims to suit individual requirements.
Equipped and veneered cocktail cabinet for rear compartment.
Media veneered cabinet to incorporate audio visual systems.
Fluorescent lighting for rear compartment.
West of England cloth upholstery for rear compartment.
Full leather trim throughout car.
Alternative wood veneers.
Curtains for rear compartment.
Fold-away veneered writing tables.
Refrigerated cool box for boot area.
Central division and rear window blinds.
Exterior colour schemes to individual requirements.

Colour schemes

Exterior colour	Single/Duotone	Interior trim
Embassy Black	Single	Bespoke
Carlton Grey	Single	
Maroon	Single	
Navy	Single	
Silver	Single	
Cream	Single	
Embassy Black	Duotone	Carlton Grey
		Silver
		Maroon
		Green
Navy	Duotone	Silver Blue

Later Coventry production: Any combination of Jaguar/Daimler standard colours could be specified, as well as bespoke colours.

Prices and production volumes

	Price new (£)	1968	1969	1970	1971	1972	1973	1974
DS420 chassis	2,369	▪	▪	▪	▪	▪	▪	▪
DS420 limousine	4,425	▪	▪	▪	▪	▪	▪	▪

	1975	1976	1977	1978	1979	1980	to 1992	Total
DS420 chassis	▪	▪	▪	▪	▪	▪	▪	903
DS420 limousine	▪	▪	▪	▪	▪	▪	▪	4,141
Total production								**5,044**

Production changes

1968
DS420 model introduced.

1981
Production moved from London to Coventry.
Nylon carpeting fitted.
GM400 auto transmission fitted instead of Borg Warner.
Thermo plastic paint finish adopted.
Steering column-mounted ignition/starter switch fitted.
Series 3 XJ steering wheel adopted.

1983
Improved air conditioning system.
Revised door locks fitted using less keys.

1984
Split-bench type seating for front (adjustable).
Auto gearbox quadrant moved to floor from steering column.
Pre-formed centre console fitted to accommodate gear lever.
E-type Series 3 handbrake fitted to centre, replacing umbrella type.
Chrome rimbellishers now extra cost option for road wheels.
Revised bumper bar over-riders (small, including rubber facings) introduced.
Rectangular horn grilles replaced circular type.
Rectangular sidelight/indicator lenses replaced circular type at front.
Rear number plate plinth revised to fluted design.

1985
Front sidelights incorporated in headlight units.
Manual choke system adopted.

1986
Series 3 XJ style front and rear rubber-faced bumper bars fitted.
Reduced depth radiator grille fitted to accommodate above.
'Daimler' scripted badge appeared on boot lid for first time.

1987
Revised siting of steering column to provide better driving position.

1989
Kent alloy wheels fitted, adapted to accept Daimler hubcaps.

1992
Daimler DS420 discontinued.

Chassis numbers

Model	Right/ Left Drive	Chassis/ Vin Nos Commencing
Daimler DS420 Limo	RHD	1M 1001
	LHD	1M 20001
Later models post '78	Vin No.	(see table 1*)

*Table 1 appears on page 316.

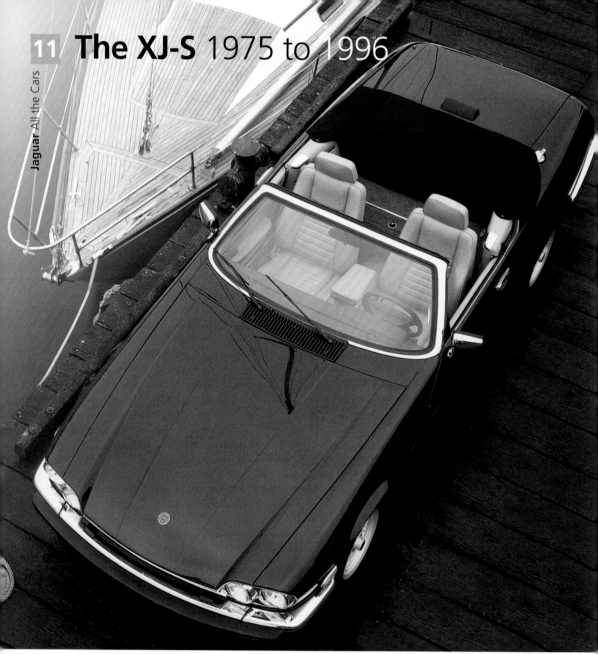

Background

With the demise of the E-type in 1974 few people realised that Jaguar would be abandoning the sports car market, for although the company had initially contemplated a direct replacement this was not to be – a situation brought about not so much by Jaguar, as by world opinion.

Most other manufacturers were abandoning the principle of an open top two-seater with rakish styling, plenty of noise, a relatively hard ride, and all the other features associated with the true sports car that marques like Jaguar, Triumph, and MG had become famous for.

Instead, changing legislation, the need for improved safety – particularly for the US market – and drivers wanting more refinement in an everyday car, forced manufacturers to think of producing coupés and grand touring cars that would cater for a wider audience and, if based on existing saloons, would be cheaper to produce and therefore more profitable.

Jaguar had, to some extent, already gone down this route with the Series 3 E-type, in that it was a much more refined car than previous Es. They had also introduced the ill-fated XJ coupé as an alternative to a four-door saloon in 1973, though it didn't actually appear until late in 1974 for 1975 delivery, and was abandoned in 1977, partly due to build problems.

This set the scene for the XJ-S or XJ 'sport', utilising the short wheelbase floorpan of the XJ saloon, essentially the same V12 engine and suspension, as well as many other mechanical and trim items, this being considered an economical way forward. Allied to this was Jaguar thinking that it would be best to move up-market with such a two-door coupé, no longer catering for a relatively small sports car audience but instead aiming at another market 'new' to Jaguar and at a much higher price. In fact the XJ-S was geared to be the most expensive production car the company had produced, so it was marketed at owners of Jensen Interceptors, Ferraris, Maseratis, and other well known luxury super-cars.

For the exterior design two basic ideas were considered, one coming from Jaguar's in-house styling department, the other from Malcolm Sayer, already well known for his work on the E-type. His design won out and was to be a radical move for Jaguar, virtually abandoning the traditional style and features normally expected from the marque. This had a negative effect on existing customers because the car was nothing like previous Jaguars – no wood veneer inside, hardly any chrome outside, avant-garde exterior styling, and not a Jaguar leaper to be found anywhere! The effect on the 'other' market was also not encouraging; Jaguar's poor 1970s reputation didn't help, and few considered that the XJ-S had the 'street cred' of, say, a Ferrari.

When launched at £8,900 it certainly wasn't cheap by Jaguar standards and was actually very close in price to competitors like the Mercedes SL and Porsche 911; and although faster than most, extreme thirst for fuel and worries over longevity proved deadly for the new car. Sales seemed reasonably encouraging for the first couple of years, but they soon started to decline, to the point where the Board at Jaguar considered dropping the whole project. This may have happened had it not been for the foresight of the new man at the helm, John Egan.

By 1981 the XJ-S had been revitalised with a more economical engine, improvements in build quality, and the restoration of some semblance of traditionalism. Sales started to rise, helped in addition by race track success in the US initially, and later in Europe courtesy of the TWR team competing in the European Touring Car Championship. In 1984 TWR won the championship and drivers' championship outright from BMW, and the popularity of the XJ-S soared.

Other models entered the range during the 1980s, offering cheaper alternatives and, with the cabriolet, a return to semi-open top motoring. Pressure from the US resulted in a full convertible, which appeared at the end of 1987 and gave another boost to a car and company

The original XJ-S cars, now known as Pre-HE, are identified by the black rubber bumper bars front and rear. For the first couple of years in production they also featured this matt black boot panel and chromed finisher to the B/C post area. All Pre-HE models had the Kent alloy wheels depicted here.

Frontal aspect of the Pre-HE XJ-S from 1975 to 1981, with black radiator grille and rubber bumper bars.

Pre-HE XJ-Ss featured no interior wood veneer, merely alloy and black. All cars from 1975 through to 1991 carried this style of bar gauge instrument binnacle.

From 1981 the car was called the XJ-S HE, identified from the side by its twin coachlines and starfish alloy wheels.

that were now in the throes of significantly better times. 1989 proved a record year for XJ-S sales, with over 10,000 being produced.

The model was totally rejuvenated in 1991 with a new bodyshell, yet greater improved quality, and a 4.0-litre engine (eventually a 6.0-litre was added as well). Year on year the XJS was improved, and even when the world became aware of a forthcoming entirely new replacement (the XK8) sales were still better than they had been in the 1970s or early 1980s.

Despite the XJ-S being considered early on as somewhat of an 'ugly duckling' it went through several revival stages, eventually earning its keep handsomely. Today it is still unique in its styling and is as instantly recognisable as the E-type. Over 115,000 were produced in its 21-year history and even its XK8 replacement is based on the same floorpan. The XJ-S turned out to be a fitting tribute to Jaguar and was perhaps the ultimate refined sporting grand tourer.

Model range and development

In simple terms there was but one model of XJ-S at its launch in September 1975, your only choices being from a very limited selection of exterior colour schemes and manual (four-speed) or three-speed automatic transmission.

Model at launch
XJ-S 5.3-litre coupé

This was the most expensive production car made by Jaguar up to that time, but for your £8,900 you got quite an inclusive package. Only available with the 5.3-litre V12 engine, now fuel injected, the XJ-S also benefited from leather upholstery, electric windows, air conditioning, and alloy wheels all as standard equipment. In terms of performance, with a 150mph plus top speed and acceleration to go with it, it was a match for anything Jaguar had ever produced before, and pretty close to most of the competition.

The downsides to the XJ-S were the body style, with its unusual 'flying buttresses' flowing down from the roof to the rear wings, and the lack of brightwork, woodwork, or even rear seat accommodation – and the price, which also reflected in the car's abysmal fuel economy! By 1980 annual sales had dwindled to just over 1,000 cars, which didn't warrant production. The manual transmission car hadn't been popular either.

Jaguar boss John Egan set about improving the concept and build quality of the XJ-S, which was effectively relaunched in 1981 as the XJ-S HE (standing for High Efficiency). The cylinder heads had been redesigned by May, and with improved combustion the V12 was now well capable of up

HE front view, with chromed grille and revised rubber-faced impact absorbing bumper bar treatment.

Rear view of HE model showing badging and rubber-faced bumper bar.

Above left: *Revised interior from the Pre-HE models, initially with burr elm woodwork, replaced from 1987 by walnut. Black fabric coverings to the centre console were also replaced by wood veneer in 1987. Steering wheel design changed to S3 XJ from S2 XJ style on Pre-HE models.*

Above right: *Starfish alloy wheels were only ever fitted to XJ-S models, initially as standard on the HE and the 3.6-litre cabriolet and then as an option on other cars up to 1991.*

to 20mpg if driven carefully. Jaguar also styled in some more traditional features like chromed topped rubber bumpers (adapted from the Series 3 saloons), a special set of Starfish alloy wheels just for this model, a swage coachline to break up the slab-sided look of the body and, inside, the return of veneer (elm). All this, accompanied by vastly improved build quality, set the XJ-S on a road to recovery and assured it of success second time around.

The next move to increase sales was by offering a wider range. A second XJ-S model was therefore launched with an alternative engine, a brand new 3.6-litre multi-valve straight six unit (AJ6) destined for a new saloon yet to appear, the XJ40. (Like Jaguar's earlier XK and V12 engines, the AJ6 was introduced in a sporting model, the XJ-S, before entering service in a saloon.) Slight changes in the standard of trim enabled the 3.6-litre XJ-S to be marked at a lower price to the top of the range V12 HE. The new model was also offered with a five-speed Getrag manual gearbox (the V12 being no longer available with any manual option) and was £2,000 cheaper to buy than the V12, offering better fuel economy. The 3.6 manual could even hold its own to 60mph against the larger-engined car.

Another new model appeared at the same time in an attempt to satisfy US demand for a convertible Jaguar. The XJ-S cabriolet introduced in 1983 offered a degree of hand finishing with a rear-section fold-away hood and front targa panels. Launched as a car to special order it was later to become available with the V12 engine as well but was never as popular as anticipated, due to the time it took to open and close the impractical top compared to the fully electrically operated concealed hoods of its competitors.

Jaguar eventually totally re-engineered the XJ-S bodyshell to create a proper two-seater convertible, announced at the end of 1987. This top of the range model, initially only available with the V12 engine, was sumptuously equipped with a fully electrically operated hood and even a glass heated rear screen. At £36,000 it was again the most expensive Jaguar you could buy and it was a hit in the US.

There was lots more publicity for the XJ-S in the 1980s of course, with three years in the European Touring Car Championship and the announcement of a sportier XJR-S special edition, initially produced by TWR themselves and later under the JaguarSport name as a joint venture with Jaguar. These cars offered a sports handling kit, improved brakes and engine manifolding, enhanced interior, and an exterior body kit if required. Jaguar also produced limited edition models specifically for different markets, like the Collection Rouge for the USA, and the Le Mans for European markets to celebrate Jaguar's 1988 and 1990 wins.

By 1989 more XJ-Ss had been produced than

Cabriolet models were introduced in 1984 with targa-top arrangement and XJ-SC badging on the boot lid.

Above left: Interior of the cabriolet model, now available with manual transmission. This car also features part-leather, part-cloth upholstery, available on all models from this time.

Above right: Rear seating was not fitted as standard on cabriolet models. Instead this box arrangement was fitted with luggage rails.

The XJS convertible from 1988, always equipped with these lattice alloy wheels as standard.

Seat design changed for the convertible, and was later fitted to other models as well. Electric seat adjustment was also available, with a generally improved trim level and walnut veneer. There were no rear seats, this new style of box arrangement being present instead, which was different to that of the cabriolet (see picture above). Note also revised steering wheel.

all the E-types ever made, and twice as many as the XK of the 1950s. However, sales started to tumble significantly in 1991 and Jaguar, without an alternative car to offer, re-engineered the XJ-S at a cost of over £50m and renamed it the XJS. This had a virtually entirely new bodyshell, though now easier to produce and galvanised. The overall styling was only subtly altered so as not to damage what was, after all, by now an established and accepted design. With smoothed out lines, improved glass area, a redesigned interior, a new 4.0-litre engine (with, later, a 6.0-litre V12 form as well), the XJS was relaunched yet again. This time there was not only the 4.0-litre coupé and convertible, but a 5.3-litre coupé and convertible and a 6.0-litre XJR-S JaguarSport performance model.

After an initial dip, sales rose again in 1993 and 1994, with yet more enhancements, the new 6.0-litre 318bhp V12 engine, changed frontal and rear styling features, and finally, in 1995, the 'Celebration' models to commemorate 60 years of the Jaguar marque and the final demise of the XJS.

Even in 1996 over 3,000 XJSs were delivered and at the time that its replacement, the XK8, was announced there were few new XJSs around in the dealers to sell. A total of 115,413 had been produced in 25 years, and the XJS had achieved Jaguar's dream of providing the ultimate grand tourer.

Several special editions were produced in the heyday of the XJ-S and many companies then and now produce modified versions, most of which commenced with TWR, the racing firm, for the European Touring Car Championship. It was TWR who produced the original Jaguar XJ-S Sport model, later adapted to the JaguarSport range (see below). Jaguar also at one time envisaged producing a Daimler XJ-S but only one was produced. A longer wheelbase model was even conceived, to provide more interior space.

A limited run of bespoke convertibles was also produced in America from standard coupé models with agreement from the factory. Manufactured by the Hess and Eisenhardt coachbuilding company, they were not only sanctioned by Jaguar but sold to special order through US dealerships. This only lasted until Jaguar introduced their own in-house convertible in 1987.

Exterior identification points

General points applicable to all XJ-Ss and XJSs

Front view

▪ Wrap-around bumper bar incorporated indicator lenses and number plate mounting in the centre (see photographs for different style post-1981).
▪ Front under-valance with air intake slatted

Lattice alloy wheels fitted from 1983, standard on V12 convertibles and as an option on all other models.

Limited edition models included the Le Mans car with US-style four headlight treatment.

The facelift model was introduced from 1991 with most body panels replaced. This convertible model shows the revised external look of these post-1991 cars, which at this time retained the rubber-faced bumper bars.

Comparison between the pre- and post-facelift models (the latter in the foreground), with revised rake to the windscreen, pillarless side windows without quarter-lights, and ...

grille, below which was a full-width black rubberised spoiler, on later models incorporated into all-enveloping bumper bar.

- Single oval headlights with surrounds featured, for UK and European cars, a conventional four headlight treatment, with chrome surround for US and Canadian models.
- Shallow radiator grille with horizontal slats, full width between headlights and central badge.
- One-piece forward-hinged bonnet, with front centrally mounted circular 'gunmetal' growler badge, swept down at front to meet radiator grille. Bonnet shaped to meet wings and headlight pods. AJ6 cars featured raised centre bonnet section to clear engine height, later adopted for all cars.
- Rear of bonnet bulkhead-mounted air intake in various finishes according to model and year.
- One-piece curved windscreen with chromed surround and twin wiper blades.

... revised side elevation. Note the rear side window changes and boot styling.

Analogue instrumentation introduced on the XJS from 1991, initially in wood veneer, later replaced by the style seen here except for V12-engined cars.

Rear view
- Rear heated screen with chromed surround following contours of roof and buttresses (coupé models).
- Flat boot panel with black-painted vertical section on early models only (see production changes).
- On boot vertical panel appropriate badging according to model and year (see photographs).
- Centre boot panel plinth contained twin reversing lights, hidden boot lock, and the name 'Jaguar' in bold lettering on a finisher surrounding boot key lock, later changed completely with facelift models (see photographs).
- Rear light units wrap around wings at base and sculptured to wing curvature at the top. Facelift models featured neutral density integrated light units (see photographs).
- Wrap-around bumper to match front, although in this case running for the entire length of rear wings to meet the rear wheel-arches.
- Twin exhaust tailpipes emerged from rear valance as on XJ saloons.

Side view
- Coupés of all ages are instantly identifiable by the flying buttress flowing down from roof panel to rear wings, on the nearside featuring concealed fuel filler cap.
- Slab-sided with waistline body crease. Later models featured swage coachlines according to model and year.
- Ford Cortina chromed flush door handles and black powder coated door and window surrounds with non-opening front quarter-lights. Facelift models abandoned door window frames, revised rear window treatment, and had new door handle design (see photographs).

More interior changes affected all models with the facelift, including a new centre console, better switchgear, and revised seating.

More changes from 1993, with all-enveloping plastic bumper bars painted to body colour. This is the later 2+2 convertible model, which necessitated a shallower rear window.

- Driver's door only mounted mirror on early cars. Later design changed and fitted mirrors both sides.
- Alloy wheels fitted to all cars of differing types according to model and year (see accompanying photographs).

XJ-S model specifics

Pre-HE coupés

- Black rubber bumper bars front and rear with no chrome finishers.
- Headlights and radiator grille with chromed surround.
- Separate under-valance black spoiler.
- Centrally mounted radiator grille depicted 'V12' emblem.
- 'XJ-S' only badging featured on boot panel.
- Matt black vertical boot panel only featured on very early cars.
- GKN Kent alloy wheels fitted.

XJ-S HE coupés

- New style rubber bumper bars front and rear incorporating chromed top finishers similar to those used on Series 3 XJ saloons. Different more prominent bumper bars featured on some US models.
- Growler badge in pewter style now fitted to forward centre area of bonnet. Side indicator repeater lenses on forward edge of front wings (larger type fitted to US and Canadian models).
- Five-spoke silver/grey Starfish alloy wheels fitted.
- Double-stripe swage coachline along entire length of body.
- Larger chrome-plated door mirrors now fitted to both doors.
- 'XJ-S' badge now moved to left-hand side from right and 'HE' badging fitted to other side of boot lid panel (later changed to 'V12').

XJ-S 3.6-litre coupés

- Growler badge in centre of radiator grille.
- New bonnet with raised centre section.
- Silver finish pepperpot alloy wheels, but Starfish were available as an option.
- '3.6' badging on right-hand side of boot lid.

Cabriolet (all models)

- Side view above door height revised with 'solid' frame, black powder coated with more pronounced B/C post with chromed leaper badge at base. Door and window surround as part of main body structure with chromed rain gutters.
- No rear wing buttresses.
- Coupé roof effectively cut away and replaced with fabric covered removable targa panels over driver and front seat passenger. Fabric-covered cross-over bar from side to side of the car, and behind it a fold-down fabric hood arrangement with Perspex rear screen.

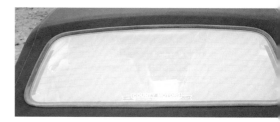

The deeper rear window of the earlier two-seater convertibles easily identifies these cars from the outside.

2+2 seating arrangement in the post-1992 convertibles.

Revised rear bumper bar treatment, which also included 'square' tailpipes.

Above left: *Later car interior, in this case a V12 with different seat stitching and, in this case, a half-wood/half-leather steering wheel, which was later also adopted for all Celebration models.*

Above right: *Five-spoke alloy wheels became available on XJS models from 1993.*

- All cabriolets fitted with either Starfish or lattice alloy wheels.
- At the rear 'XJ-SC' badging and either '3.6' or 'V12' dependent on model. Fuel filler moved to top of nearside rear wing utilising XJ Series chromed lockable cover.

Convertible models (up to 1991)
- Side view easily identifiable by the frameless construction of the windows with no quarter-lights.
- Fitted fabric hood with small rear windows that electrically descend into the body when hood mechanism operated.
- No rear wing buttresses, and fuel filler cap positioned and of the same type as on cabriolet models.
- Rear screen of glass with impregnated heating element.
- Boot badges followed coupé practice.
- All convertibles followed later coupé practice with thinner multi-coloured swage coachlines.

XJS models (post-1991 facelift)
- All cars now featured the 3.6-litre style bonnet panel with raised centre section.
- Revised style of under-valance air intake.
- Blackened radiator grille but with chrome horizontal top finisher.
- Recognisable from the side by the frameless door windows without quarter-lights and enlarged glass area to rear side windows (coupés only).
- Substantial chromed rain gutters curved to match frame of rear side windows (coupé models).
- Revised rake to front screen with thinner chromed surround.
- Lattice alloy wheels initially fitted to all models. Other styles and options became available later.
- Square design indicator repeaters now fitted to rear bottom edge of front wings (replaced by badges for some export markets).
- New style flush chromed door pulls and locks.
- More angular appearance at the rear with buttresses retained for coupé model.
- Neutral density rear lighting units now incorporate enlarged reflector units stretching across boot lid to meet centrally mounted number plate.
- Chromed surround at rear now incorporates central section for boot lock and number plate illumination.
- Stronger 'XJS' badging, also showing 'V12' badging where applicable to offside and 'Jaguar' to nearside.
- In all identification for post-facelift models, both written and badging, 'XJS' was used instead of 'XJ-S'.

XJS models (1993–6)
- An ease of identification point was the adoption of all-enveloping reinforced plastic

For a limited period in 1994 4.0-litre models gained colour-keyed brightwork around the headlights and door mirrors.

Last of the line top of the range V12 coupé with later 20-spoke alloy wheels, only fitted as standard on this model.

Last of the line 4.0-litre Celebration convertible with five-spoke alloy wheels (an alternative to the diamond-turned wheels available at this time).

Comparison frontal view of the three styles of XJ-S and XJS from the 1981 HE (centre), to facelift on the right, and Celebration on the left.

bumper bars at the front with chrome top finishers, and incorporating rectangular indicator lenses, number plate surround, under-bumper spoiler, and air intake and side reflectors at the front. Bumpers painted to body colour.

■ For a period of about a year V12 models identified by chromed surrounds to headlights and wing mirrors, with 4.0-litres identified by these areas being colour-keyed. Later changed so that all models returned to chromed finish.

■ At the rear same style of bumper bar treatment with integrated rear fog lights.

■ Square or oval exhaust tailpipes according to model.

■ Convertible rear screen altered to a smaller size to accommodate fold-down around 2+2 seating arrangement (see interior changes).

■ Most cars fitted with new five-spoke alloy wheels but others available to order.

■ From 1995 'Celebration' models featured Aerosport diamond turned alloy wheels, chromed surround to rear number plate, and restyled bonnet badge.

NB: Variations in alloy wheel type occurred several times during production and were available as extra cost options anyway. See production changes and accessories listing.

Factory special editions

■ **Collection Rouge**: Only available to the US market. Finished in Signal Red with matching diamond turned and painted lattice alloy wheels and gold coachline. US-style four headlight treatment and revised badging, with 'Collection Rouge' on boot lid and gold plated growler badge on bonnet.

■ **Classic Collection**: Only available to the US market. Similar to Collection Rouge except limited range of exterior colours, new 'Classic' badging on boot lid, and rear spoiler fitted to most cars. Revised front badging as Rouge.

■ **Le Mans**: Only available in European markets to commemorate Le Mans wins in 1988 and 1990. US four headlight treatment at front with gold growler badge on bonnet. Front spoiler painted to body colour. Twin gold coachlines along side of car and unique 'Le Mans' badging on boot panel. Lattice wheels and sports suspension fitted. Limited range of exterior paint finishes.

■ **JaguarSport XJR-S models**: Factory-build standard XJ-S shipped down to JaguarSport Bloxham works in Oxfordshire for final finishing, much of which was dependent on individual customer order. Replacement of front and rear bumpers by pre-formed plastic type painted to body colour. Front bumper incorporated indicator lighting as usual but also under-valance and air intake. Front radiator and

Unique to the XJ-S were the TWR JaguarSport models built as a joint venture between Jaguar and the TWR Company, offering a more sporty appeal at a premium price. This early example with a modified 6.0-litre engine shows typical JaguarSport options like the bodykit and wheels and slightly lower set suspension.

Revised interior for JaguarSport cars included leather-covered gear knob, special steering wheel, and badging.

Rear-end treatment for JaguarSport models included bumper kit, four exhaust tailpipes, revised badging, and spoiler.

Facelift style XJR-S by JaguarSport before production ceased at the end of 1992. Here the later style of body has been adapted to a similar specification to that of the earlier models, with new-style Sport wheels.

light surrounds black powder coated. Door mirrors colour keyed to exterior paint finish, as was rear bumper which incorporated hazard lighting and under-valance with exhaust tailpipes. Brightwork again finished to either body colour or black powder coated. Speedline alloy wheels fitted with flush centre caps hiding wheel nuts. Wider wheels and tyres to suit. Over-sills to body sill areas painted to body colour. Boot lid spoiler curving down over both rear wings with hole drilled to accommodate radio aerial. Later post-1991 facelift cars adapted to same styling basis but with revised panels. Rear boot spoiler changed so as not to infringe on radio aerial. New alloy wheels with exposed wheel nuts.

NB: Models produced by outside companies, including the initial TWR car, are not covered in this book.

Interior identification points

Pre-HE models (1975–81)

- Predominantly black trim finish to dashboard and centre console area with bright alloy areas around radio/air conditioning panel and auxiliary switch/clock panel.
- Instrumentation binnacle mounted directly in front of the driver incorporating speedometer, rev counter, and bar gauges for ancillary instruments. Row of warning lights above and below in plastic surround.
- Two-spoke steering wheel with leather surround of same design as early Series 2 saloons.
- Air conditioning ventilator layout at each end of dashboard adjustable, and in central area following Series 2 XJ format.
- Centre console layout as Series 2 saloons but with shallower slope to mid-area leading up to armrest.
- Lockable glove-box on passenger side of dashboard.
- Bucket-type seating with horizontal pleats in the leather inserts and incorporating built in headrests. Seat adjustment to allow access to rear compartment.
- Rear sculptured seat area to match style of front.
- Door panels heat embossed with full-length armrests/door pulls and built in pockets.
- Door handles and lock mechanisms as XJ saloons and lower panels incorporating carpet areas and speaker grilles.
- Rear side windows do not open.
- All Pre-HE XJ-Ss were finished in leather trim, but cloth available to special order.
- Boot trimmed in black carpet with pre-formed plastic spare wheel cover.

Later type spoiler treatment on the XJR-S model was also available for the standard cars.

Different styles of coachline were used on XJ-S models. Pre HE models had no coachline. HE and 3.6-litre cars featured this style of double line.

Twin thin opposing colour lines used on cars from 1988 on.

After facelift a single colour line was adopted.

HE and V12 models (1981–91)

- Burr elm veneered woodwork fitted to horizontal sections of dashboard and auxiliary switch panel. From 1987 also fitted to ski-slope on centre console.
- Elm woodwork cappings also fitted to revised style door trims without heat embossing in trim.
- Black vinyl replaced previous bright alloy finish around centre console area. Veneer on later cars changed to burr walnut (see production changes).
- Steering wheel of later XJ type with more rectangular centre boss and thicker rim, replaced again in 1987 by one incorporating finger grips. Two horn push buttons to centre spoke.
- Rear seating now incorporated built-in seat belt connectors.
- Boot now carpeted in grey with black soft spare wheel cover.

NB: After 1989 other changes took place according to model, such as the fitting of another (four-spoke) steering wheel, revised seating, etc. See production changes.

3.6-litre models (1983–91)

- As HE and V12 except for seats having part leather/part tweed covering to centre sections on standard models, all-leather being an extra cost option.
- Manual gearbox models featured black leather gaiter to gear lever on centre console, replacing auto transmission quadrant, and stitched leather gear knob.

Cabriolet models

- As above 3.6, HE and V12 models but door trims all leather. Revised windscreen surround to accommodate catches for targa panels. Catches also located in centre strengthening bar in roof.
- Twin targa panels made from glass fibre and upholstered inside with black circular locks initially, later chromed handles.
- Rear hood section lined and manually folded back after releasing black circular lock from strengthening bar.
- Rear seating removed and replaced by carpeted box area with two lockable lids incorporating luggage rails and, in the footwells, map pockets.
- Carpeted rear section to bulkhead.
- Black fabric envelope provided in boot to accommodate targa panels when removed from the roof.
- When hood down, a matching coloured tonneau fitted by studs and Velcro covered the hood.

Convertible models (1987–91)

- As coupés except for enhanced leather interior.

- Burr walnut veneer instead of elm.
- New seat design with stiffer bolsters and electric adjustment operated from control pads on side of centre console.
- Rear compartment featured stiffened and carpeted bulkhead area and one-piece storage box with lockable lid and luggage rail.
- Hood fully lined.

All facelift models (1991–6)

- Revised dashboard layout incorporating analogue instrumentation to binnacle in front of drive with revised ignition/starter and lighting switches.
- Centre dash section also revised with touch sensitive switchgear, new digital clock, and/or on-board computer.
- New audio/air conditioning layout. Smoother switchgear to console area, squared-off trim areas to centre console.
- Front seating similar to previous Convertible, now all with electrical adjustment on door trims.
- Frameless door windows (coupé models) with no quarter-lights.
- Rear seating amended in style to suit front, incorporating seat belt connectors. Cloth and leather trim alternatives available on coupés.
- Occasional rear seating fitted from 1992 on convertible models, necessitating a new bodyshell and revised bulkhead area behind.
- Hood amended, with a shallower window to accommodate rear seating when hood down.
- By 1994 seating style altered again with ruched leather available on certain models and two-tone dashboard trim.
- 'Celebration' models featured half wood/leather steering wheel, available on other cars as option.

Factory special editions

- **Collection Rouge**: Only available to the US market. Magnolia interior piped red, with red carpets and burr elm woodwork.
- **Classic Collection**: Only available to the US market. Leather interior matching to exterior colour, pale finishes with contrast colour piping. Walnut veneer and better quality carpeting.
- **Le Mans**: Only available to European markets. Revised type seating from the convertible in Autolux leather with contrast colour piping and carpets (better quality). Embossed 'Le Mans' name to headrests. Leather-covered steering wheel and gear knob, and door tread plates depicting car number and wins at Le Mans. Darker wood staining. Boot similarly trimmed.
- **JaguarSport XJR-S models**: Improved seating with embossed 'XJR' logos, Autolux leather, matching leather-covered steering wheel and door trims. Walnut veneer.

Technical specifications

	5.3-litre Pre-HE	5.3-litre HE
cc	5,343	5,343
Bore and stroke (mm)	90 x 70	90 x 70
Compression ratio	9:1	11.5:1
bhp	285	299
@ rpm	5,800	5,800
Torque (lb ft)	294	318
@ rpm	3,500	3,000
Fuelling	Fuel injection	Fuel injection
Transmission	GM 3-speed auto 4-speed (all synchro) limited	GM 3-speed auto
Wheel size (in)	15, alloy	15, alloy
Suspension front	Ind wishbone, coils, anti-dive	Ind wishbone, coils, anti-dive
Suspension rear	Ind lower wishbone, upper drivelink, radius arms, coil springs	Ind lower wishbone, upper drivelink, radius arms, coil springs
Brakes	4 wheel disc, rear inboard	4 wheel disc, rear inboard
Performance		
0–60mph (sec)	6.9	6.5
Top speed (mph)	153	150
Average mpg	12.8	17.9
Dimensions		
Length (in)	191.75	191.75
Width (in)	70.5	70.5
Height (in)	49.6	50.4
Wheelbase (in)	102	102
Front track (in)	58.5	58.5
Rear track (in)	58	58
Weight (cwt)	33.2	35

Technical specifications *cont …*

	6.0-litre	3.6-litre
cc	5,993	3,590
Bore and stroke (mm)	90 x 78.5	91 x 92
Compression ratio	11:1	9.6:1
bhp	308	221
@ rpm	5,350	5,100
Torque (lb ft)	355	249
@ rpm	2,850	4,000
Fuelling	Fuel injection	Fuel injection
Transmission	GM 3-speed auto	5-speed (all synchro)
		ZF 4-speed auto
Wheel size (in)	15, alloy	15, alloy
Suspension front	Ind wishbone, coils, anti-dive	Ind wishbone, coils, anti-dive
Suspension rear	Ind lower wishbone, upper drivelink, radius arms, coil springs	Ind lower wishbone, upper drivelink, radius arms, coil springs
Brakes	4 wheel disc, rear outboard	4 wheel disc, rear outboard
Performance		
0–60mph (sec)	6.6	7.2
Top speed (mph)	161	137
Average mpg		17.6
Dimensions		
Length (in)	189.75	191.75
Width (in)	70.5	70.5
Height (in)	48.8	50.4
Wheelbase (in)	102	102
Front track (in)	58.5	58.5
Rear track (in)	58	58
Weight (cwt)	36.6	32

	4.0-litre
cc	3,980
Bore and stroke (mm)	91 x 102
Compression ratio	9.5:1
bhp	223
@ rpm	4,750
Torque (lb ft)	278
@ rpm	3,650
Fuelling	Fuel injection
Transmission	5-speed (all synchro)
	ZF 4-speed auto
Wheel size (in)	15, alloy
Suspension front	Ind wishbone, coils, anti-dive
Suspension rear	Ind lower wishbone, upper
	drivelink, radius arms, coil springs
Brakes	4 wheel disc, rear inboard, later outboard
Performance	
0–60mph (sec)	7.4
Top speed (mph)	137
Average mpg	26
Dimensions	
Length (in)	191.75
Width (in)	70.5
Height (in)	49.2
Wheelbase (in)	102
Front track (in)	58.5
Rear track (in)	58
Weight (cwt)	32

Optional extras

Pre-HE models
Manual four-speed all synchromesh gearbox.
Fog/spot lights mounted underneath front
    bumper bar.
Rear seat belts.
Sundym tinted glass.
Radio/cassette or cartridge system.
Passenger side door mirror.
Mud flaps.
US four headlights with trim and surrounds.
Cloth upholstery.
Whitewall tyres.

HE, V12, and 3.6-litre coupés up to 1991
Automatic transmission (alternative to auto on
    3.6-litre engines).
Fog/spot lights mounted underneath front
    bumper bar.
Rear seat belts (early cars only).
Enhanced radio/cassette system.
Mud flaps.
US four headlights with trim and surrounds.
Cloth upholstery.
Whitewall tyres.
Lattice wheels of two sizes (dependent on
    model).
Starfish alloys (where not equipped).
Kent alloy wheels.
Cruise control.
On-board computer.
Tailored over-mats.
Headlight wash/wipe system.
Integrated hi-fi system with CD player.
Leather upholstery where cloth fitted as standard.
Boot rack with specialist fittings for skis, etc.
Wood veneer gear knob.

Cabriolets
As above plus:
Hood envelope to store hood when off the car.
Glass fibre/fabric covered hardtop with built in
    glass screen and heating element.
Wind deflector to fit on screen rail above rear
    view mirror.

Post-1991 cars
Side body mouldings painted to body colour.
Black rubber/chrome side body mouldings
    incorporated Jaguar logo.
Fog/spot lights mounted underneath front
    bumper bar.
Enhanced radio/cassette system.
Mud flaps.
US four headlights with trim and surrounds.
Cloth upholstery.
Whitewall tyres.
Cruise control.
On-board computer.
Tailored over-mats.
Headlight wash/wipe system.
Integrated hi-fi system with CD player.
Leather upholstery where cloth fitted as standard.
Boot rack with specialist fittings for skis, etc.
Wood veneer gear knob.
Sheepskin over-rugs.
Child's safety seat.
Child's booster cushion.
First aid kit for boot area.
Space-saver spare wheel.
Fire extinguisher for boot area.
Jaguar warning triangle.
Headlamp converters.
Headlamp safety covers.
Roof box (coupés only).
Mobile telephone kits.
Sports suspension option (where not standard).
Lattice wheels (two sizes).
Five-spoke wheels (alloy or chrome).
JaguarSport Speedline wheels.
Diamond turned wheels.
20-spoke wheels.

Colour schemes

Exterior colour	Details	Interior trim	Details	Interior	Details
XJ-S Pre-HE		**Leather**		**Cloth**	
Old English White	To 1977	Russet		Sand	From 1976
		Dark Blue		Garnet	From 1976
		Cinnamon		Ebony	From 1976
		Black			
Tudor White	From 1977	Russet		Sand	
		Biscuit		Garnet	
		Black		Ebony	
Dark Blue		Russet		Sand	From 1976
		Dark Blue		Ebony	From 1976
		Biscuit		Garnet	From 1976
		Black			
Cobalt Blue	From 1978	Cinnamon		Sand	
		Dark Blue		Navy	
		Black		Ebony	
British Racing Green	To 1977	Biscuit		Sand	From 1976
		Cinnamon		Ebony	From 1976
		Moss Green	1975 only		
		Black			
Racing Green Metallic	From 1977	Biscuit		Sand	
		Cinnamon		Ebony	
		Black			
Regency Red		Biscuit		Sand	From 1976
		Cinnamon		Ebony	From 1976
		Russet	1975 only		
		Black			
Damson Red	From 1977	Russet		Sand	
		Cinnamon		Garnet	
		Black		Ebony	
Black*		Russet		Sand	From 1976
		Black		Ebony	From 1976
		Cinnamon		Garnet	From 1976
		Biscuit			
Signal Red	To 1977	Biscuit		Sand	From 1976
		Russet	1975 only	Ebony	From 1976
		Black			
Sebring Red	From 1978	Biscuit		Sand	
		Dark Blue		Navy	
		Black		Ebony	
Silver*	To 1977	Russet	1975 only	Sand	From 1976
		Biscuit		Ebony	From 1976
		Dark Blue		Garnet	From 1976
		Black			
Coronet Gold	From 1978	Russet			
		Biscuit			
		Black			

Colour schemes *cont ...*

The XJS 1975 to 1996

Exterior colour	Details	Interior trim	Details	Interior	Details
Silver Frost	1976–7	Russet		Navy	
		Dark Blue		Garnet	
		Black		Ebony	
Carriage Brown		Biscuit		Sand	From 1976
		Cinnamon		Ebony	From 1976
		Black			
Chestnut Brown	From 1978	Cinnamon		Sand	
		Biscuit		Ebony	
		Black			
Squadron Blue	To 1978	Biscuit		Sand	From 1976
		Dark Blue		Navy	From 1976
		Black		Ebony	From 1976
Quartz Blue	From 1978	Biscuit		Sand	
		Dark Blue		Navy	
		Black		Ebony	
Yellow Gold	1976–7	Dark Blue		Ebony	From 1976
		Black			
Cotswold Yellow	From 1978	Dark Blue		Sand	
		Cinnamon		Navy	
		Black		Ebony	
Juniper Green	From 1976	Biscuit		Sand	
		Cinnamon		Ebony	
		Black			
Moroccan Bronze	From 1976	Biscuit		Sand	
		Cinnamon		Ebony	
		Black			
XJ-S and XJS later models		**Leather**		**Cloth**	
Tudor White	To 1987	Isis Blue		Fleet Blue	
		County Tan	To 1984		
		Mulberry	From 1984		
Portland Beige	To 1984	Burnt Umber		Graphite	
		Black			
Cobalt Blue	To 1987	Doeskin		Beige	
		Biscuit			
Racing Green	To 1985	Biscuit		Beige	
		Doeskin			
Claret	To 1987	Doeskin		Beige	
		Biscuit			
Black*		Doeskin	Plus post 1987 choice		
		Isis Blue			
		Savile Grey	From 1984		
		Charcoal	From 1987		

Exterior colour	Details	Interior trim	Details	Interior	Details
Silversand	1984–6	Doeskin		Graphite	From 1984
		Burnt Umber	To 1984		
		Black	From 1984		
Sebring Red	To 1987	Biscuit		Fleet Blue	To 1984
		Isis Blue		Beige	To 1984
		Black		Graphite	From 1984
Rhodium Silver	To 1987	County Tan	To 1984	Graphite	
		Mulberry	From 1984		
		Black			
Chestnut Brown	To 1984	County Tan		Graphite	
		Biscuit			
		Black			
Sapphire Blue (light)	To 1986	Isis Blue		Fleet Blue	
		Biscuit		Beige	
Grosvenor Brown	To 1985	County Tan	To 1984	Beige	
		Buckskin	From 1984		
		Biscuit			
Sable Brown	To 1984	Doeskin		Beige	
		Biscuit			
Coronet Gold	To 1986	Buckskin		Graphite	
		Burnt Umber	To 1984		
		Black			
Indigo Blue	To 1984	Isis Blue			
		Doeskin			
Clarendon Blue	1984–6	Savile Grey			
		Doeskin			
Cirrus Grey	1984 –6	Buckskin		Beige	
		Biscuit			
Cranberry	1984–7	Doeskin		Graphite	
		Black			
Regent Grey	1984–7	Savile Grey			
		Doeskin			
Sage Green	1984–6	Doeskin		Beige	
Antelope	1984–7	Buckskin			
		Mulberry			
		Doeskin	From 1986		
Windsor Blue	1986–7	Biscuit			
		Savile Grey			
Steel Blue	1986–7	Doeskin			
		Isis Blue			
Mineral Blue	To 1983	Biscuit			
Claret	To 1986	Doeskin			
		Biscuit			

181

Colour schemes *cont* ...

Exterior colour Single	Details	Interior trim	Details
Nimbus White	1987 only	Isis Blue†	To 1994
Westminster Blue	From 1987	Savile Grey†	To 1994
Jaguar Racing Green	To 1990	Doeskin†	To 1994
Grenadier Red	1987–91	Biscuit†	To 1992
Alpine Green	1987–90	Buckskin†	To 1994
Arctic Blue	1987–92	Mulberry†	To 1992
Bordeaux Red	1987–92	Barley†	To 1994
Crimson	1987–90	Magnolia†	To 1994
Dorchester Grey	1987–90	Cream†	From 1992
Moorland Green	1987–90	Parchment††	From 1992
Satin Beige	1987–92	Cherry Red†	1992–4
Silver Birch	1987–9	Oatmeal†	From 1994
Solent Blue	1987–94	Coffee†	From 1994
Sovereign Gold	1987 only	Nimbus Grey†	From 1994
Talisman Silver	1987–92	Regatta Blue†	From 1994
Tungsten	1987–92	Warm Charcoal†	From 1994
Glacier White	From 1988		
Signal Red	From 1988		
Savoy Grey	1990–2		
Diamond Blue	1990–4	**Tweed**	
Mica Jade Green	From 1990	Pennine Black†	1987–92
Mica Gunmetal	1990 to 1994	Chiltern Beige†	1987–92
Mica Regency Red	1990 to 1994	Cotswold†	1987–92
Brooklands Green	1991–2 only	Cheviot Grey†	1987–92
Tuscany Bronze	1991 only	**Hood**	
Meteor Red	1992 only	Blue†	
British Racing Green	From 1992	Black†	
Kingfisher Blue	From 1992	Brown†	
Platinum	From 1992	Beige†	From 1988
Silver Frost	From 1992	Burgandy†	From 1993
Oyster	From 1992	**Sculp Fabric**	
Mica Flamenco	From 1992	Doeskin†	1992–4
Mica Morocco Red	From 1992	Barley†	1992–4
Mica Rose Bronze	From 1993	Savile Grey†	1992–4
Sapphire Blue (dark)	From 1994	Isis Blue†	1992–4
Titanium	From 1994	Oatmeal†	From 1994
Ice Blue	From 1994	Coffee†	From 1994
Topaz	From 1994	Nimbus Grey†	From 1994
Steel Grey	From 1994	Regatta Blue†	From 1994

† = open choice by customer

* = special order only

Prices and production volumes

Pre-facelift models

	Price new (£)	1975	1976	1977	1978	1979	1980
XJ-S Pre-HE	8,900	■	■	■	■	■	■
XJ-S HE coupé	18,950	–	–	–	–	–	–
XJ-S V12 coupé	21,700	–	–	–	–	–	–
XJ-S V12 cabriolet	26,995	–	–	–	–	–	–
XJ-S V12 convertible	36,000	–	–	–	–	–	–
XJR-S coupé	35,000	–	–	–	–	–	–
XJ-S 3.6-litre coupé	19,248	–	–	–	–	–	–
XJ-S 3.6-litre cabriolet	20,756	–	–	–	–	–	–

	Price new (£)	1981	1982	1983	1984	1985	1986
XJ-S Pre-HE	8,900	■	–	–	–	–	–
XJ-S HE coupé	18,950	■	■	■	■	■	■
XJ-S V12 coupé	21,700	–	–	–	–	–	–
XJ-S V12 cabriolet	26,995	–	–	–	–	■	■
XJ-S V12 convertible	36,000	–	–	–	–	–	–
XJR-S coupé	35,000	–	–	–	–	–	–
XJ-S 3.6-litre coupé	19,248	–	–	■	■	■	■
XJ-S 3.6-litre cabriolet	20,756	–	–	■	■	■	■

	Price new (£)	1987	1988	1989	1990	1991	Total produced
XJ-S Pre-HE	8,900	–	–	–	–	–	15,526
XJ-S HE coupé	18,950	■	–	–	–	–	29,944
XJ-S V12 coupé	21,700	■	■	■	■	■	16,159
XJ-S V12 cabriolet	26,995	■	–	–	–	–	3,863
XJ-S V12 convertible	36,000	■	■	■	■	■	11,571
XJR-S coupé	35,000	–	■	■	■	■	448
XJ-S 3.6-litre coupé	19,248	■	■	■	■	■	8,867
XJ-S 3.6-litre cabriolet	20,756	■	–	–	–	–	1,150
Total Pre-facelift production							**87,528**

Prices and production volumes *cont ...*

	Price new (£)	1991	1992	1993	1994	1995	1996
Facelift models							
XJS V12 5.3-litre coupé	43,500	■	■	■	–	–	–
XJS V12 5.3-litre convertible	50,600	■	■	■	–	–	–
XJS V12 6.0-litre coupé	45,100	–	–	■	■	■	■
XJS V12 6.0-litre convertible	52,900	–	–	■	■	■	■
XJR-S 6.0-litre coupé	45,500	■	■	■	–	–	–
XJR-S 6.0-litre convertible	–	■	–	–	–	–	–
XJS 4.0-litre coupé	33,400	■	■	■	■	■	■
XJS 4.0-litre convertible	39,000	■	■	■	■	■	■

	Price new (£)	Total produced
XJS V12 5.3-litre coupé	43,500	1,199
XJS V12 5.3-litre convertible	50,600	3,674
XJS V12 6.0-litre coupé	45,100	774
XJS V12 6.0-litre convertible	52,900	1,787
XJR-S 6.0-litre coupé	45,500	787
XJR-S 6.0-litre convertible	–	50
XJS 4.0-litre coupé	33,400	5,667
XJS 4.0-litre convertible	39,000	13,864
Total facelift production		**27,802**
Total XJS production		**115,330**

Chassis numbers

Model	Right/ Left Drive	Chassis/ Vin Nos Commencing
XJ-S coupé	RHD	2W 1001
	LHD	2W 50001
XJ-S coupé (post 78) and all subsequent models	Later models post '78 Vin No. (see table 2*)	

*Table 2 appears on page 317.

Production changes

1975
XJ-S Pre-HE model introduced.

1976
Chromed B/C door pillar deleted.

1977
GM400 automatic transmission replaced Borg
Warner unit.

1978
Chromed radiator grille fitted.
Matt black boot panel deleted.
Manual transmission model deleted from range.

1979
Larger square type exterior door mirrors fitted.
Trim colour centre console adopted.
Radio aerial mounted to offside instead of
nearside.

1980
Rear fog lamps fitted to bumper.
P-Digital fuel injection system fitted.
Aerial now flush-fitted to rear wing.

1981
XJ-S HE model introduced.
Rear anti-roll bar deleted.
Black vinyl spare wheel cover in boot replaced
solid type.

1983
XJ-S 3.6-litre coupé and cabriolet models
introduced.

1984
Hard plastic front spoiler fitted.

1985
V12 cabriolet model introduced.
Sun visors colour-keyed to trim hereafter.
Cloth seat option became available.

1986
Introduction of H & E US-adapted convertibles.
Mark III air conditioning system fitted to all
models.
Three-point inertia reel seat-belts fitted.

1987
Wood veneered ski slopes fitted to centre
console.
Two windscreen-washer jets replaced the one
previously used.
Heated door mirrors fitted.
Stainless steel sill tread plates adopted.
Revised style of steering wheel.

Locking filler cap adopted for coupé models.
Electric lumbar support fitted to V12 models.
Sports suspension pack available for six-cylinder
models.
Rear anti-roll bar reintroduced.
3.6-litre cabriolet model deleted from range.

1988
V12 cabriolet model deleted from range.
TEVES ABS system introduced.
Side coachline stripes redesigned.
V12 convertible introduced.
XJR-S model introduced.

1989
US Collection Rouge model introduced.
XJR-S 6.0-litre model introduced.
Wipers changed to park on opposite side of
screen.
Tilt action steering column introduced.
Ignition switch moved to steering column from
dashboard.
Trim co-ordinated dash roll available.
Driver's side air bag fitted to US specification
models.
Restyled exterior door handles.

1990
Le Mans special edition introduced.
Catalytic converters standardised on all models.

1991
Facelift models introduced (XJS).

1992
4.0-litre convertible model introduced.
Driver's side air bag standardised on all cars.
Improved under-floor bracing for convertible
models.

1993
Colour-keyed plastic bumper bars fitted.
2+2 seating now fitted to convertible models.
6.0-litre V12 engine fitted to V12 models.

1994
AJ16 power unit replaced AJ6 six-cylinder unit.
Passenger side air bags fitted to all cars.

1995
Celebration models introduced.
V12-engined cars deleted from range unless to
special order.

1996
XJS production terminated.

Background

The Jaguar company had gone through some trying times in the 1970s and apart from regular upgrades of their only saloons, the XJ6/12, had not produced an entirely new car since 1968. Even after the introduction of the last version of this model, the Series 3, the company was still experiencing problems in build quality, the cars being produced by out-dated manufacturing methods which also made them too costly to build. At least some of these problems must be laid at the feet of British Leyland.

Jaguar had, however, been working on a new replacement saloon as far back as the Series 2 XJ – in fact, small-scale models had been produced as early as 1972. With so much energy being absorbed by the development of the existing XJs and the upcoming XJ-S, the 'new' project (code named XJ40) was not given the priority it deserved. Jaguar was also hampered by continuous interference from British Leyland, which at one time actually considered using the Rover V8 (ex-Buick) engine in the new car, which would have meant the end of engine production at Jaguar.

Just as Jaguar had approached Pininfarina regarding the restyling of the Series 3 XJ, they also encouraged them – and other Italian designers – to put in proposals for the new car, none of which proved suitable.

It wasn't until just before John Egan arrived on the scene at Jaguar that BL actually approved a £32m investment in a new engine (the AJ6, first seen in the XJ-S in 1983). It wasn't then until 1981 – more than three years after the Series 3 XJ had been announced – that the Board agreed to a further £80m investment in the XJ40 project after finally agreeing the exterior design from a glass fibre mock-up.

It appeared that speed was of the essence by this time and the money was approved on the undertaking that the XJ40 would be ready for launch by 1983. This was never a practical deadline and in the meantime it was fortunate that Jaguar's image improved dramatically, leading to an upsurge in sales of its existing models. This gave the company more time to develop the XJ40 into a better car. Deadlines came and went and it wasn't until the British Motor Show of 1986 that the XJ40 finally arrived, with two engine sizes (2.9-litre and 3.6-litre), two styles of trim, and a Daimler-badged model.

The XJ40 brought Jaguar up to date with all-new technology, being electronically the most technically advanced car in the world at the time (bar the ill-fated Aston Martin Lagonda). It was also quicker and cheaper to produce, more economical to run, and therefore the most significant new model since the original XJ6. Despite all that was 'new' with the car Jaguar decided to call it XJ6 again, though it was and still is widely known by its XJ40 factory code-name, which conveniently distinguishes it from its forebear.

Due to demand and other practicalities the XJ40 wasn't launched in the US until 1987, by which time it was already proving to be a great success in the UK market. Some Series 3 XJ6s had trickled through until April 1987, and Jaguar ended up with a two saloon model line-up in that the V12-engined Series 3 models would continue on into the early 1990s.

The XJ40 model range was tight but effective, even if many people considered the smaller-engined 2.9-litre car to be under-powered. This was eventually replaced in 1990 by a 3.2 version of the larger unit, which itself was enlarged to 4.0 litres in 1989.

1988 and 1989 proved to be momentous years for Jaguar because it sold more cars then than it had ever done before. Most of this was down to the XJ40, which sold 39,432 units in 1988 and 32,833 in 1989, the 40's best ever years.

As the original bodyshell of the XJ40 had never been designed to take the big V12 engine (a throw-back to Jaguar personnel deliberately 'engineering out' any chance of getting the Rover V8 in!), a V12 XJ40 didn't arrive on the scene until 1993, by which time the old Series 3 models had disappeared.

Jaguar had long been known as an 'old man's' car, and in order to redress this situation the XJ40 tried to capture a younger market with its Sport model of 1993–4. Relatively subtle changes to exterior and interior had a slight effect, but only just over 3,600 were actually sold. Jaguar also got concerned about sales late on when there was public awareness about a replacement model for the end of 1994 (the X-300). For that last year, therefore, it announced yet another model, the Gold, offering a high degree of standard equipment at a special offer price.

Along the way the joint venture with TWR, JaguarSport, produced more sporty versions of the XJ40. A very limited run of long wheelbase Majestic models was also made to order. In the valued US market several special editions were marketed, bringing back the Vanden Plas and Majestic names.

The XJ40 was a vital model to Jaguar, coming at just the right time. It saw the company out of BL control, into private ownership, and then into the Ford empire. Although only in production from 1986 to 1994 over 208,000 cars were made, and even the replacement X-300 owes much to the XJ40.

Model range and development

When one considers that the Series 3 V12 models were still produced for much of the XJ40 period,

Although exactly the same bodyshell was used for all XJ40 models, numerous changes differentiate each car. The standard XJ6 models all featured the four headlight treatment and plastic hubcaps on steel wheels. XJ6 models also used powder-coated black window surrounds as depicted here.

Top of the range Sovereign and Daimler models featured rectangular headlight units and chromed window surrounds.

Daimler styling cues involved swage line chrome trims along the entire length of the body, chromed window surrounds as Sovereign, and alloy wheels.

During the first year in production the Jaguar Sovereign model featured this black-painted boot panel like the Daimler.

the initial range of new models was comprehensive for Jaguar at this time.

Models available at launch (manual and auto transmission variants)
Jaguar XJ6 2.9-litre saloon
Jaguar XJ6 3.6-litre saloon
Jaguar Sovereign 2.9-litre saloon
Jaguar Sovereign 3.6-litre saloon
Daimler 3.6-litre saloon

The XJ6 models were effectively the base models of the range. Indeed, the 2.9-litre was offered at a price of just over £16,000 (cheaper than any Jaguar produced since 1983) in an attempt to enter the management fleet market. In neither engine size these cars did not feature such luxuries as leather upholstery, air conditioning, alloy wheels, ABS, or automatic transmission within the basic price. You did, however, get an on-board computer, the then entirely new Vehicle Condition Monitor, and a five-speed manual gearbox.

The Sovereign models were aimed fairly and squarely at traditional Jaguar customers, usually businessmen with a company-supplied vehicle. Better equipped than the outgoing Series 3 Sovereign models, you got ABS, rear ride height adjustable suspension, eight-way electrically adjustable front seats, and six-speaker hi-fi radio/cassette system. That was on top of the usual Sovereign equipment, such as air conditioning, headlight wash/wipe, cruise control, on-board computer, etc. The one things you still had to pay extra for initially were alloy wheels.

The Daimler was the most expensive and therefore top of the range vehicle, built to the usual standards by Jaguar with fluted external trim treatment and different shaping to the seating. The Sovereign and Daimler models, although utilising the same bodyshell as the XJ6s, had a different frontal lighting treatment which instantly differentiates them.

Manual and automatic transmission were offered throughout the range, the latter utilising a new 'J-gate' control quadrant, unique to Jaguar and still used to this day. This allowed a certain degree of manual control over intermediate gears.

Apart from the usual minor changes and manufacturing modifications, the range ran virtually unaltered until 1988, when a new car appeared, the XJR. Based on the 3.6-litre model, this vehicle was enhanced by the JaguarSport company at its Oxfordshire premises. According to customer requirements, the model received a new exterior paint finish, body styling kit, mechanically better brakes, stiffer suspension, and even improved engine manifolding.

From 1990 scripted badging was replaced by the embossed style shown here. XJ6 models used quite a plain rear end without much chrome adornment ...

... whereas top of the range cars from 1990 featured chrome surrounds to rear lights and enhanced boot chromes.

4.0-litre Sovereigns are identified by the extra chrome on the boot area and, normally, lattice style alloy wheels.

In 1990 the conventional production models started to change when the larger-engined cars were substantially upgraded. A new 4.0-litre version of the AJ6 power unit was adopted for this model, which brought with it improved mid-range torque. Stylistically the car gained more chrome and internally the previous all-electronic dashboard was replaced by analogue instrumentation.

The same interior treatment took effect on the last of the 2.9-litre models, which were also mechanically upgraded from 1991 with the complete replacement of this engine by a 3.2 single cam unit based on the larger twin cam engines. The later engine offered greater smoothness with enhanced performance.

Regular updates appeared each model year but it wasn't until 1993 that another new model appeared in the XJ40 range. For the first time two V12-engined cars were offered, one a Jaguar XJ12 and the other a Daimler Double Six. Equipped similarly to the Sovereign and Daimler models, there were subtle differences (see details below). The V12 engine had been significantly improved, now of 6.0 litres capacity and 318bhp. By this time the XJ40 was the only saloon model available from Jaguar, the very last Series 3 having left the factory at the end of 1992.

At the end of 1993 Jaguar announced yet another XJ40 model, the Sport, or 'S' as it became known. Trying desperately to cater for a younger market the S models (only available in six-cylinder engine form) offered colour co-ordinated exterior trim to the body, five-spoke alloy wheels, and revised interior trim, including rosewood instead of walnut veneer.

A few long wheelbase Majestic models of the XJ40 were also produced to special order, although this was never considered a proper production model. This appeared in 1994, as did the final new XJ40 model, called the Gold. Based on the standard XJ6 3.2-litre model, a special reduced exterior colour range, gold plated badge on the boot, and a mix of interiors between standard and S, and offered at a modest price, the Gold allowed Jaguar to recapture lost sales in the XJ40's final twelve months. Sales of all XJ40 models in 1994 only accounted for just over 10,000 vehicles, less than half the previous year, mostly due to public knowledge that a replacement model (the X-300) would be arriving soon.

At various times other options for XJ40 models were considered, such as a short wheelbase two-door coupé and a five-door estate car, both of which didn't progress beyond driving prototype stages. Carriage trade manufacturers also completed a number of stretched limousines, both four- and six-door variants, based on the XJ40 design, as well as hearse bodies.

Up to 1990 all XJ40s featured a digitised instrument binnacle as depicted here. This picture also shows the original style of steering wheel, prior to the fitment of air bags from 1992.

Analogue instruments appeared in 1990 for all models.

For the US market the Daimlers were, and still are, badged as Jaguar Vanden Plas.

Above left: Jaguar Sovereign models became equipped with boxwood inlays to the veneer, later also adopted for Daimler models.

Above right: For base models tweed style upholstery was fitted, along with a plainer straight grain woodwork. Air conditioning was an extra cost option initially.

The US range of XJ40 models also changed year by year, although it never received the base model XJ6s. The names Vanden Plas and Majestic were resurrected for special top of the range (Daimler equivalent) models at various times, also for the US market only.

Exterior identification points

General points applicable to all XJ40s

Front view

- Squared-off chromium-plated radiator grille with vertical slats and thick centre bar, atop of which is a growler badge.
- Matched pairs of twin headlights or rectangular single units dependent on model, with chromed surrounds.
- Rubber-faced full-width bumper bar incorporating sidelight and indicator lenses with reflectors within the wrap-around section and centrally mounted number plate area. Chrome-plated blade to top of bumper bar.
- Under-valance in body colour with black plastic air intake and spoiler. Design changed from 1992.
- Forward-hinged bonnet, quite flat in profile.
- Large bonded windscreen with chrome surround and centrally mounted single wiper.

Rear view

- Wrap-around bumper treatment as at the front incorporating red reflector and red high intensity fog lights.
- Flat boot lid with pronounced lip and vertical panel incorporating number plate and badging.
- Chromed boot lock finisher with concealed number plate lighting and boot lock button.
- Rectangular rear lighting units at extremities of body, neutral density or more lenses dependent on model and age, some with chromed surrounds.
- Centre vertical boot lid section carrying make and model badges and centrally mounted number plate with chrome surround.
- Black plastic finisher between vertical portion of boot lid and rear valance. Twin exhaust pipes emit from either side of the car below bumper level through cut-outs in valance.

Side view

- Slightly more slab-sided styling to previous Jaguar XJ6 but retaining slight 'hump' over rear wheel-arch. Six-light window styling (rear quarter-lights separate to rear door frames).
- All cars featured a trim finisher at the base of the D-post roof section where it meets the rear wing, either chrome or body colour dependent on age of car.

Until 1993 the solitary Daimler model used a similar rear interior treatment to previous models, with the addition of chromed cup-holders in the occasional veneered tables.

Above left: A simple 'D' emblem on the fluted radiator grille and Daimler badging at the rear separated European cars from the US Vanden Plas models.

Above right: Revised interior layout from 1990, with the analogue instruments and here, in this 1992 model, the new steering wheel with air bag.

Cloth replaced tweed for the interior of non-leather equipped cars, along with revised door trims.

- Side indicator repeater lights to top rear section of front wings (design changed from rectangular to square in 1991). Badges featured on US spec cars.
- Chromed rain gutter surrounds.
- Chromed or black powder coated window frames and B/C post dependent on model and year (see accompanying photographs).
- Chromed door mirrors and flush-mounted chromed door handles.
- Unusual metric-sized steel road wheels with grey plastic rimbellishers incorporating separate push-fit centre section to access wheel nuts and incorporating growler badges (changed to non-metric wheels and ventilated rimbellishers from 1991). Alloy wheels fitted as extra cost option initially, later standardised on some models. Type of wheel changed through production (see photographs).

XJ40 model specifics
XJ6 models
- Two pairs of single circular headlights with chrome surrounds within a body-coloured mounting.
- Radiator grille with chromed slats and grey growler badge.
- Steel wheels with plastic rimbellishers as standard equipment.
- Black powder coated window frames.
- 'Jaguar' and 'XJ6' scripted badges on boot lid panel.

Sovereign models
- Single rectangular sealed beam headlight units with chromed surrounds. Chromed window frames.
- Early cars fitted with steel wheels and rimbellishers, later fitted with metric-sized teardrop alloy wheels with exposed wheel nuts, also an option on early cars at extra cost. Later cars also used different alloy wheel styles (see photographs and production details).
- 'Jaguar' and 'Sovereign' badges in rectangular brushed alloy finished format. Very early Sovereign examples fitted with matt black painted vertical cover to boot lid fitted underneath badges and number plate surround.
- With the introduction of 4.0-litre models greater use of chrome at rear of car (see photographs for details).

Daimler model
- Fluted radiator grille surround with 'D' emblem badge at centre top.
- Lights and window surrounds as Sovereign.
- Scripted 'D' badging to alloy wheels. Design changed to Roulette style from 1991.
- Slim full body-length swage line chrome trims.

For the Jaguar XJ12 came a revised grille with painted slats and gold growler badge, and four headlight treatment. The Daimler Double Six version retained a chrome grille and rectangular headlights. Until the end of 1993 chromed window surrounds also featured on the XJ12, but were then changed to black powder coating.

The S (Sport) model was introduced for the 1994 model year. This was identified from the outside by its five-spoke alloy wheels in either eggshell or silver finish, red growler badges to the wheels, painted radiator grille slats, and revised coachlines.

At the rear the S model gained a painted plinth with new badging, and a choice of colour density for rear light units.

- Vertical boot lid panel matt black finished as earlier Sovereigns (later dropped) but incorporating 'Daimler' scripted badge to left-hand side.
- Low density rear light units recognisable from dark grey finish instead of red. With introduction of Daimler Double Six model in 1993 revised multi-vane alloy wheels fitted and 'Double Six' scripted badging added to rear boot area.

XJ6 3.2-litre model

- As XJ6 except fitted with ventilated silver-painted rimbellishers on new 15in steel wheels (standard equipment, alloys optional).

XJ12 model

- Frontal treatment with four headlights as XJ6 except for black centre grille vanes and gold growler badge on top.
- Wider profile tyres fitted with 16in lattice alloy wheels.
- Initially chromed plated window surrounds, later changed to black powder coated.
- At rear chromed surrounds to rear light units and boot lid, with 'XJ12' rectangular brushed alloy style badging to right-hand side.

Sport models

- As XJ6 except for body-coloured centre vanes to radiator grille.
- Five-spoke alloy wheels (silver or eggshell finished) with wider profile tyres.
- Colour-keyed door mirrors.
- Twin coachlines with 'S' logo to lower half of body sides accompanied by single gold coachline along swage.
- At the rear plastic in-fill panel to boot vertical area incorporating '3.2 S' or '4.0 S' badging.
- Contrast density rear light units fitted without chromed surrounds of later cars.

Gold model

- As XJ6 except for gold growler badge on grille top and black centre vanes. Kiwi diamond-turned alloy wheels.
- Twin gold coachlines along entire length of swage line.
- At the rear 'Gold' badging against a black rectangular background.

XJR models

- As XJ6 except for matt black centre grille vanes (later changed to egg-crate style).
- Colour-keyed front and rear bumper bars.
- Revised front under-valance and spoiler treatment.
- Initially XJ6 style four headlight treatment, replaced, when egg-crate grille came in, with rectangular lights from Sovereign model.

Revised seating style, rosewood woodwork, and contrast upholstery separated the S model from normal Jaguars.

Another new model for 1994 was the Gold with a limited range of exterior colours, new diamond-turned alloy wheels, and painted grille slats.

At the rear the Gold model featured new badging and the S style plinth.

Above left: *The S seating with horizontal pleating.*

Above right: *For the last few months the top of the range Daimler versions were offered with ruched style leather upholstery.*

- Flat design Speedline alloy wheels, later changed for ventilated type with exposed wheel nuts.
- Glass fibre sill extensions sculptured and in body colour.
- Later egg-crate grille cars featured rubbing strips along lower section of body sides.
- Chromed window surrounds or colour keyed.
- At the rear revised under-valance.
- Plastic in-fill panel to vertical section of boot and 'XJR' badging.

Interior identification points

XJ6 models

- Straight grain walnut veneer to upper section of dashboard and door cappings.
- Instrument binnacle in front of driver incorporating mixture of bar instruments and electronically driven analogue speedometer and rev counter, also TV Vehicle Condition Monitor with digital read-outs, all in a matt black surround. Completed revised analogue instrumentation binnacle fitted from 1990 within wood veneered surround.
- Supplementary switch panels flank steering column containing lighting switches on one side and on-board computer controls plus cruise control (where fitted) on the other.
- Black two-spoke steering wheel with prominent centre boss containing oval growler emblem (later changed to four-spoke incorporating air bag).
- Multi-use stalks either side of steering column operating indicators, horn, main beam, wipers, and computer mode scrolling. Designs changed through production.
- Black plastic air control vents to extreme ends of dashboard and additionally a rectangular air vent system in the centre.
- Lockable passenger side veneered glove-box incorporating vanity mirror, etc. Later deleted to accommodate passenger air bag.
- Sculptured centre console area with wood veneer incorporating heater/air conditioning controls, auxiliary switchgear, audio unit, and gear lever/automatic transmission quadrant, plus damped ashtray and armrest storage box with hinged lid.
- Handbrake sited between driver's seat and centre console, with black vinyl surround.
- Pre-formed solid door panels to match trim, with armrest pulls, pocket areas, and door-mounted audio speakers (design later changed). Chromed pull door handles. Electric window lifts on all models operated from black controls within armrest area (design changed several times throughout production).

Throughout Daimler production it was also possible to specify conventional bench-type rear seating.

Passive-style seat belts were made available for the US market.

Three different styles of indicator repeater lights were fitted to the front wings on European cars (not fitted to US spec models). The earliest rectangular type (see earlier pictures) was used until 1991, when this square type was adopted, only to be replaced on the very last cars by the inset flush style.

- Individual front seating in tweed, later changed to cloth (leather at extra cost) with vertical pleats at the rear incorporating rear lighting in the headrests (later moved to seat backs).
- Rear bench-type seat arrangement with centre fold-down armrest and initially no headrests.
- Boot area carpeted, with carpet cover to vertically mounted spare wheel, and black attaché case style tool box fitted. From 1992 spare wheel position moved to accommodate carpet-covered battery area and tool kit relocated to rear inward face of valance.

Sovereign models
- As XJ6 except for full walnut veneer interior with boxwood inlays to dashboard and door cappings.
- Instrument binnacle set against mock-wood veneer background.
- Air conditioning standard fitment.
- Leather upholstery with vertical pleating.
- Front seats electrically adjustable from switch pack on sides of centre console.
- Rear seat headrests standard.
- Enhanced audio system fitted, initially of Clarion manufacture.

Daimler models
- As Sovereign except for 'D' badging to steering wheel centre boss.
- No boxwood inlays to walnut veneer on earlier cars.
- Flatter, wider pleated all-leather seating of revised style, the front seats incorporating walnut-veneered picnic tables in the rear with chromed drinks coasters.
- Rear seating of individual style with enlarged centre fold-down armrest and console area over transmission tunnel incorporating veneer finishing and 'Daimler' scripted badge.
- Door trim design entirely different to Jaguar models with separate armrest arrangement and more pronounced door pockets.
- Wood-veneered surrounds to door window lift switches.
- Nylon over-rugs fitted to rear compartment.
- Electrically operated sun-roof panel standard fitment.
- With introduction of the Double Six model in 1993 matched leather-clad gear knob and handbrake surround were incorporated.
- From 1994 ruched leather seating of more rounded style available.

NB: US spec cars usually of the higher quality Sovereign or Daimler equipment levels. From 1990 passive seat belt arrangements were also fitted to some US models.

As with the XJ-S the JaguarSport organisation adapted production XJ40s for a more youthful market. Called the XJR, these initially featured similar body treatment to the XJ-S models, later to be adapted for normal Jaguar production with a revised grille design as shown here.

The XJR came with a bodykit and rear plinth arrangement as well.

3.2-litre model
- As XJ6 but part leather/part cloth upholstery mix introduced still with vertical pleats.
- Fitment of rear seat headrests.
- Revised door trims, later fitted to all non-Daimler models with curved armrest pulls.
- Walnut veneer added to replace straight-grain veneer.

XJ12 model
- As Sovereign except stiffer and more sculptured front seat bolsters.
- Laser-etched 'V12' gold emblem to glove-box area.
- Later style instrument binnacle, door trims, and four-spoke steering wheel.

Sport models

- As XJ6 except for seating incorporating horizontal wide pleating both front and rear with stiffer bolsters.
- Rosewood-stained maple woodwork instead of walnut veneer. No boxwood inlays.
- Matching rosewood gear knob.
- Dashboard top roll and door cappings colour keyed to rest of interior trim.

Gold model

- As XJ6 except for unique wide vertical pleating to leather seating incorporating the stiffer bolsters.
- Walnut veneer woodwork.
- Matching wooden gear knob.
- Handbrake surround and dashboard top roll/door cappings trimmed to match interior.

XJR models

- Interior trim changes dependent on individual order requirements, usually featuring magnolia leather.
- Momo four-spoke matching leather steering wheel.
- Embossed 'XJR' headrests.
- Contrast piped upholstery with contrast carpeting.
- Some later cars equipped with Daimler-style door trims, and some cars equipped with either walnut veneer or walnut with boxwood inlays.
- Leather-clad gear shift knob on all models.

1: *After the earlier plastic wheel covers (see the 2.9-litre car on page 187) this style of plastic wheel cover was adopted from 1991.*

2: *This style of plastic wheel cover then took over in 1992.*

3 and 4: *Two styles of teardrop alloy wheels were fitted to the XJ40 models, one metric size.*

5: *Lattice style wheels adopted for sport handling kit-modified cars, XJ12s, and later most 1990 Sovereign models.*

6: *Five-spoke wheels for the S model, later available for other models and XJS as well.*

7 and 8: *Later styles of alloy wheels fitted to Sovereign models, and others as optional.*

9: *Multi-spoke, as fitted to the Daimler Double Six models.*

10: *Roulette style wheel normally fitted to 4.0-litre Daimler models but also offered for other cars.*

11 and 12: *Early Speedline and later Sport wheels fitted to XJR models, the latter also being used for late model XJS cars.*

Technical specifications

	2.9-litre	3.6-litre
cc	2,919	3,590
Bore and stroke (mm)	91 x 74.8	91 x 92
Compression ratio	12.6:1	9.61
bhp	165	221
@ rpm	5,600	5,000
Torque (lb ft)	176	249
@ rpm	4,000	4,000
Fuelling	Fuel injection	Fuel injection
Transmission	Getrag 5-speed synchro ZR 4-speed auto	Getrag 5-speed synchro ZR 4-speed auto
Wheel size (in)	TD Metric alloys, later 15in alloys	TD Metric alloys, later 15in alloys
Suspension front	Ind twin wishbones anti-dive, coil springs	Ind twin wishbones anti-dive, coil springs
Suspension rear	Ind lower transverse wishbones, driveshafts upper link, anti-squat, coil springs	Ind lower transverse wishbones, driveshafts upper link, anti-squat, coil springs
Brakes	4 wheel disc, ventilated front	4 wheel disc, ventilated front
Performance		
0–60mph (sec)	10.8	7.4
Top speed (mph)	118	135
Average mpg	19.8	18.7
Dimensions		
Length (in)	196.4	196.4
Width (in)	79	79
Height (in)	54.25	54.25
Wheelbase (in)	113	113
Front track (in)	59	59
Rear track (in)	59	59
Weight (lb)	2,140	2,190

Optional extras

Side body mouldings painted to body colour.
Black rubber/chrome side body mouldings incorporated Jaguar logo.
Fog/spot lights mounted within front valance (standard on some models).
Enhanced radio/cassette system.
Mud flaps.
Cloth/tweed upholstery alternative to leather-upholstered cars.
Leather upholstery alternative to cloth/tweed-upholstered cars.
Whitewall tyres (post-1992 US cars only).
Cruise control (where not fitted as standard).
Tailored over-mats.
Headlight wash/wipe system (where not fitted as standard).
Integrated hi-fi system with CD player.

Roof rack system with specialist fittings for skis, luggage box, etc.
Wood veneer gear knob.
Sheepskin over-rugs for non-Daimler/Vanden Plas models.
Child's safety seat.
Child's booster cushion.
First aid kit for boot area.
Space-saver spare wheel.
Fire extinguisher for boot area.
Jaguar warning triangle.
Headlamp converters.
Headlamp safety covers.
Roof box.
Mobile telephone kits.
Sports suspension option (where not standard).
Stainless steel door edge guards.

	4.0-litre	6.0-litre
cc	3,980	5,993
Bore and stroke (mm)	91 x 102	90 x 78.5
Compression ratio	9.5:1	11:1
bhp	235	318
@ rpm	4,750	5,400
Torque (lb ft)	285	342
@ rpm	3,750	3,750
Fuelling	Fuel injection	Fuel injection
Transmission	Getrag 5-speed synchro ZF 4-speed auto	GM 5-speed auto
Wheel size (in)	15/16	16
Suspension front	Ind twin wishbones anti-dive, coil springs	Ind twin wishbones anti-dive, coil springs
Suspension rear	Ind lower transverse wishbones, driveshafts upper link, anti-squat, coil springs	Ind lower transverse wishbones, driveshafts upper link, anti-squat, coil springs
Brakes	4 wheel disc, ventilated front	4 wheel disc, ventilated front
Performance		
0–60mph (sec)	7.1	6.8
Top speed (mph)	138	155
Average mpg	19	12.9
Dimensions		
Length (in)	196.4	196.4
Width (in)	79	79
Height (in)	54.25	54.25
Wheelbase (in)	113	113
Front track (in)	59	59
Rear track (in)	59	59
Weight (lb)	2,290	2,415

Electrically operated sunroof (non Daimler/Vanden Plas models).
Wind deflector for sunroof.
Rear screen blinds.
Snow chains.
Electrically operated boot-mounted cooler box.
Luggage net for boot area.
Witter tow bar kit.
Cup-holders for forward centre console area.
Heated windscreen.
Ultrasonic intrusion security system.
Tool kit (later model cars not equipped as standard).
Sports suspension handling kit.
15in lattice alloy wheels.
16in lattice alloy wheels.
16in five-spoke eggshell or silver alloy wheels.
15in radial alloy wheels.

15in teardrop metric or later non-metric alloy wheels.
16in Speedline alloy wheels.
16in ventilated Speedline alloy wheels with exposed wheel nuts.
16in diamond-turned 20-spoke alloy wheels.
16in Aero alloy wheels.
16in Kiwi diamond-turned alloy wheels.
15in Roulette alloy wheels.
Air conditioning (non-equipped cars).
Anti-lock braking system (non-equipped cars).
Rear seat headrests.
Heated door lock barrels.
Limited slip differential.
Ride-height rear suspension levelling system.
Eight-way front adjustable seats.
Heated front seats.

Prices and production volumes

	Price new (£)	1986	1987	1988	1989	1990	1991
2.9 Standard/Daimler	16,495	■	■	■	■	■	–
2.9 Sovereign	22,995	■	■	■	■	■	–
3.6 Standard	18,495	■	■	■	■	–	–
3.6 Sovereign	24,995	■	■	■	■	–	–
3.6 Federal	–	■	■	■	■	–	–
3.6 Daimler	28,495	■	■	■	■	–	–
3.2 Standard	26,200	–	–	–	–	■	■
3.2 Sport	29,950	–	–	–	–	–	–
3.2 Gold	28,450	–	–	–	–	–	–
3.2 Sovereign	34,550	–	–	–	–	■	■
4.0 Standard	25,200	–	–	–	–	■	■
4.0 Sport	34,950	–	–	–	–	–	–
4.0 Gold	28,950	–	–	–	–	–	–
4.0 Sovereign	32,500	–	–	–	–	■	■
4.0 Federal	–	–	–	–	–	■	■
4.0 Daimler	36,500	–	–	–	–	■	■
XJ6 long wheelbase	52,700	–	–	–	–	–	–
6.0 Export	–	–	–	–	–	–	–
6.0 Jaguar	46,600	–	–	–	–	–	–
Daimler Double Six	51,700	–	–	–	–	–	–
6.0 long wheelbase	–	–	–	–	–	–	–
6.0 Majestic	–	–	–	–	–	–	–
Miscellaneous prototypes	–	–	–	–	–	–	–
Total production							

Colour schemes

1992	1993	1994	Total produced
–	–	–	11,191
–	–	–	2,957
–	–	–	9,349
–	–	–	49,941
–	–	–	13,319
–	–	–	10,313
■	■	■	13,056
–	■	■	3,117
–	–	■	1,499
■	■	■	3,491
■	■	■	13,585
–	–	■	500
–	–	■	23
■	■	■	50,409
■	■	■	12,864
■	■	■	8,876
■	■	■	67
–	■	■	1,325
–	■	■	1,565
–	■	■	1,102
–	–	–	101
–	–	■	50
■	–	–	33
			208,733

Exterior	Details
Glacier White	
Oyster	To 1993
Signal Red	
Black	
Regency Red	To 1993
Westminster Blue	
British Racing Green	
Kingfisher Blue	From 1991
Rose Bronze	1994 only
Flamenco Red	From 1991
Gunmetal Grey	
Morocco Red	From 1993
Dorchester Grey	
Jade Green	
Isis Blue	
Silver Frost	
Sapphire Blue	1994 only
Diamond Blue	From 1992
Platinum Grey	
Regency Red (Micra)	US Majestic only
Black Cherry	To 1993
Black Cherry (Mica)	US Majestic only
Meteor Red	To 1993
Interior (all cars)	
Doeskin	
Barley	
Savile Grey	
Isis Blue	
Cream	US Majestic only
Cherry Red	
Charcoal	
Parchment	
Magnolia	Extra Cost
Piping	**Dash top rolls**
Blue	Grey
Sage Green	Sage Green
Cherry Red	
Buckskin	
Coffee	US Majestic only

Production changes

1986
XJ40 models introduced (2.9-litre, 3.6-litre).

1988
Integrated Clarion sound systems fitted.
Heated door mirrors standardised on all cars.
Rear screen blinds and heated door locks
   standardised on Daimler.

1989
Door mirror style changed.
Rear compartment reading lights standardised on
   Sovereign models.
Boxwood inlay to walnut veneer added to
   Daimler.
XJR model introduced.

1990
4.0-litre engines replaced 3.6-litre.
ZR electronically controlled auto transmission
   with Sport and Normal modes (4.0-litre only).
New Getrag 290 manual box fitted, lever moved
   forward 15mm.
Teves ABS system replaced Girling/Bosch.
Extra chrome trim added to boot area on
   upmarket models.
Analogue instrumentation binnacle fitted to all
   models.
Indicator column stalk operation changed.
Toggle fitted to driver's door window lift button.
Dashboard top roll co-ordinated option
   available.
XJR 4.0-litre model introduced with revised
   exterior styling.

1991
US Majestic Vanden Plas model introduced.
3.2-litre model replaced 2.9-litre.
TD Metric wheels and tyres replaced by 15in.
Square style side indicator repeater lights fitted to
   front wings replaced rectangular type.

1992
Fuel filler cap gained lip for ease of opening.
Sports handling pack becomes available.
Revised front under-valance and spoiler.
Fog/spot lamps standardised on Daimler.
New style rimbellisher fitted for steel wheel
   equipped cars.
Twin electric cooling fans fitted.
Auto gearshift interlock system introduced.
Boot lid liner now carpeted, replacing board.
Battery moved to boot position.
Boot side-saddle panels reduced in size to
   increase boot space.
Full electric front seat adjustment now fitted as
   standard with headrests (Sovereign and
   Daimler).

Electric front seat height adjustment standardised
   on XJ6.
Redesigned door trim panels.

1993
Driver's air bag fitted, necessitating fitment of
   new steering wheel (four-spoke with horn
   pushes).
Redesigned air conditioning control panel.
Heated front screen available.
Full integrated security system introduced on all
   models.
Enhanced hi-fi sound system introduced with
   larger speakers.
Fabric cloth material replaced tweed on non-
   leather equipped seats.
XJ12 and Daimler Double Six models introduced.
3.2-litre Sport model introduced.

1994
4.0-litre Sport model introduced.
Passenger side air bags introduced on all models.
Space-saver spare wheel fitted as standard on all
   models.
Black-painted window frames for XJ12 model
   replaced chrome finish.
Flush front wing side indicator repeater lights
   fitted.
Shaping of column-mounted control stalks
   changed.
Flush-fitting door lock buttons fitted.
Ruched style leather seating available on Daimler
   models.
New style six-cylinder camshaft cover fitted with
   integrated oil filler cap.
Gold model introduced.
All models discontinued.

Chassis numbers

Model

XJ40 all models	Vin No. (see table 3*)

*Table 3 appears on page 317.

Background

The first new saloon model range to be produced by Jaguar under Ford ownership (code-named X-300) benefited from the latter's expertise and money, while at the same time building on the established good features of the out-going XJ40 range and previous Jaguar styling touches. Its launch played heavily on the phrase 'New Series XJ', emphasising the 'new' aspect yet still retaining the old insignia XJ, first seen on a production car back in 1968.

Introduced in September 1994, these New Series cars offered superior build quality to previous models, which meant better panel fit and finish, improved protection against corrosion, and overall better quality control. It also meant a return to more curvaceous styling, Jaguar deliberately comparing the new car with the previous Series 3 XJ. And it also meant revised interiors, if not that radically different to the XJ40 range.

Mechanically these X-300 models were no major move forward either, relying on previous Jaguar practice and building on existing success with other models. Suspension, brakes, and steering, although enhanced, could be described as merely a direct development of the XJ40 design. The 6.0-litre V12 engine used in the XJ12 and Daimler Double Six was first seen in the XJ40 in 1993. The six-cylinder AJ16 engine had also made its debut in another Jaguar, the XJS, earlier in 1994, although it had been developed with the X-300 saloon in mind. Lastly, the new cars

still carried the old-established 'XJ6' or 'XJ12' insignia or their Daimler equivalents.

In a nutshell, therefore, what the X-300 models offered was more of the same but with improved quality, a touch of retro-styling, and, perhaps more importantly, a massively improved model range. This included more sporty models to hopefully attract a younger market and, for the first time ever in a production Jaguar, a supercharged engined version.

Again building on ideas from the XJ40 range, each X-300 model carried unique styling touches and suspension geometry, since at this time these were still the only saloon cars the company produced.

The New Series saloons nevertheless had a very short production run, somewhat akin to the 2.4- and 3.4-litre compact saloons of the 1950s, and, like those models, they were replaced by similar looking, although significantly modified cars after about three years. X-300 production ceased in 1997, initially with the V12 models quietly dropping out of production. Then, in October, the whole range was replaced by the X-308 models with V8 engines.

Model range and development

The New Series Jaguars encapsulated a whole range of models based around the 3.2-litre and 4.0-litre AJ16 six-cylinder and 6.0-litre V12 power units.

Models available at launch (manual and auto available for six-cylinder models)

XJ6 saloon (3.2-litre)
XJ6 Sovereign (3.2-litre and 4.0-litre)
XJ6 Sport (3.2-litre and 4.0-litre)
XJR supercharged saloon (4.0-litre)
XJ12 saloon (6.0-litre)
Daimler Six (4.0-litre)
Daimler Double Six (6.0-litre)

This made a total of nine models, the most extensive range Jaguar had ever produced around one bodyshell design, each being specifically geared to a particular sector of the anticipated market. For example, the base XJ6 was produced down to price in the hope of catering for the fleet market and those entering Jaguar ownership for the first time. As such it did not feature alloy wheels, air conditioning, or even leather upholstery as standard equipment – in essence the same format as was offered by the lower-priced XJ40s. This was in order to maintain a competitive edge compared to the products of rival manufacturers.

In contrast Sovereign models were intended for the traditional Jaguar owner who wanted all the luxury features as standard, like air conditioning, alloy wheels, and chromed trim, plus a compliant ride for comfort. The Sport, on the other hand, catered for a younger audience, far more so than the XJ40 S had. It had colour-keyed trim to the exterior paintwork, contrasting interior trim colours and, on the driving side of things, stiffer suspension, wider wheels, and more supportive seats – a much better combination than the XJ40 offered.

The entirely new concept of a supercharged Jaguar targeted another sector of the market, those who wanted the ultimate in performance and driving experience to match the likes of the BMW M series. The most powerful model in the range, the supercharged XJR also benefited from further enhanced suspension and steering and even wider wheels. The high performance, harsher ride, and superb handling meant that to a degree luxury equipment levels were tempered.

At the top end of the price bracket were the Daimler models, designed to meet the needs of the company chairman who wanted the ultimate in luxury and, indeed, rarity, with low production numbers compared to the other models. Virtually everything was supplied as standard equipment, but with softer touring suspension. The Double Six name was retained for the V12-engined model, while the 4.0-litre was now not only a Daimler but a Daimler Six.

In 1996 long wheelbase versions of all the cars were offered at extra cost, and later became standard for the Sovereign and Daimler versions. The extra 6in of wheelbase was accommodated

The X300 is clearly identifiable from the previous XJ40 models by its more rounded front and rear corners and its lower set front. This top of the range Jaguar Sovereign model featured extra chrome (window surrounds, grille, and rear lights). It is also built on the longer wheelbase bodyshell, identified by the wider rear doors.

The XJR supercharged saloon was only built on the shorter wheelbase bodyshell, with de-chroming of exterior trim except for the bumper blades. It can also be identified not only by the badging but also by the wider Sport wheels and mesh radiator grille.

The Sport model benefited from a degree of colour keying, revised coachline treatment at the bottom of the doors near the rubbing strip, and the Dimple alloy wheels.

Subtle frontal changes affected the models. The chromed radiator grille was reserved for Jaguar Sovereign and base XJ6 models.

in the rear compartment to provide more legroom, and necessitated wider rear doors.

From their launch, the X-300 cars had never been fitted with a front passenger glove-box, a carryover from the XJ40 after the fitment of a front passenger air bag system. From 1996, however, front passenger glove-boxes were fitted under the air bag area and a kit became available to convert earlier cars to this specification. Small in size, it nevertheless met demands for more storage space.

By popular demand an extra model also entered the range in 1996, a 4.0-litre version of the standard XJ6 model becoming available. Coinciding with this, all cars received minor trim makeovers, such as revised radiator grille treatment, uprated interiors, and alternative alloy wheel options.

Also in 1996, Jaguar introduced a special limited edition Century model, to commemorate 100 years of the Daimler marque. Based on the long wheelbase Daimlers, these featured every conceivable extra including ruched leather upholstery, individually electrically adjustable rear seats, chromed alloy wheels, and bespoke paint finishes. The most expensive production model ever made by Jaguar at that time, only 100 were produced with the six-cylinder engine and another hundred with the V12 power unit.

Late in 1996 another new model appeared for the 1997 model year. This was the Executive, aimed at younger, middle-management owners. Based on the XJ6 model with enhanced Sport leather trim, half wood/leather steering wheel, wider Sport wheels and tyres, and air conditioning, the Executive helped to cultivate this new market and became the most popular model sold that year. It remained in production until the demise of the X-300.

Outside the UK the standard XJ6 was not offered, and in many markets the Daimlers were marketed under the Jaguar Vanden Plas name. Cars destined for the US also featured a revised boot lid pressing to accommodate the different style of number plate mounting and some cars were fitted with a swivel action Jaguar leaper mascot on the bonnet, illegal in the UK.

Although a concept styling exercise was produced for an X-300 estate car, this never entered production. Jaguar also produced a one-off 18ft stretched limousine based on the Daimler Six, initially used by the then Chairman, Sir Nick Scheele. This car still exists today in the Jaguar Daimler Heritage Trust. Another concept was the Daimler Corsica, utilising a short wheelbase Daimler bodyshell. Jaguar's Special Vehicle Operations department turned this into a very attractive two-door convertible as another mark of respect for the 100th anniversary of the Daimler marque in 1996, but it was never

Colour-keyed grille slats for the Sport model.

Fluted chromed grille for the Daimlers.

Rear external treatment also changed from model to model. Apart from obvious badging differences (always in different colours) models like the Sovereign and the Daimlers featured chromed surrounds to the rear lights.

Above left: *Other models did not feature the chrome trim.*

Above right: *There were no chromed screen surrounds for the Sport or XJR models.*

actually fitted with an engine. This model, too, can be found in the JDHT collection.

Worth mentioning, although strictly not of Jaguar manufacture, are the Eagle Coachworks six-door limousines and hearses produced around the X-300 models, both Jaguar and Daimler variants. Eagle, part of the Wilcox Group, purchased cars direct from Jaguar and with their approval converted them for various uses.

As mentioned above, the Daimler Double Six and XJ12 were discontinued mid-term 1997, with the other models continuing to be manufactured until the introduction of the XJ8.

Exterior identification points

General points applicable to all X-300s
Front view
- More curvaceous frontal aspect than previous models, with rounded radiator grille with growler badge top centre.
- Four headlights in two pairs with chromed bezels, the inner pair incorporating sidelights.
- All-enveloping plastic bumper bar painted in body colour with chromed top finisher. Bumper incorporating indicator lights, central number plate surround and side reflectors. Bumper also incorporates under-valance with or without integrated fog lights according to model.
- One-piece forward-hinged bonnet with curvature to match headlights and raised centre section.
- One-piece bonded windscreen with centrally mounted single wiper arm.

Side view
- Similar profile to previous XJ40 models except for greater curvature to front and rear wing extremities.
- Removal of body finisher to base of D-post roof and rear wing (now smoothed area).
- All-enveloping bumper bar treatment easily identifies models from XJ40s.
- Lower section of body length fitted to painted rubbing strips.
- Flush-mounted indicator repeater lights on front wings (or badges for some overseas markets).
- New style of rounded flush-mounted door handles, either painted or chromed in the case of Daimlers.

Rear view
- Curved and tapered rear end totally at contrast with previous XJ40 saloons.
- All-enveloping rear bumper bar matching the front but with no integrated lighting other than side reflectors and incorporating the

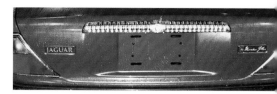

Daimlers had a shorter chromed boot plinth. As with the XJ40, US-destined Daimlers were badged as Jaguar Vanden Plas and also received a totally different boot lid pressing because of the number plate style differences.

Badge colouring changed for all models and the special limited edition Century model got even better treatment.

A mix of cloth and leather was used for Sport and XJR models unless otherwise specified. Both models also used contrast colours for other trim aspects.

Sovereign models got full leather trim and traditional walnut instead of the black-stained maple of the Sport and XJR models.

under-valance with cut-outs for exhaust system.

- Twin exhaust pipes, one emerging from either side, oval shaped chromed trims.
- Boot lid tapered vertical section incorporated indentation for number plate, and plinth finisher incorporating concealed number plate lighting and push-button boot lid lock (chromed or body colour dependent on model).
- Wrap-around rear light units at extreme sides of rear wings, Sovereign and Daimler models with chromed surrounds.
- Rectangular 'Jaguar' or 'Daimler' badges to left-hand side and model designation to right-hand side.

X-300 model specifics

XJ6 models

- Chrome surround and vertical slats to radiator grille.
- Chromed windscreen and rear screen surrounds.
- Chromed rain gutters.
- Black powder coated window frames.
- Colour coded door mirrors and door handles.
- Steel wheels with silver-painted plastic rimbellishers standard equipment (alloys at extra cost when new).
- Boot plinth chromed.
- 'Jaguar' and 'XJ6' rectangular badging on boot lid.

Sport models

- As XJ6 but with body-coloured vertical slats to the radiator grille.
- Dimple alloy wheels.
- Dual coachlines above the side rubbing strips.
- 'XJ Sport' badging to boot lid and 'Sport' badging to B/C post.
- No chromed screen surrounds.

XJR model

- As Sport except for colour co-ordinated radiator grille shell with mesh centre replacing the vanes.
- No chrome surrounds to front and rear screens.
- Matt black rain gutters.
- Sport ventilated five-spoke alloy wheels.
- Colour co-ordinated boot lid plinth.
- Larger diameter exhaust outlets.
- 'XJR' badge to central B/C post mounting between front and rear window frames. 'XJR' badging to boot lid.

Sovereign models (including XJ12)

- Chromed radiator grille.
- Chromed windscreen and rear window surrounds.
- Chromed rain gutters.
- Chromed window frames.

Standard XJ6 models did not come equipped with air conditioning or full leather trim.

From the introduction of the Daimler Century model, and continued on with the Double Six, separate heated and adjustable rear seating became the norm.

A new model for 1997 was the Executive, offering a high degree of standard equipment at a special price. The wheels fitted to the car in this photograph are not the originals.

Badging colours changed according to model.

- 14-spoke diamond-turned or 20-spoke alloy wheels, later changed.
- Chromed boot lid plinth.
- Chromed rear light cluster surrounds.
- 'Sovereign' or 'V12' badging on boot lid accompanied by 'Jaguar' on other side.

Executive model

- A cross between standard XJ6 and Sport models. Chrome was strongly featured in all areas except the window frame surrounds (matt black).
- Alloy wheels of Dimple design (like the Sport), but unlike the Sport were polished alloy without the grey finished centres.
- Chromed boot lid plinth.
- 'Executive' badging on boot lid.

Daimler models

- As Sovereign with extensive chromework around grille, glass areas, rear lights, rear plinth, etc.
- Fluted design radiator grille surround with chromed slats.
- Diamond-turned alloy wheels on Double Six, chrome on Six.
- Chromed door mirrors/door handles.
- Boot lid of shorter width to Jaguar and fluted.
- 'Daimler' badging replacing Jaguar on boot lid, and 'Six' or 'Double Six' badging.
- Sunroof standard on Double Six model.

NB: Market differences applied to some overseas cars – eg 'Vanden Plas' badging on top of range Jaguar model for the US market, using Daimler styled fluted grille, etc.

Daimler Century models

- Followed other Daimler models but were identified externally by 'Century' badging to boot lid and similar badging on some cars to bottom rear quarter of front wings.
- Chromed alloy wheels fitted unless otherwise stated by individual purchaser.

Interior identification points

General points applicable to all X-300s

- Interior layout similar to XJ40 models with more rounded seat styling.
- Bevelled edge wood veneers.
- Rounded centre console area with smooth satin finished switchgear.
- Four-spoke steering wheels incorporating prominent centre boss containing air bag.

In the case of these cars there were basically three distinct types of interior styling treatment,

There were chromed rear light surrounds for top of the range models.

Analogue instrumentation was retained on the X-300 models from the XJ40, with wood surround for the XJ6, Sovereign, XJ12, and Daimler models.

The Daimler Century model was identified by badging, chromed edge to the rubbing strips, and chromed alloy wheels.

Styling cues identified the whole range of X-300 models, all based on the same bodyshell.

two on Jaguar models plus one with variations on Daimler cars. It is better here to deal with each style of interior separately, also showing the models they were applicable to.

Sport (applicable to Sport and XJR models)
- Black stained maple woodwork.
- Aerated leather steering wheel (with or without additional wood feature).
- Two-tone contrasting upholstery colour schemes.
- Stiffer bolster seating with horizontal pleating and ventilated centre panels.

Classic (applicable to XJ6, XJ12, and Sovereign models)
- Walnut-veneered woodwork.
- Smooth leather-covered steering wheel (with or without additional wood feature).
- Seating style more rounded using vertical pleats, curved cushions with, generally, more sombre trim colour schemes, in some cases with contrast coloured piping.
- Standard XJ6 models were normally equipped with cloth centre panels to the seats, unless all leather was specifically requested by an individual purchaser.

NB: Executive models differed and were a combination of both the above styles, having walnut-veneered woodwork, a smooth leather/wood steering wheel, Sport style seating, and sombre colour scheming.

Daimler models
- Burr walnut veneer with boxwood inlays.
- Matched occasional tables built into the rear of the front seats.
- Seating style squarer with wider vertical pleats with the option of flat or ruched leather, both of a higher quality than that used on the equivalent Jaguar models.
- Century models featured ruched Autolux leather to all seats and a different style of rear seating consisting of individual seats with centre console with electrical control functions and control over the movement of the front passenger seat (when unoccupied). This type of individualised rear seating became standard equipment on all Double Six cars or an extra cost option on Daimler Sixes.

All details of trim and specification given above relate to standard production cars. Certain owners may well have specified changes to suit their individual requirements, so it is not unusual to find some more basic models with a higher specification than that described here.

Above left: *Plastic wheel covers were standard on XJ6 models.*

Above right: *Dimple wheels were standard equipment on the Sport models.*

Above left: *This wheel, adapted from the Dimple with polished finish, was fitted to the Executive model.*

Above right: *Chromed wheels fitted to the Daimler Century and later available as an extra cost option.*

Above left: *Twenty-spoke wheels fitted to the XJ12 and available as an option.*

Above right: *Kiwi fitted to later Sovereign models and available as an extra cost option.*

Above left: *An extra cost option alloy available for X-300 models.*

Above right: *Lattice wheels also available on the X-300 as an extra cost option.*

Technical specifications

	3.2-litre	4.0-litre
cc	3,239	3,980
Bore and stroke	91 x 83mm	91 x 102mm
Compression ratio	10:1	10:1
bhp	219	249
@ rpm	5,100	4,800
Torque (lb ft)	232	289
@ rpm	4,500	4,000
Fuelling	Fuel injection	Fuel injection
Transmission	Getrag 5-speed synchro ZR 4-speed auto	Getrag 5-speed synchro ZF 4-speed auto
Wheel size (in)	7 x 16 (8 x 16 Sport)	7 x 16 (8 x 16 Sport)
Suspension front	Ind unequal length wishbones, anti-dive, coil springs	Ind unequal length wishbones anti-dive, coil springs
Suspension rear	Ind double wishbones, driveshafts as upper link, anti-squat, coil springs	Ind double wishbones, driveshafts as upper link, anti-squat, coil springs
Brakes	4 wheel disc, all ventilated	4 wheel disc, all ventilated
Performance		
0–60mph (sec)	8.9 (7.9 manual)	7.8 (7 manual)
Top speed (mph)	139 (138 manual)	144 (143 manual)
Average mpg	26.9	26.8
Dimensions	**Short wheelbase**	
Length (in)	197	
Width (in)	70	
Height (in)	51	
Wheelbase (in)	112	
Front track (in)	57.25	
Rear track (in)	57	
Weight (lb)	3,968	3,968

Optional extras

Fog/spot lights mounted within front valance (standard on some models).

Enhanced radio/cassette system.

Mud flaps.

Cloth upholstery alternative to leather-upholstered cars.

Leather upholstery alternative to cloth-upholstered cars.

Cruise control (where not fitted as standard).

Tailored over-mats.

Headlight wash/wipe system (where not fitted as standard).

Integrated hi-fi system with CD auto-changer in boot.

Roof rack system with specialist fittings for skis, luggage box, etc.

Wood veneer gear knob (where not fitted as standard).

Sheepskin over-rugs for non Daimler models.

Child's safety seat.

Child's booster cushion.

First aid kit for boot area.

Space-saver spare wheel.

Fire extinguisher for boot area.

Jaguar warning triangle.

Headlamp converters.

Headlamp safety covers.

Roof box.

Mobile telephone kits.

Sports suspension option (where not standard).

Electrically operated sunroof (non Daimler/Vanden Plas models).

	Supercharged	6.0-litre
cc	3,980	5,993
Bore and stroke	91 x 102mm	90 x 78.5mm
Compression ratio	8.5:1	11:1
bhp	326	318
@ rpm	5,000	5,350
Torque (lb ft)	378	353
@ rpm	3,050	2,850
Fuelling	Fuel injection	Fuel injection
Transmission	Getrag 5-speed synchro ZF 4-speed auto	GM 5-speed auto
Wheel size (in)	8 x 17	8 x 16
Suspension front	Ind unequal length wishbones, anti-dive, coil springs	Ind unequal length wishbones, anti-dive, coil springs
Suspension rear	Ind double wishbones, driveshafts as upper link, anti-squat, coil springs	Ind double wishbones, driveshafts as upper link, anti-squat, coil springs
Brakes	4 wheel disc, all ventilated	4 wheel disc, all ventilated
Performance		
0–60mph (sec)	6.6 (5.9 manual)	6.8
Top speed (mph)	155 (155 manual)	155
Average mpg	23.4	18.4
Dimensions	**Long wheelbase**	
Length (in)	201	
Width (in)	70	
Height (in)	52	
Wheelbase (in)	116	
Front track (in)	57.25	
Rear track (in)	57	
Weight (lb)	4,134	4,354

Rear screen blinds.
Snow chains.
Electrically operated boot-mounted cooler box.
Luggage net for boot area.
Witter tow bar kit.
Cup-holders for forward centre console area.
Heated windscreen.
Ultrasonic intrusion security system.
Tool kit (mounted in under-bonnet area).
Air conditioning (non equipped cars).
Eight-way front adjustable seats (where not fitted).
Heated front seats.
Jaguar 'growler' alloy wheel centre badges, various colours.
Power folding door mirrors.
Chrome door mirror surrounds (where not fitted).

Bright rear number plate surround (chrome).
Self-dipping rear view mirror.
Wood/leather steering wheel (where not fitted).
Passenger compartment glove-box kit (pre-1996 models).
16in Dimple anthracite infill alloy wheels.
16in Turbine chromed alloy wheels.
16in Dimple (no infill) alloy wheels.
16in Turbine alloy wheels.
16in 20-spoke alloy wheels (plastic centre cap).
16in 20-spoke ally wheels (exposed wheel nuts).
16in Kiwi alloy wheels.
16in Aero alloy wheels.
16in lattice alloy wheels.
17in XJR five-spoke ally wheels (exposed wheel nuts)

Colour schemes

Exterior Colour	Details	Seats	Fascia	Piping
Glacier White	To 1996	Oatmeal (fabric)	Antelope	
Spindrift White		Coffee (fabric)	Coffee	
Signal Red	1997	Nimbus Grey (fabric)	Slate Grey	
Black†		Regatta Blue (fabric)	Warm Charcoal	
Anthracite (black)	To 1996	Black Marble Sport/Warm Charcoal	Warm Charcoal	
Westminster Blue†	1997	Grey Marble Sport/Oatmeal	Warm Charcoal	
British Racing Green†		Grey Marble Sport/Nimbus Grey	Warm Charcoal	
Kingfisher Blue		Parchment	Sage Green	Sage Green
Rose Bronze		Cream	Coffee	Coffee
Flamenco Red		Cream Sport	Warm Charcoal	
Carnival Red†	To 1996	Nimbus Grey	Slate Grey	Slate
Morocco Red	1997	Nimbus Grey Sport	Warm Charcoal	
Cabernet	To 1996	Coffee	Coffee	Cream
Jade Green	1997	Oatmeal	Antelope	Antelope
Sherwood Green		Oatmeal Sport	Warm Charcoal	
Silver Frost		Regatta Blue (fabric)	Warm Charcoal	Warm Charcoal
Sapphire Blue†		Warm Charcoal	Warm Charcoal	Nimbus Grey
Topaz (gold)		Mushroom‡	Coffee‡	Coffee‡
Ice Blue†		Silk White‡	Sage Green‡	Sage Green‡
Titanium Grey†				
Steel				
Turquoise*	To 1996	*Schemes applicable to all cars and exteriors except where indicated.*		
Aquamarine*	1997	** = only available on XJR/Sport models.*		
Antigua Blue*		*† = only colours for Executive models.*		
Nautilus Blue		*‡ = Century models only.*		
Spruce Brown				

Production changes

1994
X-300 models introduced.

1995
Long wheelbase bodyshells introduced.
(Late) Individual electrically-operated seats introduced on Daimler Double Six.
XJ6 4.0-litre standard saloon introduced.

1996
Front passenger door external key lock eliminated.
Daimler Century Six and Double Six models introduced.
Daimler Corsica Concept coupé produced.
Passenger side glove-box added to all models.
XJ6 Executive model introduced.

1997
Flatter rear seat cushion introduced on bench-seats.
Inertia three-point centre seat belt fitted.

Air conditioning standardised on 3.2-litre Sport model.
Wood/leather steering wheel standardised on all models except XJ6.
Black radiator grille vanes replaced chrome on 3.2-litre XJ6.
Long wheelbase bodyshell standardised on 4.0-litre Sovereign model.
16in 20-spoke alloys become available, standard on 4.0-litre Sovereign.
Wooden gear knob standard fitment on 4.0-litre Sovereign/Daimler models.
Electric fold-back door mirrors standardised on all Daimler models.
CD players repositioned to nearside of boot area.
(April) Last XJ12 left the production line.
(September) Production discontinued, replaced by XJ8.

Prices and production volumes

	Price new (£)	1994	1995	1996	1997	Total produced
XJ6 3.2-litre	28,950	■	■	■	–	17,346
XJ6 3.2-litre long wheelbase	33,750	–	–	■	■	747
XJ6 4.0-litre	–	–	–	■	■	2,474
XJ6 4.0-litre long wheelbase	–	–	–	■	■	203
XJ Sport 3.2-litre	29,950	■	■	■	■	7,265
XJ Sport 4.0-litre	34,450	■	■	■	■	2,534
Sovereign 3.2-litre	37,950	■	■	■	–	2,377
Sovereign 3.2-litre long wheelbase	43,250	–	–	■	■	305
Sovereign 4.0-litre	42,950	■	■	■	–	2,8490
Sovereign 4.0-litre long wheelbase	45,500	–	–	■	■	4,973
XJR	45,450	■	■	■	■	6,547
XJ12	53,450	■	■	■	■	564
XJ12 long wheelbase	–	–	–	■	■	535
XJ6 Executive 3.2-litre	34,650	–	–	■	■	–
Daimler Six	49,950	■	■	–	–	1,362
Daimler Six long wheelbase	54,750	–	–	■	■	1,330
Daimler Double Six	59,950	■	■	–	–	1,007
Daimler Double Six long wheelbase	66,450	–	–	■	■	1230
Daimler Century Six	54,750	–	–	■	–	100
Daimler Century Double Six	–	–	–	■	–	100
Vanden Plas 4.0-litre*	–	■	■	■	■	3,831
Vanden Plas 4.0-litre long wheelbase	–	■	■	■	■	7,989
Sovereign XJ12*	–	■	■	■	■	673
Sovereign XJ12 long wheelbase*	–	–	–	■	■	56
Total production						**92,038**

* *Overseas models*

Chassis numbers

Model

X-300 models	Vin No. (see table 4*)

*Table 4 appears on page 318.

Background

With the introduction of the XJ-S in 1975 Jaguar changed its policy of producing sports cars to one of making sporting grand tourers. Although not met with overall acclaim when launched, by the time the XJS went out of production in 1996 it had achieved what Jaguar had set out for it to do – to be a highly refined, effortless to drive, well-built, two-door grand tourer. It had been in production for 21 years, during which time it was constantly upgraded to meet the demands of the market and changing technology, and Jaguar needed something special to replace it. Ultimately this wouldn't become available until 1996 in the form of a car coded X-100, to be known in production as the XK8.

When Ford took Jaguar over in 1990 there was little on offer in the way of proposed new models. The XJ-S was selling better than ever, and although extensive work had been carried out on a replacement (the XJ41, also known as the F-type) the project was somewhat ill-conceived and was soon abandoned completely.

Ford had grave concerns about Jaguar's new model policy, and felt it was vital to launch new models in order to improve sales and, particularly, profitability (remembering that the XJ-S was still being built using 1970s technology). The first fruits of Ford involvement seen by the public were the replacements for the XJ40, the X-300

saloons, for although attention was turned to a replacement for the XJ-S right from the start it would take until 1996 for the car to be seen in the flesh.

The principles behind the X-100, or XK8 as we should call it now, were to build on the later success of the XJS, utilising the existing floorpan for speed and cost saving but updating the car significantly to meet the ever-increasing demands of the lucrative market for prestige sporting cars. Money for the development of the XK8 was tight, as was the schedule to bring it to production. The use of the XJS floorpan dictated the overall dimensions and interior accommodation, but the XK8 featured an entirely new body style and interior trim package plus new mechanics, not least the first use of the new AJ-V8 4.0-litre engine developed by Jaguar and produced at the Ford plant in Bridgend, Wales.

A degree of retro styling took cues from the old E-type sports car and the XJ220 Supercar that Jaguar produced on a limited basis in the early 1990s. This decision was to create a connection between the new XK and classic Jaguar sports cars, hence the rebirth of the 'XK' insignia. The totally replanned interior also retained, if anything, more of a traditional feel than its XJS and E-type predecessors. Strategically, for marketing reasons if not practicality, a 2+2 seating arrangement was retained.

Mechanically, as well as the 4.0-litre V8 engine the latest electronically controlled GM400 transmission was employed, mated to the J-gate transmission operation. An entirely new front subframe of aircraft technology design was incorporated with new front suspension and revised braking system and steering, overall a superior package to the XJS.

Enhanced creature comforts included dramatically improved rubber sealing techniques for doors and windows, particularly important for the convertible model on which, due to the constraints of the XJS floorpan, Jaguar was unable to fit an integrated metal cover over the hood when down; there was, however, a fast-action fitted hood cover. To meet the demands of the valued US market the boot was made as large as possible, promoted at the time as capable of carrying the obligatory two sets of golf clubs!

Finally launched at the British Motor Show in 1996, the XK8 found immediate success and the model range was increased thereafter. It remained in production until 2005 when it was replaced by an entirely new model.

Model range and development

When it was launched in October 1996 there were just two versions of the XK8 available.

Models available at launch (automatic transmission only)
XK8 4.0-litre coupé
XK8 4.0-litre convertible

It is perhaps significant that the opening advertising and promotional statement for the XK8 bore the words 'The Cat is Back', confirming that Jaguar had built into the new car elements of past greats such as the E-type and, of course, the XJS.

The essentials of the XK8 design are a monocoque construction bodyshell built around the existing XJS floorpan, offering two-door coupé and convertible coachwork with 2+2 seating arrangement. Although using the existing floorpan, with new technology the XK8 is built from 30 per cent less panels than the previous model but with 25 per cent more torsional stiffness. Polyurethane injection moulding is used for front and rear bumper bars, with projection technology for front lighting within a curvaceous front emulating the old E-type and XJ220 nose treatment. Smoothness of line was brought back into Jaguar sporting car styling, with a distinct lack of chromework or add-on trim.

A much lighter structure than previously, the smoothness of line made the car more attractive, stable, aerodynamic, and even easier to keep clean. 17in or 18in alloy wheels were a standard

The styling of the XK8 is unique, not being used by any other model within the Jaguar range. This 1997 example of the convertible version shows that there have been no changes in styling throughout the model's years in production. The 18in alloy wheels fitted to this example were an extra cost option on early cars.

From 1996 to mid-1997 the rear view of XK8 models did not change, but from late 1997-on, a high-level brake light was mounted on the boot lid of convertible models and within the rear screen of coupés.

Front view of XK8 models. The 2000 model year example on the left only differs from the earlier model on the right in its flush-mounted fog lamps (inset on the earlier car).

fitment, with Pirelli P-Zero tyres. The very latest rubber technology allowed for almost perfect sealing of doors and windows, the latter electrically sensored to raise a little extra when the doors were closed to grip into the rubber seals, also releasing themselves as the doors were opened.

Internally Jaguar emphasised the traditional features of woodwork with a choice of two schemes, Classic (burr walnut) and Sports (dark-stained maple with contrasting soft trim colours). Virtually nothing internally was carried over from the XJS.

Mechanically the new XK8 was a tour de force in technology. Firstly the new AJ-V8 4.0-litre engine was seen for the first time in this model. Of alloy construction with four valves per cylinder and variable cam phasing, this engine uses a specially designed management system. It achieves a very quick warm up and is mated to the ZR 5HP24 electronically controlled five-speed automatic transmission.

Its double wishbone independent front suspension has springs mounted directly to the body, and the suspension is carried in a unique aircraft technology aluminium subframe. At the rear the fully independent rear suspension with outboard brakes takes its lead from the XJ40 and later X-300 saloons and is available with Jaguar's Computer Active Technology Suspension system (CATS).

1997 was the first full production year for the XK8, during which a total of over 14,500 cars was sold worldwide, a record number, greater than any year of XJS production and more than Jaguar itself had anticipated. Although the majority of customers came from previous XJS owners, there were clear signs that the XK8 had had an effect on the sales of other cars, particularly Mercedes.

Little changed with the XK8 over the next couple of years until, in May 1998, two more models were added to the range. Called the XKR, in coupé and convertible forms, these featured the supercharged version of the AJ-V8 engine, first fitted to the XJR V8 at the launch of the XJ8 range in 1997, mated to a new Mercedes five-speed automatic transmission. The engine and transmission were essentially the same as fitted to the XJR. Producing 370bhp, the supercharged V8 was nearly ten per cent more powerful than the old V12 engine and nearly 30 per cent more powerful than the standard XK8 normally aspirated 4.0-litre.

The XKR package also included Computer Active Technology Suspension, a new Servotronic steering system, and improved brakes to match the higher performance, the car being governed to a 155mph safe maximum.

As a necessity to cope with the increased heat under the bonnet louvres were fitted to the

Above left: For the first three years standard production XK8s were fitted with these 17in Revolver alloy wheels, which were also available in chromed form to special order.

Above right: 18in Flute wheels were fitted as extra cost options.

Interior of the 'classic' XK8 models (with walnut veneer) remained visually unchanged from 1996 until the introduction of the XKR model in 1998.

The Sport interior provided greater contrasts in trim colour schemes and the use of stained maple woodwork instead of walnut.

bonnet area on each side (another throwback to E-type days) and a neat spoiler was added to the boot lid to improve aerodynamics. Along with 'Supercharged' and 'XKR' badging the more powerful models featured a mesh grille insert at the front and the XKR became the first production Jaguar to be fitted with larger wheels and tyres at the rear than at the front.

Since that time the basic structure of XK8 models has remained unchanged, although the car has been regularly upgraded in virtually every model year. In 2000, in time for the British Grand Prix at Silverstone, Jaguar announced a special edition of the XKR, called the Silverstone. This was finished in Platinum Silver externally and carried 'Silverstone' bonnet and boot badging. These cars also had 20in Detroit split-rim alloy wheels as standard equipment. The interior was also treated to unique treatment and both coupés and convertibles were produced.

In 2001 the XK8 range was revamped, with slight changes to the exterior styling including flush-mounted fog/spot lights and new badging, and internally with revised seating including, for the first time, adjustable headrests. Then in 2002 the model was enhanced again, with new zenon lighting, other minor changes to the trim package, and the adoption of a new 4.2-litre version of the AJ-V8 engine plus a supercharged version, now boasting 400bhp.

To commemorate the 100th anniversary of Sir William Lyons, the founder of the company, Jaguar introduced a limited run of XKR 100 models with unique badging, all finished in Anthracite Black paintwork.

The company also produced a one-off XKR-R with four-wheel drive, S-type rear suspension, and six-speed manual gearbox, but this did not go into production.

In 2004, further updates in exterior and interior design helped to maintain sales to the end of production. There were also other special editions for the home and US markets, like the Portfolio, Carbon Fibre and, towards the end of production, the S and Victory models.

The XK range, as covered here, came to the end of production in 2005 after an incredible lifespan. It was the most successful sporting Jaguar produced up to that time.

Exterior identification points

General points applicable to all XK models

Front view
■ Identifiable from the curvaceous frontal aspect, not seen on any other Jaguar model since the E-type and XJ220.

All XKR (supercharged) models feature a mesh grille inset. This car is fitted with R-Performance split rim alloy wheels.

All XKR models feature inset bonnet louvres.

A 'Supercharged' badge is fitted to the front nose section and boot panel of XKR models.

No front bumper bar treatment, instead an integrated pre-formed curved frontal energy absorbing panel painted to body colour, from which front wings, bonnet, and lighting flow. Centrally-mounted growler badge, separate number plate mounting, and 'mouth' either with chromed splitter bar or mesh grille, dependent on model (see pictures). From 2004, revised frontal aspect with larger 'mouth', and new-style trim and lighting.

Integrated front fog lights incorporated into the nose section, flush-mounted on later models (see pictures).

Sculptured combined headlamp/sidelight/indicator units using 'projector' technology or Xenon lights dependent upon model. Integrated headlamp wash system.

One-piece forward-hinged bonnet with raised centre section.

One-piece bonded windscreen with metal, painted surrounds.

XKR models have 'Supercharged' emblems on the instrumentation and the XKR logo embossed into the steering wheel centre.

Rear view

Tapered and curved styling treatment not featured on other Jaguar models.

Rear-hinged boot lid with curved lip (later with spoiler added, which varied according to model). Vertical-section incorporated number plate panel and lighting, initially with painted plinth cover, and later changed to chrome and with integrated push-button boot lid opening facility.

Rear light clusters formed into the shape of the rear wings, later models with chrome surround, and very late models with new style.

Pre-formed energy-absorbing one-piece bumper/valance painted to body colour, later models with more pronounced lip, different exhaust cut-outs, and variations in lower styling.

Twin exhaust pipes with chromed oval trims emitting from either side below bumper/valance, larger on XKR models and later XKRs with quadruple tailpipes.

'Jaguar' and model badging either side of the number plate surround, the latter incorporating key lock for boot lid (earlier models only). Later cars featured solid badging, which also differed according to model.

The 2004 facelift XK8 with enlarged mouth and air intake below.

Rear three-quarter view of 2000 to 2001 model year XKR coupé, depicting chromed surrounds to the rear lights and chromed boot plinth (both also applicable to XK8 models during this period).

Side view

Unique style of car with slight wedge shape to rear and tapered frontal appearance different from any other Jaguar model.

Distinct lack of chrome adornment to side of car (except for US models, where chromed door mirrors and handles applied).

Oval reflectors fitted to leading edge of front and rear wing/bumper areas.

Post-2000 to 2001 model year XKR convertible, showing the boot lid-mounted brake light (always painted to body colour) and extra brightwork at the rear.

- Indicator repeaters fitted to rear of front wings (not US cars).
- Body-coloured rubbing strips fitted to rear of front wings, running back across doors to edge of rear wings. These were deleted from 2004 model year.
- Flush-mounted door handles and locks.
- Frameless door windows, no quarter-lights, fixed rear quarter-lights (coupé). Retracting smaller rear side windows in convertibles.
- Grey-painted rain gutters on coupé models.
- Concealed fuel filler cap incorporated into rear nearside wing under flush panel, opened from electric switch on the dashboard.
- Alloy wheels fitted to all cars, dependent on market, model, and year.
- Sill area curved to underside of car up to 2004, and thereafter an over-sill of pronounced section was fitted.

XK8 model specifics
XK8 coupé
- Front air intake incorporates horizontal chrome splitter bar with two vertical grey-painted plastic over-riders on to which is normally mounted the registration plate support panel. Both the chrome splitter bar and over-riders changed style from 2004 onward with deep front valance area as well.
- 'Jaguar 4.0 litre' (later 4.2 litre) growler badge fitted to nose section.
- Inset matching fog lights fitted to all models, from 2001 flush mounted.
- Bonnet without louvres.
- Roof section forms part of whole bodyshell, flowing down to meet the rear wings at the side and incorporating a large glass (heated) rear screen with surround.
- Grey-finished window surrounds up to 2003, thereafter black finished.
- Side areas fitted with body-coloured rubbing strips, later removed.
- Sculptured sill areas with protective painted finish. From 2004 with facelift, more pronounced 'add-on' sill covers fitted.
- Rear side quarter-lights bonded with flush surrounds and do not open.
- Early cars featured a choice of just two alloy wheels types, 17in Revolver or 18in Flute. Many others supplemented the model range over the years (see photographs).
- 'XK8' scripted badge to rear wing right-hand side panel with matching 'Jaguar' badge on opposite side. Originally the 'XK8' carried the key lock to the boot lid but, from 2001, badges were changed to solid chromed type, and the boot lid key lock moved to the boot lid plinth.
- From 2001, the chromed boot lid plinth incorporated the boot lock, push-button, and number plate lighting.

Early style XK8 seating with combined headrests.

XKR seating from introduction through to 2000.

Post-2001 XK8 seating with separate adjustable headrests.

Post-2001 XKR seating with revised pleating and separate adjustable headrests.

- Boot spoiler fitted to post 2004 model year cars.
- Twin chromed tail pipes emerging from cut-outs in rear bumper/valance area. Enlarged pipes from 2004 model year.

XK8 Convertible

- As coupé above, but without steel roof section, replaced by fabric-covered hood with frame and lining, affixed from revised windscreen surround (incorporating locking mechanism. Full-width glass rear screen with heated element. Boot lid same as coupé.
- Reduced size rear quarter windows, retractable.

XKR models

- As XK8 models except nose splitter bar replaced by a full-nose mesh grille, enlarged on later facelift models from 2004.
- 'Jaguar Supercharged' growler badge to centre of nose section.
- Sculptured louvres painted to body colour, one per side, set into bonnet either side of raised area.
- 18in Double-Five original alloy wheel specified for this model, later updated several times according to model year (see accompanying pictures).
- Rubberised rear wheel-arch extensions fitted to accommodate wider track of wheels/tyres.
- Body-colour mini-spoiler fitted to boot lid area, modified on later models.
- 'Jaguar Supercharged' growler badge fitted to centre of boot lid on early cars.
- 'XKR' scripted badges match those of XK8s above, later also changed to rectangular solid type.
- Larger bore exhaust pipe trims compared to XK8 models. Later models featured quadruple pipe system (from 2004).
- Larger rear boot spoiler fitted from 2004.

Special Edition models
Silverstone
- Only finished in Platinum Silver exterior paint with appropriate re-badging.

XKR100
- Only finished in Anthracite Black exterior paint with appropriate badging and sill tread plates.

Carbon Fibre
- 2004/05 model with quad exhaust pipes and 20in split-rim alloy wheels.

Portfolio (US)
- Only finished in choice of Coronado Blue or Jupiter Red.
- 20in split-rim alloy wheels.

Above left: Limited edition Silverstone models all featured unique badging.

Above right: Silverstone model interiors are all in black with contrast piping.

Current coupé model XK8. Apart from the Gemini alloy wheels, (standard on XK8 models) the only differentiating point from earlier cars are the chromed and 'jewelled' rear light units.

Above left: Revised rear lighting of the modern 'jewelled' type on the current XK8 and R models, along with revised embossed badging.

Above right: Interior enhancements for current models include the option of contrast leather trim and R-Performance options like the alloy gear knob. When satellite navigation is fitted, a centrally mounted TV screen and controls replace auxiliary gauges on the dashboard.

Victory (US)

- Leading up to the end of production. Available in special option colours – Black Copper, Frost Blue, Bay Blue, or Satin Silver, as well as normal Jaguar colourways.
- Chromed finish 19in Atlas alloy wheels for normally-aspirated model, 20in Victory alloys for XKR versions.

4.2 S

- The European equivalent of the Victory (above) with 4.2 S badging.
- Atlas alloy wheels, not chromed for European models.

Interior identification points

General points applicable to all models

- Full-width wood-veneered dashboard in oval shape (originally Walnut or Grey-stained Maple, later options included Birds Eye Maple and Piano Black), with primary instrumentation in front of the driver, deeply inset with auxiliary gauges in the centre of the dashboard mounted below the air-conditioning outlets. When fitted with satellite navigation, the screen replaces these gauges.
- Secondary air vents placed at either end of the dashboard, all outlets black plastic finished.
- On-board computer control pod sited on driver's side, next to the rev counter.
- Auxiliary warning lights within main instruments.
- Four-spoke steering wheel, either entirely leather clad or half leather/half wood veneer. Incorporates horn push and driver's air bag, and embossed Jaguar growler head. Side controls for operation of audio system. High-spec models incorporate similar side controls for cruise control.
- Centre console (similar design and layout to X-300 saloons), incorporating digital air conditioning controls and read-out, auxiliary lighting, seat heating (where fitted), traction control, headlight adjustment, and audio unit. This area around the sound system controls was modified in post-2004 models. J-gate transmission quadrant with black surround incorporating buttons for 'Sport' mode and (where fitted) cruise control. Flush-mounted ashtray with damped lid, behind which is the centre console arm-rest and glove box. Cup-holders in arm-rest (where fitted).
- Passenger side airbag situated under veneered dash panel, below which is the glove box with lid, trimmed to match interior of the car.

The later facelift XKR model with enlarged mesh grille and under-valance.

Very late XKR rear, incorporating the quadruple exhaust tailpipes, revised, deeper bumper/valance and 'R' badging.

4.2 S model from 2005 with revised seating, alternative veneer choice and inset navigational system replacing the auxiliary gauges.

- Soft door side trims incorporating chromed door handles. Door pulls incorporating pocket fitted with wood-veneered window switch pack.
- Front door panel audio speakers fitted behind trim panels, with tweeter speakers (Premium Sound system only) fitted in forward portion of door top window channel area.
- Reclining seats with integral headrests trimmed in leather (some part-cloth on earlier Sport spec models) with electric adjustment controlled from the side of the seat. Post 2001 models with more substantial seating incorporating separate, adjustable headrests. Different seat style options from 2004 on.
- Rear bench-style sculptured occasional seating with seat belts, flanked by speaker grilles in rear side panels. On coupé models large rear parcel shelf incorporates woofer speaker and grille.

NB: Interior differences between coupé and convertible models are restricted to the hood operation button on the centre console, shaping of the rear quarter windows, and slight differences to the trim layout to accommodate the lined hood and mechanism.

XK model specifics
XKR models
- 'Supercharged' legend incorporated into main instruments in front of driver. 'XKR' logo embossed into centre steering wheel air bag boss (later changed to stylized 'R').
- Contrast seat stitching to XK8 models.
- Style of seating upholstery changed in 2001 model year, and then later from 2004 with the option of Recaro seating available in two-tone trim colourways.
- From 2004, stylised 'R' badging featured on rear of car.
- From 2002, chromed/trimmed 'R' J-gate control knob fitted.

Trim styles
- Originally there were two styles of interior trim levels, affecting all models, except special editions. These were:

Classic
- High-quality walnut veneer woodwork.
- Complimenting upholstery trim colours.
- Matching leather or wood-veneered/leather steering wheel.
- Matching wooden gear knob.

Sport
- Dark-stained maple woodwork.
- Leather-covered steering wheel.
- Contrasting two-tone upholstery schemes.

Very late 4.2-litre naturally aspirated V8 engine installation in the XK8.

- Leather-covered gear knob.
- From 2004 Sport trim was no longer offered (and had never been offered in the US market), replaced with a wider range of trim options including veneers.

Silverstone model
- The main difference between this model and other XKR models is in the upholstery – black with red piping to leather and carpets.

XKR100 model
- Black trim only.

Carbon Fibre model
- Carbon fibre dashboard replacing veneer.
- Recaro sports seating.

Portfolio model
- High-quality burr walnut interior woodwork.
- Matching leather trim with high-quality stitching, piping, and carpet edges to match exterior blue or red of models, including steering wheels.

Victory/S models
- Elm veneer interior for XK8s, carbon fibre interior trim on XKR versions only.
- Polished sill tread plates.

NB: There is also a range R-Performance options available for the XK models. For further information consult the options listing.

1: *When 19in and 20in alloy wheels are fitted to XK models a special black rubber insert is fitted to the wheel-arch.*

2: *18-inch Double Five, standard fit on XKR at launch.*

3: *These Sport wheels were never fitted as standard but were available as an option.*

4: *17in Gemini wheel (standard equipment on later model XK8s).*

5: *18in Centaur wheel (later alternative to Flute and Double Five wheels).*

6: *19in Apollo (2003/4 option).*

7: *18in Hydra (later XKR standard wheel).*

8: *20in Detroit (R-Performance split-rim wheel).*

9: *20in Montreal (R-Performance split-rim wheel).*

10: *20in Paris (R-Performance split-rim wheel).*

11: *17in Lamina (standard for XK8s, 2004 on).*

12: *18in Impeller (later optional).*

13: *19in Atlas (final fit XK8 S/Victory, and others optional).*

14: *18in Aris (2004/5 standard higher spec XK8 models, others optional).*

15: *20in Sepang (R-Performance split-rim wheel, only for post 2004 model year cars).*

16: *The Victory wheels fitted to the very last Victory special edition models destined for the US market.*

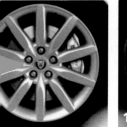

Technical specifications

	4.0-litre	4.0-litre supercharged
cc	3,996	3,996
Bore and stroke (mm)	86 x 86	86 x 86
Compression ratio	10.75:1	9:1
bhp	290	370
@ rpm	6,100	6,150
Torque (lb ft)	290	387
@ rpm	4,250	3,600
Fuelling	Fuel injection	Fuel injection
Transmission	5-speed auto	5-speed auto
Wheel size (in)	17 or 18	18 or 19
Suspension front	Ind unequal length wishbones, anti-dive, coil springs	Ind unequal length wishbones, anti-dive, coil springs
Rear suspension	Ind double wishbones, driveshafts as upper links, anti-squat, coil springs, CATS optional	Ind double wishbones, driveshafts as upper links, anti-squat, coil springs
Brakes	4 wheel disc, all ventilated	4 wheel disc, all ventilated
Performance		
0–60mph (sec)	6.5	5.2
Top speed (mph)	155	155
Average mpg	23	23
Dimensions		
Length (in)	187	187
Width (in)	72	72
Height (in)	51	51
Wheelbase (in)	102	102
Front track (in)	57	57
Rear track (in)	57	57
Weight (lb)	3,560 (3,759 convertible)	3,616 (3,814 convertible)

Optional extras

Mud flaps.
Cruise control (where not fitted as standard).
Tailored over-mats.
Headlight power-wash system.
Premium hi-fi system with CD auto-changer in boot.
Child's safety seat.
Child's booster cushion.
First aid kit for boot area.
Space-saver spare wheel.
Full-size spare wheel.
Fire extinguisher for boot area.
Jaguar warning triangle.
Headlamp converters.
Headlamp safety covers.
Mobile telephone kits.
Snow chains.
Luggage net for boot area.
Witter tow bar kit.
Cup-holders for forward centre console area.
Heated windscreen.
Ultrasonic intrusion security system.

Tool kit roll.
Heated front seats.
Jaguar 'growler' alloy wheel centre badges, various colours.
Power folding door mirrors.
Chrome door mirror surrounds (where not fitted).
Bright rear number plate surround (chrome).
Self-dipping rear view mirror.
Wood/leather steering wheel (where not fitted).
Fog lamp protective covers.
Wind deflector (convertible models only).
Tailored front seat covers.
Boot-mounted carrier.
Luggage box for boot mounting on carrier.
Boot rack ski holder.
Boot rack Cycle/Mountain Bike holder.
Various options of fitted luggage for the boot.
Round alloy gear knob.
Satellite navigation system (later cars).
Reverse park aid.
Auxiliary power socket.
Tracker security system.
Aspheric door mirrors.

	4.2-litre	4.2-litre supercharged
cc	4,196	4,196
Bore and stroke (mm)	96 x 90.3	96 x 90.3
Compression ratio	11:1	9:1
bhp	300	400
@ rpm	6,000	6,100
Torque (lb ft)	310	408
@ rpm	4,100	3,500
Fuelling	Fuel injection	Fuel injection
Transmission	6-speed auto	6-speed auto
Wheel size (in)	17, 18, or 19	17, 18,19, or 20
Suspension front	Ind unequal length wishbones, anti-dive, coil springs	Ind unequal length wishbones, anti-dive, coil springs
Rear suspension	Ind double wishbones, driveshafts as upper links, anti-squat, coil springs, CATS optional	Ind double wishbones, driveshafts as upper links, anti-squat, coil springs
Brakes	4 wheel disc, all ventilated	4 wheel disc, all ventilated
Performance		
0–60mph (sec)	6.1	5.2
Top speed (mph)	155	155
Average mpg	24.9	22.9
Dimensions		
Length (in)	187	187
Width (in)	72	72
Height (in)	51	51
Wheelbase (in)	102	102
Front track (in)	57	57
Rear track (in)	57	57
Weight (lb)	3,715 (3,913 convertible)	3,825 (4,001 convertible)

Lockable boot-mounted security box.
Adaptive cruise control.
Xenon headlight units (where not fitted).
Heated rear screen.
Rear spoiler.
Air filtration system to air conditioning.
Cold climate pack.
Birds Eye Maple veneer (2004 as alternative to walnut veneer).
Burr Elm veneer (2004 as alternative to walnut veneer).
Piano Black finish (2004 as alternative to walnut veneer).
Memory pack of interior trim additions.
Technology pack of Adaptive cruise control, speed limiter, Alpine sound system, and navigational system.
18in seven-spoke Sports alloy wheels (exposed wheel nuts).
17in XJR five-spoke alloy wheels (exposed wheel nuts).
17in five-spoke Revolver chromed alloy wheels.
18in Apollo alloy wheels (later cars).

17in XJR style five-spoke alloy wheels.
17in Lamina five-spoke alloy wheels (later cars).
18in Impeller alloy wheels (later cars).
18in seven-flute alloy wheels.
17in Gemini five-spoke double flute alloy wheels (post-2002).
18in Centaur seven-spoke alloy wheels (post-2002).
18in Hydra alloy wheels (standard on XKR post-2002).
18in Aris (2004/05 model year optional choice).
19in Atlas (2004/05 model year optional choice).

R-Performance specifics
18in Milan split rim alloy wheels.
18in Winter alloy wheels.
20in Paris split rim alloy wheels.
20in Detroit split rim alloy wheels.
20in Montreal nine-spoke alloy wheels (post-2002).
20in Sepang (only applicable to facelift models, post 2004).
Brembo brakes.
XK handling pack (XK8 models only).

Colour schemes

Exterior Colours	Details	Interior Sport	Fascia	Details
Spindrift White	To 2001	Charcoal	Charcoal	
Sherwood Green	To 1999	Ivory	Charcoal	
Antigua Blue	To 2000	Oatmeal	Charcoal	To 2002
Anthracite (black)	To 2002	Nimbus	Charcoal	2000–2
Titanium Grey	1996/7, 2000	Dove	Charcoal	From 2003
British Racing Green	To 2004	Cranberry	Charcoal	From 2003
Aquamarine*	To 1998	Cranberry/Charcoal	contrast	From 2003
Topaz (gold)	To 2004	Heritage Tan	Charcoal	From 2003
Carnival Red	To 2003	Heritage Tan/Charcoal	contrast	From 2003
Sapphire Blue	To 2002			
Ice Blue	To 1997			
Meteorite Silver	1997–2000			
Amaranth (Purle)	1997–9	**Veneer**		
Phoenix Red	1999–2004	Grey Maple		
(first year XKR only)		Burr Walnut	option	2003–4
Alpine Green	1999–2000	Grey Stain		2003–4
Emerald Green	2000–2	Carbon Fibre		From 2004
Mistral	2000–2	Burr Elm		From 2004
Westminster Blue	2000–2	Piano Black	option	From 2004
Pacific Blue	2000–4			
Seafrost	2000–4			
Platinum	From 2000			
White Onyx	2001–4			
Roman Bronze	2001–2			
Zircon	2003–4			
Jaguar Racing Green	From 2003			
Quartz	From 2003			
Adriatic Blue	2003–4			
Slate	2003–4			
Ebony	2003–4			
Midnight	From 2003			
Ultraviolet Blue	2004			
Salsa Red	2004			
Radiance Red	2003–4			
Satin Silver*	2005			
Bay Blue*	2005			
Frost Blue*	2005			
Copper Black*	2005			

* = Relates to Victory and S models only for 2005 model year

*All interior colour schemes optional
with exterior paint finishes.*

Interior Classic	Fascia	Details	Hood	Details
Teal	Dark Teal	To 1999	Black	
Cashmere	Sable	To 2004	Blue	
Ivory	Sable		Green	To 2004
Charcoal	Charcoal		Stone	To 1999
Oatmeal	Antelope	To 2002	Dark Beige	
Nimbus	Slate	2000–4	Light Beige	2000-4
Dove		From 2003	Sable or Flint	
Cranberry		2003–4		
Cranberry/Charcoal	contrast	2003–4		
Heritage Tan		2003–4		
Heritage Tan/Charcoal	contrast	2003–4		
Veneer				
Grey Maple	option	From 2003		
Burr Walnut				

Seating Style	Details
Classic	Standard on XK8s to 2005
Sport	Standard on XKRs ans better spec'd XK8s to 2005
Sport Luxury	New-style standard seating from 2005
Recaro	Standard on higher spec'd XKRs

Prices and production volumes

	Price New(£)	1995	1996	1997	1998	1999	2000
XK8 4.0-litre coupé	47,950	■	■	■	■	■	■
XK8 4.0-litre convertible	54,950	■	■	■	■	■	■
XKR coupé	60,105	–	–	–	–	■	■
XKR convertible	67,105	–	–	–	–	■	■
XKR Silverstone coupé	67,310	–	–	–	–	–	■
XKR Silverstone convertible	72,710	–	–	–	–	–	■

	Price New(£)	2001	2002	2003	2004	2005	Total
XK8 4.0-litre coupé	47,950	■	■	–	–	–	19,748*
XK8 4.0-litre convertible	54,950	■	■	–	–	–	46,770*
XKR coupé	60,105	■	■	–	–	–	9,478*
XKR convertible	67,105	■	■	–	–	–	13,620*
XKR Silverstone coupé	67,310	–	–	–	–	–	233
XKR Silverstone convertible	72,710	–	–	–	–	–	325
XKR 100 coupé	69,950	■	–	–	–	–	100
XKR 100 convertible	74,950	■	–	–	–	–	100
XK8 4.2-litre coupé	48,700	–	■	■	■	■	–
XK8 4.2-litre convertible	55,345	–	■	■	■	■	–
XKR 4.2-litre coupé	56,695	–	■	■	■	■	–
XKR 4.2-litre convertible	63,345	–	■	■	■	■	–
XKR Carbon Fibre coupé	64,650	–	–	–	■	■	–
XKR Carbon Fibre con.	71,450	–	–	–	■	■	–
XK Portfolio convertible	66,645	–	–	–	■	–	–
XK8 Victory/S coupé	50,000	–	–	–	–	■	–
XK8 Victory/S convertible	56,800	–	–	–	–	■	–
XKR Victory/S coupé	60,000	–	–	–	–	■	–
XKR S convertible	66,800	–	–	–	–	■	–

(*includes special editions)

Production changes

1996
XK8 coupé/convertible introduced.

1997
Boot-mounted high level brake light fitted.

1998
XKR models became available.

1999
Stiffening pillar added to seat belt anchorage/B post area on convertibles.
Servotronic power steering system from XKR now fitted to XK8 models.
Air assisted fuel injectors fitted to V8 engines.
Continually variable cam timing replaced two-stage phasing on 4.0-litre engines.
Electronic cruise control actuation fitted.

2000
Adaptive cruise control fitted to XKR model.
Satellite navigation system available on XK models.
Rain sensing wipers available for XKR models only.
Enhanced Alpine 320-watt Premium sound system for all models.
Electric seat belt tensioners added to all models.
XJR engine enhanced with new engine management system.
CD system standardised on all XK models.
XKR Silverstone Special Edition introduced.

2001
XK8/R facelift, flush-mounted front fog lamps in revised nose section.
XK8 revised front 'splitter' bar design.
New lens style rear light clusters with chromed surrounds.
Chrome boot plinth now incorporating external boot lid catch.
Revised rear bumper with deeper skirt.
Towing eye now fitted behind bumper under concealed flap.
Larger chromed exhaust tailpipes.
Adaptive Restraint Technology fitted.
Reinforced front side-members in bodyshell for extra stiffness.

New front seat design with separate headrests and extra electrical adjustment.
XKR 100 introduced to commemorate 100th anniversary of founder of company.

2002
4.2-litre engines replace 4.0-litre.
ZR 6-speed automatic transmission fitted to all models.
XKR standardised with larger Brembo ventilated disc brakes.
CATS suspension standardised on all XK models.
Emergency Brake Assist technology added.
Revised rear 'solid' badging.
Zenon headlights standardised on all models.
Leaping cat mascot on passenger side air bag door.
Recaro racing seats now available as extra cost option.

2004
Styling makeover for final production period, incorporating enlarged nose area, over-sills, and front and rear bumper/valance treatment.
Removal of side mouldings, black window surrounds, rear spoiler added to XK8, and larger spoiler for XKR models.
Revised exhaust treatment according to model.
Addition of driver-controlled Automatic Speed Limiter System.
Availability of special technology and premium packs to further enhance specification.

2005
Range rationalised with final production special editions, plus reduction of paint, interior finishes.
Production discontinued.

Chassis numbers

Model

Model	
XK8 models	Vin No. (see table 6*)

*Table 6 appears on page 319.

The **XJ8 saloons** 1997 to 2002

Background

After the success, though limited production period, of the X-300 range introduced under Ford influence, in September 1997 the next generation of XJ saloons appeared to replace it. Coded X-308, this was the first time that the designation XJ8 was seen, as the essence of the new models was the AJ-V8 engine, first seen in the XK8 a year earlier. As well as the 4.0-litre V8, both normally aspirated and supercharged, there was a new 3.2-litre version for entry level models.

Mechanically the XJ8s were improved in other areas, with better gearbox, suspension upgrades, and improved steering areas. Stylistically they looked very similar to the X-300 but were in fact different in many areas, not least in having an entirely new interior layout. Build quality was improved yet again over the previous model.

Following on from the success of the X-300, an expansive range of cars was offered, from a base 3.2-litre V8 through to the supercharged XJR version, with a model built to suit most buyer's requirements. Just as there were two Daimler models in the X-300 range, so there were for the XJ8, only this time both would utilise V8 power units and one would be of the supercharged type, making the Daimler Super V8 the fastest production Daimler ever produced.

However, just as the X-300 range had a relatively short production run, so too did the XJ8 range, which only lasted until 2002. Even so, during this time the range was changed several times and all the cars gained a unique reputation for quality and longevity, more so than any previous Jaguar saloon models.

The last XJ8s left the production line in mid-2002 prior to the launch of their replacements, coded X-350. There would be gap of nearly 12 months before the new cars were available to the public, during which time the last remaining examples of the XJ8 were sold through, marking the end of another Jaguar era.

The all-new technology of the replacement X-350s will see the flagship range of Jaguar models through more years than the X-308.

Model range and development

The XJ8 encapsulated a whole range of models very similar to the outgoing X-300 cars, based around the 3.2-litre and 4.0-litre V8 engines.

Models available at launch
XJ8 saloon (3.2-litre)
XJ8 Sovereign (4.0-litre)
XJ8 Sport (3.2-litre)
XJ8 4.0-litre
XJR supercharged saloon (4.0-litre)
Daimler Eight (4.0-litre)
Daimler Super V8 (Supercharged 4.0-litre)

This total of eight models was one less than was available for the X-300 range, but each one was specifically geared to a particular sector of the anticipated market. The base XJ6 3.2-litre (or Executive, as it was also known and later designated) was an ideal entry level into Jaguar flagship motoring. Ideal for those who wanted the prestige of a big luxury saloon but at a bargain price, it nevertheless offered such items as air conditioning, alloy wheels, and leather upholstery as standard equipment. The XJ8 4.0-litre was initially more or less a larger-engined version of the XJ8, though later it became equipped as a Sport model but retained the exterior chrome trim and interior veneer.

The Sport was similarly priced and roughly to the same specification but offered a slightly stiffer ride, wider tyres and wheels, colour keying of exterior trim, and a more youthful interior, again all in leather. In contrast the Sovereign model was, as usual, intended for the traditional Jaguar owner who wanted all the luxury features as standard with the benefit of lots of chrome and detail.

The supercharged XJR took up the mantle of the six-cylinder model but offered significantly better performance and refinement and was again intended for the BMW M5 and similar market. The most powerful model in the range, it also benefited from further enhanced suspension and steering and even wider wheels. As before, the high performance, a harsher ride, and superb handling meant that to a degree luxury equipment levels were tempered.

At the top of the range were the Daimler models, to meet the needs of the company chairman who wanted the ultimate in luxury and, once again, rarity, production numbers being low compared to the other models. It was also thought that with the demise of the V12 Jaguar, the Daimlers would cater for a slightly wider market this time. Virtually everything was supplied as standard equipment, but with softer touring suspension and slight alterations to exterior and interior trim to differentiate them from Jaguars. The Daimler Eight used the normally aspirated 4.0-litre engine and, indeed, met and exceeded the specification of the equivalent Jaguar Sovereign. The Super V8 offered XJR performance with slightly softer suspension, the longer wheelbase bodyshell, and an enhanced interior.

Short and long wheelbase bodyshells were still available, although the short version was earmarked for the XJ8, Sport, and XJR models, while the majority of Sovereigns and Daimlers were supplied with the longer shell.

Outside the UK the same principles applied for the XJ8 as had with the X-300 models, namely the base models were not offered and the Daimler model range was called Jaguar Vanden Plas.

Little happened to the range over the next couple of years, although at one time the 3.2-litre Sport was dropped, at which time the 4.0-litre XJ8 was upgraded to become a mix of luxury saloon and sport model. Later the 3.2-litre Sport returned due to popular demand, and thereafter it stayed in production until the end.

In the last year of production (2002) Jaguar introduced a new model to the range, effectively

External styling changes from the previous XJ6/12 (X-300) models to the XJ8 range are subtle. Side views of both cars show the XJ8 model (on the right) with oval reflectors set into the front and rear bumper bars.

An unusual view of the XJ8 shows the chromed bumper blades at the front. Previous models enjoyed a single full-width blade.

Frontal differences between the 1994–7 six- and twelve-cylinder models and the V8s are shown in the more rounded valance air intake, circular fog lamps, oval indicator lenses, differing styles of headlights, and the more rounded exterior to the radiator grille.

Rear differences were the styling 'lip' to the bumper bar/valance and revised badging of the V8 (on the left).

bringing together trim aspects of the 3.2 with the Sovereign model. Called the SE (Special Equipment), a high degree of standard interior accommodation was offered, all for less than £36,000, making it a very attractive proposition in this sector of the market.

Minor changes took place to all models throughout production. Specifications were enhanced and such items as alloy wheel design changed regularly to meet fashion needs.

No other special versions of the X-308 were produced although, as with the X-300, the Eagle Coachworks produced four- and six-door limousines and hearses, both Jaguar and Daimler variants.

The XJ8 proved a vital flagship model range to Jaguar, even after the launch of the new and smaller S-type and X-type models from 1999 on. These were arguably the best cars Jaguar had built up to that time.

Exterior identification points

XJ8 model

- Chrome trim to radiator grille, screen surrounds, rain gutters, waistline trims and boot plinth.
- Matt black window frames.
- Colour co-ordinated door mirrors and handles.
- Grey plastic vertical slats to the radiator grille.
- Distinctive halogen headlights with chrome centre spot and vertical rib.
- A single contrasting swage coachline.
- 'Jaguar' and XJ8' badging to boot lid.
- 20-spoke alloy wheels standard equipment, with plastic centre caps to cover wheel nuts incorporating grey Jaguar growler emblems.
- For later updates on 4.0-litre models see detailed photographs.

Sport model

- As XJ8 except for:
- Black vertical slats to the radiator grille, radiator grille surround colour keyed to exterior paint finish.
- Dual coachline above the side rubbing strips.
- Matt black finished rain gutters and front and rear screen surrounds.
- Dimple alloy wheels.
- 'Jaguar' and 'XJ Sport' badging to boot lid and 'V8' badging to B/C post.

XJR model

- As Sport except for:
- Colour co-ordinated radiator grille shell with mesh centre replacing the vanes.
- Sport ventilated five-spoke alloy wheels.
- Larger exhaust outlets.
- 'Jaguar' and 'XJR' badging to boot lid.

Boot badge legends and backgound colours changed from the previous X-300 models. For example, most XJ8 badges are based on a grey background (Daimlers being the exception). The 'Executive' badge only applied from 2001.

The B/C pillars between the doors always show the 'V8' insignia, unlike X-300 models, which show 'V12', 'Sport', 'XJR', etc, according to model.

The XJ8's interior was 90 per cent changed from that of the X-300, with curved dashboard, inset instruments (like the XK8), and curved centre console surround. This car is an XJ8 model (the half-wood/half-leather steering wheel was an extra-cost option). The same style applied to Executive and SE models.

Above left: XJ8 consoles are more rounded than on the X-300, and include an integrated audio/telephone pad. This is a post-1999 model, with a leather-clad gear selector surround instead of the black plastic used on earlier models.

Above right: XJ8 4.0-litre interior with revised seat cushions, as used from 2000 on. These models were available with or without dark stained maple woodwork.

Sovereign models, like the Daimler cars, enjoyed full chroming, including window frames and radiator grille.

The supercharged model is easily identifiable by its mesh radiator grille insert and lack of chrome trim.

Sport models featured de-chroming like the XJR, but had the grille centre vane panel painted in grey.

Daimler models like the one on the left included fluted grille and chromed door handles/door mirrors. The XJ8 (later the Executive model) is on the right, with different grille treatment.

One of the last Executive models, the SE shared much of its specification with the Sovereign, and had a chromed grille but no chromed door frames.

The rear view of XJ8 Executive and SE models shows a chromed boot plinth and relevant badging but no chromed surrounds to the rear light units. A high-level brake light in the rear screen is fitted to all XJ V8 models.

As with the previous models, V8 Daimlers used a shorter fluted chromed boot plinth.

Rear aspect of the XJR model shows a painted boot plinth (also applicable to Sport models) and larger exhaust tailpipes.

Sovereign model

■ All-chrome exterior trim including window frames, front and rear screens, and rear light cluster surrounds.
■ A choice of alloy wheels (see photographs).
■ 'V8' script to B/C post, 'Jaguar' and 'Sovereign' badging to rear boot lid.

Daimler models

■ As Sovereign except for:
■ Fluted design radiator grille surround and boot plinth (and of shorter width to Jaguar type).
■ Sunroof standard on Super V8.
■ Unique alloy wheels (see photographs) and chromed door mirrors/door handles.
■ 'Daimler' badging replacing Jaguar on boot lid, 'Eight' or 'Super V8' badging also on boot lid.

SE model

■ As XJ8 except for 'SE' badging on boot lid and reverse park aid equipment fitted as standard to rear bumper.

NB: Market differences applied to some overseas cars: eg 'Vanden Plas' badging, use of Daimler grille to Jaguar models, etc.

A wide variety of alloy wheel designs were available throughout production, many of which could have been specified by buyers upon initial purchase. A chromed mesh radiator grille was also made available later in production for the XJR model, so some cars were fitted with this from new.

Interior identification points

General points applicable to all XK models

■ Sunroof standard on Super V8.
■ Curved dashboard with main instruments deeply inset in front of the driver with on-board computer control panel. Black plastic air conditioning outlets, one either side of dashboard, plus centre vent area flanking circular clock. Centre console of similar appearance to previous models although more curved in style with integrated audio system and auxiliary switch gear for heated seats (where fitted), traction control (where fitted), headlight adjustment, and air conditioning controls with digital temperature read-out and telephone pad controls.
■ Veneered centre console containing J-gate gear shift mounted initially in black plastic surround, later changed to leather. Switches incorporated for Sport gearbox mode and cruise control (where fitted).
■ Concealed trim flush-mounted damped ashtray arrangement as XK8.

Above left: Interior view of the Sport model with dark stained maple woodwork and high contrast interior colour schemes. The similar style seating to X-300 Sport models was different to later 4.0-litre XJ8 cars (see the picture on page 230). All XJ8 models had leather upholstery. This early car shows the black plastic surround to the gear lever area, later changed to stitched leather.

Above right: Front interior of the Daimler model. All Daimlers featured better quality, burr walnut veneering, with boxwood inlays as seen in the passenger side fascia and door panel.

Rear compartment of Daimler Super V8. Veneered picnic tables and boxwood inlays are standard to all models, while the split-seating arrangement is standard on the Super V8 and optional on the Eight.

Above left: Twenty-spoke alloy wheels were fitted to XJ8 models for two years, and were optional on others.

Above right: Dimple alloys, previously fitted to X-300 Sport models, continued on all XJ8 Sport cars.

Above left: The Cosmic alloy was never fitted as standard equipment but was available as an option to other alloy wheels on XJ8 models.

Above right: The Crown alloy wheels normally fitted to Daimler models were also available on Jaguars, but with a growler emblem in the centre.

- Centre armrest incorporating lid and storage area.
- Steering wheel of four-spoke design common to all Jaguars of this era, either leather-covered or wood/leather-covered incorporating air bag and horn push. Auxiliary switch packs to either side of steering wheel for audio controls, telephone, and cruise control (where fitted).
- Passenger side glove-box of larger dimensions to previous X-300 model.
- Door trim panels incorporating full-length armrests, window lift controls, and map pockets with shaped wood-veneered cappings.
- Curved front seats, all electrically operated, with vertical pleats and integrated stitching.
- Matching rear bench arrangement with fitted headrests and fold down centre armrest.

XJ8 model
- Initially 3.2-litre and later SE plus early 4.0-litre models. As above but with figured walnut veneer to dashboard, centre console ski-slope, and door cappings.
- Complimentary trim finishes in two-tone and normal vertically pleated seating.

Sport model
- As XJ8 except for
- Dark-stained maple woodwork throughout.
- Contrast two-tone upholstery and squarer more supportive sports front seats with wider horizontal pleating and aerated sections. No lumbar support available.
- Rear bench seating to match.

Sovereign model
- As XJ8 except for burr walnut veneer woodwork throughout. Wood veneer finish to door window lift switch packs.

Later 4.0-litre models
- A mix of Sport and Sovereign, incorporating walnut veneer woodwork but with slightly revised sports seating with horizontal pleats (see photographs).

XJR model
- As Sport.

Daimler models
- As Sovereign except for:
- Boxwood inlay to woodwork, higher quality burr walnut veneer woodwork throughout.
- More rounded seating with wider pleats in higher quality leather.
- Colour-keyed items such as handbrake surround and gear knob.
- Walnut-veneered picnic tables behind front seats.
- Only available on longer wheelbase models, primarily for Super V8, individualised rear

Above: *The complete range of later alloy wheels fitted and available on XJ8 models.*

Left: *The Penta five-spoke fluted wheel was another alloy available on XJ models.*

seating arrangement with extended centre console between seats and following on from front armrest area, incorporating wood-veneered panel and electric switchgear for electrically adjustable seating.

All details of trim and specification given above relate to standard production cars. Certain owners may well have specified changes to suit their individual requirements, so it is not unusual to find some more basic models with a higher specification than that described here.

Technical specifications

	3.2-litre	4.0-litre
cc	3,248	3,996
Bore and stroke (mm)	86 x 70	86 x 86
Compression ratio	10.5:1	10.75:1
bhp	240	290
@ rpm	6,350	6,100
Torque (lb ft)	233	290
@ rpm	4,350	4,250
Fuelling	Fuel injection	Fuel injection
Transmission	ZR 5-speed auto	ZF 5-speed auto
Wheel size (in)	16, alloy	17, alloy
Suspension front	Ind unequal length wishbones, anti-dive, coil springs	Ind unequal length wishbones, anti-dive, coil springs
Suspension rear	Ind double wishbones, driveshafts as upper links, anti-squat, coil springs, CATS optional	Ind double wishbones, driveshafts as upper links, anti-squat, coil springs, CATS optional
Brakes	4 wheel disc, all ventilated	4 wheel disc, all ventilated
Performance		
0–60mph (sec)	8.1	6.9
Top speed (mph)	140	150
Average mpg	23.5	23.7
Dimensions		
Length (in)	197 (201 long wheelbase)	197 (201 long wheelbase)
Width (in)	69	69
Height (in)	51 (52 long wheelbase)	51 (52 long wheelbase)
Wheelbase (in)	112 (116 long wheelbase)	112 (116 long wheelbase)
Front track (in)	57	57
Rear track (in)	57	57
Weight (lb)	3,769	3,769

Optional extras

Mud flaps.
Cruise control (where not fitted as standard).
Tailored over-mats.
Headlight power-wash system.
Premium hi-fi system with CD auto-changer in boot.
Child's safety seat.
Child's booster cushion.
First aid kit for boot area.
Space-saver spare wheel.
Full-size spare wheel.
Fire extinguisher for boot area.
Jaguar warning triangle.
Headlamp converters.
Headlamp safety covers.
Mobile telephone kits.
Snow chains.
Luggage net for boot area.
Witter tow bar kit.
Cup-holders for forward centre console area.
Heated windscreen.

Ultrasonic intrusion security system.
Additional zip-fastening tool kit.
Heated front seats (where not fitted).
Jaguar 'growler' alloy wheel centre badges, various colours.
Power folding door mirrors.
Chrome door mirror surrounds (where not fitted).
Bright rear number plate surround (chrome).
Self-dipping rear view mirror.
Wood/leather steering wheel (where not fitted).
Fog lamp protective covers.
Tailored front seat covers.
Boot cargo net.
Boot luggage hooks.
Luggage retainer clips and/or straps.
Roof-mounted rack.
Two-bar roof rack carrier.
Ski/cycle holders.
Luggage frame for roof rack.
Compact, Sport or large roof box.
Various options of fitted luggage for the boot.

	4.0-litre supercharged
cc	3,996
Bore and stroke (mm)	86 x 86
Compression ratio	9:1
bhp	370
@ rpm	6,150
Torque (lb ft)	387
@ rpm	3,600
Fuelling	Fuel injection
Transmission	ZF 5-speed auto
Wheel size (in)	18, alloy
Suspension front	Ind unequal length wishbones, anti-dive, coil springs
Suspension rear	Ind double wishbones, driveshafts as upper links, anti-squat, coil springs, CATS
Brakes	4 wheel disc, all ventilated
Performance	
0–60mph (sec)	5.3
Top speed (mph)	155
Average mpg	21.6
Dimensions	
Length (in)	197
Width (in)	69
Height (in)	51
Wheelbase (in)	112
Front track (in)	57
Rear track (in)	57
Weight (lb)	3,913

Round alloy gear knob.
Satellite navigation system (later cars).
Reverse park aid (where not fitted).
Auxiliary power socket.
Tracker security system.
Aspheric door mirrors.
Lockable boot-mounted security box.
Xenon headlight units (where not fitted).
Air filtration system to air conditioning.
Engine block heater.
Cold climate pack.
Electric sunroof (where not fitted).
Rear window blinds.
Deflector for sunroof.
CATS suspension package (where not fitted).
Chromed grille surround (where not fitted).
Alternative woodwork veneers (according to model).
16in 20-spoke alloy wheels (plastic centre caps).
16in Dimple with anthracite infill alloy wheels.
16in Dimple alloy wheels (plain).

16in Crown alloy wheels (centre cap covers).
16in Starburst alloy wheels.
16in Cosmic five double spoke alloy wheels.
16in Lunar seven-spoke alloy wheels (later models).
16in Eclipse five-spoke alloy wheels (later models).
16in multi-spoke Corona alloy wheels (later models).
17in XJR Sport alloy wheels (exposed wheel nuts).
17in Celtic ten-spoke alloy wheels (later models).
18in Penta five-spoke alloy wheels (later models).
18in seven-flute alloy wheels.
18in Asteroid seven-spoke alloy wheels (later standard XJR model).

R-Performance specifics
18in Milan split rim alloy wheels.
18in Winter alloy wheels.
19in Montreal alloy wheels (later models).
Brembo brakes.
XK handling pack (XK8 models only).

Colour schemes

Exterior	Details	Models applicable	Interior Sport/XJR	Fascia	Details
Spindrift White	To 2001	Non Sport/XJR until 2000	Charcoal	Charcoal	
Sherwood Green	To 2000	Non Sport/XJR	Ivory	Charcoal	
Seafront		Non Sport/XJR until 2000	Oatmeal	Charcoal	
Anthracite (black)			Nimbus	Charcoal	To 2002
Titanium Grey	To 2002	Non Sport/XJR until 2000			
British Racing Green					
Aquamarine	To 1999	Sport/XJR			
Topaz (gold)		Non Sport/XJR until 2000			
Carnival Red		Spot/XJR until 2000			
Sapphire Blue					
Mistral	To 2002	Non Sport/XJR until 2000			
Meteorite Silver	To 2000				
Amaranth (purple)	To 2000	Non Sport/XJR	**Veneer**		
Westminster Blue		Non Sport/XJR until 2000	Grey Maple		
Madeira (Maroon)	To 2000	Non Sport/XJR	Figured Walnut	option	From 2001
Spruce Green	To 1999	Non Sport/XJR	Burr Walnut	option	From 2001
Alpine Green	1999–2001	Non Sport/XJR until 2000			
Emerald Green	1999–2002	Non Sport/XJR until 2000			
Antigua Blue	1999–2000				
Platinum Grey	From 2000				
Pacific Blue	From 2000				
White Onyx	From 2001				
Roman Bronze	2001–2				
Slate Grey	2002 only				
Quartz	2002 only				
Aspen Green	2002 only				
Zircon	2002 only				

*Interior colour schemes applicable to
all Sport/XJR model exterior colours.*

Interior XJ8/Sovereign/ Daimler	Fascia	Details	Contrast Piping
Oatmeal	Antelope		Antelope
Cashmere	Sable	To 2002	Sable
Ivory	Sable		Sable
Charcoal	Charcoal		Nimbus
Nimbus	Slate	Sovereign/Daimler	Slate
Catkin	Pine	Sovereign/Daimler	Pine
Cranberry/Charcoal	contrast		
Heritage Tan			
Heritage Tan/Charcoal	contrast		
Veneer			
Figured Walnut			
Burr Walnut		Sovereign/Daimler	

Interior colour schemes applicable to all XJ, Sovereign, and Daimler exterior colours except where indicated.

Prices and production volumes

	Price new (£)	1997	1998	1999	2000
XJ8 3.2-litre	35,675	■	■	■	■
XJ8 3.2-litre long wheelbase	–	■	■	■	■
XJ8 3.2-litre Sovereign	–	■	■	■	■
XJ8 3.2-litre Sovereign long wheelbase	–	■	■	■	■
3.2-litre Sport	34,475	■	■	■	–
XJ8 3.2-litre Executive	35,950	–	–	–	■
XJ8 3.2-litre SE	35,950	–	–	–	–
XJ8 4.0-litre	40,975	■	■	■	■
XJ8 4.0-litre long wheelbase	–	■	■	■	■
XJ8 4.0-litre Sovereign	43,950	■	■	■	■
XJ8 4.0-litre Sovereign long wheelbase	46,575	■	■	■	■
XJ8 4.0-litre SE	40,950	–	–	–	–
XJR	50,675	■	■	■	■
XJR 100	58,935	–	–	–	–
4.0-litre Vanden Plas	–	–	–	■	■
4.0-litre Vanden Plas long wheelbase	–	■	■	■	■
4.0-litre VDP S/C long wheelbase	–	–	■	■	■
Daimler Eight	–	■	■	■	■
Daimler Eight long wheelbase	52,575	■	■	■	■
Daimler Super V8	–	–	■	■	■
Daimler Super V8 long wheelbase	62,775	■	■	■	■
Total production					

Production changes

1997
XJ8 models introduced.

1999
Chrome external trim pack available as extra cost option for XJR model.
Short wheelbase Sovereign model becomes available.
Improved clock graphics on dashboard.
Soft-stitched colour-keyed gearbox surround replaced plastic on centre console.

Repositioned switch-pack on front passenger seat for rear adjustment.
Burr walnut option for XJR model.
Servotronic power-steering system from XKR fitted to all saloons.
Air-assisted fuel injectors fitted to all V8 engines.
Continually variable cam timing replaced two-stage phasing on 4.0-litre engines.
Electronic cruise control actuation fitted.

2001	2002	Total produced
■	–	20,235 Inc Exe/SE
■	■	771
■	■	2,095
■	■	385
■	■	1,108
■	■	
–	■	
■	■	8,369
■	■	148
■	■	36,635 Inc SE
■	■	11,566
–	■	
■	■	15,203 Inc long wheelbase
■	–	100
–	–	1
■	■	21,080
■	■	788
■	■	164
■	■	2,119
■	■	76
■	■	2,387
		126,260

NB: Use of Sovereign name varies by model and by world market.

Larger XKR style brake discs fitted to XJR model.
Sports pack became available for Sovereign models with wider alloy wheels.

2000
Satellite navigation system becomes available as extra cost option on any model.
Rain sensing wipers available on all models except XJ8 Executive.
Enhanced Alpine 320-watt Premium sound system for all models.

Improved sports seating for Sport and XJR saloons with longer cushion and improved lateral support.
XJR engine enhanced with new engine management system.
XJ8 3.2/4.0-litre models gain 12-way electric front seat adjustment as standard equipment.
XJ8 3.2/4.0-litre models gain all chromed window surrounds as standard equipment.
XJ8 3.2/4.0-litre models gain rear compartment cigar lighter and boot mounted warning triangle.
Rain sensing wipers/CD player/heated windscreen standard on Sovereign models.
XJR standard equipment now included cruise control, 12-way seat adjustment, and rain sensing wipers.
XJR standard equipment also included heated screen, CD, rear cigar lighter, tool kit, and warning triangle.
XJR standard equipment also included carpet mats, and new Asteroid alloy wheels.
320-watt Premium sound system standardised on Daimler Eight.
3.2-litre Sport model discontinued from range.

2001
3.2-litre Sport model reintroduced.
Standard XJ8 model now badged as 'Executive'.
'Executive' now fitted as standard with rain sensing wipers, CD, cruise control, and reverse park aid.
Sovereign model gains heated front seats and reverse park aid as standard equipment.
Reverse park aid fitted as standard to all Daimler models.
XJR 100 model introduced to commemorate 100th anniversary of founder of company.

2002
3.2-litre SE (Special Equipment) model introduced.
4.0-litre SE model replaces previous 4.0-litre XJ8.
Daimler and Sovereign models now made to special order only.
(End) Production of all XJ8 (X308s) discontinued.

Chassis numbers

Model

X-308 models	Vin No. (see table 5*)

*Table 5 appears on page 318.

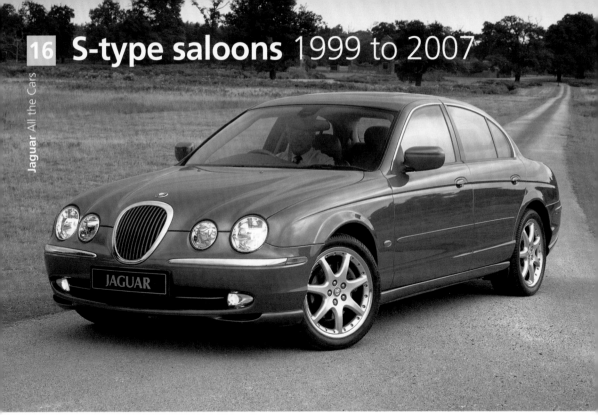

Background

It was in the mid-1950s that Jaguar recognised the potential expansion to their market if they produced a smaller luxury saloon model for those who didn't need or want a gargantuan prestige car like the Mark VII. Although there were plenty of 'medium' sized saloons around from car makers like Ford, Humber, Riley, Wolseley and others, the only company to have successfully produced a small prestige saloon in a similar class to Jaguar was Daimler (at that time still an independent company), with its Century model. Of quality manufacture, it had the image, but was a little staid and lacked somewhat on the performance front.

At the end of 1955 Jaguar introduced its legendary 2.4-litre saloon which marked a turning point in company policy, utilising new technology and offering the motor car buying public a smaller, cheaper, and more economical option, something Jaguar hadn't done since the old post-war 1.75-litre saloon had been dropped. This led the company to further success, widening their product range, market sector and, of course, profitability –exactly what the current S-type has achieved for Jaguar today. The 2.4-litre model led to the Mark 2, then extra models like the 1960s S-type, 420, and also Daimler models, and again as then, the new S-type range has expanded since its introduction in 1999; and, of course, the X-type stems from the same stable.

So successful was Jaguar in this 'new' market in the 1950s and 1960s that many other companies entered it, not least the likes of BMW, who stole the show from Jaguar in the 1980s. In contrast Jaguar took a different route with the introduction of the XJ6 in 1968 that led to a one-model policy which in itself was successful, although many mourned the passing of the sporting small 'compact' luxury models, particularly the Mark 2.

For many different reasons, not least the lack of resources and finance, Jaguar stayed with their one-saloon range throughout the life of the Series XJs, the XJ40, and the X-300/X-308, until 1999, when, after over 30 years without a smaller car, the company announced the launch of the S-type, revisiting a name from the 1960s.

Starting at a modest £26,000, the S-type was an all-new car, built at the Jaguar Castle Bromwich factory in Birmingham, the first complete Jaguar to be built there (the facility was normally used for building and painting bodies for other models in the Jaguar range). It used an all-new floorpan jointly developed with Ford (and also used by Lincoln in America), and both a new V6 engine of 3.0 litres capacity and the AJ-V8 V8 power unit used in the XK8 and XJ. There were new gearboxes, both manual and automatic, new front and rear suspensions and steering, and an entirely new body style built with the latest technology.

The very curvaceous body style was like nothing else on the market, with a multiplicity of shapes and body lines created by the very latest in body press techniques. A slight retro look was achieved with the radiator grille, a mix of racing C-type from the 1950s and Mark 2 from the 1960s. The very curved body line also, in other areas, echoes Jaguars of the past, particularly around the roof line. To go with this an all-new interior layout was part of the package, again with the latest electronics technology, even down to voice activation of some controls for the better equipped models.

The S-type became Jaguar's most successful model produced in its first couple of years, and the range has developed to include more models. It has turned out to be a fabulous addition to the range of saloons offered by Jaguar. It not only catered for a new sector of the market, which normally purchased cars like the BMW 5 Series and E class Mercedes, but also for those wishing to down-size from larger cars. It therefore found new markets that the company hadn't catered for in years, and hardly had any effect on the sales of other Jaguars.

All S-types are instantly identifiable from any other Jaguar model by the frontal treatment. This first generation car (1999–2002) shows the Mark 2/C-type radiator style treatment. Fog lights were an extra cost option on base models. The bonnet badge proclaimed the engine size (3.0- or 4.0-litre).

Model range and development

Models available at launch
S-type 3.0-litre saloon (manual or automatic)
S-type 3.0-litre SE (Special Equipment) (manual or automatic)
S-type 4.0-litre saloon (automatic)

The S-type was the most important new model since the introduction of the XJ6 in 1968, but despite its all-new technology and design it took a mere three years to get into production. The basis of its design and styling was carried through on all models, the only differences being in equipment specification and engine size, following established Jaguar practice.

All S-types featured the then unique swan neck front suspension design and new rear suspension with integrated parts from the Fords part bin. The 4.0-litre model used the existing AJ-V8 power unit from the XJ and XK8, which featured the existing ZF automatic transmission mated to the J-gate operation. No manual option was available. The new 3.0-litre V6 engine was also unique to Jaguar, although it was initially built in Canada. A very refined responsive unit, this was either mated to a Ford four-speed automatic transmission, again with J-gate operation, or a brand new Ford-built five-speed manual gearbox.

Visually the S-type was all new, with very curvaceous styling that was quicker, easier, and

Again, the rear view is entirely different to all other Jaguar models, with pronounced curvature to the boot surround. All cars have 'S-type' badging, 3.0-litre models without an engine size whereas later cars show the 'V8' insignia where applicable.

The only identifying features from the side, between the early S-types and the 2002 models are in the design of the door mirrors and a different choice of alloy wheels, but at the end of 2001 the side rubbing strips were removed.

lighter to produce than any previous Jaguar bodyshell. The styling is still unique and makes the car instantly recognisable on the road compared to any other car from any manufacturer. The interior design was all new too, and although not universally liked by many Jaguar traditionalists, the whole interior would be replanned for later production.

The state of interior trim varies dramatically according to how much the S-type buyer wants to spend, even the Special Equipment models being available with a host of extra cost options including satellite navigational systems, voice recognition operation of key controls, and so on.

Apart from minor production alterations, the S-type range remained unchanged until 2001, when a new model, the Sport, was added. Based on experience gained with the larger XJ range, the Sport offered an alternative for a younger market. It had colour co-ordinated exterior trim, a dark-stained maple interior, and the usual features such as sports seating and other minor differences in trim.

The next and most major change to the S-type range to date came in 2002, when all the models underwent a complete revamp. They received minor changes to exterior trim plus a completely new interior layout, copied from the then still new X-type and emulated in the latest X-350 models. Mechanically there were also a number of changes. Bodies were now laser welded for extra strength and higher strength steels were used in key areas. Although the 3.0-litre models remained virtually unchanged, there was a new 2.5-litre V6-engined version at a lower price, the engine being taken from the X-type saloon although still, in the case of the S-type, in rear-wheel drive form. At the same time, following on from work done on the XK8s, the 4.0-litre engines were upgraded to 4.2-litre capacity, improving their performance.

A supercharged 4.2-litre S-type also became available. This comes with a special structural 'shear ring' around the back seat area to provide a further seven per cent improvement in torsional strength to aid the vehicle's performance and handling characteristics. It also has all the usual supercharged Jaguar features, like mesh radiator grille, colour-keyed exterior trim, revised interior, and stiffer suspension layout. Lastly, all 4.2-litre S-types received a brand new ZF six-speed automatic transmission, offering the ultimate in gear change refinement.

The model continued to develop with enhanced equipment levels. In 2002 electrically adjustable foot pedals were fitted to all models.

In 2004 the bodywork was facelifted and featured a lighter, aluminium bonnet, revised bumper treatment, complete revised rear-end styling, and the removal of the side rubbing strips. Other changes included a wider range of

Facelift model from 2004 on. Note in particular the revised shaping to the front and rear bumper areas and blades, the slightly taller rear end, more prominent, less sculptured sills and overall cleaner lines.

Prior to 2002 the grille area looked like this (except for colour-coding for the Sport model). This particular car is equipped with a spring-loaded 'leaper' mascot instead of the conventional growler litre badge at this time. These leapers were only fitted to S-types for certain markets, not including the UK.

Cloth interior was standard on 3.0-litre models and, later, on 2.5-litre cars, although leather could be specified. The style of seating applied to all early models, although Sports seats could be specified.

alloy wheels, new styling for the door mirrors and, most important, the launch of the first diesel S-type, using the 2.7-litre engine covered in the 'Jaguar engines' chapter.

In 2005 the 2.5-litre engine S-types were dropped from the range and Jaguar started to offer limited editions like the XS from 2006, providing a degree of sportiness to the exterior design with revised bumper bar and spoiler treatment. For 2007 the Spirit became the base model but with extra equipment as standard, like leather upholstery and automatic transmission, and all models adopted similar frontal styling to the R model during the run-down in production to make way for the replacement model, the XF. The S-type finally ended production in 2007.

Exterior identification points

General points applicable to all S-type models

Front view

▪ Curvaceous frontal aspect instantly recognisable and different from any other Jaguar model.
▪ Oval radiator grill with chrome or painted surround, later incorporating growler badge.
▪ Four separate headlight units in spherical style, outer units incorporating side and indicator lights.
▪ All-enveloping pre-formed energy-absorbing bumper/valance arrangement mating with front wings and upper panel surround. This incorporates number plate surround, behind which is lower air intake area with splitter bar or other design according to model and year. Multi-curved one-piece rearward-hinged bonnet shaped around grille and lights, originally in steel, later changed to aluminium. Bonnet originally incorporated growler badging with litre indication, later dropped.
▪ One-piece curved windscreen with twin wiper blades.

Rear view

▪ Bonded and curved one-piece rear screen with heated element.
▪ High level brake warning light within rear screen.
▪ One-piece rear-hinged boot lid, differing in shape according to year model and, in some models, incorporating rear spoiler.
▪ Rear number plate surround in centre of boot lid with chromed finisher and lock/illumination panel.
▪ Oval rear light units, changed according to model year, with jewelled lenses.
▪ All-enveloping rear bumper bar treatment with chromed blades to match the front, but altered dependent on model year and specification.

Above left: Interior dashboard layout used until 2002, in this case with the optional satellite navigational system with screen. The half-wood/half-leather steering wheel was optional.

Above right: This console shows the manual transmission (not available on 4.0-litre models) and the alternative layout used for cars not equipped with a navigational system.

This rear compartment shot shows the different style and pleating of Sports seats.

Post 2004 S-type frontal appearance. The style of bumper/valance varies according to model, this one applying to the conventional saloon and diesel model.

■ Twin exhaust pipes with chromed trims, differing according to engine size and type.

Side view
■ Heavily swaged sides with pronounced curvature to roof section and front wing area.
■ Flush-mounted, colour-keyed door handles.
■ Sculptured and colour-keyed front door mirrors (different design on facelift models).
■ Flush-mounted indicator repeater lights at rear of front wings, and colour-keyed rubbing strips along the side (deleted on post-2001 models).
■ Sculptured sills (design changed with facelift models).
■ Limousine-style door frames that curve into the roof section.
■ Black side-window surrounds.
■ Alloy wheels fitted to all models, size and style being dependent on model year and specification.

S-type model specifics
Standard and SE models (1999–2002)
■ Radiator grille with grey plastic vertical slats.
■ Chromed bumper bar blades.
■ Fog lights initially standard equipment on SE model only.
■ 7in x 16in Classic alloy wheels standard on 3.0-litre, 7.5in x 16in Dynamic for SE and 4.0-litre, with other options at extra cost (see photographs).

Sport model (up to 2002 model year)
■ Radiator grille colour keyed to body paint.
■ Colour-keyed bumper bar blades.
■ 7.5in x 17in Sport alloy wheels fitted.
■ Colour-keyed boot lid plinth.
■ Colour-keyed rear bumper bar blades.

S-type model changes (2002–3)
■ As others above except for the following styling changes:
■ Xenon lighting treatment at the front instantly recognisable from the smaller light units internally.
■ Radiator grille surround incorporating circular growler badge at the top, eliminating the need for a badge on top of the bonnet.
■ Removal of side rubbing strips (from 2002 model year).
■ Rounded style of door mirrors fitted.
■ Chromed window surrounds (dependent upon model).
■ Revised style badging on the boot lid.

S-type R model
■ As 2002 model year styling changes except for:
■ Radiator grille colour keyed to body paint, incorporating mesh insert.

The introduction of the Sport model brought about de-chroming of exterior trim front and rear for ease of identification.

Sport interior with high contrast upholstery.

Revised S-type from 2002, showing amended grille and badging, light units, door mirrors, later style wheels, additional chrome at top of doors, and the plain sides without rubbing strips.

- Colour-keyed bumper blades and other colour co-ordinating as Sport model.
- Zeus 18in alloy wheels as standard.
- 'R-Performance' badging on boot lid.

S-type model changes (2004–7)
- Exterior facelift incorporating slightly wider and lower radiator grille with revised vanes (where applicable).
- Simpler design to front and rear bumper/valance (design varying according to model).
- Subtle changes to the curvature of bonnet panel.
- More prominent and less sculptured sill panels.
- Revised rear lighting treatment and boot panel.
- Wider boot finisher panel with concealed lock.
- From 2006 a uniform frontal styling approach was carried out with mesh grille and R style bumper/valance treatment.

XS model
- A later, special edition model, not available in 4.2-litre form.
- 18in Mercury alloy wheels.
- Lower front spoiler.
- Upper and lower bright mesh grilles.
- Boot lid spoiler.
- Exhaust pipe trail trims.
- Aluminium interior trim.
- Only available in Midnight, Platinum, Quartz or Ultraviolet colours.

Interior identification points

General points applicable to all S-types
Pre-2002
- One-piece dashboard assembly incorporating semi-circular centre console area vertically mounted in metal painted grey.
- Centre console incorporating integrated audio system, cassette holder box, damped ashtray, and auxiliary switches for air conditioning, etc, with digital readout for clock, audio, and air conditioning temperatures. Where equipped with navigational system, TV screen and controls replace cassette box. Damped ashtray below with J-gate transmission control in veneered surround with auxiliary switches for Sport mode and cruise control (where fitted). Cup-holder with flush mounted lid, armrest incorporating lift lid and storage area. Handbrake built into passenger side of console area.
- Complete instrument binnacle in front of driver, also incorporating warning lighting and illumination.
- Air conditioning vents in grey plastic either side of the dashboard and centrally mounted vents as well.

S-type R models only appeared from 2002 so have the new-style front. Note the new bumper bar/under valance style applicable to this model.

As at the front, the S-type R model had de-chromed trim at the rear, plus a boot spoiler and special badging.

A virtually new interior for all S-types from 2002 takes styling cues from X-type models. All S-types are now equipped with an electronic handbrake, operated from the chromed half-moon button between the gear lever surround and the centre console glove-box.

- On-board computer control pack set into dashboard beside binnacle.
- Passenger side glove-box underneath veneered panel concealing passenger air bag.
- Maple veneer woodwork to top of dashboard, gear surround section of centre console, and door trims.
- Four-spoke leather or leather/wood steering wheel incorporating air bag and horn push centre boss. Side of wheel controls for audio system, telephone, and cruise control (where fitted).
- Door trims sculptured with veneered inserts and wood surrounds to window lift controls. Door pulls/armrests and pre-formed pocket areas. Chrome-finished door handles with integrated lock mechanisms.
- Choice of seat styling dependent on model, all based on separate electrically adjustable front seats and bench-style rear with centre armrest.

Post-2002 (identifying differences from earlier cars)

- Dashboard assembly and layout similar to X-type and X-350 saloons, curved top roll with revised instrument binnacle in front of driver.
- Centre console of curved design with new upholstered areas between the seats. Centre console incorporating integrated audio system, cassette holder box, damped ashtray, and auxiliary switches for air conditioning, etc, with digital readout for clock, audio, and air conditioning temperatures on larger screen area. Satin black finished switch gear and no grey metal finishes like previous models. Where equipped with navigational system, large TV screen and controls replace 'manual' switches relying on touch-sensitive controls visible on TV screen. J-gate transmission control in veneered

Above left: *New-style grille from 2002, featuring integrated growler badge. The Sport model still has a colour-keyed surround, all other models chromed except for the R model, with mesh insert.*

Above right: *New-style front light units help to identify 2002 models and beyond from earlier cars.*

Side view of an early S-type R with much wider and larger diameter wheels/tyres.

Very late S-type model with sporting kit, later adopted for the XS model.

surround with auxiliary switches for Sport mode and cruise control (where fitted). Cup-holder with flush-mounted lid, armrest incorporating lift lid and storage area. Handbrake now merely a chromed moon-shaped pull lever in centre at rear of console (conventional handbrake on manual transmission cars).

- Dual zone air conditioning system.
- Four-spoke leather or leather/wood steering wheel as X-type, incorporating air bag and horn push centre boss. Side of wheel controls for audio system, telephone, and cruise control (where fitted).
- Revised seat styling dependent on model, with stiffer bolsters.
- Electrically adjustable foot pedal arrangement from switch on steering column side.
- From 2003 a wider range of interior options became available, including later Figured Alloy and Piano Black as an alternative to wood veneer.
- Non-perforated leather trim brought in from 2006 to replace Classic style. All models thereafter supplied with leather trim (no cloth option).

Model specifics

Standard and SE models
- Bird's eye stained maple veneered woodwork.
- Leather or cloth seating with vertical pleats and forward-curved stitching.
- Leather or wood/leather steering wheel.

Sport model
- Bird's eye grey-stained maple veneered woodwork.
- Leather sports steering wheel.
- Stiffer bolster aerated upholstery seating.

S-type R model
- Bird's eye grey-stained maple veneered woodwork.
- Warm charcoal trim with another contrasting colour.
- Thick leather ribbed sports steering wheel.
- Unique R-Performance seats with horizontal pleating, contrast colour upholstery centre sections fitted with headrests using Isofix seat bracketry.
- Contrast colour upholstery door panels in warm charcoal and another colour.
- Leather and alloy finished gear knob.
- Fitted foot mats as standard to match upholstery.

All details of trim and specification given above relate to standard production cars. Certain owners may well have specified changes to suit their individual requirements, so it is not unusual to find some more basic models with a higher specification than that described here.

Revised, clearer instrumentation from 2004 included two message centres in the main dials.

Dashboard treatment is entirely different on 2002 models from previous S-types. This particular car is equipped with satellite navigational equipment, with the large central screen, touch sensitive controls, and voice activation.

Above left: *Alternative centre console layout for cars not equipped with satellite navigation.*

Above right: *Alternative centre console layout for standard cars without CD player and enhanced air conditioning system.*

1: *Classic alloy wheels, original standard equipment for the 3.0 litre models;* 2: *Dynamic alloy wheels, normally standard on SE models, but an option on other models;* 3: *Sport wheels, an option for all earlier models;* 4: *Helios, the standard 16in wheels on 2.5-litre models;* 5: *Herakles, the standard wheels on Sport models up to 2004.* 6: *Spirit alloy wheels, standard fit on SE models up to 2004;* 7: *17in Kronos wheels were a standard fit on 4.2-litre SE and 2.7-litre diesel models;* 8: *Zeus wheels fitted to the S-type R models;* 9: *Juno 17in wheels, standard from 2004 on all SE models;* 10: *Aurora 17in wheels, standard on 2.5-litre S model;* 11: *Triton 18in wheels, standard from 2004 on all Sport models and on SEs in 2007;* 12: *Mercury 18in wheels, standard on XS models;* 13: *Vulcan 18in wheels, standard on post 2004 R model;* 14: *Indianapolis 18in wheels, extra cost option post 2004 models;* 15: *Monaco 18in wheels, extra cost option post 2004 models;* 16: *Melbourne 18in wheels, extra cost option post 2004 models;* 17: *Antares 17in wheels became standard fit on SE models in 2006;* 18: *Valencia 18in wheels, extra cost option from 2006;* 19: *The larger 19in Barcelona wheels came in 2007, just for the R model.*

Technical specifications

	2.5-litre	2.7-litre diesel
cc	2,497	2,720
Bore and stroke (mm)	81.65 x 79.5	81 x 86
Compression ratio	10.5:1	17:1
bhp	201	206
@ rpm	6,800	4,000
Torque (lb ft)	184	320
@ rpm	4,000	1,900
Fuelling	Fuel injection	Fuel injection
Transmission	ZF 5-speed auto Ford 5-speed synchro	ZF 6-speed automatic
Wheel size (in)	16 or 17, alloy	16, 17, or 18
Suspension front	Ind double wishbones, alloy control arms, anti dive, coil springs	Ind double wishbones, alloy control arms, anti-dive, coil springs
Suspension rear	Ind double wishbones, alloy control arms, co-axial coil springs CATS optional	Ind double wishbones, alloy control arms, co-axial coil springs CATS optional
Brakes	4 wheel disc, all ventilated	4-wheel discs, all ventilated
Performance		
0–60mph (sec)	8.2	8.1
Top speed (mph)	142	143
Average mpg	25.4	36
Dimensions		
Length (in)	189	189
Width (in)	69	69
Height (in)	55	55
Wheelbase (in)	113	113
Front track (in)	60	60
Rear track (in)	60	60
Weight (lb)	3,572	3,947

Technical specifications *cont ...*

	3.0-litre	4.0-litre
cc	2,967	3,996
Bore and stroke (mm)	89 x 79.5	86 x 86
Compression ratio	10.5:1	10.75:1
bhp	240	281
@ rpm	6,800	6,100
Torque (lb ft)	221	287
@ rpm	4,500	4,300
Fuelling	Fuel injection	Fuel injection
Transmission	ZF 5-speed auto Ford 5-speed synchro	ZF 5-speed auto
Wheel size (in)	16 or 17, alloy	16 or 17, alloy
Suspension front	Ind double wishbones, alloy control arms, anti dive, coil springs	Ind double wishbones, alloy control arms, anti dive, coil springs
Suspension rear	Ind double wishbones, alloy control arms, co-axial coil springs CATS optional	Ind double wishbones, alloy control arms, co-axial coil springs CATS optional
Brakes	4 wheel disc, all ventilated	4 wheel disc, all ventilated
Performance		
0–60mph (sec)	6.9 manual, 7.6 auto	6.6
Top speed (mph)	146	150
Average mpg	22.7	24.5
Dimensions		
Length (in)	189	189
Width (in)	69	69
Height (in)	55	55
Wheelbase (in)	113	113
Front track (in)	60	60
Rear track (in)	60	60
Weight (lb)	3,610	3,805

	4.2-litre	4.2-litre supercharged
cc	4,196	4,196
Bore and stroke (mm)	86 x 90.3	86 x 90.3
Compression ratio	11:1	9:1
bhp	300	400
@ rpm	6,000	6,100
Torque (lb ft)	310	408
@ rpm	4,100	3,500
Fuelling	Fuel injection	Fuel injection
Transmission	ZF 6-speed auto	ZF 6-speed auto
		Ford 5-speed synchro
Wheel size (in)	17 or 18, alloy	17 or 18, alloy
Suspension front	Ind double wishbones, alloy control arms, anti dive, coil springs	Ind double wishbones, alloy control arms, anti dive, coil springs
Suspension rear	Ind double wishbones, alloy control arms, co-axial coil springs CATS optional	Ind double wishbones, alloy control arms, co-axial coil springs CATS optional
Brakes	4 wheel disc, all ventilated	4 wheel disc, all ventilated
Performance		
0–60mph (sec)	6.2	5.3
Top speed (mph)	155	155
Average mpg	22.5	22.5
Dimensions		
Length (in)	189	189
Width (in)	69	69
Height (in)	55	55
Wheelbase (in)	113	113
Front track (in)	60	60
Rear track (in)	60	60
Weight (lb)	3,826	3,969

Optional extras

Automatic transmission (where not fitted, 2.5/3.0 models only).

Manual transmission (2.5/3.0 models only).

Mud flaps.

Cruise control (where not fitted as standard).

Tailored over-mats.

Lambswool over-mats.

Fitted seat-covers.

Headlight power-wash system.

Premium hi-fi system with CD auto-changer in boot.

Child's safety seat.

Child's booster cushion.

First aid kit for boot area.

Space-saver spare wheel.

Full-size spare wheel.

Fire extinguisher for boot area.

Jaguar warning triangle.

Headlamp converters.

Headlamp safety covers.

Mobile telephone kits.

Snow chains.

Luggage net for boot area.

Witter tow bar kit.

Heated windscreen.

Ultrasonic intrusion security system.

Additional zip-fastening tool kit.

Heated front seats (where not fitted).

Jaguar 'growler' alloy wheel centre badges, various colours.

Power folding door mirrors.

Sculptured rear number plate.

Self-dipping rear view mirror.

Wood/leather steering wheel (where not fitted).

Front fog lamps (early cars only).

Fog lamp protective covers.

Boot cargo net.

Boot luggage hooks.

Luggage retainer clips and/or straps.

Roof mounted rack.

Two-bar roof rack carrier.

Ski/cycle holders.

Luggage frame for roof rack.

Compact, Sport, or large roof box.

Various options of fitted luggage for the boot.

Round alloy gear knob.

Satellite navigation system (later cars).

Reverse park aid (where not fitted).

Auxiliary power socket.

Tracker security system.

Aspheric door mirrors.

Lockable boot mounted security box.

Air filtration system to air conditioning.

Engine block heater.

Cold climate pack.

Electric sunroof (where not fitted).

Rear window blind.

Deflector for sunroof.

Xenon headlights (later models only).

Rain sensing wipers.

Leather upholstery (2.5/3.0-litre models only).

Electrically adjustable foot pedal box (where not fitted, later cars only).

Ski-hatch.

CATS suspension package (where not fitted).

16in Classic seven-spoke alloy wheels.

16in Dynamic five-spoke alloy wheels.

16in Spirit ten-spoke alloy wheels.

16in Helios ten-spoke alloy wheels (later models).

16in Artemis alloy wheels (later models).

17in Sport ten-spoke alloy wheels.

17in Kronos six double spoke alloy wheels (later models).

17in Herakles five-spoke alloy wheels (later models).

18in Zeus five-spoke alloy wheels (later models).

Post 2004 options of dashboard treatment including Piano Black and Aluminium, along with alternative veneer finishes.

With later 'Premium' specification models, option of contrast colour piping to leather upholstery, bespoke gear knobs, and higher-quality veneering.

Polished alloy gear knobs for automatic transmission models.

Front and rear parking sensors.

Sport collection incorporating front spoiler, upper and lower bright or black mesh grilles.

Juno 17in wheels, later models.

Aurora 17in wheels, later model.

Triton 18in wheels, later models.

Mercury 18in wheels later models.

Vulcan 18in wheels later model.

Indianapolis wheels, later models.

Monaco 18in wheels, later models.

Melbourne 18in wheels later models.

Antares 17in wheels, later models.

Barcelona 19in wheels, later models.

Valencia 18in wheels, later models.

R-Performance specifics

18in Monaco split rim alloy wheels.

18in Indianapolis split rim alloy wheels.

Brembo brakes.

Colour schemes

Exterior	Details	Interior	Fascia	Details
Spindrift White	To 2001	Almond	Mink	To 2002
Pacific Blue	From 2002		Charcoal	
Seafront		Cashmere	Sable	To 2002
Anthracite (black)	To 2002		Charcoal	
Titanium Grey	To 2002	Pewter	Granite	To 2002
British Racing Green		Charcoal	Charcoal	
Emerald Green	To 2002	Ivory (leather only)	Sable	
Topaz (gold)			Charcoal	
Carnival Red	To 2003	Sand	Sable	2003 only
Sapphire Blue	To 2002	Dove		From 2003
Mistral	To 2002	Cranberry		2003 only
Meteorite Silver	To 2000	Cranberry/Charcoal	contrast	2003 only
Alpine Green	To 2001	Heritage Tan		2003 only
Westminster Blue	To 2002	Heritage Tan/Charcoal	contrast	2003 only
Platinum Grey	From 2000	Champagne		From 2004
White Onyx	From 2001	Dove/Graphite		From 2004
Roman Bronze	2001 only	Dove/Warm Charcoal		From 2004
Slate Grey	From 2002	Light Sand/Charcoal		From 2004
Quartz	From 2003			
Aspen Green	2002 only			

Zircon	From 2002	Veneers		Details
Ebony	From 2003	Grey maple		To 2004
Jaguar Racing Green	From 2003	Bronze maple		To 2004
Adriatic Blue	2003 only	Aluminium		From 2004
Midnight	From 2003	Bronze Stained Madonna		From 2004
Ultraviolet Blue	From 2004	Burr Walnut		From 2004
Radiance Red	From 2004	Grey Stained Birds Eye Maple		From 2004
Indigo	From 2006	Satin Mahogany		From 2006
Winter Gold	From 2006			

16 Prices and production volumes

	Price New(£)	1998	1999	2000	2001	2002	2003
2.5-litre	24,950	–	–	–	–	■	■
2.5-litre Sport	27,450	–	–	–	–	■	■
2.5-litre SE	28,900	–	–	–	–	■	■
3.0-litre	26,700	–	■	■	■	–	–
3.0-litre Sport	30,600	–	■	■	■	■	■
3.0-litre SE	31,150	–	■	■	■	■	■
4.0-litre	35,350	–	■	■	■	–	–
4.0-litre Sport	38,400	–	–	■	■	–	–
4.2-litre	36,000	–	–	–	–	■	■
4.2-litre R	47,400	–	–	–	–	■	■
Total production		**290**	**53,002**	**53,523**	**38,325**	**36,150**	**31,920**

	Price New(£)	2004	2005	2006	2007	Total produced
2.5-litre	24,950	■	–	–	–	–
2.5-litre Sport	27,450	■	–	–	–	–
2.5-litre S	–	■	–	–	–	–
2.5-litre SE	28,900	■	–	–	–	–
3.0-litre	26,700	■	■	■	–	–
3.0-litre Spirit	28,995	–	–	■	■	–
3.0-litre S	29,277	–	■	■	–	–
3.0-litre Sport	30,600	■	■	–	–	–
3.0-litre XS	31,995	–	■	■	■	–
3.0-litre SE	31,150	■	■	■	■	–
2.7-litre D	29,347	■	■	■	–	–
2.7-litre Spirit	29,995	–	–	–	■	–
2.7-litre D S	30,697	–	■	■	–	–
2.7-litre D Sport	–	■	■	–	–	–
2.7-litre D XS	30,947	–	■	■	■	–
2.7-litre D SE	30,947	■	■	■	■	–
4.2-litre Sport	37,552	■	■	–	–	–
4.2-litre SE	36,452	■	■	■	–	–
4.2-litre R	–	■	■	■	■	–
Total production		**26,567**	**23,868**	**16,701**	**11,040**	**291,386**

Production changes

1999
S-type 3.0-litre and 4.0-litre models introduced.

2001
Dynamic Stability Control (DSC) standardised on all models.

Improved ZF steering system fitted to all models.

Sports pack including CATS suspension available for all models.

Rear door sill tread plates fitted.

CD players now fitted to boot area instead of glove-box.

Boot under-floor area revised to accommodate tools and jack.

New boot lid liner with pull strap.

Side body mouldings discontinued.

Sport model introduced.

2002
Facelifted exterior with revised grille incorporating badge.

Facelifted exterior with chromed window surrounds, new door mirrors, and rear badging.

New interior layout similar to X-type.

Electrically adjustable foot-pedal box.

Enhanced seat design.

Improved Alpine 140-watt or Premium 320-watt sound systems.

Side air bags fitted.

Adaptive Restraint Technology fitted.

ZR 6-speed automatic transmission fitted to all models.

4.2-litre V8 engines replace 4.0-litre models.

Automatic handbrake system fitted.

New double wishbone front suspension.

Revised rear subframe.

Larger diameter disc brakes fitted to all models.

New 2.5-litre model introduced.

New supercharged 4.0-litre S-type R model introduced.

2004
Exterior facelift to body style with new frontal and rear-end treatment, lighting and sills.

Availability of 2.7-litre diesel engine. Rationalisation of model range. Aluminum interior rim added as an alternative to wood veneers.

2005
Special edition XS models were introduced to replace the Sport models. All 2.5-litre production ceased. All new models now featured the R style bumper and mesh grille treatment.

2006
Range rationalised again with Spirit model replacing standard cars but with extra specification.

2007
Production of S-type ceased, to make way for the replacement XF model.

Chassis numbers

Model

Model	
S-type (1999 on) models	Vin No. (see table 7*)

*Table 7 appears on page 319.

Jaguar All the Cars

Background

As mentioned in the preceding chapter, for many years Jaguar offered just one saloon model range in different formats. Then in 1999 came the S-type, which opened up a new market for smaller cars. At the time of the S-type launch, however, an even smaller model was under development. Coded X-400, this was to become the X-type.

The X-type represented entirely new territory for Jaguar, as the smallest cars it had previously produced had been the 2.4-litre and its progeny, more akin to the current S-type in size, stature, and market sector. Jaguar's decision to enter a new market place with a smaller car was motivated by two factors: firstly, the general appeal of smaller cars to the motoring public, offering cheaper prices and better economy; and secondly, the need to develop a 'family' of cars, something competitors like BMW had been very good at.

This 'family' concept was necessary in order that Jaguar could encourage new markets for its cars – younger buyers who, hopefully, would aspire to other Jaguar models and stay loyal to the brand. Typically a young sales executive would be able to accommodate a 2.0-litre X-type within his company benefits package; then, as he progressed through the organisation and became a sales manager, he would choose an S-type. Perhaps at director level an XJ6 might be acceptable, and so on.

The X-type was therefore conceived to hit important growth areas in the market for under 40-year-olds, and to offer not only a viable but a better alternative to cars like BMW's 3 Series, the Audi A4, and others. Jaguar was targeting what it called 'The New Jag Generation', consisting for the most part of people who had never before considered buying a new Jaguar.

Launched in the 2001 model year, the X-type was the smallest car Jaguar had ever commercially produced. Starting at a modest £22,000, it was built at the ex-Ford factory in Halewood, Merseyside, the first British Jaguar not to be built in the West Midlands. Converting the workforce and its manufacturing ethos from Ford Escorts to X-types was a major feat for Jaguar, and many other X-type based models will doubtless appear from this production facility in the future.

Although the X-type is another all-new car the Ford parts bin has once again been raided, and development alongside the Ford Mondeo in some key areas allowed Jaguar to achieve a quick yet successful fix. Introduced as just a four-door saloon, another entirely new innovation for Jaguar was that all original X-type models were equipped with four-wheel drive. Engine options were taken from the S-type in the form of the 3.0-litre V6 power unit, adapted for the four-wheel drive layout, and Jaguar developed a smaller 2.5-litre V6 version from the same unit. Automatic and manual gearboxes followed S-type practice.

The body style took key cues from the XJ range, with conventional Jaguar front end treatment accompanied by a slightly wedge-shaped profile to provide more boot space, and a higher roof level to provide more interior accommodation. Features of S-type design were keyed into the X-type too, such as the all-enveloping bumper bar treatment and the very latest body pressing and assembly techniques.

The X-type provided Jaguar with a four model line-up, and since its launch it achieved record sales. New models were added, including the Indianapolis, in both engine sizes, and in 2003 the diesel option became available in 2.0-litre form. This was also supplemented later by the 2.2-litre diesel option, available with a new six-speed manual transmission.

The body range was expanded with the introduction of the first production Jaguar Estate Car, available in all engine sizes and trims. Later special editions have included the Spirit and XS, and for 2008 the bodywork received a major facelift to give a more sporting appeal to the frontal aspect, as well as changes to exterior trim, the rear bumper area, and the interior.

From the 2008 model year a six-speed automatic transmission with sequential change became available on the 2.2-litre diesel engine cars, which necessitated a major rework of the floor pan and other areas of the car.

At the time of writing, no new model is planned to replace the X-type, production of which was terminated at the end of 2009.

Model range and development

The range of X-type models introduced in 2001 was quite extensive.

Models available at launch (manual and automatic transmissions)
X-type 2.5-litre saloon (Classic)
X-type 2.5-litre Sport
X-type 2.5-litre SE (Special Equipment)
X-type 3.0-litre Sport
X-type 3.0-litre SE (Special Equipment)

All X-types featured a development of the S-type suspension and steering layout, but adapted, of course, for the four-wheel drive system. The 2.5-litre engine provided good performance and smooth refinement at a lower cost, making X-type ownership available to a different category of driver, yet retaining the smoothness of a six-cylinder unit. The 3.0-litre, on the other hand, provided enhanced performance, both over the 2.5 and the equivalent S-type model, particularly so because of the smaller and lighter body.

On the pre-facelift models the only external differences in X-type models are in the radiator grille/bumper bar treatment and alloy wheels fitted. This is an early SE model which, like the Standard saloon, has chromed grille, bumper blades, and window surrounds.

The Sport models have colour co-ordinated exterior trim features throughout.

An early 2.0-litre Sport model with black window surrounds and conventional alloy wheels.

Visually the X-type showed its connection with previous Jaguar heritage by its typical four headlight and curvaceous frontal aspect treatment, whilst the interior, although all new, also offered a degree of retro-styling in its use of typical Jaguar features.

The principles behind the X-type range were based on price, allowing the purchaser to choose between excellent performance and a relatively good turn of speed dependent on budget and, perhaps, insurance. With three choices of specification – standard (now known as Classic), SE, and Sport – this gave a wide variety of options and price. Essentially the basic X-type models are determined squarely by price. Although they include standard features like air conditioning and four-wheel drive, owners have to pay extra for leather upholstery and other traditional details normally associated with a Jaguar. So, in 2002 you could be driving your first new Jaguar for just £22,000, a very competitive price for that important advantage over the competition – four-wheel drive.

In contrast, the Sport offers something different, for the younger market or for those wishing either to stand out or to get away from Jaguar's previous 'old man's' image. Different seating and interior trim finishes allied to de-chroming of the exterior trim make for a more sporty appearance and feel. At the other end of the scale are the Special Equipment (SE) models, offering a high degree of standard equipment, including leather upholstery, chrome, and so on. So, something for everyone who wants a smaller but luxurious car and the prestige of the Jaguar name.

Right from the start Jaguar made little secret of the fact that the X-type range would be built on over a number of years, and the next phase came in 2002 with the launch of another new engine size. This 2.0-litre V6 power unit, designed by Jaguar from its existing 2.5-litre engine, is fitted to the X-type but with only front-wheel drive, it being felt that four-wheel drive would be too much of a drag on its performance. This new model, available in all three trim options, opened up yet another new market for Jaguar. Strategically priced at £19,995 it also broke new ground as, pro rata, it was the cheapest production Jaguar ever produced. This 'new' market also brings in company car ownership, where engine capacity and price are important issues.

Next came a special edition model which appeared at the 2002 British Motor Show in the form of the X-type Indianapolis. Essentially a 2.5- or 3.0-litre Sport X-type with a lot of standard features and a new colour scheme combination, this is perhaps the start of many more 'special' models to come from the X-type stable.

Another new engine added to the X-type range was the 2.0-litre diesel unit in 2003, and

The Indianapolis, one of the X-type special editions, shown in one of only three external colour schemes available and with the unique alloy wheels which could also have been purchased separately for other models.

Rear view of pre-facelift model; boot spoilers only applied to the Sport and Indianapolis models at the time. The boot plinth and bumper bar blades were chromed on other models.

This interior view of the Sport model shows the different pleating to the seat faces and the high contrast trim colours.

this was the first Jaguar production car to be fitted with an oil engine. Different from the other X-types at this time, the 2.0-litre models offered only front-wheel drive instead of AWD (all-wheel drive). An even more dramatic addition took place in 2004 with the Estate Car version of the X-types becoming available, and then in 2005 a further new engine, another diesel, this time of 2.2-litre capacity, also front-wheel drive.

As with the medium-sized S-type model, the X-type range has included some other special edition models, the Spirit and the XS. The whole range was stylistically facelifted in 2007 with a new, more aggressive style of frontal aspect, and other trim changes. By this time the 2.0-litre and 2.5-litre petrol engine models had been discontinued.

Exterior identification points

General points applicable to all X-types
Front view
- ■ Frontal view initially adapted from the larger XJ saloon styling, facelifted in 2007 with more prominent grille and bumper/valance area.
- ■ Four elliptical reflector headlamp units (with the option of Xenon units), incorporating side and indicator lights.
- ■ Horizontal radiator grille with body colour/chromed surround and vertical slats of mesh inserts according to model and year. Initially a conventional growler badge featured, but from 2007 this changed in style.
- ■ All-enveloping pre-formed plastic front bumper/valance area, incorporating number plate mounting, blades, air intake with splitter bar, and integrated fog lamps. Designs vary according to model and year.
- ■ One-piece rear-hinged sculptured bonnet.
- ■ One-piece bonded windscreen with surround finisher and twin wiper blades.

Rear view
- ■ Wraparound rear screen with surround, incorporating high-mounted rear brake light.
- ■ One-piece rear-hinged boot lid incorporating spoiler. Centrally-mounted Jaguar plinth, later models with lengthened 'signature' panel, incorporating boot lock and number plate lighting.
- ■ Styled rear light units to match bodywork, with current technology lenses.
- ■ One-piece all-enveloping rear bumper/valance unit, varying in design and finish according to model and year.
- ■ Unique 'X-type' style badge and scripted engine capacity according to model.

The X-type Estate Car follows all the trim specifications of the saloon models.

The very practical way in which the tailgate operates on the X-type estate models.

Interior of standard and SE leather-upholstered models. Note the different seat style to Sport models and the lighter veneer finish.

Side view

- ▨ A combination of traditional Jaguar profile with slightly raised rear end, and pronounced uplift over rear wheelarch area.
- ▨ Flush-mounted door handles in body colour.
- ▨ Body-colour front door mirrors.
- ▨ Deep swage-line at waist level with body-painted rubbing strip on earlier models to the lower section of front, rear wings, and door areas.
- ▨ Indicator repeaters at rear of each front wing.
- ▨ Limousine-style door frames with no rain gutters.
- ▨ Alloy wheels fitted to all models, dependent on specification and year.

X-type specifics

Unless indicated otherwise, identification points apply to cars of all engine sizes.

Standard (Classic) models

- ▨ Chromed bumper bar blades.
- ▨ Chromed radiator grille.
- ▨ 16in Calcos alloy wheels, standard original fit.

Sport Models

- ▨ Body-coloured grille surround and boot lid finisher.
- ▨ Body-coloured bumper bar blades front and rear.
- ▨ Black finish to door window surrounds.
- ▨ 17in Andros or 18in Aruba alloy wheels, standard original fit.

Indianapolis model

- ▨ Only available in three exterior paint finishes.
- ▨ Body-coloured radiator grille surround with mesh insert.
- ▨ Body-coloured bumper bar blades front and rear.
- ▨ Body-coloured boot plinth/spoiler.
- ▨ 18in x 15-spoke Indianapolis alloy wheels.

SE models

- ▨ Chrome finished radiator grille and rear boot finisher.
- ▨ 16in Tobago or 17in Cayman alloy wheels, standard original fit.
- ▨ Chromed bumper bar blades.

S models

- ▨ As classic model except for alloy wheels.
- ▨ 17in Andros alloy wheels.

Sport Premium models

- ▨ Black mesh radiator grille insert with body-coloured surround.
- ▨ Body-coloured boot lid 'signature' finisher.
- ▨ Headlight powerwash, standard equipment.
- ▨ Heated front windscreen, standard equipment.

The centre console design varies according to specification. This car is equipped with satellite navigation, hence the screen.

Sport interior with non-leather seat facings and non-satellite navigation centre console.

Rear interior of Sport non leather-upholstered car. Seat pleating varies from Sport to standard.

- Rear spoiler.
- 18in Aruba alloy wheels.

Sovereign models
- As SE model but with additional heated windscreen.
- 17in Cayman alloy wheels.

Spirit/XS models
- 18in Aruba alloy wheels.
- Front spoiler.
- Upper and lower black mesh grille.
- Sill appliqués.
- Boot lid spoiler.

Interior identification points

General points applicable to all X-types
- Dashboard assembly and layout similar to S-type and X-350 saloons, curved top roll with instrument binnacle in front of driver.
- Centre console of curved design with upholstered areas between the seats. Incorporates integrated audio system, damped ashtray, and auxiliary switches for air conditioning, etc, with digital readout for clock and audio. Satin black finished switch gear. Where equipped with automatic air conditioning system a separate digital read-out screen features at top of centre console, replacing three rotary controls. Where navigational system fitted, large TV screen relying on touch-sensitive controls visible on screen replaces other screen read-outs. J-gate or gear lever transmission control in surround of varying finishes (see specifics). Cup-holder with flush-mounted lid, armrest incorporating lift lid, and storage area. Handbrake situated within rear of console.
- Four-spoke leather or leather/wood steering wheel as later S-type incorporating air bag and horn push centre boss with growler badge. Side of wheel controls for audio system, telephone, and cruise control (where fitted).
- Individual front seat styling dependent on model.
- Rear bench-seat arrangement to match.
- Door trim panels softly upholstered with inserts, window lift switchpacks, door arm rests, integral pockets, and audio speakers. Chromed door locks.

Model specifics
Standard (Classic) models
- Bird's eye maple veneer until 2004, then replaced by bronze-stained sapele.
- Manually adjusted cloth seating.
- Vinyl trim coloured steering wheel.

An X-type fitted with the Sports Collection pack of trim detail showing spoilers, sill appliqués, and black mesh grilles.

The facelift X-type model showing the more pronounced front end treatment, revised sill and rubbing strip design, and new style door mirrors.

Rear of the facelift model showing new style bumper area and trim on boot lid. Note from facelift, an aerodynamic radio antenna is fitted.

Example of later facelift interior trim with carbon fibre and aluminium instead of wood veneer and re-design to gear knob and surround.

- Complementary colour scheming to all interior areas.
- Manually-operated rear door windows (2.0-litre models only).
- Single-slot CD player.
- Soft vinyl gear knob.

Sport models

- Bird's eye maple veneer.
- Cloth centre seat panels with leather outside panels and horizontal pleating.
- Centre armrest with cup holders.
- Perforated leather gear knob.
- Electrically-adjustable front seats (both).
- Twin rear head restraints.
- Sports leather steering wheel.

SE models

- As Classic models above plus:
- Door inserts to match facia.
- Leather gear knob.
- Rear head restraints.
- Centre armrest with cup holders.
- Trip computer with message centre.

Indianapolis model

- Mottled effect maple veneering to woodwork on dashboard.
- Alcantara-trimmed central areas of seats with leather outside areas, and stiffer bolsters to front seats, and horizontal pleating.
- Centre armrest with cup-holders.
- Sport leather-clad aerated steering wheel.
- Driver's seat four-way seat adjustment, passenger height adjustment.
- Alcantara-trimmed centre areas of door trim panels.
- Electrically-operated windows at front only.
- Automatic climate control system with digital screen.
- Single-slot CD player.
- Sports leather/alloy gear knob.
- Warm charcoal-coloured upper fascia with flint-coloured carpets.

S models

- As Classic models above plus:
- Choice of grey stained maple or bronze sapele veneers.
- Leather gear knob.
- Rear centre armrest with cup holders.
- Half cloth/leather seat trim.
- Electrically-adjustable seats at front.
- Electrically-controlled front and rear windows.

Sport Premium models

- As Sport models plus:
- Carbon fibre facia trim.
- Perforated leather grip steering wheel.
- Sport perforated leather gear knob.
- Alcantara seat trimming.

Very late model alternative soft grain leather option to seating, with needle diamond stitching pattern.

The 2.0-litre V6 S model offers a higher degree of specification to the normal car at a special price.

Interior of the Indianapolis model, with unique veneer figuring to the woodwork and Alcantara seat trimming.

- Electrically-adjustable and heated front seating.
- Six-disc CD player.
- Cold climate pack.
- Trip computer with message centre.
- Aruba alloy wheels.

Sovereign models
- As SE plus the following:
- Half leather/veneer steering wheel.
- Walnut veneer.
- Six-disc CD player.
- Alpine Premium sound system.
- Satellite navigational system.
- Jaguar Voice system.

All details of trim and specification given above relate to standard production cars. Certain owners may well have specified changes to suit their individual requirements, so it is not unusual to find some more basic models with a higher specification than that described here.

X-type 2004 model changes
With the introduction of the diesel-engined version in 2003 came subtle styling changes to the whole X-type.

Exterior
- Classic and Sport models now incorporates body-colour bumper bar blades (no longer chrome).
- Matt black B & C pillar window surrounds on Classic models.
- Chromed vertical radiator grille vanes on SE models.
- Rear boot lid finisher now widened.
- Boot release button moved from top centre of finisher to underneath.
- 'Crystal' design side indicator lenses on all models.
- 'D' badging on boot lid for the diesel-engined models.

Interior
- Soft-touch material used on the parcel shelf area.
- Fore and aft tilting for front seat headrests added.
- Re-shaping of front seats to allow for more space in centre console area.
- Twin cup holders standardised on all models in centre console area.
- Two additional sound system speakers for models equipped with standard audio system.
- Enhanced 320-watt Premium sound system with ten speakers.
- Black background (instead of green) for instruments.
- Outside temperature warning light fitted to instrument binnacle.

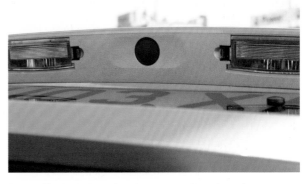

Revised siting for the boot release button, now underneath out of sight.

The mid-term rear-end treatment (pre-facelift) with elongated boot signature plinth. Note this is a diesel model displaying less prominent exhaust tailpipes.

Another new move for Jaguar is the availability of carbon-fibre instead of wood veneer in the X-type, affecting all models from 2004 model year.

X-type 2005/2006 model changes

• Sports Collection now available to enhance the styling of the models. This incorporated a front spoiler, black mesh grilles, de-chroming pack, sill appliqués, boot lid spoiler, revised rear valance, and exhaust tail pipe trims, much of which subsequently appeared on the XS model.

X-type 2007 model changes

▨ The X-type models were facelifted in 2007, providing the following changes:

▨ More prominent and squarer horizontal radiator grille with wide mesh grille and new-style growler badge.

▨ Smoother-finish bumper bar/valance area with larger air intake and inset fog lights.

▨ New-style, flatter side rubbing strips.

▨ Full-width boot lid 'signature' panel.

▨ Revised style to rear bumper bar/valance area and tail pipe arrangements.

▨ Revised seating style (according to model).

Alcantara (mock suede) trim, once only available on the Indianapolis X-type, is now available for all X-type models.

Twin cup holders identify the interior of the 2004 model-year X-types from the earlier models.

The fully enclosing cover on top of the diesel engine makes it instantly identifiable from petrol versions.

1: *16in X7 wheel, original standard equipment on 2.0-litre standard and SE models.*

2: *16in X10 wheel, original standard equipment on 2.5-litre standard and SE models.*

3: *17in X7 Flute wheel, original standard equipment on the 3.0-litre SE.*

4: *17in X-Sport wheel, original standard equipment on all Sport models.*

5: *The original X5 wheel. Unique at the time to 3.0-litre cars, later replaced by X7 (see above).*

6: *16in Calcos wheels, the standard wheels from 2004 for all standard (classic) models.*

7: *16in Tobago wheels, the standard fit from 2004 on 2.0-litre SE models.*

8: *17in Cayman wheels, the standard fit from 2004 on 2.5-litre and 3.0-litre SE models.*

9: *17in Andros wheels, the standard fit on 2.0-litre and 2.2-litre Sport models from 2004.*

10: *18in Aruba wheels, the standard fit on 2.5-litre and 3.0-litre Sport models from 2004, and on the special edition XS models. (This wheel was also available in an 18in split-rim form as an extra cost option).*

11: *18in R-Performance Melbourne split-rim wheels, available from 2004 as an extra cost option.*

12: *16in Saba wheels became the standard wheel on standard (classic) models from 2006.*

13: *17in Belize wheels became the standard fit on S models from 2006.*

14: *18in Proteus wheels became the standard fit on Sport Premium models from 2006.*

15: *16in Antares wheels became available in 2006 replacing all other 16in wheels.*

16: *17in Bermuda alloy wheels became available in 2006 as a supplementary wheel to the only other 17in wheel available then, the Belize.*

17: *New R-Performance 18in Valencia split-rim alloy wheels became available in 2006, replacing the Melbourne.*

18: *17in Barbados wheels were introduced with the facelift models from the 2008 model year, fitted as standard to all SE models.*

19: *18in Abaco wheels, were introduced with the facelift models from the 2008 model year, fitted as standard to all Sport Premium models.*

Technical specifications

	2.0-litre	2.5-litre
cc	2,099	2,495
Bore and stroke (mm)	81.6 x 66.8	81.6 x 79.5
Compression ratio	10.75:1	10.3:1
bhp	157	194
@ rpm	6,800	6,800
Torque (lb ft)	148	180
@ rpm	4,100	3,000
Fuelling	Fuel injection	Fuel injection
Transmission	Ford 5-speed synchro Ford 5-speed auto front-wheel drive	Ford 5-speed synchro Ford 5-speed auto 6-speed manual option (from late 2005) 4-wheel drive
Wheel size (in)	16, 18 (from 2006), alloy	16 or 17, 18 (from 2006), alloy
Suspension front	Ind double wishbones, alloy control arms, anti dive, coil springs	Ind double wishbones, alloy control arms, anti dive, coil springs
Suspension rear	Ind double wishbones, alloy control arms, co-axial coil springs	Ind double wishbones, alloy control arms, co-axial coil springs
Brakes	4 wheel disc, all ventilated	4 wheel disc, all ventilated
Performance		
0–60mph (sec)	8.9 manual, 10.4 auto	7.9 manual, 8.5 auto
Top speed (mph)	130	140
Average mpg	30.7	29.5
Dimensions		
Length (in)	183, 186 estate	183, 186 estate
Width (in)	68	68
Height (in)	53, 58 estate	53, 53 estate
Wheelbase (in)	104	104
Front track (in)	60	60
Rear track (in)	60	60
Weight (lb)	3,197	3,428

	3.0-litre	2.0-litre diesel
cc	2,967	1,998
Bore and stroke (mm)	89 x 7.5	86.0 x 86.0
Compression ratio	10.5:1	18.2: 1
bhp	231	128
@ rpm	6,800	3,800
Torque (lb ft)	209	243
@ rpm	3,000	1,800
Fuelling	Fuel injection	Common rail fuel injection
Transmission	Ford 5-speed synchro Ford 5-speed auto 6-speed manual option (from late 2005) 4-wheel drive	Ford 5-speed synchro 6-speed manual option (from late 2005)
Wheel size (in)	16 or 17, 18 (from 2006), alloy	16,17, 18, (from 2006), alloy
Suspension front	Ind double wishbones, alloy control arms, anti dive, coil springs	Ind double wishbones, alloy control arms, anti dive, coil springs
Suspension rear	Ind double wishbones, alloy control arms, co-axial coil springs	Ind double wishbones, alloy control arms, co-axial coil springs
Brakes	4 wheel disc, all ventilated	4 wheel disc, all ventilated
Performance		
0–60mph (sec)	6.6 manual, 7.1 auto	9.5
Top speed (mph)	146	125
Average mpg	27.5	50.3
Dimensions		
Length (in)	183, 186 estate	183, 186 estate
Width (in)	68	68
Height (in)	53, 58 estate	53, 58 estate
Wheelbase (in)	104	104
Front track (in)	60	60
Rear track (in)	60	60
Weight (lb)	3,428	3,311

Technical specifications *cont ...*

	2.2-litre diesel
cc	2,198
Bore and stroke (mm)	86 x 94.6
Compression ratio	17.5 to 1
bhp	155
@ rpm	3,500
Torque (lb ft)	360
@ rpm	1,800
Fuelling	Fuel injection
Transmission	6-speed manual gear
	6-speed automatic with sequential change (from 2008)
Wheel size	16, 17 or 18 alloy
Suspension front	Ind double wishbones, alloy control arms, anti dive, coil springs.
Suspension rear	Ind double wishbones, alloy control arms, co-axial coil springs.
Brakes	4 wheel disc, all ventilated
Performance	
0–60mph (sec)	8.5
Top speed (mph)	137
Average mpg	47
Dimensions	
Length (in)	183 (186 estate car)
Width (in)	68
Height (in)	53 (58 estate car)
Wheelbase (in)	104
Front track (in)	60
Rear track (in)	60
Weight (lb)	3,473

Colour schemes

Exterior	Details	Interior	Details
White Onyx	To 2008	Ivory	To 2004 (reintroduced in 2006)
Pacific Blue	To 2006	Sand	To 2003
Phoenix Red	To 2003	Dove	To 2003
Anthracite (black)	To 2003	Charcoal	
Titanium Grey	To 2003	Cranberry	Cloth only 2003
British Racing Green	To 2007	Heritage Tan	To 2004
Emerald Green	To 2003	Champagne	2003–7
Topaz (gold)	To 2006	Stone	2003–7
Carnival Red	To 2003	Spice (red)	From 2008
Adriatic Blue	To 2003	Barley	From 2008
Westminster Blue	To 2003	Oyster (non-seating)	From 2008
Platinum Grey	To 2007	**Veneers**	
Quartz	2003–7	Grey maple	To 2003
Ebony	From 2003	Carbon fibre	From 2002
Zircon	To 2007	Bird's-eye maple	
Jaguar Racing Green	To 2008	Bronzed Stained Sapele	2003–7
Ultaviolet Blue	2003–7	Piano Black	From 2004
Radiance Red	2003–7	Burr Walnut	From 2005
Salsa Red	2003–5	Rosewood	From 2008
Midnight	2005–8	**Contrast Piping**	
Indigo	From 2006	Mocha	2005–7 (only Sovereign models)
Winter Gold	From 2006	Stone	2005–7 (only Sovereign models)
Glacier Blue	From 2007	Charcoal	From 2008
Shadow Grey	From 2007	Barley	From 2008
Liquid Silver	From 2007	Oyster	From 2008
Chilli Red	From 2007	**Seat Style**	
Ultimate Black	From 2008	Classic	Vertical pleating (cloth or
Emerald Fire (green)	From 2008		leather, from 2008 changed to
Tekite Grey	From 2008		horizontal pleating
Lazuli Blue	From 2008	Sports	Horizontal pleating (cloth,
Ionian Blue	From 2008		leather, Alcantera or perforated)
Porcelain	From 2008	Sports Premium	Diamond stitching from 2008

17 Prices and production volumes

	Price New (£)	2001	2002	2003	2004	2005	2006
2.0-litre petrol	19,995	–	■	■	■	■	–
(Estate)	20,447	–	–	–	■	■	–
2.0-litre diesel	19,995	–	–	■	■	■	■
(Estate)	20,472	–	–	–	■	■	■
2.0-litre diesel XS	22,995	–	–	–	–	–	■
2.0-litre Sport petrol	22,245	–	■	■	■	–	–
(Estate)	22,702	–	–	–	■	–	–
2.0-litre Sport D	22,245	–	–	■	■	■	■
(Estate)	22,727	–	–	–	■	■	■
2.0-litre SE petrol	22,995	–	■	■	■	■	–
(Estate)	23,347	–	–	–	■	■	–
2.0-litre SE D	22,995	–	–	■	■	■	■
(Estate)	23,372	–	–	–	■	■	■
2.0-litre V6 S	20,995	–	–	–	■	■	–
2.0-litre diesel S	20,332	–	–	–	–	■	■
(Estate)	21,472	–	–	–	–	■	■
2.0-litre Sp/Prem D	27,000	–	–	–	–	–	–
(Estate)	28,400	–	–	–	–	–	–
2.0-litre Sov D	28,000	–	–	–	–	–	–
(Estate)	29,400	–	–	–	–	–	–
2.2-litre Sport D	22,302	–	–	–	–	■	■
(Estate)	23,472	–	–	–	–	■	■
2.2-litre SE D	25,302	–	–	–	–	■	■
(Estate)	26,472	–	–	–	–	■	■
2.2-litre S/Prem D	27,802	–	–	–	–	■	■
(Estate)	28,972	–	–	–	–	■	■
2.2-litre Sov D	27,802	–	–	–	–	■	■
(Estate)	28,972	–	–	–	–	■	■
2.2-litre diesel S	22,500	–	–	–	–	–	–
(Estate)	23,900	–	–	–	–	–	–
2.5-litre	22,000	■	■	■	■	–	–
(Estate)	23,202	–	–	–	■	–	–
2.5-litre XS	24,770	–	–	–	–	–	■
2.5-litre Sport	24,000	■	■	■	■	■	■
(Estate)	25,552	–	–	–	■	■	■

2007	2008	2009	Total produced (to 2008)
–	–	–	(1) 49,762
–	–	–	(5) 1,587
■	–	–	(4) 55,615
■	–	–	(8) 16,747
–	–	–	(4)
–	–	–	(1)
–	–	–	(5)
■	–	–	(4)
■	–	–	(8)
–	–	–	(1)
–	–	–	(5)
■	■	■	(4)
■	■	■	(8)
–	–	–	(1)
■	■	■	(4)
■	■	■	(8)
–	■	■	(4)
–	■	■	(8)
–	■	■	(4)
–	■	■	(8)
■	–	–	(9) 31,294
■	–	–	(9)
■	■	■	(9)
■	■	■	(9)
■	■	■	(9)
■	■	■	(9)
■	■	■	(9)
■	■	■	(9)
–	■	■	(9)
–	■	■	(9)
–	–	–	(2) 99,939
–	–	–	(6) 4,306
–	–	–	(2)
■	–	–	(2)
■	–	–	(6)

Automatic transmission (where not fitted).
Manual transmission.
Mud flaps.
Cruise control.
Tailored over-mats.
Lambswool over-mats.
Fitted seat-covers.
Headlight power-wash system.
Premium hi-fi system with CD auto-changer in boot.
Child's safety seat.
Child's booster cushion.
First aid kit for boot area.
Space-saver spare wheel.
Full-size spare wheel.
Fire extinguisher for boot area.
Jaguar warning triangle.
Headlamp converters.
Headlamp safety covers.
Mobile telephone kits.
Snow chains.
Luggage net for boot area.
Witter tow bar kit.
Heated windscreen.
Ultrasonic intrusion security system.
Additional zip-fastening tool kit.
Heated front seats (where not fitted).
Jaguar 'growler' alloy wheel centre badges, various colours.
Power folding door mirrors.
Self-dipping rear view mirror.
Wood/leather steering wheel (where not fitted).
Fog lamp protective covers.
Boot cargo net.
Boot luggage hooks.
Luggage retainer clips and/or straps.
Roof-mounted rack.
Two-bar roof rack carrier.
Front parking sensors.
Alcantara upholstery.
Carbon fibre trim.
Piano black trim detail.
Ski/cycle holders.
Luggage frame for roof rack.
Compact, Sport, or large roof box.
Various options of fitted luggage for the boot.
Round alloy gear knob.
Satellite navigation system.
Reverse park aid.
Tracker security system.
Aspheric door mirrors.
Lockable boot mounted security box.
Air filtration system to air conditioning.
Engine block heater.
Cold climate pack.
Electric sunroof.
Rear window blind.
Deflector for sunroof.

Prices and production volumes *cont ...*

	Price New (£)	2001	2002	2003	2004	2005	2006
2.5-litre SE	24,750	■	■	■	■	■	■
(Estate)	26,552	–	–	–	■	■	■
2.5-litre S	22,052	–	–	–	–	■	■
(Estate)	23,222	–	–	–	–	■	■
3.0-litre Sport	25,500	■	■	■	■	–	–
(Estate)	27,052	–	–	–	■	–	–
3.0-litre SE	26,250	■	■	■	■	–	–
(Estate)	28,052	–	–	–	■	–	–
2.5-litre Indianapolis	27,500	–	–	■	–	–	–
3.0-litre Indianapolis	29,000	–	–	■	–	–	–
3.0-litre S/Prem	29,277	–	–	–	–	■	■
(Estate)	30,447	–	–	–	–	■	■
3.0-litre Sov	29,277	–	–	–	–	■	■
(Estate)	30,447	–	–	–	–	■	■
Total production (to 2008)	Total includes 79 miscellaneous models and prototypes						

Production changes

2001
X-type 2.5-litre and 3.0-litre models introduced.

2002
2.0-litre models introduced.
Indianapolis models introduced.

2003
2.0-litre diesel models introduced.
Last of Indianapolis special editions produced.

2004
Introduction of estate models.
Cosmetic changes to interior and exterior trim.

2005
2.0-litre petrol engine models phased out.
2.2-litre diesel engines introduced.
S models increased.
Introduction of Sport Premium range.

2006
Spirit and XS limited editions introduced.

2007
2.5-litre and 3.0-litre petrol engines discontinued.

2008
Facelift models introduced.
General model range contraction.

2009
Production ceased.

Chassis numbers

Model

X-type models	Vin No. (see table 8*)

*Table 8 appears on page 320.

Optional extras *cont …* 17

2007	2008	2009	Total produced (to 2008)
■	−	−	(2)
■	−	−	(6)
■	−	−	(2)
■	−	−	(6)
−	−	−	(3) 91,595
−	−	−	(7) 4,382
−	−	−	(3)
−	−	−	(7)
−	−	−	(2)
−	−	−	(3)
■	−	−	(3)
■	−	−	(7)
■	−	−	(3)
■	−	−	(7)
			355,306

Xenon headlights.
Rain sensing wipers.
Leather upholstery (where not fitted).
Ski-hatch.
Ten-way electrically adjustable front seats.
Rear door electric window operation (where not fitted).
Sport perforated leather seating.
Air conditioning with pollen filters.
Front compartment cup-holder.
Dynamic stability control.
CATS suspension package (where not fitted).
16in X-7 seven-spoke alloy wheels.
16in X-10 ten-spoke alloy wheels.
17in X-7 Flute alloy wheels.
17in X-Sport alloy wheels.
16in Calcos, Tobago, Saba or Antares alloy wheels.
17in Cayman, Andros, Belize, Bermuda or Barbados alloy wheels.
18in Aruba, Proteus and Abaco alloy wheels.

R-Performance specifics
18in Monaco split rim alloy wheels.
18in Indianapolis split rim alloy wheels.
Brembo brakes.
Handling pack.
R-Performance Melbourne and Valencia split rim alloy wheels.
Sports collection trim pack.

XJ6 and XJ8 saloons (X-350)
2003 to 2009

Background

If Jaguar's model range has been known for two things, they are the company's superbly styled sports cars and its refined saloons, and since the introduction of the original XJ6 back in 1968 over one million saloons carrying that XJ insignia have been produced.

Just as the XJ40 saw Jaguar out of BL control, the X-300 replacement was the first car produced under Ford control, heralding in better build quality, and the X-308 brought about the change from straight-six and V12 power units to an all-V8 line-up. The success of the XJ's heritage cannot be over-stated, particularly when one considers that until 1999 it was the only saloon body-shape available from Jaguar. It was therefore fitting that Jaguar decided to retain the XJ insignia for its current flagship saloons, and at the same time to reintroduce another XJ6.

Code-named X-350, this entirely new XJ was announced in 2003, a major leap forward for Jaguar. Although initially utilising the engine line-up from other models, for the first time in a production model the XJs were fitted with an all-aluminium body structure featuring highly sophisticated bonding and riveting methods. If that was not enough, there are the air suspension system, dynamic stability control, the latest development of Jaguar's Computer Active Technology suspension, adaptive cruise control, multi-media system, voice activation of some controls, additional air bags, and even a heated steering wheel!

Even the exterior styling of the X-350 warrants special appreciation. Whilst, importantly, maintaining strong links to previous models, the overall design boasts many new features and provides for more interior space and luggage accommodation. Internally it is all new. Following a similar design style to the X-type and later S-types, it has many more features and a host of specifications and trim levels to suit what has now become a very lucrative and sophisticated market.

And that was the essence of the X-350. More than any previous XJ, this car had to cater for a more demanding customer – someone with a statement to make, who wanted the very best in quality and technology – and it proved a more than even match of the competition.

Instead of a Daimler model, there was a Super V8 Jaguar variant when the car was introduced in April 2003 (and models badged 'Vanden Plas' for the States), but a Daimler version was offered at the end of 2005 for a limited period. At that time XJs were offered with a choice of four engines – 3.0-litre, 3.5-litre, 4.2-litre and 4.2-litre supercharged. The 3.5-litre variant was dropped in 2008 and a 2.7-litre diesel version was offered from 2005. Then, in 2007, the model was facelifted to provide a more contemporary, aggressive look to the styling, along with other trim changes.

In 2009 the X-350 was discontinued to make way for another, entirely new XJ saloon for the 2010 model year.

Model range and development

No fewer than ten models were initially launched in the X-350 range.

Models available at launch

XJ6 saloon
XJ6 Sport
XJ6 SE (Special Equipment)
XJ8 saloon (3.5-litre V8)
XJ8 Sport (3.5-litre V8)
XJ8 SE (Special Equipment 3.5-litre V8)
XJ8 Sport (4.2-litre V8)
XJ8 SE (Special Equipment 4.2-litre V8)
XJR saloon (supercharged 4.2-litre)
Super V8 (supercharged 4.2-litre)

This is an impressive line-up, being a wider range than offered with the previous X-308 cars and, pro-rata, better value for money, given the high tech nature of the new models. It is worth spending a moment examining these new cars in some detail, as they are so significantly different to any previous XJ.

Firstly, as regards the styling, Jaguar had to take note of common criticisms levied at previous XJs, such as lack of headroom, rear compartment legroom, or even boot space. Also, research had shown that people are now bigger overall, so more space was wanted for everyone, including the driver. The styling of the X-350 had to accommodate this without losing the very essence of 'Jaguarism' in the design.

The bodywork is all-aluminium, incorporating aircraft technology in epoxy bonding and riveting, resulting in the car being 40 per cent lighter and 60 per cent stiffer than the previous XJ8. Mechanically, the cars utilise very similar suspension to the S-type, but with a sophisticated air suspension system which even alters the height of the vehicle to meet the requirements of the surface being driven on. Along with other features like emergency brake assist, voice-activated controls, electronic parking brake, and bi-xenon headlights, the X-350 is the most adventurous and lavishly equipped car Jaguar have ever produced. It is designed to create an overall air of quality, down to special features like a self-closing boot panel and one-touch bonnet closure.

Stylistically the bodywork takes its main cue from the X-type in a much larger form, yet retains touches everywhere you look from previous Jaguar models, even back to the Series saloons of the 1960s and 1970s. It is also the best-built Jaguar to date, with text-book panel gaps and finish, a tribute to the company.

This initial range was extensive, based around four engine options; the existing S-type 3.0-litre

Pre-facelift X-350 XJ6 and XJ8s are identifiable from previous X-300 and XJ8 models by the taller roof, protruding door handles (always chromed), limousine-style flush-fitting door frames, and the taller rear end. This is an XJ6 example, which uses the black centre grille slats.

Pre-facelift radiator slatted grille applied to standard models, SE, and some Sovereign models.

Mesh grille originally applied to XJR model only, later adopted for Sport and Sport Premium.

V6, a new 3.5-litre V8 configuration, and the 4.2-litre V8 in normally aspirated and supercharged form. The 3.0-litre signified the reintroduction of the XJ6 insignia, previously used from 1968 to 1997. This model effectively took over from the previous 3.2-litre X-308 Executive, but it was now also available in Sport and SE (Special Equipment) forms. Strategically priced, it was the most popular 'entry' model in the UK at the time, sitting nicely alongside the lower-priced sector from the competition.

For those who wanted better performance, the 3.5-litre V8 was offered within the same range of models, and the larger 4.2-litre engine's models were only available in Sport form to special order. The most lavishly equipped, top of the range model at the time was the Super V8, which included many of the features normally associated with previous Daimler models.

From 2004, model designations and specification started to change. The first was an extra model, the 3.5-litre Sport Premium, offering a higher level of equipment than the Sport model. Later in the same year the 3.0-litre and 4.2-litre Sovereign models were added, and long wheelbase versions were offered.

A new 2.7-litre diesel engine version, the TDVi, was introduced in 2005 in Executive (replacing the standard XJ models), Sovereign and Sports Premium versions, and the SE models and Sport model were discontinued.

For the 2006 model year a solitary Daimler model became available for a limited period of time in long wheelbase Super Eight (supercharged) form. Another special model was the Portfolio, based on a concept primarily aimed at the US market. This singularly finished car saw the XJ through the final phases of production at the old Browns Lane, Coventry factory in 2006, after which all subsequent X-350s were produced at the Castle Bromwich plant near Birmingham.

Apart from minor trim changes, the next and final stage of development came with a facelift in 2007 with a redesigned front and rear end, enhanced interiors, and model rationalisation. The facelift, although initially offered with all engine sizes, by 2008 for the 2009 model year, the 3.0-litre petrol engine was 'officially' dropped from the range, but some were still produced.

Production of the X-350 range was phased out in 2009 to make way for the 2010 entirely new XJ saloons.

Exterior identification points

General points applicable to all X-350s
From whatever angle you view them, these models are significantly different to previous cars – larger in overall dimensions, with less frontal over-range,

Side view of the pre-facelift X-350 standard wheelbase model, emphasising the raised haunches at the rear.

Long wheelbase equivalent model showing the aesthetically pleasing lines eliminating the usual need to just extend the rear door area.

Rear view of typical pre-facelift X-350 showing the extra chrome applying to none-Sport and R models.

Typical boot badging on the X-350 models, common to all models; only the supercharged models have a coloured 'R' emblem.

Leather interiors apply to all models, with style varying according to model. This shows a standard/Executive XJ6 model with leather-clad steering wheel.

a higher roofline, and a more pronounced wedge-shaped profile from front to rear.

Front view

■ Four headlamp treatment, slightly elliptical in shape, the inner pair slightly smaller.
■ Traditional XJ-shaped radiator grille, surround in chrome on standard, SE, and Super V8 models, body-coloured on Sport and XJR, initially with mesh insert for Sport, Sport Premium, and XJR models, cross-slat insert in black on standard, or chrome on SE/Super V8 models. Facelift models have a more angular grille profile, all models in body colour, with bright mesh insert, also applicable to all models, the centre vane incorporated a pronounced, contemporary growler badge.
■ Integrated front bumper bar/valance also forming part of upper structure around lights and radiator grille. Pre-formed and energy-absorbing, with number plate mounting, enlarged oval air intake beneath with splitter bar, and built-in fog lights. Facelift models have a more pronounced front bumper/valance arrangement with deep mesh under-grille and circular fog lamps. Chromed bumper bar blades from earlier cars now removed.
■ Individual chromed bumper bar blade finishers.
■ One-piece curved and shaped rear-hinged bonnet with raised centre section.
■ One-piece curved windscreen with black or chrome surround, from 2005 bonded without surround. Twin wiper arms.

Rear view

■ All-enveloping rear bumper, combined valance treatment as front. Facelift bumpers have a deeper and smoother finish without chromed bumper blades.
■ Reverse park sensors fitted to all rear bumpers.
■ Twin exhaust pipes emitting either side of the valance, chromed trims.
■ One-piece tapered boot panel, rear-hinged, with pronounced horizontal swage and wide 'Jaguar' plinth incorporating boot lock and concealed number plate lighting. Boot plinth chromed on standard, SE, Super V8, and Sovereign models; body colour on others. Rectangular chromed boot badges, vary according to model.
■ Facelift models incorporate a full boot-width 'signature' panel, chromed on all models except Sport Premium and XJR. New style boot badging.
■ Triangular rear light clusters with unique LED lighting.
■ Rear curved screen with high-level brake light, black or chromed surrounds, from 2005 bonded without surrounds.

Typical Sport interior with contrast trim and revised rectangular pleat sections in the seating.

XJR interior with dark stained maple like the Sport, but revised seating.

Above left: XJR rear compartment showing different style seat treatment. The multi-media control panel is situated in the centre armrest.

Above right: Rear compartment of the Daimler model showing screens for the multi-media system and inset lap-top tables. Soft grain leather trim also applied to the Super V8 Jaguar model.

Side view

- More pronounced 'wedge' shape of profile.
- Less frontal body overhang.
- Raised and curved roof area with no rain gutters and pronounced rake to front screen.
- Limousine-style door frame surrounds with black window surrounds and full roof length finishers in chrome on all models except Sport, Sport Premium, and XJR (high gloss black).
- Protruding 'chunky' door handles.
- Waist-height swage line and, at the lower level, body-colour rubbing strips (discontinued in 2006) extending from front wing-mounted indicator repeater light to rear doors.
- No quarter-lights in front doors, non-opening quarter-lights in rear doors, no windows in rear quarters.
- Fuel filler in rear wing with flush cover.
- Alloy wheels fitted to all models, varying dependent upon model and specification.
- Facelift models all feature more sculptured sill areas, revised door mirrors incorporating indicator tell-tails and 'signature' vertical air vent at the rear of each front wing.

X-350 model specifics

The same specification applies to any engine size, the only external difference being the boot lid badging.

Pre-facelift (2007) models

XJ6 models

- Horizontal and vertical black-painted slats to radiator grille with chrome surround.
- Chromed window surrounds.
- Chromed boot plinth.
- Halogen headlights.
- 17in Elegant alloy wheels.
- 'XJ6' badge on boot lid.

Sport models

- Body coloured radiator grille surround, initially with black slatted inner grille, in 2005 changed to black mesh finish.
- Black window surrounds.
- Body-coloured boot plinth.
- Bi-xenon headlights.
- 18in Dynamic alloy wheels.
- 'XJ Sport' badging on boot lid.

Special Equipment models

- Horizontal and vertical chromed slats to radiator grille with chromed surround.
- Chromed window surrounds.
- Chromed boot plinth.
- Halogen headlights.
- 18in Luxury alloy wheels.
- 'SE' badging on boot lid.

The instrument display for X350 models is entirely new compared to the previous X308 style.

The facelifted XJ exterior with much revised frontal aspect. Note the enlarged lower grille area, more pronounced radiator grille and badge area, new fog lamps, new style to bumper/valance, cleaner looking sides and the 'signature' vertical air vent in the front wing.

The newer smoother look of the post 2006 models without the side rubbing strips and with flush-bonding of the front and rear screens.

Above left: *Centre console of XJR model showing dark stained maple woodwork and unique R style gear lever knob.*

Above right: *Walnut veneer for XJ6, SE, and Super V8 models. All X350 models are equipped with the electronic handbrake previously seen on S-type models. It is operated by the half-moon chrome button to the rear of the gear lever.*

XJR models
- Mesh insert to radiator grille with body-coloured surround.
- Black window surrounds.
- Body-coloured boot plinth.
- Bi-xenon headlights.
- 19in Performance alloy wheels.
- New style 'R-Performance' badging on boot lid.

Super V8 models
- Chromed grille surround with horizontal and vertical chromed slats until 2004, when changed to a bright finish mesh insert.
- Chromed window surrounds.
- Chromed boot plinth.
- Bi-xenon headlights.
- Heated front windscreen.
- Front distance park sensors.
- 18in Prestige alloy wheels.
- 'Super V8' badging on boot lid.

Sovereign models
- As SE models except with Bi-xenon headlights, 19in Custom alloy wheels, 'Sovereign' rear boot badging.

Sport Premium models
- As Sport models but including front headlight wash system, heated front screen, and 19in Custom alloy wheels.

Long-Wheelbase models
- Amended profile to roof line to accommodate the extra length.
- Wider front and rear doors.
- Not available in some models unless by special order.
- Additional 'L' to rear badging.

Daimler models
- Built as Super V8 model with following amendments:
- Fluted chromed radiator grille surround with chromed vertical slats and 'D' emblem at centre-top.
- Rapier 18in alloy wheels.
- Chromed door mirrors.
- Fluted chromed rear boot signature panel.
- 'Daimler' badging to boot lid.

Facelift models
- All the facelift models carry many of the same features except for:
- Halogen lighting for XJ6, Xenon all other models.
- No headlamp washers, standard equipment on XJ6 models.
- Badging and alloy wheel types differ according to model.

The rare Daimler Super V8 model showing the unique fluted radiator grille treatment.

Rear view of the facelifted XJ model. Note the smoother and lower bumper/valance area, revised 'signature' panel on the boot lid.

Unique door handle style, always chromed, on X-350 models.

- Daimler facelift model retained traditional grille treatment but gained the revised bumper bar/under valance and lower grille of the Jaguar models.

Interior identification points

General points applicable to all X-350s

- General style of dashboard follows current X-type and S-type theme with instrument binnacle in front of driver, air conditioning vents to either side and centre of dashboard.
- Centrally mounted analogue clock in dashboard between air conditioning vents.
- Wood veneer features to dashboard top, door cappings, and other areas dependent on model.
- Four-spoke steering wheel with air bag centre boss, Jaguar growler badge, and finger tip controls for audio system, telephone, and cruise control (where fitted).
- Soft-trimmed centre console with auxiliary control buttons, large digital read-out screen for audio/air conditioning information (also used for satellite navigation equipment when installed). Satin black finish.
- Damped ashtray.
- Traditional J-gate controls with different styles of gear knob dependent on model.
- One-touch chromed handbrake pull instead of conventional handbrake.
- Centre armrest with cup-holders, etc.
- Door trims in soft upholstery with window switch packs, chromed door handles, armrests/pulls, and integrated door pockets plus wood cappings.
- Individual style seats of differing types and upholstery dependent on model, all electrically operated.
- Rear seat arrangement to match front, again dependent on model.

Model specifics

As with previous XJ practice there are differing types of trim, in this case four styles, which are best covered individually with appropriate models indicated.

Classic (Standard) XJ6/SE and Sovereign models

- Complementary trim colour schemes with matching upper fascia area.
- Standard leather-clad steering wheel, half wood veneer on SE/Sovereign models.
- Burr walnut veneer woodwork on fascia, centre console area, door cappings, and gear knob.
- Leather seating with horizontal pleats (XJ6) or vertical pleats (SE and Sovereign models).

- Fixed rear bench-seat with triple headrests to match front upholstery.

Sport/Sport Premium models

- Dashboard top roll, steering wheel, and door top rails always finished in charcoal.
- Leather-clad steering wheel, late changed to R-Performance style.
- Contrast colour trim schemes to door inner trim panels and seat centres or all-charcoal finish.
- Grey-stained maple veneer woodwork.
- Perforated leather seating with 'window pane' style panelling and stiffer bolsters.
- Wooden gear knob.

Super V8

- Complimentary trim colour schemes with matching upper fascia area.
- Complimentary coloured leather and burr walnut heated steering wheel.
- Navigational 'steer' screen in centre console.
- Fixed front compartment telephone.
- Burr walnut veneer woodwork on fascia, centre console area, door cappings, and gear knob.
- Ruched leather seating with horizontal pleated panels, with or without contrast piping.
- Rear bench-seat electrically adjustable with multi-media centre in centre armrest area.

Long wheelbase models

- As above, dependent on model variant plus:
- Electrically-heated rear bench seat with electric seat adjustment and memory, standard on Super V8 and Daimler models only.
- Heated steering wheel, standard only on Super V8 and Daimler models.
- Rear multi-media centre, standard only on super V8 and Daimler models.
- Rear laptop tables set into the front seat backs, standard only on Daimler model.

Portfolio model

- This was a limited-edition model based on an initial concept on the X-308 saloon. This was available, primarily for the US market, but was also available in other markets by order. All cars were finished with black interior to a totally different style from other XJ models.

All details of trim and specification given above relate to standard production cars. Certain owners may well have specified changes to suit their individual requirements, so it is not unusual to find some more basic models with a higher specification than that described here. From 2006 a wider range of interior finishes was available to replace the conventional maple or walnut veneers. Check details in pictures and colour schemes.

1: *17in Elegant wheels, original fitment on XJ6 models, deleted in 2004.*

2: *18in Dynamic wheels were fitted as standard on Sport and SE models until 2005.*

3: *18in Luxury alloys, original fitment on SE and, in 2004, for XJ6.*

4: *18in Prestige alloys were the standard fit on Super V8 models up to 2004.*

5: *19in Performance alloy wheels were standard equipment on XJR models to 2005.*

6: *20in Sepang alloy wheels were standard on Portfolio models, optional on Daimler models, and an extra-cost option on all others.*

7: *19in Custom wheels, initially an extra-cost option became standard on Sport Premium models, and for 2004 on Sovereign model.*

8: *18in Rapier wheels became the standard fit on Sovereign and Super V8 models from 2005, and then on the Daimler model.*

9: *18in Tucana wheels became the standard fit on XJ6 models from 2005.*

10: *19in Sabre wheels became the standard fit on XJR models from 2005.*

11: *19in Polaris wheels, initially fitted to facelift Sovereign models, became an extra cost option for 2008/9 model years.*

12: *19in Carelia wheels – the standard fit on Executive facelift models.*

13: *20in Cremona wheels were only fitted to Sport Premium and XJR models in 2008.*

14: *20in Takoba wheels were standard fit on Sovereign and Super V8 models during the last year of production.*

15: *20in Callisto wheels were original fitment on Executive, Sport Premium, Sovereign, and XJR models from 2008 up to the end of production.*

16: *The unique 19in Vela alloy wheel produced for the facelift Daimler model only.*

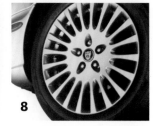

Technical specifications

	2.7-litre diesel	3.0-litre
cc	2,722	2,967
Bore and stroke (mm)	81 x 88	89 x 79.5
Compression ratio	17.3 to 1	10.5:1
bhp	204	240
@ rpm	4,000	6,800
Torque (lb ft)	321	221
@ rpm	1,900	4,100
Fuelling	Fuel injection	Fuel injection
Transmission	ZF 6-speed auto	ZF 6-speed auto
Wheel size (in)	18 (variable)	17 or 18, alloy
Suspension front	Ind double wishbones, coil springs air suspension standard	Ind unequal length double wishbones, anti dive, coil springs, air suspension standard
Suspension rear	Ind double wishbones, coil springs, air suspension standard	Ind double wishbones, coil springs, air suspension standard
Brakes	4 wheel disc, all ventilated	4 wheel disc, all ventilated
Performance		
0–60mph (sec)	7.8	7.8
Top speed (mph)	141	145
Average mpg	35	27
Dimensions		
Length (in)	199	199
Width (in)	73	73
Height (in)	55	55
Wheelbase (in)	117	117
Front track (in)	61	61
Rear track (in)	60	60
Weight (lb)	3,657	3,406

Optional extras

Air suspension (selected models only).
De-chromed exterior trim pack (selected models only).
Power fold-back mirrors (where not fitted).
Headlamp power-wash (where not fitted).
Heated front screen.
Front distance park aid (where not fitted).
Electric sunroof.
Variable heated seat cushions (where not fitted).
16-way electrically adjustable front seats (selected models only).
Wood/leather steering wheel (where not fitted).
Heated wood/leather steering wheel.
Four-zone climate control system.

Adaptive cruise control.
Lambswool over-rugs.
Ski-hatch.
Rear sunblind (electric).
Side manually-operated window blinds.
Premium sound system.
Telephone installations.
Voice activation control.
Satellite navigation system.
Rear-mounted multi-media system with TV screens.
Electrochromatic rear-view mirror with compass.
Mud flaps.
Tailored over-mats.
Child's safety seat.

	3.5-litre	4.2-litre
cc	3,555	4,196
Bore and stroke (mm)	86 x 76.5	86 x 90.3
Compression ratio	11:1	11:1
bhp	262	300
@ rpm	6,250	6,000
Torque (lb ft)	254	310
@ rpm	4,200	4,100
Fuelling	Fuel injection	Fuel injection
Transmission	ZF 6-speed auto	ZF 6-speed auto
Wheel size (in)	17 or 18, alloy	18, alloy
Suspension front	Ind unequal length double wishbones, anti dive, coil springs, air suspension standard	Ind unequal length double wishbones, anti dive, coil springs, air suspension standard
Suspension rear	Ind double wishbones, coil springs, air suspension standard	Ind double wishbones, coil springs, air suspension standard
Brakes	4 wheel disc, all ventilated	4 wheel disc, all ventilated
Performance		
0–60mph (sec)	7.3	6.3
Top speed (mph)	150	155
Average mpg	26.5	26
Dimensions		
Length (in)	199	199
Width (in)	73	73
Height (in)	55	55
Wheelbase (in)	117	117
Front track (in)	61	61
Rear track (in)	60	60
Weight (lb)	3,560	3,560

Child's booster cushion.
First aid kit for boot area.
Space-saver spare wheel.
Full-size spare wheel.
Fire extinguisher for boot area.
Jaguar warning triangle.
Headlamp converters.
Headlamp safety covers.
Snow chains.
Luggage net for boot area.
Witter tow bar kit.
Tracker security system.
Alternative woodwork veneers (according to model).

Long wheelbase bodyshell to special order on non-production models.
Tyre pressure monitoring system.
Wheels options (dependent on model and standard equipment):
17in Elegant.
18in Dynamic, Luxury, Prestige, Rapier, and Tucana.
19in Performance, Custom, Sabre, Polaris, and Carelia.
20in Sepang, Cremona, Takoba, and Callisto.

R-Performance option
20in Sepang split rim alloy wheels.

Technical specifications *cont ...*

	4.2-litre supercharged
cc	4,196
Bore and stroke (mm)	86 x 90.3
Compression ratio	9:1
bhp	400
@ rpm	6,100
Torque (lb ft)	408
@ rpm	3,500
Fuelling	Fuel injection
Transmission	ZF 6-speed auto
Wheel size (in)	18 or 19, alloy
Suspension front	Ind unequal length double wishbones, anti dive, coil springs, air suspension standard
Suspension rear	Ind double wishbones, coil springs, air suspension standard
Brakes	4 wheel disc, all ventilated
Performance	
0–60mph (sec)	5
Top speed (mph)	155
Average mpg	23
Dimensions	
Length (in)	199
Width (in)	73
Height (in)	55
Wheelbase (in)	117
Front track (in)	61
Rear track (in)	60
Weight (lb)	3,671

Variances

Long wheelbase models:

Weight (lb)	3,560
Length (in)	205
Wheelbase (in)	124

Colour schemes

Exterior	Details	Interior	Details	Contrast piping	Details
White Onyx	To 2007	Ivory		Charcoal	
Jaguar Racing Green	To 2007	Sand	Until 2005	Sable	To 2007
British Racing Green	To 2007	Dove	2004–8	Granite	To 2008
Radiance Red		Charcoal		Charcoal	
Pacific Blue	To 2007	Cranberry		Mocha	From 2007
Platinum Grey	To 2007	Champagne	2004–8	Navy	From 2008
Quartz	To 2007				
Ultraviolet Blue	To 2007	**Fascias**	**Details**	**Stitching**	**Details**
Seafrost	To 2007	Mocha		Black	To 2008
Slate	To 2007	Granite	To 2008	Heritage Tan	To 2005
Topaz	To 2007	Charcoal		Cranberry	To 2006
Ebony		Navy	From 2008	Warm Charcoal	From 2008
Zircon	To 2007			Granite	From 2008
Midnight	From 2004			Dove	From 2008
Winter Gold	From 2006				
Indigo	From 2006	**Contrasts**		**Details**	
Botanical Green	From 2007	Ivory/Charcoal		To 2005	
Emerald Fire	From 2007	Heritage Tan/Charcoal		To 2005	
Vapour Grey	From 2007	Cranberry/Charcoal		To 2005	
Frost Blue	From 2007				
Blue Prism	2007	**Veneers**		**Details**	
Azure Blue	From 2008	Burr walnut			
Ultimate Black	From 2007	Grey-stained maple			
Pearl Grey	From 2007	Aluminium		From 2006	
Lunar Grey	From 2007	Elm		From 2007	
Liquid Silver	From 2007	Satin American Walnut		2007–8	
Porcelain	From 2007	Rich Oak		From 2008	
Garnett	From 2006*	Burr walnut with Boxwood inlay		Only applicable to Daimler model	

* = Daimler model only

Prices and production volumes

	Price new (£)	2003	2004	2005
XJ6 3.0 litre SWB	£39,000	■	■	■
XJ6 3.0 litre LWB	Sp order	–	–	■
XJ6 3.0 litre Sport SWB	£42,250	■	■	–
XJ6 3.0 lirtre SE/Sov SWB	£42,250	■	■	■
XJ6 3.0 litre Sov LWB	£45,750	–	–	■
XJ6 2.7 litre TDV SWB	£43,272	–	–	■
XJ6 2.7 litre TDV LWB	£46,770	–	–	–
XJ6 2.7 litre Prem Sp SWB	£49,272	–	–	■
XJ6 2.7 litre Sov SWB	£49,272	–	–	■
XJ6 2.7 litre Sov LWB	£52,770	–	–	–
XJ8 3.5 litre SWB	£41,550	■	■	■
XJ8 3.5 litre LWB	Sp order	–	■	■
XJ8 3.5 litre Sport SWB	£44,802	■	■	■
XJ8 3.5 litre SE SWB	£48,000	■	■	■
XJ8 3.5 litre Sp Prem	£47,302	–	■	■
XJ8 4.2 litre SWB	£51,500	■	■	■
XJ8 4.2 litre LWB	£60,375	–	■	■
XJ8 4.2 litre Sport SWB	Sp order	■	–	–
XJ8 4.2 litre SE/Sov SWB	£57,902	■	■	■
XJ8 4.2 litre SE/Sov LWB	£61,995	–	■	■
XJ8 4.2 litre VDP SWB	USA	■	■	–
XJ8 4.2 litre VDP LWB	USA	–	■	■
XJ8 4.2 litre Super V8 SWB	£68,500	■	■	■
XJ8 4.2 litre Super V8 LWB	£71,975	–	■	■
XJR 4.2 litre S/charged SWB	£58,500	■	■	■
XJR 4.2 litre S/c VDP LWB*	£61,277	–	■	■
Daimler Super V8	£79,277	–	–	■
Total production		**27,811**	**15,100**	**13,594**

* = this figure includes Portfolio model

Chassis numbers

Model	
X-350 models	Vin No. (see table 9*)

*Table 9 appears on page 320.

2006	2007	2008	2009	Total produced
■	■	■	■	4,861
■	■	■	■	476
–	–	–	–	626
■	■	■	■	4,512
■	■	■	■	2,233
■	■	■	■	3,647
■	■	■	■	230
■	■	■	–	780
■	■	■	■	3,453
■	■	■	■	696
■	■	■	–	981
■	■	■	–	225
■	–	–	–	523
■	■	■	–	3,890
■	■	■	–	747
■	■	■	–	15,840
■	■	–	–	8,836
–	–	–	–	190
■	■	■	■	6,322
■	■	■	■	1,735
–	–	–	–	4,194
■	■	■	■	6,872
■	■	■	■	1,309
■	■	■	–	943
■	■	■	■	7,316
■	■	■	–	1,277
■	■	■	–	853
10,032	**10,270**	**5,912**	**837**	**83,566**

Background

Jaguar's new sports car (replacing the 1996–2005 XK8 and XKR models) was announced in October 2005 ready for the 2006 model year. Taking strong cues from the ALC (Aluminium Lightweight Coupé) concept car, the New XK, as it was called, also inherited many technical features from the X-350 saloons.

Unusual for a sports car, the New XK was designed as a convertible first to ensure the maximum rigidity possible, and the body construction of all aluminium followed the same processes as the big XJ saloon. The new car was, therefore, not only 20 per cent lighter than the outgoing XK8 but was also an astonishing 50 per cent stiffer. Despite this high-tech move forward with outstanding contemporary styling, the car was initially launched with the existing 4.2-litre AJ-V8 engine, developing 300bhp but with multi-hole injectors to the fuel injection system, mated to the ZF six-speed automatic transmission.

Innovative features included keyless entry and start facilities, active front lighting that followed the steering, sequential gear-shift operation from steering wheel mounted paddles and, in the case of the convertible, a fully retracting hood under an aluminium tonneau closing panel.

Key safety features included automatically deploying rollover bars at the rear of the cockpit, and, unique at the time, a pyrotechnic deployable bonnet system which in the event of accidental collision with a pedestrian would instantly raise the height of the bonnet above the hard areas beneath to provide a softer impact. Larger brakes with an improved overall braking system, with modified steering and suspension, completed the new package.

Announced as both 2+2 coupé and convertible, the New XK continued to provide excellent boot accommodation (suitable for the obligatory two sets of golf clubs!). The interior was a complete redesign with clearer instruments, new layout, and many more creature comforts than previous models.

It wasn't until a year later for the 2007 model year that the XKR variants were announced, also in coupé and convertible form. Now boasting a 420bhp supercharged engine, improved brakes and suspension, subtle trim changes differentiated the XKRs from the normally aspirated XK models.

Towards the end of 2007 the Portfolio was announced as a special edition to the XKR range, but only as a coupé model, (later added to the convertible range in 2008). Then, at the Geneva Motor Show in March 2008, Jaguar announced the XKR-S, based on the XKR but with improved performance and aerodynamics. In 2008 the XK60 was announced as the replacement for the basic XK models with higher spec equipment levels and revised trim.

Then, in 2009, for the 2010 model year the XK was effectively re-launched with an all-new 5.0-litre V8 engine in both normally-aspirated and supercharged forms, with a large degree of interior and exterior trim changes, plus other mechanical refinements. At the time of writing the XK is still in production.

Model range and development

The New XK was promoted at launch as *'the car that demands your immediate attention'*.

Models available at launch
New XK 4.2-litre 2+2 coupé
New XK 4.2-litre 2+2 convertible

The principles of this virtually entirely new Jaguar sports still lay in a monocoque construction, but now of ultra-lightweight aluminium and, unlike the previous XK8, was neither designed for nor used in any other model. Here was a much lighter, more aerodynamic car, more economical to produce and maintain, and economical to run, with styling that was contemporary and 'sharp', yet retaining many of the features well known to Jaguar sports cars since the 1960s.

It was offered with a choice of 18in, 19in or 20in alloy wheels and the option of run-flat tyres and a tyre-pressure monitoring system. Standard equipment included Xenon headlights, reverse parking aid, and auto-locking system upon leaving the car. The New XK was the first Jaguar to carry the now well-known 'signature' wing vents in the front wings.

Internally the cars were fitted out to a very high standard, with a choice of wood veneer or alloy finishes, standard equipment cruise control, and a sophisticated security system.

Direct comparison between the latest XK and the previous 1996 model.

Always conceived as a convertible, this is an early example with the 20in Santa alloy wheels showing the clean lines of the hood.

Early XK frontal aspect with smoother treatment to the under-bumper area, inset fog lights, and chrome 'splitter' bar to the grille area.

Rear view of an early XK convertible with discreet spoiler with built in brake-light.

The drive train followed that of the X-350 saloons (without air suspension) and some design elements from the S-type models. Incorporated was a four-channel ABS system with analogue control and Electronic Brakeforce Distribution ensuring the correct balance of braking forces spread across all four wheels.

One of the most interesting aspects of the new car was the 'sound', produced by the exhaust system and by a complex valve system which allowed a degree of noise to enter the cockpit of the car.

The first customer cars were delivered in 2006 and it wasn't until 2007 that the XKR supercharged version came to the marketplace. The new engine supplied 420bhp with 560Nm of torque, providing an incredible acceleration time of under 5sec to 60mph. Springs and shock absorbers were uprated for this model along with a recalibration of the CATS (Computer Active Technology Suspension) package.

Subtle exterior changes to differentiate the XKR from the XK included new-style bumper treatment and grille, louvres set into the bonnet, the alloy finish to the front wing side vents, and the four exhaust pipes instead of two. Internally the XKR was identifiable by its revised trim and seating.

Towards the end of 2007 the Portfolio was announced as a special edition to the XKR range, but only as a coupé model. Cosmetically it was only available in black (or also silver for UK and Swiss markets) but had unique front-end treatment with alloy finished grille, vents, and unique bonnet louvres. Along with interior trim changes, mechanically it has an enlarged braking system.

At the Geneva Motor Show in 2008 Jaguar announced their next 'special' XK, the XKR-S. Although essentially still based on the XKR model, the engine management system was recalibrated along with tweaks to the suspension and aerodynamics, to improve performance. Jaguar claimed a top speed of 174mph, making it the fastest Jaguar production car since the XJ220 supercar in the 1990s. The massive disc brakes and six-pot calipers were a carryover from the Portfolio model mentioned above. On sale through 2008, production was limited to just 200 cars, all for the European market.

In 2008 the XK60 was announced as the replacement for the basic XK (non-supercharged models), in both coupé and convertible forms. The new car offered extra equipment levels as standard, including 20in alloy wheels, alloy gear knob and surround, and enhanced exterior front, rear and side trims.

At the Geneva Motor Show in 2009 the XKs received a major boost with the replacement of the above models with the 2010 model year cars, the highlight of which was the fitment of new

The early coupé model with sculptured rear tailgate emphasising the pronounced haunches of the car.

The distinctive interior treatment, totally different from previous XKs with great use of alloy finishes. This car is equipped with the burr walnut veneering.

With the introduction of the XKR models, came revisions to the front and rear styling and different finish to items like the side 'signature' vents. Note also the louvres added to the bonnet for XKR models only.

AJ-V8 Gen III 5.0-litre V8 engines providing a 23 per cent increase in performance and 12 per cent increase in torque over the previous 4.2-litre units. Other mechanical upgrades included steering and brakes and the adoption of a JaguarDrive control system for gear changes. Offered in both normally-aspirated and supercharged forms, in both convertible and coupé, there are three models now: the XK, the XKR, and the XK Portfolio (the latter with a higher trim specification), all with exterior and interior changes to the previous models.

Side view of the 2008 Portfolio convertible, with 20in Cremona alloy wheels and enlarged braking system.

Exterior identification points

General points applicable to XK models (up to 2010 model range)

Front view

- Curvaceous frontal aspect emulating previous XK but with more pronounced nose and lower under-bumper incorporating spoiler and lower grille area.
- Nose incorporates mesh insert, in front of which is a chromed splitter bar with centrally-mounted growler badge.
- Xenon headlights incorporating side light and indicator units sculptured into front wing areas.
- Standard fit insert fog lights.
- One-piece forward-hinged bonnet with pronounced power-bulge in centre.
- One-piece bonded windscreen with twin wipers.

Revised XK frontal view for 2008 models.

Rear view

- Severely tapering rear-end styling.
- Rear-hinged boot lid terminating at tonneau panel on convertible model.
- Rear-hinged tailgate incorporating rear screen on coupé model.
- Number plate surround indent in boot with Jaguar 'signature' chromed panel incorporating illumination and boot lock control.
- Rear light clusters matching the front lighting moulded into the side of each rear wing, incorporating digital light techniques.
- Twin chromed exhaust tailpipes, one emitting from each side below bumper/valance area.
- Chromed 'XK' and '4.2' badging each side of the boot panel.
- Pronounced and sculptured body-colour rear bumper/valance panel with reverse parking aid.

Side view

- Inset body-coloured vertical air vents 'signature' panels at rear of each front wing which also incorporate 'Jaguar' badging and indicator repeater lenses.

The very latest XKR, equipped with the 5.0-litre engine and, in this case, with Nevis 20in wheels.

- Simple waist height swage line running the length of the car.
- Pronounced sculptured sills.
- Pronouced body-colour door handle/pulls.
- Frameless door glass.
- Concealed fuel filler cap incorporated into the rear nearside wing, with flush cover.

XKR specifics
Front view
- Revised styling to front bumper/valance area with colour-keyed finish to fog light housings.
- Nose incorporates mesh insert to both the grille and under-grille areas without the chromed splitter bar of the XK and a larger, centrally-mounted growler badge.
- Louvred air vents set into bonnet top.

Rear view
- Restyling to rear bumper/valance area to accommodate:
- Four chromed exhaust tailpipes, two emitting from each side below the bumper/valance area.
- Chromed and coloured 'R' badging, on right-hand side of the boot panel.
- Alloy-finished rear 'signature' panel.
- Rear spoiler added to boot lid incorporating high-level brake light.

Side view
- Inset alloy-finished vertical air vents 'signature' panels at rear of each front wing which also incorporate 'Jaguar' badging and indicator repeater lenses.
- Black R brake calipers visible through alloy wheels.

Portfolio specifics
Additional to R specification.
- Portfolio models only available in Celestial Black paint finish (or Liquid Silver for UK and Swiss markets). Became available as a convertible model from 2008.

Front view
- Reshaped front bumper area incorporating aluminium-finished grilles and fog light areas.
- Revised bonnet louvres.

Rear view
- Satin-finished alloy rear 'signature' panel.

Side view
- Inset polished alloy-finished vertical air vent 'signature' panels at rear of each front wing.
- 20in polished Cremona alloy wheels.
- Six-pot, red 'R' brake calipers with cross-drilled brake discs visible.

XKR-S Specifics (additional to Portfolio models)
- Only available in Ultimate Black exterior paint finish.

Front view
- Revised frontal bumper/valance treatment with aerodynamic 'lip'.
- Contrast finish to grilles and spoiler/splitter.

Rear view
- Unique 'R-S' badging to right-hand side of boot lid.
- Revised more prominent spoiler.
- Rear diffuser panel below bumper level in contrast colour.

Side view
- 10mm ride-height reduction compared to other XKR models.
- Sill extensions in contrast colour.
- 20in Vortext forged alloy wheels.

XK60 Specifics
Front view
- Revised front bumper/valance treatment with bright mesh grilles, circular inset fog lights and sculptured spoiler.
- Chrome splitter no longer featured.

Rear view
- Revised rear valance with diffuser.
- Revised tailpipe finishers.

Side view
- Chrome-finished front wing-mounted 'signature' vents.
- Sill appliqués.

2010 model year specifics
Front view
- New front-end treatment with larger under-grille area (finished in black on XK and Portfolio) with chromed detailing to different shaped inserts and upper mesh grille.
- Chrome lower mesh grille on XKR models.

Rear view
- LED rear light clusters with integrated fog lights and twin reversing lights (only one on previous models.)
- Chromed boot 'signature' panel now standard on all models.
- Revised shape lower bumper/valance on XKR model with new-style exhaust tailpipes.
- 18in Venus alloy wheels standard on XK models.
- 19in Caravela alloy wheels standard on Portfolio models.
- 19in Tamana alloy wheels standard on XKR models.

Side view

- LED side indicator repeater lights in front wings.
- Revised colour 'signature' vents in front wings.
- LED repeater lights within the door mirrors.
- Chrome detailing on window surrounds.

Interior identification points

General points applicable to XK models up to 2010 model year

- Full-width dashboard area split into three areas, instrument binnacle in front of driver, pronounced centre console area incorporating multi-media, air-con, and auxiliary controls leading to console between the front seats holding the gear select, 'start' button, and handbrake control, and the passenger area with trim and glove compartment.
- Air-conditioning air vents in centre of dash area, plus auxiliary vents, one either side of dash area.
- Main instrument binnacle incorporates inset speedometer, rev counter, and auxiliary fuel bar gauge plus message centre.
- Centre console area incorporates air-conditioning controls, audio system plus touch-screen for satellite navigational system, and TV tuner (where fitted).
- Three-spoke steering wheel in a choice of finishes incorporating paddle controls for gear-shift and thumb controls for audio system, telephone, and cruise control.
- Choice of wood veneer or alloy finish to dash and trim areas.
- Soft door trim areas incorporating door pulls, chromed door handles, and switch packs for windows/mirrors.
- All seats trimmed in perforated leather with horizontal and vertical panel stitching.
- Each front seat contains electrically-adjustable head restraints and full seat electric controls from side of seats.

XKR specifics

- XKR badging to main instruments.
- Unique alloy 'weave' finish to dash and console area as standard equipment.
- R seating with stiff bolsters and larger panels with horizontal stitching plus heavily embossed seat back side panels.
- R performance gear knob.

Portfolio specifics

- Additional to XKR:
- Engine-spun alloy dash panel finish or US Satin walnut alternative.
- Alloy and leather gear knob.
- Soft-grab door handles.

Above left: The centre console area of the early new XK showing the conventional J-gate gear change system, in this case with Poplar veneer surround. Note also the red 'start' button, at the time unique to the XK.

Above right: Showing the alloy finished interior. Note the sportier seating compared to the previous picture.

The XKR interior with alloy finish veneer, revised gear-knob, and the different seat style.

Above left: XKR Portfolio with different alloy-style finish and gear-knob.

Above right: The revised interior of the XKR for the 2010 model year. Note the contrasting use of Piano Black finish to the alloy, the JaguarDrive control for gear changes, and the leather stitched centre spoke to the steering wheel.

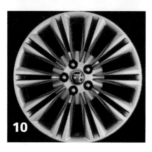

- Contrast leather stitching to all trim.
- Leather-edged carpet over-mats.
- 'Portfolio' treadplates.
- Soft grain interior trim in choice of only two colour schemes (ivory or charcoal).
- Bowers & Wilkins hi-fi sound system.

XKR-S specifics
- Piano Black veneer.
- Revised, recalibrated instrument pack.
- Alston charcoal headlining.
- Contrast stitched leather steering wheel.
- Bright alloy foot pedals.
- XKR-S 'branded' headrests, mats, and treadplates.

XK60 specifics
- Alloy gear-knob and surround.

2010 model year specifics
- Centre console now incorporates JaguarDrive gear selector control.
- Suede cloth headlining for XKR coupé model.
- Bright sill treadplates applicable to all models.
- Leather-wrapped lower spoke steering wheel.
- White instrument illumination for XK and Portfolio models.
- Red instrument pointers for XKR models.
- Heated and cooled front seats standard on all models.
- Saddle-stitched and soft padded door pulls and casings.
- Chromed highlight door pack switches.
- Soft-grain leather with contrast stitching on Portfolio and XKR models.
- Option of Ebony veneer for Portfolio model.

1: *18in Venus wheels, standard fit on XK.*

2: *19in Carelia wheels, an option to 2009.*

3: *20in Senta wheels, an option to 2009.*

4: *19in Sabre wheels, a run-flat wheel available to 2009.*

5: *19in Jupiter wheels, available mid-2007–late-2009.*

6: *20in Cremona wheels, available mid-2007–2009.*

7: *20in Pegasus wheels (2007–2009).*

8: *20in Nevis R-Performance wheels from 2010.*

9: *19in Caravela wheels, an option in 2010.*

10: *19in Artura wheels, an option in 2010.*

11: *20in Kalimnos, standard on Portfolio and optional on XK/XKR in 2010.*

Technical specifications

	4.2-litre	4.2-litre supercharged
cc	4,196	4,196
Bore and stroke (mm)	86 x 90	86 x 90
Compression ratio	11 to 1	9 to 1
bhp	298	420
@ rpm	6,000	6,250
Max torque (lb ft)	310	413
@ rpm	4,100	4,000
Fuelling	Fuel injection	Fuel injection
Transmission	6-speed auto sequential	6-speed auto sequential
Wheel size (in)	19/20 alloy	19/20 alloy
Suspension front	Ind unequal length wishbones, coil springs	Ind unequal length wishbones, coil springs
Suspension (rear)	Ind unequal length wishbones, coil springs	Ind unequal length wishbones, coil springs
Brakes	4-wheel disc, all ventilated	4-wheel disc, all ventilated
Performance		
0–60mph (sec)	5.9	4.9
Top speed (mph)	155	155
Average mpg	25	22
Dimensions		
Length (in)	189	189
Width (in)	74	74
Height (in)	52	52
Wheelbase (in)	108	108
Front track (in)	61	61
Rear track (in)	61	61
Weight (lb)	3,516	3,691

Technical specifications *cont ...*

	5.0-litre	5.0-litre supercharged
cc	5,000	5,000
Bore and stroke (mm)	92.5 x 93	92.5 x 93
Compression ratio	11.5 to 1	9.5 to 1
bhp	385	510
@ rpm	6,500	6,500
Max torque (lb ft)	385	510
@ rpm	6,500	6,500
Fuelling	Fuel injection	Fuel injection
Transmission	6-speed auto sequential	6-speed auto sequential
Wheel size (in)	19/20	19/20
Suspension front	Ind unequal length wishbones, coil springs	Ind unequal length wishbones, coil springs
Suspension rear	Ind unequal length wishbones, coil springs	Ind unequal length wishbones, coil springs
Brakes	4-wheel disc, all ventilated	4-wheel disc, all ventilated
Performance		
0–60mph (sec)	5.2	4.6
Top speed (mph)	155	155
Average mpg	25	23
Dimensions		
Length (in)	189	189
Width (in)	75	75
Height (in)	52	52
Wheelbase (in)	108	108
Front track (in)	61	61
Rear track (in)	63	63
Weight (lb)	3,651	3,865

Optional extras

Black or Bright finish mesh grilles.
Square stainless steel exhaust trim pipes.
Bright finish door mirror covers.
Bright finish front wing 'signature' vents.
Brush aluminium or chromed gear knobs.
Tailored over-carpet mats.
Aluminium drilled pedal pads.
Wind deflector for convertible models.
18in Venus alloy wheels.
19in Carelia, Caravela, Artura, Tamana, or Saba alloy wheels.
20in Senta, Kalimnos, or Nevis alloy wheels.
Tyre pressure monitoring system.
Keyless entry.
Alternative veneer dash trims.
TV tuner.
DVD audio system.

Bowers & Wilkins Premium hi-fi system.
Active front lighting.
Power fold-back door mirrors.
Front park assist system with interior touch-screen information.
Soft-grain leather seat facings.
ACC cruise control.
Premium surround-sound hi-fi system.
Bowers & Wilkins hi-fi system.
Upgrade styling kit.
Garage door opener.
Heated windscreen.
Heated door mirrors.
R-Performance interior (2010 on)
Choice of veneer.
Chromed bonnet louvres.

Colour schemes

Exterior	Details
British Racing Green	To 2008
Jaguar Racing Green	To 2008
White Onyx	To 2007
Porcelain	From 2007
Seafrost	To 2007
Liquid Silver	
Lunar Grey	From 2007
Quartz	To 2007
Slate Grey	To 2008
Vapour Grey	From 2008
Pearl Grey	From 2008
Zircon	To 2007
Frost Blue	From 2007
Ultraviolet Blue	To 2007
Blue Prism	From 2007
Azure Blue	From 2008
Indigo	
Midnight	To 2008
Ebony	
Salsa Red	To 2009 all models (from 2010 XKR only)
Radiance Red	
Winter Gold	
Celestial Black	To 2009 (Portfolio only)
Ultimate Black	XKR-S model (then XKR from 2009)
Claret	From 2010
Spectrum Blue	From 2010
Kyanite Blue	From 2010 (XKR only)
Botanical Green	From 2008
Emerald Fire	From 2008

Hood colours (convertibles)	Details
Beige	
Dark Beige	To 2008
Blue	
Black	
Dark Grey	From 2008
Dark Brown	From 2008 Portfolio only (2010 including XKR)
Burgandy	From 2008 Portfolio only (2010 including XKR)
Dark Green	From 2008 Portfolio only (2010 including XKR)

Leather seat colours	
Caramel	
Ivory	
Warm Charcoal	

Trim colours	
Ivory	
Caramel	
Slate Blue	
Warm Charcoal	
Oyster	2010 on (XKR & Portfolio only)

Contrast stitching	
Ivory	
Charcoal	
Slate Blue	

Veneers	
Burr Walnut	
Poplar	To 2008
Aluminium	
Weave Aluminium	To 2009 (XKR only)
Engine-spun alloy	To 2009 (Portfolio only)
Piano Black	Initially XKR-S, from 2008 XKR
Satin American Walnut	2008–9
Rich Oak	From 2010 (XK & Portfolio only)
Knurled Aluminium	From 2010 (XK & Portfolio only)
Dark Mesh	From 2010 (XKR only)
Dark Oak	From 2010 (XKR only)
Ebony	From 2010 (Portfolio only)

Prices and production years

	Price new (£)	2006	2007	2008	2009	2010
XK coupé	59,232	■	■	■	–	■
XK8 convertible	65,232	■	■	■	–	■
XKR coupé	66,732	–	■	■	■	■
XKR convertible	72,732	–	■	■	■	■
XKR Portfolio coupé	75,597	–	■	■	■	■
XKR Portfolio convertible	78,232	–	–	■	■	–
XK8 Portfolio coupé		–	–	–	–	■
XK8 Portfolio convertible		–	–	–	–	■
XKR-S coupé	79,995	–	–	■	■	–
XK60 coupé	60,995	–	–	■	■	–
XK60 convertible	66,995	–	–	■	■	–

Alloy wheel options

18in Venus
Standard fit XK models.

19in Carelia
To late 2009.

19in Sabre
Run-flat to late 2009.

19in Jupiter
Mid-2007–9.

19in Artura
Painted, chromed or run-flat (from 2010).

19in Caravela
Standard fit 2008/9 on for Portfolio models.

19in Tamana
Standard fit 2010 on for non-UK XKR models.

20in Senta
To late 2009.

20in Cremona
Mid-2007–9 (polished for Portfolio models).

20in Vortext
Only for XKR-S model.

20in Pegasus
2007–9.

20in Kalimnos
Standard fit 2010 on Portfolio models.

20in Nevis
R-Performance (standard on XKR from 2010).

Background

The Jaguar XF (an entirely new production model identification for the company) was announced in 2007 as a direct replacement for the outgoing S-type model that had been in production from 1999. Although carrying much of the S-type's architecture, including engines/transmissions, the suspension has been a direct development of that used in the new XK sports cars. Although built of steel, use has been made of the latest technology metals like high-carbon, dual-phase, hot-formed boron, and bake-hardened steels. New technology also allowed the use of slimmer A and B posts, not only for improved safety but also for better visibility, and the XF incorporates the pedestrian contact system, first used on the new XK sports car.

The most striking aspects of the XF were the entirely new body style and interior, and the sophisticated systems. Available in just one body style – four-door but with a coupé style to the rear of the roof area – the general styling of the car owed nothing to previous Jaguar models and has provided the stimulus for all future Jaguar 'in-house' designing.

Introduced with the previous 2.7-litre diesel, 3.0-litre and 4.2-litre petrol engines, there was also a supercharged version. The XF became the first Jaguar saloon to offer the new JaguarDrive gear-change system, as well as paddle controls on the steering wheel. With its sophisticated on-board equipment and state-of-the-art safety features, the XF became an immediate class leader and proved a success for the company.

At the beginning of 2009 a new model was announced – the XF Diesel S. The main change came in the engine, with the very latest derivative of the 2.7-litre unit, now of 3.0-litre capacity (AJ-V6D Gen III). Providing 275bhp with a massive 600Nm of torque, acceleration times and top speed were much improved, as was fuel consumption (12 per cent better than the previous 2.7-litre model). This car replaced the previous diesel models and was also available as a more luxurious Portfolio version.

Early in 2009, for the 2010 model year, the biggest changes to date took place in the XF range. Jaguar announced their new 5.0-litre AJ-V8 Gen III engines for these cars at the same time as the XKs, effectively replacing the 4.2-litre and 3.0-litre petrol engines. Along with many visual changes, both inside and out, the XF has been much improved in economy, emissions, and performance. Luxury Portfolio models have also been added to the range. The XF continues as a current production model, built at Castle Bromwich in the West Midlands of England.

Model range and development

Although of the standard three-box, four-door saloon principle, the XF provided Jaguar with a new 'house-style' with a near-coupé approach to roof design and a striking new frontal and rear aspect. With a severe sloping front end and a high rear section, this gave excellent aerodynamics with a drag coefficient of 0.29 resulting in excellent fuel economy, low wind noise levels, and high stability at speed. The high rear end also meant that the XF, for the first time in many years, provided better luggage accommodation than most of its rivals.

Models available at launch
XF Luxury 2.7-litre diesel
XF Luxury 3.0-litre petrol
XF Premium Luxury 2.7-litre diesel
XF Premium Luxury 3.0-litre petrol
XF Premium Luxury 4.2-litre petrol
SV8 4.2-litre supercharged petrol

The XF was the first Jaguar to feature the entirely new JaguarDrive system operated from a single aluminium control in the centre console, which rises when the ignition is switched on, and with a simple twist selects the gear required. The system offers different modes that interact with the engine and gearbox to change the characteristics of engine, transmission shifts, and brake interventions, depending on driving conditions and circumstances. The one gearbox fitted to the XF is the ZF six-speed with sequential change.

Technically the XF is very advanced, and standard equipment levels include Emergency Brake Assist, Electronic Brakeforce Distribution, Anti-Lock Braking, Traction Control, Dynamic Stability Control, Cornering Brake Control, and Engine Drag Torque Control.

Initially available with a wide choice of 17in, 18in, 19in and 20in alloy wheels, the XF was the first car of its class to be available with the larger 20in alloys. Externally the XF was also the first Jaguar saloon to be fitted with the 'signature' front wing vents, and it saw the reintroduction of a prominent leaper mascot, although this time on the boot lid instead of the bonnet!

Internally the cars are very well appointed with a high specification regardless of model. Retaining many of the traditional features expected of a Jaguar, these have been combined with contemporary looks and feel, like the mix of wood veneer with alloy finish for example.

The range remained unchanged until the end of 2008 when a new model was announced, the XF Diesel S. Effectively replacing the previous

The striking frontal aspect of the XF moves the company away from previous practice. Mesh grille with new growler badge, single headlights, and large under-valance air intakes.

The high back-end of the XF with unique lighting, enlarged 'signature' chromed finisher and unusually styled exhaust tailpipes.

The XFR with revised, more pronounced frontal treatment incorporating chrome-finished air vents.

2.7-litre diesel models, the big change came with the introduction of the new, more fuel efficient 3.0-litre diesel engine. Providing a 10 per cent reduction in emissions and performance of 0–60mph in under 6sec, a key feature of the new engine is the parallel sequential turbocharger system, the first of its type to be fitted to the V-formation engine. For most everyday driving a variable geometry primary turbocharger does all the work, while a smaller, fixed-geometry secondary turbo is brought on line within 30 milliseconds, boosting the engine output when necessary.

The Diesel S was distinguishable from other models by the standard fit 19in wheel, a boot spoiler and 'S' badging.

The range was not altered again until early in 2009 when Jaguar announced their revised XF range for the 2010 model year. The biggest change came in the range of engines available. Out went the 3.0-litre petrol unit and both 4.2-litre engines. The 3.0-litre diesel, first seen a year earlier, was retained as an 'S' model and a more standard model. To replace the 4.2-litre units, a new highly efficient 5.0-litre engine became the option in normally-aspirated or supercharged form. The model range included a choice of Luxury, Premium Luxury, Portfolio, and XFR options.

Exterior identification points

General points applicable to all XF models

Front view
- Curvaceous frontal aspect unique to this model.
- Bold radiator grille with chromed surround incorporating bright mesh centre with Jaguar growler badge.
- One-piece light clusters incorporating a single headlight, fog light, and side/indicator lenses. Bi-Xenon lighting for Luxury Premium and SV8; halogen all other models.
- Full width bumper/under valance incorporating central mesh area and, either side air intakes with chromed splitter bars.
- One-piece forward-hinged bonnet with pronounced power-bulge in centre, sloping down to meet the light units and grille.
- One-piece bonded windscreen with twin wipers.

Rear view
- Much taller rear end compared to other Jaguar models, with severe sloping coupé-style roof section and wide haunches.
- One-piece, severely raked, bonded rear screen.
- Rear-hinged boot panel incorporating reflector sections of the rear lights, illuminated number plate area, and with a Jaguar chromed leaper emblem centrally mounted.
- Chromed full-width 'signature' finisher 'Jaguar' legend.
- Rear bumper/valance area wraps around to form part of rear wings area, incorporating cut-out areas for new-style square exhaust tail trims in chrome.
- Rear light clusters matching wrapping around the rear wings incorporating the latest LED technology.
- Chromed 'XF' and litre-badging, each side of the boot panel.

Side view
- Coupé style roof line mated to conventional four-door arrangement forming a sloping forward wedge design.
- Pronounced styling line starting near the base of the front wing, following through the door areas, shallowing out near the rear wheel-arch.
- Black window frames with one-piece chrome edging incorporated into limousine-style door frames.
- Body-coloured door mirrors incorporating indicator repeater lights.
- Front wing mounted 'signature' vents.
- Concealed fuel filler cap incorporated into the rear nearside wing, with flush cover.
- 17in Libra alloy wheels, standard fit on Luxury models.
- 18in Cygnus alloy wheels, standard fit on Premium Luxury models.
- 20in Volans alloy wheels, standard fit on SV8 model.

Diesel S specifics
- 'S' badging at rear.
- Boot spoiler.
- 19in Artura alloy wheels.

The Diesel S model when launched, equipped here with 20in Senta alloy wheels.

2010 model year specifics
XFR (replacing SV8)
Front view

▨ More pronounced bumper/under valance incorporating a larger central mesh grille area painted black.

▨ Chrome surround side air ducts and lip to under-panel area.

▨ Painted louvres to the bonnet area like those used on the XK sports car.

Rear view

▨ Special enlarged aerodynamic spoiler.

▨ 'R' badging.

▨ Revised style to rear bumper/under valance area, all now in body paint colour.

▨ Four exhaust pipes of revised design.

Side view

▨ Sill extensions.

▨ Revised styling to door mirrors incorporating LED lighting.

▨ R-Performance brake calipers visible through wheels.

Other 2010 model year specifics
3.0-litre V6 diesel

▨ Luxury trim – 18in Venus alloy wheels (19in Artura alloy wheels on S).

▨ Premium Luxury trim – 19in Carelia alloy wheels (20in Senta alloy wheels on S).

▨ Portfolio trim – 20in Selena alloy wheels (also on S).

5.0-litre V8 petrol

▨ Portfolio trim – 20in Selena alloy wheels.

▨ XFR trim – 20in Nevis alloy wheels.

NB: All 2010 models feature digital LED rear lighting.

Interior identification points

General points applicable to XF models up to 2010 model year

▨ Full width dashboard area with instrument binnacle (containing speedometer, rev counter, and auxiliary gauges/read-outs) directly in front of the driver.

▨ Leather steering wheel with three spokes finished in alloy, containing controls for cruise control, telephone operation, and audio controls. Centre boss leather area with Jaguar growler badge. Paddle gear-shift controls behind steering wheel.

▨ Centre dash section in alloy finish with air-conditioning vents flanking centre screen area for on-board controls/sat-nav, etc.

Entirely new dash layout treatment with a contemporary mix of veneer and alloy. Unique to the XF are the air-conditioning vents that open automatically when the engine is started, and the touch-sensitive panel to open the glove-box.

JaguarDrive control for gear changes, the substantial alloy knob rises when the engine is started. Also note, just ahead of this, the black 'starter button'. This interior is equipped with the Rich Oak veneer.

Unique phosphor blue lighting is used in several areas of the XF, including the door panels.

XFR interior in Dark Oak veneer. Note the different seat style and steering wheel from other models.

- Passenger dash area in matching alloy finish and containing concealed airbag area and air-conditioning outlet.
- Extensive centre console area featuring switchgear, ashtray, cup-holder, and JaguarDriver control.
- Wood veneer finish to centre console area and along the edge of the dash area, full width.
- Soft finish door trim areas incorporating door pulls, chromed door handles, speaker grilles, and switch packs for windows/mirrors. Wood veneer inset panels and phosphor blue subdued lighting.
- All seats trimmed in leather with horizontal and vertical panel stitching.
- Each front seat contains electrically-adjustable head restraints and full seat electric controls from side of seats.

XFR specifics
- Salsa and Kyanite Blue exterior paint finishes unique to this model.
- Dark oak veneer.
- Embossed 'R' logos in seats.
- Rear of front seat map pockets.
- Dark mesh alloy dash with 'R' logo.
- Instruments with red pointer dials.

Portfolio specifics
- Vented, heated, and cooled seating.
- Rear of front seat map pockets.
- Suedecloth premium headlining.
- Contrast stitching to upper door trims and instrument surround.
- Premium carpet mats with contrast piped edges and embroidered Jaguar legend.

1: *17in Libra wheels for Luxury models to 2009.*

2: *18in Venus wheels – standard fit on 3.0-litre diesel Luxury model.*

3: *18in Cygnus wheels for Premium Luxury models to 2009.*

4: *19in Carelia wheels – standard fit for 3.0-litre diesel Premium Luxury models.*

5: *Optional extra 19in Auriga wheels.*

6: *20in Volans wheels for SV8 model.*

7: *20in Selena wheels – standard fit for Portfolio models.*

8: *20in Nevis wheels for XFR model.*

9: *20in Senta wheels. Standard fit on 3.0-litre Diesel S Premium Luxury from 2009; otherwise optional.*

10: *19in Artura wheels, standard on Luxury Diesel S and optional on standard Diesel.*

Technical specifications

	2.7-litre diesel	3.0-litre petrol
cc	2,720	2,967
Bore and stroke (mm)	81 x 88	89 x 79.5
Compression ratio	17:1	10.5:1
bhp	207	238
@ rpm	4,000	6,800
Torque (lb ft)	320	216
@ rpm	1,900	4,100
Fuelling	Fuel injection	Fuel injection
Transmission	ZF 6-speed auto sequential	ZF 6-speed auto sequential
Wheel size (in)	17, 18, 19, 20	17, 18, 19, 20
Suspension front	Ind double wishbones, alloy control arms, anti-dive, coil springs	Ind double wishbones, alloy control arms, anti-dive, coil springs
Suspension rear	Ind double wishbones, alloy control arms co-axial coil springs (CATSI)	Ind double wishbones, alloy control arms, co-axial coil springs (CATSI)
Brakes	4-wheel disc, all ventilated	4-wheel disc, all ventilated
Performance		
0–60mph (sec)	7.7	7.9
Top speed (mph)	143	148
Average mpg	37.6	26.8
Dimensions		
Length (in)	195	195
Width (in)	74	74
Height (in)	57.5	57.5
Wheelbase (in)	114.5	114.5
Front track (in)	61	61
Rear track (in)	63	63
Weight (lb)	3,904	3,702

Optional extras

Chromed side 'signature' vents.
Boot spoiler.
Bright alloy finished foot pedals.
Illuminated sill treadplates.
Luggage compartment finisher.
Rear screen connectivity system.
R-Performance aerodynamic pack.
R-Performance interior trim.
Black or Bright finish mesh grilles.
Square stainless steel exhaust trim pipes.
Bright finish door mirror covers.
Brush aluminium or chromed gear knobs.
Tailored over-carpet mats.
Tyre-pressure monitoring system.
Keyless entry.
Alternative veneer dash trims.

TV tuner.
DVD audio system.
B & W Premium hi-fi system.
Front park assist system with interior touch-screen information.
Soft-grain leather seat facings.
ACC cruise control.
Garage door opener.
Heated windscreen.

Alloy wheel options:
17in Libra.
18in Cygnus and Venus.
19in Carelia, Auriga, and Artura.
20in Selena, Volans, Senta, and Nevis.

	3.0-litre diesel	4.2-litre petrol
cc	2,993	4,196
Bore and stroke (mm)	84 x 90	86 x 90
Compression ratio	16:1	11:1
bhp	240 (275 S)	298
@ rpm	4,000	6,000
Torque (lb ft)	369 (443 S)	303
@ rpm	2,000	4,100
Fuelling	Fuel injection	Fuel injection
Transmission	ZF 6-speed auto sequential	6-speed auto sequential
Wheel size (in)	18, 19, 20	19, 20
Suspension front	Ind double wishbones, alloy alloy control arms, anti-dive, coil springs	Ind unequal length wishbones, coil springs
Suspension rear	Ind double wishbones, alloy control arms, co-axial coil springs (CATSI)	Ind unequal length wishbones, coil springs
Brakes	4-wheel disc, all ventilated	4-wheel disc, all ventilated
Performance		
0–60mph (sec)	6.7 (5.9 S)	6.2
Top speed (mph)	149 (155 S)	155
Average mpg	42	25
Dimensions		
Length (in)	195	195
Width (in)	74	74
Height (in)	57.5	57.5
Wheelbase (in)	114.5	114.5
Front track (in)	61	61
Rear track (in)	63	63
Weight (lb)	4,012	3,856

Technical specifications *cont ...*

	4.2-litre supercharged	5.0-litre
cc	4,196	5,000
Bore and stroke (mm)	86 x 90	92.5 x 93
Compression ratio	9:1	11.5:1
bhp	416	385
@ rpm	6,250	6,500
Torque (lb ft)	413	380
@ rpm	4,000	3,500
Fuelling	Fuel injection	Fuel injection
Transmission	6-speed auto sequential	6-speed auto sequential
Wheel size (in)	19, 20	19, 20
Suspension front	Ind unequal length wishbones, coil springs	Ind unequal length wishbones, coil springs
Suspension rear	Ind unequal length wishbones, coil springs	Ind unequal length wishbones, coil springs
Brakes	4-wheel disc, all ventilated	4-wheel disc, all ventilated
Performance		
0–60mph (sec)	5.1	5.5
Top speed (mph)	155	155
Average mpg	22	25
Dimensions		
Length (in)	189	189
Width (in)	74	75
Height (in)	52	52
Wheelbase (in)	108	108
Front track (in)	61	61
Rear track (in)	61	63
Weight (lb)	4,061	3,924

Alloy wheel options

17in Libra
Standard fit on Luxury models to 2009.

18in Venus
Optional fit (in 2009 standard fit on 3.0-litre Diesel Luxury).

18in Cygnus
Standard fit on Premium Luxury models to 2009.

19in Carelia
Optional fit (in 2009 standard fit on 3.0-litre Diesel Premium Luxury).

19in Auriga
Optional fit.

19in Artura
2009 standard fit on 3.0-litre Diesel S Luxury.

20in Volans
Standard fit on SV8.

20in Selena
Optional fit (in 2009 standard fit on Portfolio).

20in Senta
Optional fit (in 2009 standard fit 3.0-litre Diesel S Premium Luxury).

20in Nevis
Standard fit on XFR.

	5.0-litre supercharged
cc	5,000
Bore and stroke (mm)	92.5 x 93
Compression ratio	9.5:1
bhp	510
@ rpm	6,500
Torque (lb ft)	461
@ rpm	5,500
Fuelling	Fuel injection
Transmission	6-speed auto sequential
Wheel size (in)	19, 20
Suspension front	Ind unequal length wishbones, coil springs
Suspension rear	Ind unequal length wishbones, coil springs
Brakes	4-wheel disc, all ventilated
Performance	
0–60mph (sec)	4.7
Top speed (mph)	155
Average mpg	24
Dimensions	
Length (in)	189
Width (in)	75
Height (in)	52
Wheelbase (in)	108
Front track (in)	61
Rear track (in)	63
Weight (lb)	4,369

Prices and production years

	Price new (£)	2007	2008	2009	2010
2.7-litre diesel	33,900	▪	▪	▪	–
3.0-litre petrol	33,900	▪	▪	▪	–
3.0-litre diesel	33,900	–	–	▪	▪
3.0-litre diesel S	37,500	–	–	▪	▪
4.2-litre petrol	45,500	▪	▪	▪	–
4.2-litre SV8	54,900	▪	▪	▪	–
5.0-litre petrol	49,900	–	–	▪	▪
5.0-litre XFR	59,900	–	–	▪	▪

Colour schemes

Exterior	Details	Seat trim/ Upper fascia	Details	Seat/ Trim style
Porcelain		Spice		Bond grain leather
Botanical Green		Oyster		Softgrain leather
Emerald Fire		Truffle		R-Performance
Vapour Grey		Ivory		
Frost Blue		Champagne		
Azure Blue	Until mid-2009	Dove		
Indigo		Warm Charcoal		
Midnight	Until mid-2008	Barley	From 2009	
Ultimate Black	From mid-2008	Red Zone (XFR)	From 2009	
Ebony		London Tan (XFR)	From 2009	
Pearl Grey				
Lunar Grey				
Liquid Silver				
Winter Gold				
Radiance	Until 2009			
Spectrum Blue	From 2009			
Claret	From 2009			
Kyanite Blue	From 2009 (XFR only)			
Salsa	From 2009 (XFR only)			

Contrast stitching	Details	Veneers	Details	
Spice		Satin Aluminium	All cars to 2009	
Ivory	From 2009	Knurled Aluminium	From 2009	
Barley	From 2009	Dark Mesh	From 2009 (XFR only)	
Red Zone	From 2009	Satin American Walnut		
London Tan	From 2009	Burr Walnut		
		Rich Oak		
		Figured Ebony	Portfolio models only	
		Dark Oak	XFR only	

Background

The Jaguar XJ insignia and flagship of the range continues with the advent of a car with a different ethos to previous XJ models. Announced in 2009 the new car, although a direct replacement for the X-350 models, is much more contemporary and shows no styling connection to the previous models that shared the XJ name.

The most striking aspects of the body style incorporate some cues from the medium sized XF model but take things much further with a more pronounced frontal aspect with larger grille and a 'coupe' style roof. Key features include a panoramic glass roof, an integral part of the all-new XJ's design concept, enabling the car to have a lower, more streamlined roofline, while dramatically enhancing the feeling of light and space inside.

The new bodyshell provides a drag coefficient of just 0.29 and is claimed to be made from 50 per cent recycled materials. For the first time in production of any XJ, the new car is available in both conventional and long wheelbase form, the latter providing an additional 125mm of legroom.

Constructed using Jaguar's aerospace-inspired aluminium body technology, the XJ is lighter than its rivals by at least 150kg. Technologies developed for the XJ significantly improve performance, handling and economy, while also delivering increased strength, refinement and safety. Other features include air suspension, Adaptive Dynamics (continuously variable damping), Active Differential Control and quick-ratio power steering.

The XJ launched with a range of four engines – 3.0-litre diesel, 5.0-litre normally aspirated petrol, 5.0-litre supercharged petrol and, for the Portfolio model only, the range topping 5.0-litre 510bhp supercharged petrol unit. All models incorporate the JaguarDrive gear-change system with steering wheel mounted paddle controls and sophisticated braking, suspension and steering equipment, much of which follows the practice of the latest XK sports car models.

The cabin, although unmistakably Jaguar, is of an entirely new design, blending elegance with contemporary design features. Three specification levels – Luxury, Premium Luxury and Portfolio are offered plus the Supersports model, which is even better equipped but only available with the most powerful engine.

As well as an entirely new interior design and layout, the very latest technology has been incorporated including a 'virtual' instrument display, split viewing screen in the centre console so that front seat passenger and driver can view different images at the same time, interactive voice control system, DVD hard drive system and laminated glass all round.

The car is comprehensively equipped with a range of active safety aids including: an Anti-lock Braking System (ABS), Dynamic Stability Control (DSC), Cornering Brake Control (CBC), Understeer Control, Electronic Brakeforce Distribution (EBD), Electronic Traction Control (ETC), Emergency Brake Assist (EBA), Engine Drag Torque Control and, for vehicles fitted with Adaptive Cruise Control (ACC), Electronic Brake Pre-fill and, not least, the Pedestrian Contact Sensing system first seen on the XK sports car, with the automatically deployable bonnet to help safeguard pedestrians from injury.

Models available at launch:

XJ6 3.0 litre Diesel	Luxury	Short Wheelbase
		Long Wheelbase
	Premium Luxury	Short Wheelbase
		Long Wheelbase
	Portfolio	Short Wheelbase
		Long Wheelbase
XJ8 5.0 litre (normally aspirated)	Premium Luxury	Short Wheelbase
		Long Wheelbase
	Portfolio	Short Wheelbase
		Long Wheelbase
XJ8 5.0 litre (supercharged)	Premium Luxury	Short Wheelbase
		Long Wheelbase
	Portfolio	Short Wheelbase
		Long Wheelbase
	Supersports	Short Wheelbase
		Long Wheelbase

Exterior identification points

General points applicable to all XJ models

Front View

- Curvaceous frontal aspect, pronounced mesh radiator grille with chrome surround incorporating the new style Jaguar growler head.
- One piece light clusters wrapping around to the sides of the car, incorporating Xenon swivelling headlights plus fog lights and side/indicator lenses.
- Full width bumper/under valance moulded into the body with mesh undergrille and chromed splitter bars to air intakes.
- One-piece forward hinged bonnet with pronounced power-bulge in centre, sloping down to the front panel of the car.
- One-piece bonded windscreen with twin wipers.

Rear View

- Coupe style 'moon roof' area sweeping down to sharply raked rear screen meeting the boot lid.

Arguably the most luxurious interior for Jaguar yet with wrap-around wood veneer, a strong emphasis on chrome and metal. Note the return to circular air vents and the Swiss styled clock.

A complete departure in Jaguar styling with a much plainer rear end but with prominent 'leaper' emblem, the number plate now mounted before boot level and the 'claw style' rear light units.

The contemporary fontal aspect of the XJ echoes the medium sized XF but with a more forward facing and larger grille. Note the headlights, similar to those used on the XK sports car and the tall, swept-back windscreen.

- D-post areas of roof covered in black finish giving the effect of a 'floating' roof.
- Tall rear end with plain one-piece boot lid with little adornment except for large chromed leaper in the centre and XJ insignia to the left-hand side.
- Rear bumper/valance area (incorporating the rear registration plate and lighting) wraps around to form part of rear wings area incorporating cut-out areas for new style square exhaust tail trims in chrome. Horizontal chrome finisher to this panel.
- Rear light clusters flow vertically over the top of the rear wings, styled to look similar to a jaguar claw and using the latest LED technology.

Side View
- Coupé-style roof line with extremely raked front and rear screens for maximum effect.
- Pronounced styling line starting at the base of the front wing, following through the door areas and tapering out at the rear.
- Black window frames with one-piece chrome edging incorporated into limousine style door frames.
- Front door mirrors incorporating indicator repeater lights.
- Front wing mounted horizontal 'signature' vents.
- Concealed fuel filler cap incorporated into the rear nearside wing with flush cover.
- A maximum choice of six alloy wheels designs, dependent on market.

2010 Model Year Specifics
Exterior points carry through the entire range except for:

Exterior View

Luxury Models:	19" Aleutian Alloy Wheels
Premium Luxury:	19" Toba Alloy Wheels + Metallic Paintwork
Portfolio:	20" Kasuga Alloy Wheels + Metallic Paintwork + Rear Camera Aid.
Supersports:	20" Metavia Alloy Wheels + Metallic Paintwork + Rear Camera Aid.

Interior identification points

General points applicable to all current XJ models:
- All-leather-wrapped instrument panel sitting low across the vehicle. At the sides of the cabin, a bold section of wood veneer sweeps forward from the doors to meet at the front of the car below screen level.

- Virtual digital instrument display in front of cover that is interactive and changes dependent on driving mode, and using phosphor blue lighting.
- 3-spoke leather-covered steering wheel (veneer option) with centre chromed leaper, incorporating minor controls for various operations and gear change paddles.
- Circular chrome on metal eye-ball air con vents at either side of dashboard with two prominent pod mounted vents in the centre of the dashboard area.
- Wide centre console area incorporating operational screen, auxiliary controls and JaguarDrive control.
- Electrically locked glove box to passenger side of dash area.
- All-leather seating with contrasting piping, electrically controlled and heated/ventilated according to model.
- Door panels incorporate wood veneer panels to match the rest of the car.
- Soft-finish door trim areas incorporating door pulls, chromed door handles, speaker grilles and switch packs for windows/mirrors.

The Moon Roof which has tinted, reflective glass and opens outwards electrically to eliminate any loss of headroom. Note also the embossed Jaguar emblems in the headrests.

Portfolio interior with contrast stitching and walnut veneer.

Technical specifications

	3.0-litre Diesel	5.0-litre
cc	2,993	5,000
Bore & Stoke (mm)	84 x 90	92.5 x 93
Compression ratio	16:1	11.5:1
Bhp	275	385
@ rpm	4,000	6,500
Max Torque	600	380
@ rpm	2,000	3,500
Fuelling	Fuel injection	Fuel injection
Transmission	ZF 6-speed auto, Sequential	6-speed auto, Sequential
Wheel size (in)	18in, 19in, 20in	18in, 19in, 20in
Suspension (front)	Ind double wishbones, alloy control arms, anti-dive, coil springs	Ind. Unequal length wishbones, coil springs
Suspension (rear)	Ind double wishbones, alloy control arms, Co-axial coil springs (CATSI)	Ind. Unequal length wishbones, coil springs
Brakes	4-wheel discs, all ventilated	4-wheel discs, all ventilated
Performance		
0 to 60mph (sec)	6.0	5.4
Top speed (mph)	155	155
Average mpg	Not yet assessed	Not yet assessed
Dimensions		
Length (in)	201.7 swb, 206.6. lwb	201.7 swb, 206.6. lwb
Width (in)	83.1	83.1
Height (in)	57	57
Wheelbase (in)	119.4. swb, 124.3. lwb	119.4 swb, 124.3 lwb
Front track (in)	64	64
Rear track (in)	63.1	63.1
Weight (lb)	3960 Swb, 3998 lwb	3870 swb, 3909 lwb

Optional extras

Dependent on individual model specification.
Driver assistance pack (forward alert, Adaptive cruise control, blind spot monitor, Emergency brake assist, Active seat belts).
Option to delete XJ badging from rear of car.
Privacy glass.
Air quality monitoring system.
Front ashtray and cigar lighter.
Wood and Leather heated steering wheel.
DAB radio.
Whitefire emitter and headphones.
Chromed door mirror covers.
Pesonalised signature.

Locking wheel nuts.
Rear number plate surround.
Wheelarch splash guards.
Boot interior finisher, illuminated.
Alloy pedal kit.
Garage door opener.
TV tuner
Rear Seat Entertainment Centre.
Adaptive front lighting.
Rear Camera Parking system.
Rear Business Trays
Softgrain leather front seating with heating/cooling system.

	5.0-litre Supercharged	5.0-litre Supersports
cc	5,000	5,000
Bore & Stoke (mm)	92.5 x 93	92.5 x 93
Compression ratio	9.5:1	9.5:1
Bhp	470	510
@ rpm	6,500	6,500
Max Torque	424	461
@ rpm	2,500–5,500	2,500–5,500
Fuelling	Fuel injection	Fuel injection
Transmission	6-speed auto, Sequential	6-speed auto, Sequential
Wheel size (in)	18in, 19in, 20in	18in, 19in, 20in
Suspension (front)	Ind. Unequal length wishbones, coil springs	Ind. Unequal length wishbones, coil springs
Suspension (rear)	Ind. Unequal length wishbones, coil springs	Ind. Unequal length wishbones, coil springs
Brakes	4-wheel discs, all ventilated	4-wheel discs, all ventilated
Performance		
0 to 60mph (sec)	4.9	4.7
Top speed (mph)	155	155
Average mpg	Not yet assessed	Not yet assessed
Dimensions		
Length (in)	201.7 swb, 206.6. lwb	201.7 swb, 206.6. lwb
Width (in)	83.1	83.1
Height (in)	57	57
Wheelbase (in)	119.4 swb, 124.3 lwb	119.4 swb, 124.3 lwb
Front track (in)	64	64
Rear track (in)	63.1	63.1
Weight (lb)	4172 swb, 4223 lwb	4172 swb, 4223 lwb

Softgrain leather rear seating with
   heating/cooling system.
Leather heated steering wheel.
Leather & Wood heated steering wheel.
Dual view functionality centre console screen.
Bowers & Wilkins 1,200 watt Hi-Fi system.
Tyre pressure monitoring system.
Spike Spyder Traction System.
Illuminated Tread Plates.
Parking aid kit.
Keyless entry.
600 watt Premium Sound System.

Alloy Wheels:-
18" Meru
19" Aleutian
19" Toba
19" Toba (polished)
20" Amirante
20" Kasuga
20" Kasuga (polished)
20" Orona
20" Orona (polished)

Colour schemes

Exterior
Cashmere
Claret
Ultimate Black
Indigo
Frost Blue
Spectrum Blue
Pearl Grey
Vapour Grey
Lunar Grey
Liquid Silver
Caviar
Botanical Green
Ebony
Porcelaine

Seats	Facia	Headlining	Stitching	Veneers
Cashmere	Truffle	Canvas		Carbon Fibre
Jet	Jet	Ivory		Burr Walnut
				Satin American Walnut

Prices and production years

Model	Style	Wheelbase	Price new (£)
3.0 litre	Luxury	SWB	52,500
		LWB	55,500
	Premium Luxury	SWB	55,900
		LWB	58,900
	Portfolio	SWB	62,900
		LWB	65,900
5.0 litre	Premium Luxury	SWB	62,900
		LWB	65,900
	Portfolio	SWB	69,900
		LWB	72,900
5.0 litre S/c	Supersports	SWB	85,000
		LWB	88,000

Post-war Jaguar production graph

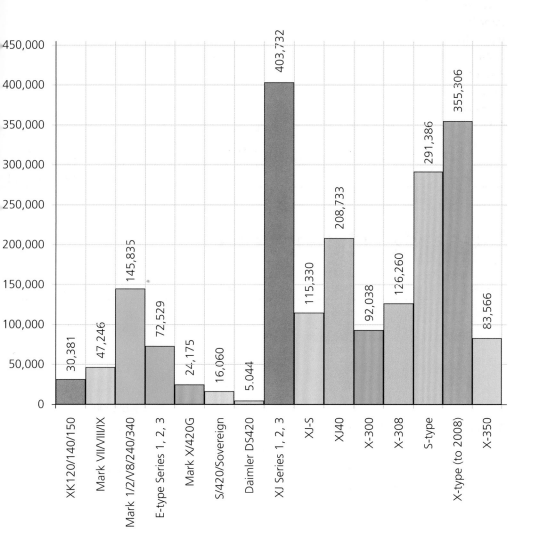

Chassis number identification

Special Notes

Jaguar and Daimler derivatives covered in this publication were identified with individual Chassis Numbers which are relatively easy to understand and applied to all markets with only numerical changes for left hand drive and right hand drive cars. This criteria applied until 1978.

Changes in the way the world recognised vehicles came into effect from 1979 and in readiness for this and subsequently Jaguar have used the internationally recognised VIN number system (Vehicle Identification Number). This system indicates a number of separate issues relating to each particular model produced giving much greater detail. The structure of the VIN numbers changes slightly according to model range therefore it is not practical to list all Vin numbers for the models covered. The tables below will provide the detail required however.

Table One

Applicable to XJ Series 3 saloons and DS420 limousines (post 1978)

Example Vin No. SAJJDALW4EM300001

The details behind each alpha/numeric (or set) is as follows:

SAJ	Manufacturer	(SAJ – Jaguar) (SAD – Daimler)	**W**	Engine	(K – 3.4/4.2 litre) (L,N,P.R.S or T – other 4.2 variants) (V – 5.3 litre) (W, X or Y – other 5.3 variants)
J	Marque	(J – Jaguar) (D – Daimler)			
D	Model	(A – XJ6) (B – XJ12) (C – Sovereign) (D – Double Six) (E – Limousine)	**4**	Transmission/ Steering	(3 – Auto rhd) (4 – Auto lhd) (7 – Manual rhd) (8 – Manual lhd)
A	Specification	(A – Baseline model) (G – Japanese VDP) (J – Japanese) (L – Canadian) (N – Canadian VDP) (R – Vanden Plas) (V – USA) (Y – USA)	**E**	Model Year	(e.g. B – 1981, C – 1982, H – 1987, J – 1988, etc.)
			M	Emission System*	(e.g. A,B,C,F,M,P or R)
			300001	Serial No.	Ascending number based on production.
L	Body Type	(L – 4 door saloon) (T – 4 door limousine) (W – Hearse)			

* Also using letter C up to 1987 model year to denote cars produced at Browns Lane Plant in Coventry.

Table Two

Applicable to XJ-S models from 1978 and all subsequent XJS models

Example Vin No. SAJJNAEW4EP100001

The details behind each alpha/numeric (or set) is as follows:

SAJ	Manufacturer	(SAJ – Jaguar)
J	Marque	(J – Jaguar)
N	Model	(N – XJS) (S – XJR-S) (T – Special Editions)
A	Specification	(A – Baseline model) (J – Japanese) (K – Japanese with airbag) (L – Canadian) (M – Canadian with airbag) (V – USA) (W – USA with airbag) (Y – USA with passive belts)
E	Body Type	(C – Cabriolet) (D – Convertible) (E – Coupé) (F – 2 + 2 Convertible)
W	Engine	(B – 3.6 litre) (C,D or E – 3.6 litre post ECS) (K,V,W,X,Y or Z – 5.3 litre) (S – 6.0 litre)
4	Transmission/ Steering	(3 – Auto rhd) (4 – Auto lhd) (7 – Manual rhd) (8 – Manual lhd)
E	Model Year	(A – original XJ-S) (B – HE or US 1981 model year) (C – AJ6 or US 1982 model year) (D – V12 Con or US 1983 model year) (E – Facelift or US 1984 model year) (F to P US model years from 1985 to 1993)
P	Emission System*	(e.g. A,B,C,E,F, etc to T)
100001	Serial No.	Ascending number based on production.

Also using letter C up to 1987 model year to denote cars produced at Browns Lane Plant in Coventry.

Table Three

Applicable to XJ40 models

Example Vin No. SAJJFALD3AJ500001

The details behind each alpha/numeric (or set) is as follows:

SAJ	Manufacturer	(SAJ – Jaguar)
J	Marque	(J – Jaguar) (D – Daimler)
F	Model	(F – XJ6) (H – Sovereign or XJ12) (K – VDP, Daimler DD6 or Sov V12) (M – Majestic) (P – XJR)
A	Specification	(A – Baseline model) (J – Japanese) (K – Japanese with airbag) (L – Canadian) (M – Canadian with airbag) (V – USA) (W – USA with airbag) (Y – USA with passive belts)
L	Body Type	(L – Saloon) (M – Long Wheelbase Saloon)
D	Engine	(B,C,D or E – 3.6 litre) (F or J – 2.9 litre) (G – 2.9 litre or 3.2 litre) (H – 2.9 litre or 3.6 litre) (S – 6.0 litre)
3	Transmission/ Steering	(3 – Auto rhd) (4 – Auto lhd) (7 – Manual rhd) (8 – Manual lhd)
A	Model Year	(A – original XJ40) (USA, Canada & Korea model year: e.g. H – 1987 to P – 1993)
J	Emission System	(e.g. A,B,C,E,F, etc to T)
500001	Serial No.	Ascending number based on production.

All the Cars

Chassis number identification

Table Four

Applicable to X-300 models

Example Vin No. SAJJFALD3SJ500001

The details behind each alpha/numeric (or set) is as follows:

SAJ	Manufacturer	(SAJ – Jaguar)
J	Marque	(J – Jaguar) (D – Daimler)
F	Model	(F – XJ6) (H – Sovereign or XJ12) (J – Executive) (K – VDP, Daimler DD6 or Sov V12) (M – Majestic) (P – XJR or Sport)
A	Specification	(A – Baseline model) (K – Japanese) (F,G,or N – Canadian) (D,E,X or V – USA) (S,P or T – Mexico)
L	Body Type	(L – Saloon) (M – Long Wheelbase Saloon) (N – Long Wheelbase Saloon, 4 seater)
D	Engine	(L, D or E – 4.0 litre) (F – Supercharged) (G – 3.2 litre) (S – 6.0 litre)
3	Transmission/Steering	(3 – Auto rhd) (4 – Auto lhd) (7 – Manual rhd) (8 – Manual lhd)
S	Model Year	(S – 1995) (T – 1996) (V – 1997)
J	Emission System	(e.g. C,J,N,P or R)
500001	Serial No.	Ascending number based on production.

Table Five

Applicable to X-308 models

Example Vin No. SAJJFALD3SJ500001

The details behind each alpha/numeric (or set) is as follows:

SAJ	Manufacturer	(SAJ – Jaguar)
J	Marque	(J – Jaguar) (D – Daimler)
F	Model	(F – XJ8) (H – Sovereign) (K – VDP & Daimler) (P – XJR or Sport)
A	Specification	(A – Baseline model) (K – Japanese) (F,G or N – Canadian) (D,E or X – USA) (P,S or X – Mexico)
L	Body Type	(L – Saloon) (M – Long Wheelbase Saloon) (N – Long Wheelbase Saloon, 4 seater)
D	Engine	(L,D or E – 4.0 litre) (F – Supercharged) (G – 3.2 litre) (S – 6.0 litre)
3	Transmission/Steering	(3 – Auto rhd) (4 – Auto lhd)
S	Model Year	(W – 1998, Y – 2000, 1 – 2001, etc.)
J	Emission System	(e.g. A, through to X)
500001	Serial No.	Ascending number based on production.

Table Six

Applicable to XK8 models

Example Vin No. SAJJGAED3WJ014080

The details behind each alpha/numeric (or set) is as follows:

SAJ	Manufacturer	(SAJ – Jaguar)
J	Marque	(J – Jaguar)
G	Model	(G – XK, all)
A	Specification	(A – Baseline model) (K – Japanese) (F,G or N – Canadian) (D,E or X – USA) (P,S or X – Mexico)
E	Body Type	(E – Coupé) (F – Convertible)
D	Engine	(D, E or F – 4.0 litre) (L – Supercharged)
3	Transmission/Steering	(3 – Auto rhd) (4 – Auto lhd)
W	Model Year	(W – 1998, Y – 2000, 1 – 2001, etc.)
J	Emission System	(e.g. A, through to X)
014080	Serial No.	Ascending number based on production.